A Short History of the
Confederate States of America

BOOKS BY SEA RAVEN PRESS

AMERICAN CIVIL WAR
Abraham Lincoln Was a Liberal, Jefferson Davis Was a Conservative: The Missing Key to Understanding the American Civil War
Confederacy 101: Amazing Facts You Never Knew About America's Oldest Political Tradition
Confederate Blood and Treasure: An Interview With Lochlainn Seabrook
Everything You Were Taught About African-Americans and the Civil War is Wrong, Ask a Southerner!
Everything You Were Taught About the Civil War is Wrong, Ask a Southerner!
Give This Book to a Yankee! A Southern Guide to the Civil War For Northerners
Lincoln's War: The Real Cause, the Real Winner, the Real Loser
The Great Yankee Coverup: What the North Doesn't Want You to Know About Lincoln's War!
The Ultimate Civil War Quiz Book: How Much Do You Really Know About America's Most Misunderstood Conflict?
Women in Gray: A Tribute to the Ladies Who Supported the Southern Confederacy

CONFEDERATE MONUMENTS
Confederate Monuments: Why Every American Should Honor Confederate Soldiers and Their Memorials

CONFEDERATE FLAG
Confederate Flag Facts: What Every American Should Know About Dixie's Southern Cross
What the Confederate Flag Means To Me: Americans Speak Out in Defense of Southern Honor, History, and Heritage

SECESSION
All We Ask Is To Be Let Alone: The Southern Secession Fact Book

SLAVERY
Everything You Were Taught About American Slavery is Wrong, Ask a Southerner!
Slavery 101: Amazing Facts You Never Knew About America's "Peculiar Institution"

CHILDREN
Honest Jeff and Dishonest Abe: A Southern Children's Guide to the Civil War
Saddle, Sword, and Gun: A Biography of Nathan Bedford Forrest For Teens

NATHAN BEDFORD FORREST
A Rebel Born: A Defense of Nathan Bedford Forrest - Confederate General, American Legend (winner of the 2011 Jefferson Davis Historical Gold Medal)
A Rebel Born: The Screenplay (film about N. B. Forrest)
Forrest! 99 Reasons to Love Nathan Bedford Forrest
Give 'Em Hell Boys! The Complete Military Correspondence of Nathan Bedford Forrest
I Rode With Forrest! Confederate Soldiers Who Served With the World's Greatest Cavalry Leader
Nathan Bedford Forrest and African-Americans: Yankee Myth, Confederate Fact
Nathan Bedford Forrest and the Battle of Fort Pillow: Yankee Myth, Confederate Fact
Nathan Bedford Forrest and the Ku Klux Klan: Yankee Myth, Confederate Fact
Nathan Bedford Forrest: Southern Hero, American Patriot - Honoring a Confederate Icon and the Old South
Saddle, Sword, and Gun: A Biography of Nathan Bedford Forrest For Teens
The God of War: Nathan Bedford Forrest As He Was Seen By His Contemporaries
The Quotable Nathan Bedford Forrest: Selections From the Writings and Speeches of the Confederacy's Most Brilliant Cavalryman

QUOTABLE SERIES
The Alexander H. Stephens Reader: Excerpts From the Works of a Confederate Founding Father
The Quotable Alexander H. Stephens: Selections From the Writings and Speeches of the Confederacy's First Vice President
The Quotable Jefferson Davis: Selections From the Writings and Speeches of the Confederacy's First President
The Quotable Nathan Bedford Forrest: Selections From the Writings and Speeches of the Confederacy's Most Brilliant Cavalryman
The Quotable Robert E. Lee: Selections From the Writings and Speeches of the South's Most Beloved Civil War General
The Quotable Stonewall Jackson: Selections From the Writings and Speeches of the South's Most Famous General
The Unquotable Abraham Lincoln: The President's Quotes They Don't Want You To Know!

CONSTITUTIONAL HISTORY
The Articles of Confederation Explained: A Clause-by-Clause Study of America's First Constitution
The Constitution of the Confederate States of America Explained: A Clause-by-Clause Study of the South's Magna Carta

VICTORIAN CONFEDERATE LITERATURE
Rise Up and Call Them Blessed: Victorian Tributes to the Confederate Soldier, 1861-1901
The God of War: Nathan Bedford Forrest As He Was Seen By His Contemporaries
The Old Rebel: Robert E. Lee As He Was Seen By His Contemporaries
Victorian Confederate Poetry: The Southern Cause in Verse, 1861-1901

ABRAHAM LINCOLN
Abraham Lincoln: The Southern View - Demythologizing America's Sixteenth President
Lincolnology: The Real Abraham Lincoln Revealed in His Own Words - A Study of Lincoln's Suppressed, Misinterpreted, and Forgotten Writings and Speeches
Lincoln's War: The Real Cause, the Real Winner, the Real Loser
The Great Impersonator! 99 Reasons to Dislike Abraham Lincoln
The Unholy Crusade: Lincoln's Legacy of Destruction in the American South
The Unquotable Abraham Lincoln: The President's Quotes They Don't Want You To Know!

CIVIL WAR BATTLES
Encyclopedia of the Battle of Franklin - A Comprehensive Guide to the Conflict that Changed the Civil War
Nathan Bedford Forrest and the Battle of Fort Pillow: Yankee Myth, Confederate Fact
The Battle of Franklin: Recollections of Confederate and Union Soldiers
The Battle of Nashville: Recollections of Confederate and Union Soldiers
The Battle of Spring Hill: Recollections of Confederate and Union Soldiers

NATURAL HISTORY
North America's Amazing Mammals: An Encyclopedia for the Whole Family
The Concise Book of Owls: A Guide to Nature's Most Mysterious Birds
The Concise Book of Tigers: A Guide to Nature's Most Remarkable Cats

PARANORMAL
Carnton Plantation Ghost Stories: True Tales of the Unexplained from Tennessee's Most Haunted Civil War House!
UFOs and Aliens: The Complete Guidebook

FAMILY HISTORIES
The Blakeneys: An Etymological, Ethnological, and Genealogical Study - Uncovering the Mysterious Origins of the Blakeney Family and Name
The Caudills: An Etymological, Ethnological, and Genealogical Study - Exploring the Name and National Origins of a European-American Family
The McGavocks of Carnton Plantation: A Southern History - Celebrating One of Dixie's Most Noble Confederate Families and Their Tennessee Home

MIND, BODY, SPIRIT
Autobiography of a Non-Yogi: A Scientist's Journey From Hinduism to Christianity
Britannia Rules: Goddess-Worship in Ancient Anglo-Celtic Society - An Academic Look at the United Kingdom's Matricentric Spiritual Past
Christ Is All and In All: Rediscovering Your Divine Nature and the Kingdom Within
Christmas Before Christianity: How the Birthday of the "Sun" Became the Birthday of the "Son"
Jesus and the Gospel of Q: Christ's Pre-Christian Teachings As Recorded in the New Testament
Jesus and the Law of Attraction: The Bible-Based Guide to Creating Perfect Health, Wealth, and Happiness Following Christ's Simple Formula
Seabrook's Bible Dictionary of Traditional and Mystical Christian Doctrines
The Bible and the Law of Attraction: 99 Teachings of Jesus, the Apostles, and the Prophets
The Book of Kelle: An Introduction to Goddess-Worship and the Great Celtic Mother-Goddess Kelle, Original Blessed Lady of Ireland
The Divine Three Manual: How to Heal Yourself Safely and Simply Using Earth's Natural Resources
The Goddess Dictionary of Words and Phrases: Introducing a New Core Vocabulary for the Women's Spirituality Movement
The Hormesis Effect: The Miraculous Healing Power of Radioactive Stones

WOMEN
Aphrodite's Trade: The Hidden History of Prostitution Unveiled
Princess Diana: Modern Day Moon-Goddess - A Psychoanalytical and Mythological Look at Diana Spencer's Life, Marriage, and Death
Women in Gray: A Tribute to the Ladies Who Supported the Southern Confederacy

REPRINTS
A Short History of the Confederate States of America (author Jefferson Davis; editor Lochlainn Seabrook)
Prison Life of Jefferson Davis (author John J. Craven; editor Lochlainn Seabrook)

Five-Star Books & Gifts From the Heart of the American South!

SeaRavenPress.com

A Short History of the

CONFEDERATE STATES OF AMERICA

JEFFERSON DAVIS
ORIGINALLY PUBLISHED POSTHUMOUSLY IN 1890

THIS EDITION EDITED & ARRANGED BY AUTHOR-HISTORIAN, "THE VOICE OF THE TRADITIONAL SOUTH," COLONEL
LOCHLAINN SEABROOK
JEFFERSON DAVIS HISTORICAL GOLD MEDAL WINNER

This is a Sea Raven Press Reprint
Not one word has been added to or subtracted from the original text

2020

Sea Raven Press, Nashville, Tennessee, USA

A Sea Raven Press Reprint published by
Sea Raven Press, Cassidy Ravensdale, President
PO Box 1484, Spring Hill, Tennessee 37174-1484 USA
SeaRavenPress.com • searavenpress@gmail.com

Original text by Jefferson Davis (1808-1889)
This book was first published posthumously in 1890 by the Belford Company, New York.
In our reprint not one word has been added to or subtracted from the original text.

Copyright © collection, editing, & arrangement Lochlainn Seabrook, 2020
in accordance with U.S. and international copyright laws and regulations, as stated and protected under the Berne Union for the Protection of Literary and Artistic Property (Berne Convention), and the Universal Copyright Convention (the UCC). All rights reserved under the Pan-American and International Copyright Conventions.

1st SRP paperback edition, 1st printing, October 2020 • ISBN: 978-1-943737-86-4
1st SRP hardcover edition, 1st printing, October 2020 • ISBN: 978-1-943737-87-1

ISBN: 978-1-943737-86-4 (paperback)
Library of Congress Control Number: 2020946160

This work is the copyrighted intellectual property of Lochlainn Seabrook and has been registered with the Copyright Office at the Library of Congress in Washington, D.C., USA. No part of this work (including text, covers, drawings, photos, illustrations, maps, images, diagrams, etc.), in whole or in part, may be used, reproduced, stored in a retrieval system, or transmitted, in any form or by any means now known or hereafter invented, without written permission from the publisher. The sale, duplication, hire, lending, copying, digitalization, or reproduction of this material, in any manner or form whatsoever, is also prohibited, and is a violation of federal, civil, and digital copyright law, which provides severe civil and criminal penalties for any violations.

A Short History of the Confederate States of America, by Jefferson Davis (1890). This reprint edition published by Sea Raven Press (2020); edited by Lochlainn Seabrook (2020).

Front and back cover design and art, book design, layout, and interior art by Lochlainn Seabrook
All images, graphic design, graphic art, and illustrations copyright © Lochlainn Seabrook
All images selected, placed, manipulated, and/or created by Lochlainn Seabrook
Davis image on page 7 courtesy Percival Beacroft, Trustee of the Papers of Jefferson Davis
Cover image: Jefferson Davis, courtesy U.S. Library of Congress

All persons who approve of the authority and principles of the literary works of Sea Raven Press, and realize our benefits as a means of reeducating the world about the South and the Confederacy, are hereby requested to avidly recommend our books to others and to vigorously cooperate in extending their reach, scope, and influence around the globe. Thank you.

The views on the American "Civil War" documented in this book are those of the publisher.

PRINTED & MANUFACTURED IN OCCUPIED TENNESSEE, FORMER CONFEDERATE STATES OF AMERICA

Lochlainn Seabrook's Dedication

To the Confederacy's greatest chief executive.

Jefferson Davis' Epigraph

Prosperum et felix scelus virtus vocatur.

SENECA THE YOUNGER
1ˢᵗ Century A.D.

(Editor's translation: "Prosperous and successful crime goes by the name of virtue.")

CONTENTS

Notes to the Reader - 13
Preface, by Lochlainn Seabrook - 19
Editor's Introduction, by Lochlainn Seabrook - 21
Introduction, by Jefferson Davis - 37

PART 1: BEFORE SECESSION

CHAPTER 1: CAUSES OF THE WAR BETWEEN THE STATES - 47
CHAPTER 2: NEGRO SLAVERY & THE SLAVE-TRADE - 50
CHAPTER 3: THE EXTENSION OF SLAVERY - 52
CHAPTER 4: THE MISSOURI COMPROMISE - 54
CHAPTER 5: THE COMPROMISE MEASURES - 57
CHAPTER 6: POLITICS IN MISSISSIPPI - 59
CHAPTER 7: THE KANSAS- NEBRASKA TROUBLES - 61
CHAPTER 8: THE ABOLITION MOVEMENT - 64
CHAPTER 9: THE JOHN BROWN RAID - 67
CHAPTER 10: A RETROSPECT - 69
CHAPTER 11: PRELIMINARY PREPARATIONS FOR DEFENCE - 73
CHAPTER 12: THE CLOSE OF 1860 - 76
CHAPTER 13: SECESSION OF SOUTH CAROLINA - 78
CHAPTER 14: GENERAL PRINCIPLES - 85
CHAPTER 15: THE RIGHT OF SECESSION - 87

PART 2: SECESSION & CONFEDERATION

CHAPTER 16: EARLY DAYS OF SECESSION - 93
CHAPTER 17: FORT SUMTER - 96
CHAPTER 18: PROGRESS OF SECESSION - 99
CHAPTER 19: THE CONFEDERATE CABINET & CONGRESS - 101
CHAPTER 20: SOME NORTHERN PROTESTS - 104
CHAPTER 21: THE CONFEDERATE CONSTITUTION - 105
CHAPTER 22: NEGOTIATIONS WITH THE FEDERAL GOVERNMENT - 108
CHAPTER 23: BOMBARDMENT OF FORT SUMTER - 111

PART 3: THE WAR

CHAPTER 24: SOUTH CAROLINA, MARYLAND, & VIRGINIA - 115
CHAPTER 25: CONFEDERATE PREPARATIONS FOR DEFENCE - 117
CHAPTER 26: ORGANIZATION OF OUR RESOURCES - 119
CHAPTER 27: FEDERAL OPPRESSIONS IN MARYLAND - 122
CHAPTER 28: THE BATTLE OF MANASSAS - 127
CHAPTER 29: NEUTRALITY OF KENTUCKY - 131
CHAPTER 30: THE CONTEST IN MISSOURI - 134
CHAPTER 31: GENERAL ALBERT SIDNEY JOHNSTON - 136
CHAPTER 32: FEDERAL OUTRAGES IN MISSOURI - 138
CHAPTER 33: MISSOURI DISARMED - 141
CHAPTER 34: MILITARY OPERATIONS IN MISSOURI - 144

CHAPTER 35: CONFEDERATE AID TO MISSOURI - 147
CHAPTER 36: OPERATIONS OF GENERALS WISE, FLOYD & LEE - 150
CHAPTER 37: ARREST OF MASON & SLIDELL - 154
CHAPTER 38: OUR DEFICIENT ORDNANCE SUPPLIES - 157
CHAPTER 39: THE CONFEDERATE FINANCIAL SYSTEM - 167
CHAPTER 40: REFORMS IN THE MILITARY LEGISLATION - 170
CHAPTER 41: FEDERAL HOSTILITIES & USURPATIONS - 172
CHAPTER 42: FORTS HENRY & DONELSON SURRENDERED - 177
CHAPTER 43: TRANS-MISSISSIPPI MILITARY OPERATIONS - 185
CHAPTER 44: THE BATTLE OF SHILOH - 189
CHAPTER 45: FURTHER MILITARY EVENTS IN THE WEST - 194
CHAPTER 46: NAVAL OPERATIONS IN THE EAST - 197
CHAPTER 47: OPENING OF THE PENINSULAR CAMPAIGN - 200
CHAPTER 48: JACKSON'S SHENANDOAH CAMPAIGN - 207
CHAPTER 49: THE BATTLE OF SEVEN PINES - 216
CHAPTER 50: THE BATTLE OF NEW COLD HARBOR - 221
CHAPTER 51: THE BATTLES OF FRAZER'S FARM & MALVERN HILL - 229
CHAPTER 52: FEDERAL LEGISLATIVE USURPATIONS - 239
CHAPTER 53: FEDERAL EXECUTIVE USURPATIONS - 242
CHAPTER 54: CONFEDERATE NAVAL OPERATIONS - 247
CHAPTER 55: CONFEDERATE NAVAL OPERATIONS IN THE WEST - 260
CHAPTER 56: NAVAL AFFAIRS IN THE WEST - 270
CHAPTER 57: THE CONFEDERATE NAVY ON THE HIGH SEAS - 281
CHAPTER 58: FEDERAL APPEALS TO EUROPE NOT TO AID "PIRATES" - 299
CHAPTER 59: THE MILITARY GOVERNMENT OF STATES - 306
CHAPTER 60: PROGRESS OF CENTRALIZATION - 311
CHAPTER 61: MILITARY OPERATIONS IN VIRGINIA - 316
CHAPTER 62: WAR TRANSFERRED TO THE FRONTIER - 326
CHAPTER 63: THE BATTLE OF ANTIETAM - 330
CHAPTER 64: TREASURY REGULATIONS & THE COTTON FARMING - 338
CHAPTER 65: MILITARY OPERATIONS IN VIRGINIA - 342
CHAPTER 66: OUR FOREIGN RELATIONS - 354
CHAPTER 67: MILITARY OPERATIONS IN THE WEST - 361
CHAPTER 68: NAVAL & MILITARY OPERATIONS ON THE MISSISSIPPI - 367
CHAPTER 69: THE CAMPAIGN AGAINST VICKSBURG - 374
CHAPTER 70: THE DEFENCE OF VICKSBURG - 377
CHAPTER 71: SURRENDER OF PORT HUDSON - 380
CHAPTER 72: THE BATTLE OF CHICKAMAUGA - 381
CHAPTER 73: MISSIONARY RIDGE - 385
CHAPTER 74: THE BATTLE OF GETTYSBURG - 387
CHAPTER 75: AFTER GETTYSBURG - 393
CHAPTER 76: THE SUBJUGATION OF TENNESSEE & LOUISIANA - 395
CHAPTER 77: THE SUBJUGATION OF MARYLAND - 400
CHAPTER 78: THE SUBJUGATION OF KENTUCKY - 404
CHAPTER 79: THE SUBJUGATION OF MISSOURI - 409
CHAPTER 80: THE SUBJUGATION OF THE STATE OF NEW YORK - 411
CHAPTER 81: THE MILITARY COMMISSION AT WASHINGTON - 418
CHAPTER 82: FREE SPEECH SUPPRESSED IN THE NORTH - 422
CHAPTER 83: MILITARY OPERATIONS IN VIRGINIA - 424
CHAPTER 84: BUTLER BOTTLED UP - 427
CHAPTER 85: THE BATTLES OF THE WILDERNESS - 432
CHAPTER 86: EARLY'S ADVANCE ON WASHINGTON & CHAMBERSBURG - 441
CHAPTER 87: BATTLE OF WINCHESTER - 447

CHAPTER 88: MILITARY OPERATIONS AFTER WINCHESTER - 450
CHAPTER 89: THE RED RIVER CAMPAIGN - 455
CHAPTER 90: FORT PILLOW - 457
CHAPTER 91: JOHNSTON'S RETROGRESSIVE CAMPAIGN - 459
CHAPTER 92: FALL OF ATLANTA - 463
CHAPTER 93: HOOD'S CAMPAIGN FROM ATLANTA TO NASHVILLE - 466
CHAPTER 94: SHERMAN'S MARCH TO THE SEA - 469
CHAPTER 95: THE BATTLE OF NASHVILLE - 474
CHAPTER 96: EXCHANGE OF PRISONERS - 476
CHAPTER 97: FEDERAL BARBARITIES & THREATENED RETALIATION - 481
CHAPTER 98: MISSION OF VICE-PRESIDENT STEPHENS - 484
CHAPTER 99: WAR PRISONS, NORTHERN & SOUTHERN - 487
CHAPTER 100: ABORTIVE NEGOTIATIONS - 492
CHAPTER 101: SHERMAN'S MARCH NORTHWARD - 500
CHAPTER 102: SIEGE OF PETERSBURG - 504
CHAPTER 103: FORT FISHER - 511
CHAPTER 104: EVACUATION OF PETERSBURG - 513
CHAPTER 105: EVACUATION OF RICHMOND - 516
CHAPTER 106: THE SURRENDER AT APPOMATTOX - 518
CHAPTER 107: EVACUATION OF RICHMOND - 521
CHAPTER 108: SURRENDER OF GENERAL JOHNSTON - 524
CHAPTER 109: CAPTURE OF PRESIDENT DAVIS - 528
CHAPTER 110: THE COST OF THE WAR & THE NORTHERN METHODS OF WARFARE - 536
CHAPTER 111: RE-ESTABLISHMENT OF THE UNION BY FORCE - 541

Learn More About Lincoln's War - 543

Why the South fought . . .

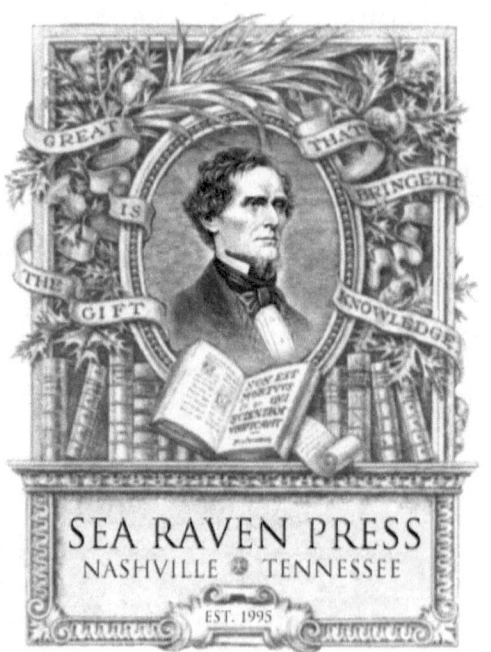

NOTES TO THE READER
From the Editor

THE TWO MAIN POLITICAL PARTIES IN 1860
☛ *A Short History of the Confederate States of America* will not make sense unless one first grasps the easily demonstrable fact that in 1860 the two major political parties—the Democrats and the newly formed Republicans—were the opposite of what they are today. In other words, the Democrats of the mid 19th Century were Conservatives, akin to the Republican Party of today, while the Republicans of the mid 19th Century were Liberals, akin to the Democratic Party of today.[1]

The author's cousin, Confederate Vice President and Democrat Alexander H. Stephens: a Southern Conservative.

Thus, the Confederacy's Democratic president, Jefferson Davis (the author of this book), was a Conservative (with libertarian leanings); the Union's Republican president, Abraham Lincoln, was a Liberal (with socialistic leanings).[2] This is why, in the mid 1800s, the Democrat Party, the Conservative party, called itself "the States' Rights Party."[3] The Left, as is well-known, has always detested states rights, for they interfere with the progressive's goal of establishing a large monolithic central government that totally dominates and controls the citizenry (as in Cuba). Hence, in his autobiography, *Mein Kampf*, national socialist Adolf Hitler heartily lauded Lincoln's destruction of states rights in the South.[4]

As further proof of my assertion that the two major parties were reversed in 1860, the Democrats of the Civil War period referred to themselves as "conservatives," "confederates," "anti-centralists," or

---

1. Thomas E. Woods Jr., *The Politically Incorrect Guide to American History*. Washington, D.C.: Regnery, 2004, p. 47.
2. On Lincoln's socialistic, Marxist, and communist thoughts, ideas, tendencies, cabinet members, Union generals, friends, and associates, see my books: 1) *Lincoln's War: The Real Cause, The Real Winner, the Real Loser*; 2) *Abraham Lincoln Was a Liberal, Jefferson Davis Was a Conservative: The Missing Key to Understanding the American Civil War*; 3) *Abraham Lincoln: The Southern View*. Also see Burke McCarty (ed.), *Little Sermons in Socialism by Abraham Lincoln*. Chicago, IL: The Chicago Daily Socialist, 1910; Earl Browder, *Lincoln and the Communists*. New York, NY: Workers Library Publishers, Inc., 1936.
3. Supra, p. 60. See also John William Jones, *The Davis Memorial Volume; Or Our Dead President, Jefferson Davis and the World's Tribute to His Memory*. Richmond, VA: B. F. Johnson, 1889, pp. 144, 200-201, 273.
4. Lochlainn Seabrook, *Abraham Lincoln: The Southern View*. 2007. Franklin, TN: Sea Raven Press, 2013 paperback ed., pp. 299-300.

"constitutionalists" (the latter because they favored strict adherence to the original Constitution—which tacitly guaranteed states' rights—as created by the Founding Fathers), while the Civil War Republicans called themselves "liberals," "nationalists," "centralists," or "consolidationists" (the latter three because they wanted to nationalize the central government and consolidate political power in Washington, D.C.).[5]

In this very book, Davis, who referred to the 1860 Democrats as "the conservative power of the country,"[6] explained the two main political parties at the time this way:

> . . . the names adopted by political parties in the United States have not always been strictly significant of their principles. In general terms it may be said that the old Federal party [Liberal] inclined to nationalism [then a term for big government], or consolidation [that is, consolidation of power in the Federal government], and that the Whig party [liberalistic], which succeeded it, although not identical with it, was favorable, in the main, to a strong Central Government [liberalism and socialism]. On the other hand, its opponent, the Republican [Conservative], afterward known as the Democratic party [until the election of 1896, when the two parties reversed, becoming the parties we know today], was dominated by the idea of the sovereignty of the States and the federal or confederate character of the Union [known as Americanism or conservatism]. Although other elements have entered into its organization at different periods, this has been its vital, cardinal, and abiding principle.[7]

Since this idea is new to most of my readers, let us further demystify it by viewing it from the perspective of the American Revolutionary War. If Davis and his conservative Southern constituents (the Democrats of 1861) had been alive in 1775, they would have sided with George Washington and the American colonists, who sought to secede from the tyrannical government of Great Britain; if Lincoln and his Liberal Northern constituents (the Republicans of 1861) had been alive at that time, they would have sided with King George III and the English monarchy, who sought to maintain the American colonies as possessions of the British Empire. It is due to this very comparison that we Southerners often refer to our secession from the U.S. as the Second Declaration of Independence and the "Civil War" as the Second

---

5. See Lochlainn Seabrook, *The Alexander H. Stephens Reader: Excerpts From the Works of a Confederate Founding Father*. Spring Hill, TN: Sea Raven Press, 2013, passim; Edward Alfred Pollard, *The Lost Cause*. New York, NY: E. B. Treat and Co., 1867, p. 178; John Hope Franklin, *Reconstruction After the Civil War*. Chicago, IL: University of Chicago Press, 1961, pp. 101, 111, 130, 149; John G. Nicolay and John Hay (eds.), *Abraham Lincoln: Complete Works*. 12 vols. 1894. New York, NY: The Century Co., 1907 ed., Vol. 1, p. 627.
6. Supra, p. 72.
7. Supra, pp. 68-69.

American Revolutionary War.

As noted, without a basic understanding of these facts, the War for Southern Independence will forever remain incomprehensible. Indeed, in any study of America's antebellum, bellum, and postbellum periods, this knowledge is crucial. For a full discussion of these topics see in particular my books, 1) *Abraham Lincoln Was a Liberal, Jefferson Davis Was a Conservative: The Missing Key to Understanding the American Civil War*; 2) *Lincoln's War: The Real Cause, the Real Winner, the Real Loser*; 3) *Abraham Lincoln: The Southern View*.

FAITHFULNESS TO DAVIS' TEXT

☛ In writing *A Short History of the Confederate States of America*, President Davis assumed that his readers would have a good working knowledge of American history, of politics, and in particular, of the War for Southern Independence. He could not have known that, thanks to today's America's Left-wing run public school system (a remnant of Reconstruction), many modern students lack even a basic knowledge of American history; and what little they are taught by their mostly progressive (i.e., anti-South) teachers are biased fairy tales meant to, not educate, but further injure and humiliate Dixie and carry on the vicious South-shaming that was started by their Liberal Yankee forebears. This overt Left-wing indoctrination of our children, masquerading as "education," is what I refer to as fake history.

Naturally, as a 21st-Century Southern historian, there were many clarifications and explanations I could have appended to Davis' text, items that would have greatly benefitted the modern reader. For example, he often leaves out the first name and national affiliation (Confederate or Union) of the many politicians and military officers he references. Late 19th-Century Victorians would have been familiar with such individuals, but in our time they are thoroughly foreign to most people.

Despite this, I resisted the temptation to add explanatory footnotes of my own to Davis' text.

In order to preserve the authenticity of *A Short History of the Confederate States of America*, I have also retained Davis' original spellings, formatting, and punctuation. These include such items as British-English spellings, long-running paragraphs, obsolete words, outdated military terms (in particular pertaining to rank, weapons, and equipment), unusual hyphenations, and various literary devices peculiar to the Victorian Era. Note that all bracketed words, notes, and sentences, are Davis'.

Where the Confederate chief executive misspells personal names, I have made the necessary corrections in order to prevent confusion (for example, some names, like Breckinridge, he spells differently on several occasions). Davis' original work, like all books, includes a number of typos, which, where discovered, I have taken the liberty to rectify. Lastly, Davis neglected to add an index or a bibliography, and I have been faithful to these two omissions as well.

There is a singular curiosity in Davis' book that warrants mentioning: toward the end he has given two separate chapters, 105 and 107, the same name ("Evacuation of Richmond"). Whether this was intentional or an oversight (perhaps the result of his age at the time, late 70s, early 80s), is unknown. In any event, in keeping with my policy of textual noninterference, I have left these two chapters as is.

The end result is what I believe to be an accurately rendered manuscript, one that carefully preserves every word of text from Davis' original 1890 book without the intrusive addition of modern commentary.

In short, nothing has been added, nothing has been subtracted. This includes the footnotes (from his introduction to chapter 111), which are the President's and his alone.

ARTISTIC & EDITORIAL CHANGES

☛ Naturally, as editor, I have redone Davis' book in my own visual and artistic style, selecting different fonts as well as creating a new cover, all which differ greatly from his 1890 edition. However, I have retained Davis' 12 original illustrations, as well as their captions and chronological order. The only changes made here were altering the page placement (to what I consider more logical positions) and cleaning up images that had lost much of their clarity and luster after 130 years.

In addition to these modifications, there is one area where I have taken editorial licence with Davis' writing, and that is with his chapter numbering system. He divides his work into three parts, beginning each section with "Chapter 1." From a scholar's, researcher's, and reader's point of view I find this arrangement unnecessarily cumbersome, as Davis' version contains three "Chapter 1s," three "Chapter 2s," three "Chapter 3s," and so on.

In my edition I have retained the three parts of Davis' original work, but have numbered his chapters consecutively, from the beginning to end of the book. Thus both his Part 1 and my Part 1 have 15 chapters. But while his Part 2 begins with Chapter 1, mine starts with Chapter 16; while his Part 3 starts with Chapter 1, mine begins with Chapter 24; while his final chapter is 88, mine is Chapter 111. These subtle changes, which do no harm to the text, will make it easier for today's reader to navigate Davis' lengthy and highly detailed work.

LEARN MORE

☛ Lincoln's War on the Constitution and the American people can never be fully understood without a thorough knowledge of the South's perspective. For those who are interested in additional material from Dixie's viewpoint, please see my comprehensive histories listed on pages 2 and 3.

Keep Your Body, Mind, & Spirit Vibrating at Their Highest Level

YOU CAN DO SO BY READING THE BOOKS OF

SEA RAVEN PRESS

There is nothing that will so perfectly keep your body, mind, and spirit in a healthy condition as to think wisely and positively. Hence you should not only read this book, but also the other books that we offer. They will quicken your physical, mental, and spiritual vibrations, enabling you to maintain a position in society as a healthy erudite person.

KEEP YOURSELF WELL-INFORMED!

The well-informed person is always at the head of the procession, while the ignorant, the lazy, and the unthoughtful hang onto the rear. If you are a Spiritual man or woman, do yourself a great favor: read Sea Raven Press books and stay well posted on the Truth. It is almost criminal for one to remain in ignorance while the opportunity to gain knowledge is open to all at a nominal price.

We invite you to visit our Webstore for a wide selection of wholesome, family-friendly, well-researched, educational books for all ages. You will be glad you did!

Five-Star Books & Gifts From the Heart of the American South

SeaRavenPress.com

U.D.C. MOTTO, 1921

PREFACE

REVIVING A MASTERPIECE

WHY did I choose to resuscitate and edit President Jefferson Davis' glorious volume *A Short History of the Confederate States of America*? Not only am I an ardent admirer of the Confederate chief executive, but he and I are distant cousins. We also share spiritual (Christian), regional (Southern), constitutional (Confederate), and political views (Conservative), for my Southern ancestors, the Democrats of the mid 19th-Century, were Conservatives (as noted, the Republicans of the mid 19th-Century were Liberals).

These are personal reasons, however. My primary purpose in republishing this work is educational, for no one understood the birth, life, and suppression of the Confederacy as clearly as Davis did, an individual who not only lived through the War, but helmed the new republic, then survived Lee's surrender by 24 years. Nearly a century and a half later, his crystalline words remain one of the best chronicles of what actually transpired between the Southern Confederacy and the Northern Union those many years ago—something completely missing from histories penned by the Left and its biased South-hating historians.

Jefferson Davis (1808-1889), the first, but not the last, President of the Confederate States of America.

Works by Conservative Americans like Jefferson Davis are invaluable and thus must be preserved for posterity. I am honored and proud to help contribute to this effort. *Deo Vindice.* L.S.

Editor's Introduction
by Lochlainn Seabrook

Understanding Lincoln's War in Light of Current Events

AS I edit this book (Autumn 2020), a communist uprising is taking place across not only America, but the entire world. Naturally, the Left-wing hatred for anything and everything Southern, traditional, Christian, and particularly Confederate, is on daily display in every corner of the U.S. Progressives have always detested the old Southern Confederacy. Why? In great part because an innate aspect of confederacies are the political powers known as *states rights*, one of the greatest barriers to the birth and expansion of Left-wing ideologies like socialism and communism (just one reason we modern freedom-loving Southerners continue to endorse and espouse this tradition).

In the concocted name of "social justice," Confederate monuments are being torn down, Confederate gravestones are regularly defaced, the names of Confederate heroes are being removed from street signs and schools, and the Confederate Battle Flag is being ridiculed, burned, and banned like never before. And while the statues of Confederate politicians (many, like Davis, who were also U.S. politicians) are quietly being removed from the Capitol building (Davis' statue being just one example), and while several American military branches are outlawing Confederate flags and other Southern symbols on their bases, at this very moment a bill is being submitted to Congress that will require the removal of anything remotely connected to the Southern Confederacy from all *public* property throughout the U.S. Though Confederate memorabilia displayed on *private* property will still be protected, from this time forward it will presumably be unlawful on land owned by the U.S. government.[8]

President Davis' *A Short History of the Confederate States of America* is irrefutable testimony, in black and white, that the American socialist-communist uprising of 2020 is nothing but a continuance of the socialist-communist uprising of 1861, a conflict which Liberal historians (many who are socialists and communists themselves) disingenuously call the "Civil War" (a conspiracy of gargantuan proportions that I discuss at length in my book *The Great Yankee Coverup*). Davis readily exposes these facts for all to see.

Between 1860 and 1877 (the year Reconstruction ended) Northern Republicans (then America's main Liberal party) methodically trampled over the Constitution, violating law after law to forward their ultimate goal: the destruction of states rights and the installation of big government at

---

8. For a detailed examination of the importance of Confederate history, see Lochlainn Seabrook, *Confederate Monuments: Why Every American Should Honor Confederate Soldiers and Their Memorials*. Spring Hill, TN: Sea Raven Press, 2018.

Washington, D.C.—or what Davis called, in the language of his day, "the establishment of the monarchial or consolidated form" of government.[9]

Big government Liberal Abraham Lincoln, who viewed "the sovereignty of the people and of the several and distinct States" as little more than "a weakness and an enthusiasm of the [founding] fathers,"[10] referred to the type of government he desired as a "National Union." However, the Founding generation specifically rejected the idea of forming the U.S. as a nation, and actually voted against the concept,[11] describing our country, as George Washington and other Founders did, as a "Confederate Republic."[12]

The Left, obsessed with the destruction of states rights and their replacement with the centralization of *all* governmental power at Washington, have been trying to rid our country of state sovereignty ever since. The South, and her devoted attachment to that "corner-stone of the Union, the independence of the States,"[13] was all that was standing in the Left's way. This desire on the part of the North "lay at the foundation of the war,"[14] which is why Lincoln sent 75,000 invaders into the South in 1861. It was in response to this "monstrous usurpation"[15] that the South took up arms.

What actually occurred between April 12, 1861, and April 9, 1865, has been completely whitewashed from our history books. Fortunately for us, Davis cataloged this period in *A Short History of the Confederate States of America*, using his personal experiences, exemplary mind, home library, wartime friends, and photographic memory to assemble the facts. According to Davis, the following is a but a partial list of the many crimes, outrages, atrocities, and barbarities inflicted by Lincoln, his administration, and his military (along with many Yankee politicians), on the South—and also the North—during the War:

- The overthrow and destruction of all the state governments of the Northern states (by Lincoln's personal order).
- The general suppression, under threat of violence or arrest, of free speech and freedom of the press across the North and South.
- Reducing both Southern and Northern states "to the condition of a conquered province."[16]
- Issuing a proclamation declaring that, in Lincoln's judgment, "the public safety required that the privilege of the writ of *habeas corpus* should be suspended

---

9. Supra, p. 476.
10. Supra, p. 476.
11. Lochlainn Seabrook, *All We Ask is to be Let Alone: The Southern Secession Fact Book*. Spring Hill, TN: Sea Raven Press, 2017, pp. 58-60.
12. Lochlainn Seabrook, *Confederate Flag Facts: What Every American Should Know About Dixie's Southern Cross*. Spring Hill, TN: Sea Raven Press, 2016, p. 27.
13. Supra, p. 477.
14. Supra, p. 477.
15. Supra, p. 476.
16. Supra, p. 329.

throughout the United States. . . ."[17] Of this gross illegality Davis writes: "No autocrat ever issued an edict more destructive of the natural right to personal liberty."[18]
- Issuing a proclamation declaring the inhabitants of the South to be "in insurrection,"[19] which effectively permitted the Union to seize any and all commercials goods coming in or going out of the Confederacy—along with the confiscation of the vehicles or vessels they were being transported in.
- Issuing falsehoods about the Confederacy throughout Europe in an attempt to insure that European countries did not recognize the South as an independent power.
- Issuing falsehoods about "the agents of the Confederate States in Canada," claiming, for example, that they planned, on election day, 1864, to send "an invasion of voters from Canada to colonize different points"[20] throughout the Union in order to dissuade people from voting for Lincoln. In another instance the U.S. State Department "issued a despatch saying that information had been received from the British Provinces that there was a conspiracy to set fire to the principal cities in the Northern States on the day of the Presidential election."[21] This type of blatant disinformation was used as justification by Lincoln to intervene, with military force, in the 1864 election in an attempt to sway the outcome in his favor. (Like many of his other connivances, it worked.)
- The mass burning of Southern homes, nearly all containing non-combatants (mainly helpless women, children, and elderly men), as well as the theft of the owners' property.
- The frequent use of baseless slander and defamation of Southerners of note, with the two-fold intention of creating division and strife throughout Dixie and falsifying the historical record to confuse future historians. A ridiculous and mendacious charge brought against Davis, for instance, was that of "inciting and encouraging"[22] the assassination of Lincoln.
- The fabricated accusations, unlawful arrests, harsh imprisonments, fake "trials," and horrific executions of innocent Southerners, such as William B. Mumford, Mary Surratt, and Henry Wirz.
- In states like Louisiana, forcing "aged and peaceful citizens, unresisting captives, and non-combatants"[23] to do hard labor while in chains.
- Lincoln's imprisonment of ordinary Southern citizens in cold, dark, damp dungeons and remote isolated fortresses.
- Sherman's order at Atlanta requiring "the immediate expulsion from their homes and only means of subsistence of thousands of unoffending women

---

17. Supra, p. 413.
18. Supra, p. 414.
19. Supra, pp. 338, 340.
20. Supra, p. 416.
21. Supra, p. 416.
22. Supra, p. 418.
23. Supra, p. 307.

and children, whose husbands and fathers were either in the army, in Northern prisons, or had died in battle."[24] (Union soldiers later sent to guard the womenfolk that had been expelled from their homes, robbed them of what little goods they had been allowed to bring with them. These included clothing, jewelry, and assorted "trinkets.")

- Sherman's burning of Atlanta. Of this heinous crime Davis writes: "Not a house was spared, not even a church."[25]
- The North's issuance, in 1862, of an order stating that the U.S. government had the right "to seize and use any property, real or personal, which may be necessary or convenient for their several commands for supplies or for other military purposes." Davis calls this a "system of plunder."[26]
- The violent seizure and arrest of Yankee Democrats (at that time, Conservatives), such as former Right-wing Ohio Representative Clement L. Vallandigham, who were illegally tried before military commissions (they were citizens, not military personnel) and deported south to the Confederacy—all for merely commenting publicly on Lincoln's unconstitutional acts.
- In New York countless citizens were arrested and imprisoned for criticizing or even questioning Lincoln. By Lincoln's own order, Davis writes, "the Constitution, the laws, the courts, the Executive of the state . . . were subverted, turned aside from the end for which they were instituted, and all the specific arrangements were of no avail to secure this guaranteed right of its citizens. Probably every one of the prisoners was entirely innocent of any act whatever that was criminal under the laws of either the State or the United States. . . . Finally, the prison in New York harbor became so full that many prisoners were sent to Fort Warren, in Boston harbor."[27]
- Lincoln's use of "degrading punishment" for "selling medicine to the sick soldiers of the Confederacy."[28]
- Lincoln's complete disregard of every type of voting law, with "fraud and falsehood triumphing over popular rights and fundamental law."[29]
- The North's intimidation, harassment, beatings, torture, and even murder of innocent nonresisting Southerners (including women and children).
- The stripping of the constitutional rights of everyday law-abiding citizens; this included being divested of firearms, arrested without warrant, and convicted and imprisoned without trial.
- In Missouri, where "the State organization was subjugated to do the will of the usurper and to disregard the will of the sovereign people,"[30] Lincoln had

---

24. Supra, p. 466.
25. Supra, p. 469.
26. Supra, p. 481.
27. Supra, p. 412.
28. Supra, p. 307.
29. Supra, p. 314.
30. Supra, p. 410.

the governor charged with treason, then "proceeded to declare the State offices vacant and to elect a provisional Governor and other officers entirely subservient to the will and interests of the administration at Washington."[31]
- The disarmament and disbandment of state militias in order to prevent "rebellion" against the Union.
- The murder of Confederate officers, like Colonel John L. Owen, who died by order of Yankee General John Pope. (Davis notes that he had been "credibly informed that many other Federal officers within the Confederacy had been guilty of felonies and capital offences.")[32]
- The attempt by numerous Union officers, such as General David Hunter and General John W. Phelps, to start a race war by arming black slaves and encouraging them to murder their former white owners.
- Occupying the office of the independent telegraph line by a military force "in the name of the Government of the United States."[33]
- Lincoln's removal of tens of thousands of Southern families from their plundered homes, who were then "left to starve in the street or subsist on charity."[34]
- Lincoln's brutal suppression of citizens who organized in opposition to him, and which he labeled "insurrectionary movements."[35]
- Lincoln's suppression of nearly 400 Northern, conservative-leaning (i.e., anti-Lincoln) newspapers; not only were these newspapers censored, but their printing presses were destroyed, their offices were closed and sold, and their owners were jailed. Among the many states where these 1st Amendment outrages occurred were New Hampshire, Pennsylvania, Ohio, Wisconsin, and Vermont.
- After much of Maryland was subjugated and placed under martial law, the U.S. government began arbitrarily terrorizing her citizens. For example individuals were arrested and even deported for "rendering assistance to wounded Confederate soldiers" or for "expressing treasonable sentiments"—that is, statements criticizing Lincoln's dictatorial actions. In one instance two Marylanders were charged and arrested simply for "cheering for Jefferson Davis."[36]
- In Baltimore the 2nd Amendment was suspended, owning firearms was made illegal, and Union soldiers ransacked private homes in search of weapons, which they seized and piled by their thousands into "large wagons."[37]
- To expedite its lawbreaking in Maryland, the Lincoln administration had the state's judges arrested and exiled from their cities and counties.

---

31. Supra, p. 409.
32. Supra, p. 482.
33. Supra, p. 415.
34. Supra, p. 308.
35. Supra, p. 142.
36. Supra, p. 401.
37. Supra, p. 401.

- Many parts of Maryland were placed under strict military occupation, some of which entailed armed Yankee soldiers standing guard at the polls, intimidating citizens into voting for Liberals and the Union. "Thus," says Davis, "was the State Government of Maryland subjugated and made an instrument of destruction to the people; thus were their rights ruthlessly violated, and property, millions of dollars in value, annihilated."[38]
- Lincoln's arrest of "treasonable or seditious" individuals, who were then required to take an oath of allegiance to the Government of the United States—or be imprisoned or exiled.[39]
- Lincoln's issuance of a "paper blockade" of the entire Southern coastline, one that happened to be completely ineffective. This made the blockade a violation of both maritime and international law.[40]
- Lincoln's arbitrary arrest of Confederate officers and soldiers, who "were kept in confinement, sometimes in irons or doomed to cells, without charge or trial."[41]
- The North's imprisonment of clergymen, school-teachers, and editors, as well as "large numbers of private citizens,"[42] who refused to take the U.S. oath of Allegiance—and who were held against their wills until they did so.
- Yankee "pillage and arson" attacks on quiet villages, crimes that still stand "prominent for savage cruelties against defenceless women and children."[43]
- The North's confiscation, plunder, and takeover of large Southern plantations, after which their black servants (known derogatorily as "slaves" in the North and as "contraband" by the U.S. army) were forced to continue working for their new Yankee owners under armed Union soldiers.
- The North's use of murder and the violent destruction of property to instill fear and compliance in the Southern populace.
- In Tennessee the unalienable rights of her citizens "were systematically denied, freedom of speech was suppressed, freedom of the press was suspended, personal liberty was destroyed. Citizens were arrested, imprisoned, and exiled without the process of law."[44]
- The U.S. military's invasion of private homes, whose contents were ransacked and whose owners were purposefully terrorized. Many such houses, after being capriciously pillaged for valuables, were bombed, then set on fire and burned to the ground. This resulted in thousands of homeless families roaming the South as refugees in their own country.
- The subjection of Southern females, from young to old, to vulgar speech and "vile insults" from Union soldiers.[45]

---

38. Supra, p. 403.
39. Supra, p. 306.
40. Supra, p. 356.
41. Supra, p. 485.
42. Supra, p. 306.
43. Supra, p. 370.
44. Supra, pp. 397-398.
45. Supra, p. 307.

- The forced removal of contented black Southern servants from their homes, who were then left to "wander helpless on the highway."[46]
- The intentional and unlawful fragmentation of a Confederate state (Virginia) into two separate states, the new one ("West" Virginia), which was turned into a Union state for the purpose of accruing additional electoral votes for Lincoln in the 1864 election.
- The North's immediate execution (without trial) of any Southern citizen believed to be guilty of shooting at a Union soldier. (If found guilty, the individual's house was burned and the remaining inhabitants were imprisoned—again, without due process.)
- The needless destruction of not only private Southern homes, but also Southern barns, mills, factories, furnaces, fences, and farm equipment, such as reapers and thrashing-machines.
- The destruction of millions of bushels of harvested farm products, such as corn and wheat, as well as tons of hay.
- The wanton burning and spoilation of Southern croplands, destroyed in such a way as to render them useless for future planting.
- The wholesale theft of thousands of farm animals, including livestock such as horses, cattle, sheep, and hogs.
- The Union army's flagrant robbery of Southern households, absconding with such items as furniture, dishes, silverware, money, and bonds.
- The Union army's routine search of private houses for "ammunition and arms of every description,"[47] which were then seized, rendering the citizenry defenseless.
- In Louisiana "the Government of the State was subverted, the Constitution of the State in part set aside, and the sovereignty of the people trampled down by a power that had no rightful authority for such acts."[48]
- The emancipation of Southern "slaves" (at the time still legally considered "private property" under the Constitution) in an effort to destabilize the Southern economy and disrupt Southern society.
- The nullification of state military bills, which were then replaced by the draconian military laws of the Lincoln administration.
- The demilitarization of state "Home Guards," which Lincoln considered "illegal organizations."[49]
- Trying and executing Southern citizens, like William B. Mumford, for merely flying the Confederate Flag.
- In Kentucky, which Lincoln placed under martial law, the U.S. military openly and brazenly interfered with elections "under the intimidation of the bayonets." Here, "a [Union] military force was stationed at the polls to sustain and enforce the action of some of the servants of the Government

---

46. Supra, p. 308.
47. Supra, p. 123.
48. Supra, p. 399.
49. Supra, p. 142.

of the United States, in order to overawe the judges of election, secure the administration of a rigid oath of allegiance, and thereby the rejection of as many opposition votes as possible."[50]
- After suspending the writ of *habeas corpus* in the Bluegrass State, Lincoln had "a large number of eminent Kentuckians, of all professions and pursuits, . . . arrested and imprisoned. A group of persons, consisting of judges, magistrates, wealthy merchants, and young women, were banished from the State without having been allowed a hearing or trial, or any opportunity to vindicate themselves."[51]
- The incitement of black servants to insurrection "by every license and encouragement" possible,[52] the Left's usual ploy to instigate a fake race war, thereby dividing and weakening the populace.
- Lincoln's practice of withholding medicines from the sick, including Southern women and children.
- The tearing of "helpless" Southern women from their homes and placing them in solitary confinement—some in fortresses and prisons, others on hot barren islands.
- The feeding of "loathsome rations" to Southern citizens while imprisoned.[53]
- The blockading of all Southern ports, with the intent of preventing food, clothing, and medicines from reaching the Southern citizenry.
- The outright robbing of Southern banks by Union soldiers.
- Breaking and entering of Southern courthouses and stealing public records.
- The arrest and imprisonment of entire state legislatures, after which their state assemblies were dissolved.
- The jailing of individuals whose public opinions ran counter to those of Lincoln and his administration.[54]

Every item listed here—a small part of what Davis called the policies of "pillage and expatriation"—is constitutionally, nationally, or civilly illegal, and hence a crime, many of the highest and most felonious magnitude. But this did not stop Lincoln and his minions from engaging in "numerous usurpations and violations of constitutional principles and laws."[55] These tactics included,

> invasions with military force, the expulsion of lawful State Governments, the assumption by the State Convention of unlawful powers, the election and introduction of persons into offices not vacant, and the declaration of martial law without any authority for it.[56]

---

50. Supra, p. 404.
51. Supra, p. 406.
52. Supra, p. 308.
53. Supra, p. 307.
54. Each of the items in this list is touched upon or discussed in detail by Davis in the present book.
55. Supra, p. 409.
56. My paraphrasal of Davis (see supra, p. 409).

As is clear, it was not just the South that Lincoln invaded and attacked. In every Northern state as well, Davis writes,

> "the sovereignty of the people was entirely disregarded, and the operation of the institutions which had been established for the protection of their rights was suspended or nullified by a military force of the Government of the United States."[57]

During the latter half of the War, having not yet been able to pressure the seceded Southern states back into the Union by physical force, the U.S. government stepped up its practice of imposing its iron will on the South. Davis describes the situation this way:

> "Plunder and devastation of the property of non-combatants, destruction of private dwellings, and even of edifices devoted to the worship of God; expeditions organized for the sole purpose of sacking cities, consigning them to the flames, killing the unarmed inhabitants, and inflicting horrible outrages on women and children, were some of the constantly recurring atrocities of the invader."[58]

Clearly the North's intent was to force every state to comply with its Left-wing worldview—even though this was unconstitutional—all under "the pretext of a restoration of the Union."[59] According to Davis, Lincoln desired and received "the subjugation of *every* State, either by voluntary submission or conquest" via military occupation.[60] To achieve this "the Government of the United States . . . broke through every restraint of the Constitution, of national law, of justice, and of humanity."[61]

Lincoln's aim? The establishment of "the absolute sovereignty of the General Government" across the entire U.S. and C.S. For those commonwealths resisting the North's Left-wing tyranny, this meant nothing less than "the extinguishment of the independence and sovereignty of the State."[62] This was all part of what the North innocently called "State reconstruction,"[63] but what we here in the South call "State deconstruction."

We have uncovered the true motive behind the North's war on the South: the desire to destroy states rights, and even the states themselves (as left-leaning Founders, like Alexander Hamilton, wished),[64] and replace them with a

---

57. Supra, p. 416.
58. Supra, p. 537.
59. Supra, p. 492.
60. Supra, p. 142.
61. Supra, p. 172.
62. Supra, p. 142.
63. Supra, p. 306.
64. Lochlainn Seabrook, *Abraham Lincoln: The Southern View*. 2007. Franklin, TN: Sea Raven Press, 2013 paperback ed., p. 48.

monolithic "big government" that controls the entire country from Washington—a pernicious operation that 19th-Century Liberals called the "American System").[65] Thus the North fought to overturn the constitutional liberty of the states. Yet, as Davis wrote at the time, "the purpose of the Confederate States in the existing war" is to maintain "the constitutional liberty" of its member states.[66]

And here is the clearest evidence of who was in the right and who was in the wrong. Davis declares:

> "Unhesitatingly it may be said that all the conduct of the Confederate States pertaining to the war consisted in just efforts to preserve to themselves and their posterity rights and protections guaranteed to them in the Constitution of the United States, and that the actions of the Federal Government consisted in efforts to suppress those rights, destroy those protections, and subjugate us into compliance with its arbitrary will; and that this conduct on their part involved the subversion of the Constitution and the destruction of the fundamental principles of liberty."[67]

In short, the South fought to preserve the Constitution, the North fought to destroy it.

Through a process that Davis rightly calls "a reign of terror and unbridled despotism,"[68] brute force, trickery, duplicity, thuggery, and fraud helped the Liberal North secure Lincoln in the White House, launch an illicit War on the Conservative South, and hamper the efforts of the Confederacy to defend herself against the unlawful invasion of her territory.

Using minorities (in this case African Americans) as political pawns, was the Victorian Left's standard procedure before, during, and after the War, a practice that continues to this day. Out of this racist policy came the Yankee myths that the "war was over slavery," that "the South fought to preserve and extend slavery," and that "the North fought to destroy slavery"—though there is not a single shred of evidence for any of this, and plenty contradicting it.[69] It was the Left who also produced the overt falsehoods that "secession is illegal," that "the Confederacy was unconstitutional," and that Southerners were "traitors and racists."[70]

This discussion begs the question: from where did such radical ideas, Far-left policies, overt lies, and sinister outrages derive?

---

65. Lochlainn Seabrook, *Lincoln's War: The Real Cause, the Real Winner, the Real Loser.* Spring Hill, TN: Sea Raven Press, 2016, p. 24.
66. Supra, p. 149.
67. Supra, p. 241.
68. Supra, p. 123.
69. For an in-depth discussion on these topics, see Lochlainn Seabrook, *Everything You Were Taught About American Slavery War is Wrong, Ask a Southerner!* Spring Hill, TN: Sea Raven Press, 2015.
70. For an in-depth discussion on these topics, see Lochlainn Seabrook, *All We Ask is to be Let Alone: The Southern Secession Fact Book.* Spring Hill, TN: Sea Raven Press, 2017.

During my lifetime, Liberals (that is, Democrats) have never promoted subversion of the Constitution, the destruction of capitalism, or the overthrow of our very country. Democrat President John F. Kennedy, for example, publicly promoted the traditional (Right-wing) idea that one should aid his country rather than asking for the country's aid, a concept espoused by Conservatives since the dawn of America.

And what about the Left's burning hatred of the Southern Confederacy today? Is this a *liberal Democratic* notion? In 1978, Democrat President Jimmy Carter, certainly one of our most progressive chief executives, restored U.S. citizenship to President Davis (the author of this book), a status that had been illegally stripped from the Southern statesman over 100 years earlier by Lincoln.[71] During the 1992 election, the campaign badges of Democratic candidates Bill Clinton and Al Gore bore a bright Confederate Battle Flag with their names proudly emblazoned on them. Where was the Left's abhorrence of the Confederacy just 28 years ago?

Let us ask again: where did the extreme Far-left notions that permeated the mind of big government Liberal Lincoln and his progressive administration originate? From the mind of "Honest Abe"? Hardly. Davis is emphatic that the Lincoln administration hoped to conceal the facts that

> "the contest on the part of the central [U.S.] Government was for empire—for its absolute supremacy over the State Governments; that the Constitution was rolled up and laid away among the old archives; and that the conditions of their liberty in the future were to be decided by the sword or by 'national' control of the ballot-box."[72]

These are not the acts and policies of everyday Liberal politics. These are the doctrines of *radical, militant, fanatics*; destructive, tradition-hating and often violent activists who operate on the outer left extremes of the political spectrum: the realm of anarchists, syndicalists, and nihilists.

From the beginning to the end of the War, there is unmistakable evidence of the nefarious influence of *anti-American outsiders* surrounding Lincoln; men who, according to Davis, put enormous "pressure"[73] on him to both foment war on the South and, later, pretend that slavery was the cause of the conflict. Indeed, Davis calls this pressure "organized."[74] Who would have "organized" a movement to "pressure" Lincoln into destroying the South, which would, quite notably, also destroy, or at least greatly weaken, states rights?

Is it possible that this Far-left organization was created by and comprised of socialists and communists? The Union's many appalling war crimes have all

---

71. Lochlainn Seabrook, *Everything You Were Taught About the Civil War is Wrong, Ask a Southerner!* 2010. Spring Hill, TN: Sea Raven Press, 2019 ed, p. 208.
72. Supra, p. 303.
73. Supra, p. 242.
74. Supra, p. 242.

the hallmarks of an extremist and revolutionary ideology. But where would we find such individuals in 1860s America? We would find them working in the Lincoln administration and leading the Union armies!

Because it has been hidden from the public most people are not aware that Lincoln surrounded himself with a veritable community of socialists and communists, men such as: Carl Schurz, Charles A. Dana, Friedrich K. F. Hecker, Reinhold Solger, Casper Butz, Friedrich Kapp, Joseph Wedemeyer, August Willich, Fritz Jacobi, Robert Rosa, Max Weber, Francis Channing Barlow, Fritz Anneke, Anselm Albert, Charles Zagonyi, Alexander Sandor Asboth, George Duncan Wells, Alexander Schimmelfennig, Isidor Bush, Franz Sigel, Gustav Von Struve, Johan Fiala, Albin Francisco Schoepf, Henry Ramming, Peter Joseph Osterhaus, Allan Pinkerton, Julius Stahel, Ludwig Blenker, and Friedrich Salomon, among countless others. Many of these men were cohorts, acquaintances, and close associates of Karl Marx and Friedrich Engels, the authors of *The Communist Manifesto*, written in 1848. Lincoln himself considered a number of these individuals "good friends."[75]

Why did Lincoln encircle himself and his armies and administration with revolutionaries, many of them foreigners with subversive anti-American ideas and violent personal histories?

Though he was not a socialist himself, Lincoln displayed a great affinity for socialism and even various aspects of communism, which is why socialists and communists have long been attracted to him, even writing books about Lincoln's socialist and communist views, policies, and activities.[76]

This deep interest in Far-left ideologies certainly explains why Lincoln often spoke at socialist meetings and why he "gratefully accepted" an honorary membership from a socialist organization.[77] It explains why he disliked the Constitution,[78] why he so easily violated the First, Second, and Fourth Amendments (among many others), and why he devoted so much of his time and energy to enlarging the Federal government while he was in office.[79]

It explains why he has always been admired by national socialists like Adolf Hitler, by anarchists like Mikhail Bakunin, and by Marxists like Marx, the founder of modern communism. It also explains why Lincoln was an enthusiastic supporter of revolutions, revolutionary ideas, and revolutionary

---

75. Lochlainn Seabrook, *Lincoln's War: The Real Cause, the Real Winner, the Real Loser*. Spring Hill, TN: Sea Raven Press, 2016, pp. 76-77.
76. See e.g., Burke McCarty, *Little Sermons in Socialism by Abraham Lincoln*. Chicago, IL: The Chicago Daily Socialist, 1910; Earl Browder, *Lincoln and the Communists*. New York, NY: Workers Library Publishers, Inc., 1936.
77. Lochlainn Seabrook, *Abraham Lincoln Was a Liberal, Jefferson Davis Was Conservative: The Missing Key to Understanding the American Civil War*. Spring Hill, TN: Sea Raven Press, 2017, p. 104.
78. Lochlainn Seabrook, *Abraham Lincoln Was a Liberal, Jefferson Davis Was Conservative: The Missing Key to Understanding the American Civil War*. Spring Hill, TN: Sea Raven Press, 2017, p. 90.
79. Lochlainn Seabrook, *Abraham Lincoln: The Southern View*. 2007. Franklin, TN: Sea Raven Press, 2013 paperback ed., pp. 511-512.

leaders, such as those who headed the failed 1848 socialist revolts in Europe;[80] it is why, in July 1861, Lincoln specifically asked European revolutionary Giuseppe Garibaldi to head the Union army; it is why in the 1930s, American communists formed a military organization called "The Abraham Lincoln Battalion," and it is why the 1939 Communist Party Convention in Chicago, Illinois, affectionately displayed an enormous image of Lincoln over the center of its stage, flanked by pictures of Russian communist dictators Vladimir Lenin on one side and Joseph Stalin on the other.[81]

While, due to the Left's wholesale revision of American history, most non-Southerners are not aware of it, it is no secret here in the South that the Lincoln administration provided a warmly receptive home for disaffected socialists and militant communists. The evidence is plain to see for those willing to look.

Let us bear in mind that someone on the extreme left in Lincoln's Republican Party (then the Liberal party) was called a "radical," which is a synonym for such words as left-winger, leftist, liberal, progressive, and of course, socialist and communist.[82]

More proof. On July 12, 1864, in yet another Southern attempt to end the war, Confederate commissioners corresponded—not with a Republican (Liberal) official from the Lincoln administration, but—with Horace Greeley, a confirmed socialist.[83]

Then there are those revealing statements uttered by the Confederate president himself. For instance, Davis mentions a mysterious comment made by Lincoln in early 1865 concerning his discomfort due to "the extreme men in Congress and elsewhere, who wished to drive him into harsher measures than he was inclined to adopt."[84] Davis also stresses the fact that Union General Francis P. Blair seemed to believe that the U.S. Congress was "infected by a cabal undermining the Executive in his efforts successfully to prosecute the war" according to his own dictates.[85]

Who were these "extreme men"? Why did they dislike the lenient manner (in their eyes) in which Lincoln was "prosecuting the war"? Who were the members of the strange underground "cabal" that was "infecting" the White House? And moreover, what was its purpose?

We must also ask why Davis referred to Lincoln's avalanche of

---

80. European revolutionaries who were involved in this short-lived uprising were called "Forty-Eighters."
81. For more on these topics, see Lochlainn Seabrook, *Lincoln's War: The Real Cause, the Real Winner, the Real Loser*. Spring Hill, TN: Sea Raven Press, 2016; Lochlainn Seabrook, *Abraham Lincoln Was a Liberal, Jefferson Davis Was a Conservative: The Missing Key to Understanding the American Civil War*. Spring Hill, TN: Sea Raven Press, 2017.
82. Other synonyms for the word "radical" include: anarchist, insurgent, revolutionary, extremist, agitator, nonbeliever, iconoclast, dissident, reactionary, insurrectionist, rioter, propagandist, firebrand, revolter, malcontent, reactionary, reformer, heretic, revisionist, rabble-rouser, troublemaker, provocateur, disrupter, and resister. Most of these words have long been associated with the Far-left—and still are.
83. Supra, p. 493.
84. Supra, p. 495.
85. Supra, p. 496.

unconstitutional acts as "the wheels of revolution."⁸⁶ What type of revolution was he speaking of, and who were the revolutionaries behind it? The definition of a revolution is "the sudden and often violent overthrow of an established government or political system by radical citizens."

There is only one thing Lincoln could have been trying to overthrow, and that is the U.S. Constitution: a document that guarantees *the independence of the States*—an all-important political concept that, as noted earlier, Davis called "the corner-stone of the Union."⁸⁷

Tragically, for the patriotic, Conservative, freedom-loving South, Lincoln did not like the Constitution,⁸⁸ and neither did most of his Liberal associates, many who variously referred to it as an "agreement with hell," a "scrap of paper," a "covenant with death and a league with hell," "hate's polluted rag," and "a thing of nothing, which must be changed." Left-leaning Alexander Hamilton called it a "frail and worthless fabric," while radical Yankee progressive William Lloyd Garrison angrily burned a copy of the Constitution in the public square.⁸⁹

Yes, Lincoln's ultimate target was the Constitution, but his ultimate goal was the elimination of states rights—still one of the major objectives of both American socialists and American communists.

Adding up all of the various factors we have covered, it seems clear that the American "Civil War" included many elements long associated with Bolshevik revolutions. I am speaking here of sociopolitical uprisings led by radical liberals, socialists, anarchists, and communists; the same type of revolutions that exploded in Europe in 1848, in Russia in 1917, and, most recently, in the U.S. in 2020.

If I am correct—and I believe that the evidence presented here suggests as much—then the American "Civil War," the "War of the Constitution," as Robert E. Lee correctly called it, was a mid 19th-Century socialist-communist uprising masquerading as a Liberal Yankee movement to "restore the Union." This covert insurrection was carefully manipulated by a secret "cabal" of "extreme men" (mainly German socialists and communists) who used Lincoln and his administration as a front to hide their conspiratorial plot to overthrow and destroy the U.S. Constitution and install a socialistic-style "big government" in Washington. As I write in my book, *Lincoln's War: The Real Cause, the Real Winner, the Real Loser*:

> "We will recall that many of the Union officers who led these unlawful campaigns against their fellow Americans were 'Forty-Eighters,' disgruntled foreign socialists and communists, radical immigrants who had come to the U.S. after their left-wing

---

86. Supra, p. 242.
87. Supra, p. 477.
88. Lochlainn Seabrook, *Abraham Lincoln: The Southern View*. 2007. Franklin, TN: Sea Raven Press, 2013 paperback ed., pp. 67-68.
89. Lochlainn Seabrook, *All We Ask is to be Let Alone: The Southern Secession Fact Book*. Spring Hill, TN: Sea Raven Press, 2017, p. 239.

revolution failed in Europe in 1848. Naturally, all of them gravitated to Liberal Lincoln and the North, rightly viewing Conservative Davis and the South as the arch enemies of their ultimate plan: "the reconstruction of a social [that is, socialist] world" in America.[90]

How deeply was Lincoln himself involved? We will never know. He certainly proved by his actions and words, however, that he supported despotic, unconstitutional, authoritarian ideas as well as outright revolution and violence. Many fellow Yankees, in fact, recognized these traits *during the War*. On September 8, 1900, at Grand Rapids, Michigan, for instance, New Yorker and future American president Theodore Roosevelt acknowledged that between 1861 and 1865,

> "on every hand Lincoln was denounced as a tyrant, a shedder of blood, a foe to liberty, a would be dictator, a founder of an empire—one orator saying, 'We also have our emperor, Lincoln, who can tell stale jokes while the land is running red with the blood of brothers.' Even after Lincoln's death the assault was kept up."[91]

Adding weight to my theory that Liberal Lincoln and his Left-wing administration were involved in fomenting socialism, if not communism, is the following public statement, issued by American socialist Norman Mattoon Thomas in 1944:

> "The American people will never knowingly adopt socialism. But, under the name of 'liberalism,' they will adopt every fragment of the socialist program, until one day America will be a socialist nation, without knowing how it happened. . . . I no longer need to run as a Presidential Candidate for the Socialist Party. The Democratic Party [by then Liberal] has adopted our platform."[92]

This view seems to have been current during Lincoln's presidential tenure, if not before. After all, Lincoln's Republican Party (a mid 19th-Century liberal party that was in no way connected to the conservative Democratic-Republican Party of Thomas Jefferson) was founded in 1854 by hard left radicals. One of these revolutionaries, South-hating Yankee Galusha A. Grow—nicknamed "the Father of the Republican Party" (of 1854)—was known by his conservative critics as a "socialist" and as a chief representative of the "workingman's idealism." The actual founder of the 1854 Republican Party was Alvan Earle

---

90. Lochlainn Seabrook, *Lincoln's War: The Real Cause, the Real Winner, the Real Loser.* Spring Hill, TN: Sea Raven Press, 2016, p. 114.
91. Lochlainn Seabrook, *Abraham Lincoln: The Southern View.* 2007. Franklin, TN: Sea Raven Press, 2013 paperback ed., p. 475.
92. While this quote is often attributed to Thomas, its origins may lie in the writings and speeches of earlier socialists.

Bovay, who had ties to socialists, like radical English-American socialist George Henry Evans, as well as communists, such as *The Communist Manifesto* authors Marx and Engels. All were rabid radicals who hated the South, pushed for an emancipation proclamation, and urged a civil war against the South.[93]

Norman Mattoon Thomas need not have worried, however. By 1892, fifty-two years before he uttered his now famous words, socialism had already become firmly ensconced in the American consciousness. It was in that year that American socialist Francis Bellamy wrote and published what was to become the U.S. Pledge of Allegiance. The originally godless vow contained—and still does—three thoroughly un-American and anti-American words (italicized) that are guaranteed to the warm the heart of any states rights-hating communist:

> "I pledge allegiance to my Flag and the Republic for which it stands, *one nation, indivisible*, with liberty and justice for all."

In 1933, some 41 years later, the Liberal who launched the modern American welfare state, President Franklin Delano Roosevelt, instigated his "New Deal" programs, which greatly enlarged the U.S. Federal government, centralized additional political power in Washington, and further undermined states rights. The result? The ongoing erosion of the Constitution—the ultimate objective of the Left. And from whence did the term "New Deal" derive? Not from the Roosevelt administration. It was coined in 1865 to describe Lincoln's socialist domestic policies.[94]

Wherever one looks, when it comes to American socialism and American communism one will find the name Abraham Lincoln—if you search deeply enough.

In *A Short History of the Confederate States of America*, Southern icon Jefferson Davis perfectly describes what happens when men like Lincoln attain political power, detailing the dire consequences that arise when the blight of Left-wing radicalism infestates society. Fortunately, the Conservative Confederate president not only tells us how to prevent liberal outbreaks, progressive contagions, socialist infections, communist plagues, and revolutionary epidemics, but also how to cure these "pathogens" if and when they germinate.

The question is, will we listen and act upon Davis' sage warnings and advice? The future of the United States of America depends on it.

Lochlainn Seabrook
Nashville, Tennessee, USA
October 2020, *In Nobis Regnat Christus*

---

93. Lochlainn Seabrook, *Abraham Lincoln Was a Liberal, Jefferson Davis Was Conservative: The Missing Key to Understanding the American Civil War*. Spring Hill, TN: Sea Raven Press, 2017, pp. 77-79.
94. Lochlainn Seabrook, *Abraham Lincoln: The Southern View*. 2007. Franklin, TN: Sea Raven Press, 2013 paperback ed., pp. 510-511.

INTRODUCTION

by JEFFERSON DAVIS

THE vindication of the Southern States for their Ordinances of Secession in 1861 involves two considerations, namely: their rightful power to withdraw from the Union into which they had entered by voluntary compact; and the causes that justified the exercise of that power.

In treating this question in its twofold aspect, the legal and the moral, it is not intended to vex the weary ear by adducing time-worn arguments; but, believing the case to be one which must be adjusted finally by historical facts, the candid reader is asked, without favor or prejudice, to make a decision on the unquestionable record.

The British Colonies of North America—subsequently the United States—had a common allegiance to the British Crown. Otherwise they were as distinct from one another as they were from Canada, Nova Scotia, and the American islands owned by Great Britain. When, by the violation of both charter and inalienable rights, for which neither redress nor security against repetition could be obtained, some of the colonies decided to sever their connection with the British Crown, they formed an alliance, declared themselves free and independent States, and, with their united strength, made such vigorous resistance to the efforts of the Mother Country to reduce them to subjection that, finally, a Treaty of Peace was made, in September, 1783, in the following words:

> "ARTICLE I. His Britannic Majesty acknowledges the said United States, viz : New Hampshire, Massachusetts Bay, Rhode Island and Providence Plantations, Connecticut and New York, New Jersey, Pennsylvania, Delaware, Maryland, Virginia, North Carolina, South Carolina, and Georgia, to be free, sovereign, and independent States; that he treats with them as such," etc., etc.

It has been contended that, although the States were severally named, the recognition was to the Union, not merely as the negotiating agent, but as the supreme authority.

The fallacy of this assumption is shown by the provisions of Articles V. and VII., recognizing the separate, independent power of the respective States to provide for the restitution of all estates, rights, and properties which had been confiscated, belonging to real British subjects; and also of the estates, rights, and properties of persons resident in districts in the possession of His Majesty's arms, and who had not borne arms against the said United States, etc.

> "ARTICLE XII. There shall be a firm and perpetual peace between His Britannic Majesty and the said States, and between the subjects of the one and the citizens of the other. . . And His Britannic Majesty shall also order and cause all archives, records, deeds, and papers belonging to any of the said States, or to their citizens, which, in the course of the war, may have fallen into the hands of his, officers, to be forthwith restored and delivered to the proper States and persons to whom they belonged."

The States, now recognized as free and independent, had, in November, 1777, agreed upon "Articles of Confederation and Perpetual Union," which were referred to the Legislatures of the several States, and, being duly approved, were adopted by the Congress on the 9th day of July, 1778.

From these "Articles of Confederation and Perpetual Union" the subjoined extracts are made:

> "ARTICLE I. The style of this Confederacy shall be, the United States of America."

> "ARTICLE II. Each State retains its sovereignty, freedom, and independence, and every power, jurisdiction, and right which is not by the Confederation delegated to the United States in Congress assembled."

> "ARTICLE X. In determining questions in the United States, in Congress assembled, each State shall have one vote."

> "ARTICLE XIII. Each State shall abide by the determinations of the United States, in Congress assembled, on all questions which by this Confederation is submitted to them. And the articles of this Confederation shall be inviolably observed by every State, and the Union shall be perpetual; nor shall any alteration at any time hereafter be made in any of them, unless such alteration be agreed to in a Congress of the United States and be afterward confirmed by the Legislature of every State."

Our heroic ancestors, against fearful odds, had staked all that men hold most dear in the War for Independence. By unexampled sacrifices they gained that priceless possession. But a long, exhausting war left them poor and heavily encumbered by debts, to provide for which the Confederation had little power. The western lands, for the time unproductive of revenue but of great prospective value, were covered by claims of several States. These were, in some cases, conflicting, and, because of vaguely defined territorial limits and questionable title, the controversies were of such difficult adjustment that they continued after the war had ended.

Happily, the patriotism of the people came to the relief of the General Government and terminated the disputes by the cession of unoccupied lands to be disposed of for the public good.

The Congress applied to the States for a grant of power to regulate foreign trade and commerce, and to impose duties on imports to obtain the needed revenue. It was not found possible to obtain the unanimous assent of the States, and the current of events, including the hostile commercial policy of England, rendering the grant more and more obviously necessary to the general welfare, the Congress, on February 21, 1787,

> "Resolved, That it is expedient that, on the second Monday of May next, a convention of delegates, who shall have been appointed by the several States, be held in Philadelphia, for the sole and express purpose of revising the Articles of Confederation, and reporting to Congress and the several legislatures such alterations and provisions thereon as shall, when agreed to in Congress and confirmed by the States, render the Federal Constitution adequate to the exigencies of Government and the preservation of the Union."

This resolution has been quoted at length because it declares the sole purpose to be to revise the Articles of Confederation and recognizes the supremacy of the States as the power to confirm the resolution to be submitted to their several legislatures. And it is to be remembered that it required the unanimous assent of the States to make any alteration in the Articles of Confederation.

When the delegates met in convention, discussion developed the impracticability of amending the Articles of Confederation so as to make them adequate to the exigencies of government, and the convention proceeded to devise a new form of Federal Constitution. There was a well-grounded apprehension that no instrument granting the powers deemed essential would receive unanimous confirmation by the States; and it was provided, by Article XII, that

> "The ratification of the Convention of nine States shall be sufficient for the establishment of the Constitution between the States so ratifying the same."

Therefore the names of the States were not written in the preamble, as they had been in the first draft of the Constitution, and as had been done in the Articles of Confederation, but only the general expression, "We, the People of the United States," which could mean no more or less than the people of the ratifying States.

If it be asked how could nine States consistently secede from the "Confederation and Perpetual Union," of which they were a component part, and the terms of which Union could not be altered unless such alteration should "be confirmed by the Legislature of every State," it is submitted, as an answer to the question, that the States, that is, the people of each State, had never surrendered their Sovereignty, and, by virtue of it, if the Government failed to fulfil the end for which it was established, they had the unalienable right to "alter or to abolish it, and to institute a new government, laying its foundation on such principles and organizing its powers in such form, as to them should seem most likely to effect their safety and happiness."

In Convention it was agreed that such States as chose, not less than nine in number, might establish a new form of government; which necessarily involved separation from some of their associates in the Union which they had covenanted should be perpetual. George Washington presided over their Convention, and transmitted the Constitution drafted by it to the several States, to be ratified or rejected by the people of each State in convention assembled.

The duty assigned to him was not perfunctorily performed; but, deeply anxious for the formation of the more perfect Union projected, which rested on the power of a State to secede from the old Union, and to accede to the new one—as provided by the closing Article (VII.) of the Constitution as submitted to the States—he exerted his great influence to secure ratification by the requisite number of States for the "establishment of the Constitution between the States so ratifying the same." In one of his letters he asks "what the opponents of the Constitution in Virginia would do if nine other States should accede to the Constitution ?"[95]

After a time the Constitution was ratified by eleven States, and the "more perfect Union" was organized, leaving two States—North Carolina and Rhode Island—sole representatives of the Confederation which had raised the Colonies to statehood and independence. The position of these two States conclusively proves that the sovereignty of each State was an admitted fact, and that it was a voluntary compact to which their assent was requested and from which it was withheld.

The power of the States, in whole or in part, to withdraw from the Union of the Confederation, in 1787, has been conceded by the succeeding generations, and the causes which led to the act have, in like manner, been admitted to be an all-sufficient justification.

And this fact suggests the inquiry, Did the States, by the adoption of the new form of government, deprive themselves of that power? and if not, did there exist, in 1861, justifiable causes for its exercise?

Article X, in amendment of the Constitution (the more entitled to consideration because it was one of the conditions on which the Constitution was ratified), is in these words:

> "The powers not delegated to the United States by the Constitution, nor prohibited by it to the States, are reserved to the States respectively or to the people."

If nowhere is to be found the delegation by the States of sovereignty to the United States, that remained with the States, severally, to be exercised thereafter as it had been in 1787.

Elbridge Gerry, of Massachusetts, said, in reference to the power of nine States to withdraw from the Confederation: "If nine out of thirteen can dissolve the compact, six out of nine will be just as able to dissolve the new one hereafter." Certainly the act of withdrawal, as provided, was to be by the States severally. The number agreeing to withdraw involved the power to maintain the new government, not the right of each to

---

95. See his letter to Lafayette.

separate itself from the old one. That was a function of Sovereignty, and the terms of the Constitution recognized the right of each State to exercise it; and to Mr. Gerry's contention it might be answered, the power inherently belongs not to a majority, but to each State.

It has sometimes been argued that the powers delegated by the States to the Federal Government included such as were only exercised by sovereigns. It suffices for the present to say that so did those which had been delegated to the Congress of the Confederation.

The consideration of the second branch of the inquiry involves a comparison between the causes which led to secession in 1787 and 1861. In the former case the inefficiency of the Articles of Confederation for some of the purposes of the General Government was presented as the reason for requiring its amendment; and the Convention, when it assembled, proceeded to draft a new form of government which, being submitted and adopted, became the Constitution for a more perfect Union. In the latter case, the destruction of the balance of power which existed when the Constitution was adopted, and subsequent legislation for sectional advantages rather than the general welfare, together with gross and persistent violations of obligations which the States had assumed in the formation of the compact of Union, added to increasing hostility, shamefully displayed, and culminating in invasion, had at length created a feeling that the fraternity in which the Union was founded had ceased to exist—that the Union was no longer one of the heart. In these circumstances a president was elected by a strictly sectional vote—a man who had declared that the Union could not continue to exist "half slave, half free;" whose party dogma was the exclusion of slave-holders from the territory belonging in common to the States, and whose partisans hurled bitterest denunciations and derisive anathemas on the flag of the Union.

The South, as a minority, was naturally attached to the Constitution, as a guarantee of equal rights and protection to public and private interests. Her sons had gathered much glory under the flag of the Union; it was an emblem of free and independent States, and was the object of pride and affection to her people. A very large majority of her people believed secession to be a remedy that could be peacefully exercised. The Southern States, one after another, passed Ordinances of Secession, but they made no adequate preparations for war, because it was generally believed none were necessary. At the instance of Virginia, leading now for peace as she had led for war in the revolutionary era, a call was issued inviting the States to a convention for the purpose of securing peace to the Union. The Convention met at Washington, D. C., on February 4, 1861, a majority of Northern and Northwestern States and eight of the Southern States being represented. The effort of the wise and patriotic members to secure some proper adjustment of existing issues proved unsuccessful.

The States that had seceded met at Montgomery, Ala., February 4, 1861, formed a Provisional Government by their delegates in Congress assembled, and by them a president and a vice-president were elected, and the Provisional Government was inaugurated on the 18th of the same month.

Immediately thereafter commissioners were sent to Washington with authority to negotiate with the Federal Government for a settlement of all issues between it and the seceded States on the basis of equality and goodwill. These efforts, which continued to the expiration of Mr. Buchanan's term and into the administration of Mr. Lincoln, proved as unproductive of the desired fruit as had the Peace Congress; and yet there were not wanting those among us who believed that the Federal Government, having no grant in the Constitution to use force against a State, would not attempt invasion, but, as did General Jackson, would limit their operations to collecting revenue from the outside of Southern ports.

Confederate Capitol at Richmond.

PART 1
BEFORE SECESSION

Chapter 1

Causes of the War Between the States

IGNORANCE and credulity have enabled unscrupulous partisans so to mislead public opinion, both at home and abroad, as to create the belief that the institution of African slavery was the chief cause, instead of being a mere incident in the group of causes, which led to war. In keeping with the first misrepresentation was that of the position assigned to the belligerent parties. Thus, the North is represented as having fought for the emancipation of the African slaves, and the South for the increase and extension of the institution of African servitude as it existed in the Southern States. Therein is a twofold fallacy. First, the dominant party at the North, in 1861, through their exponent, President Lincoln, declared, in his inaugural message, as follows:

> "I have no purpose, directly or indirectly, to interfere with the institution of slavery in the States where it exists. I believe I have no lawful right to do so; and I have no inclination to do so."

This declaration was reinforced by quoting from the platform of the political convention which nominated him, an emphatic resolution, in these words:

> "Resolved, that the maintenance inviolate of the rights of the States, and especially the right of each State to order and control its own domestic institutions according to its own judgment exclusively, is essential to that balance of power on which the perfection and endurance of our political fabric depends; and we denounce the lawless invasion, by armed force, of the soil of any State or Territory, no matter under what pretext, as among the gravest of crimes."

Fitly, as to time and occasion, was the armed invasion of a State denounced as among the gravest of crimes, and so it remains, whether or not a State's secession should be an accomplished fact. If the State were still in the Union, it was a crime against the Constitution, which did not grant power to coerce a State (indeed the convention which formed that Constitution refused to give that power); if a State had withdrawn from the Union, it was a crime against humanity and justice to make war upon a neighbor's late associate for the exercise of that sovereign right: in either case it was a crime against the hopes of mankind in destroying the fairest prospect for the success of federative government and substituting the theory of force for that of consent.

When Mr. Lincoln endorsed that resolution and incorporated it in his inaugural the effect was like a rift in the cloud while the storm and darkness were gathering, and the words closely following were the more cheering because of the prevalent belief in his rugged honesty. Pity that the confidence should have been impaired by subsequent passages in his address, and that the past and passing acts and avowals of his party gave no reasonable expectation that he would be able to execute his declared policy!

Federation had so generally proved a failure that the world had become distrustful of it; but its success in the United States had revived the hopes of those who saw in it the best mode of securing community welfare and happiness. It was therefore most proper to denounce as among the grandest of crimes the armed invasion of any State; for their conquest would be the extinguishment of the beacon which was illuminating the world by the rays of federal liberty.

If additional evidence be needed to prove that "emancipation" was not an original purpose, it may be found not only in the inaugural, but also in the fact that President Lincoln subsequently defended the issuance of his emancipation proclamation, in 1863, on the ground of "military necessity." Therefore, the North could not have entered upon the war to abolish Slavery. Developments in the course of the war cannot be transplanted to its beginning, and then be made to do duty as the cause.

The Southern States could not have contemplated war as a means of defending her citizens against the evasion of their duty by the Northern States in the matter of fugitives from service or labor, nor because of lawless criminals who were secretly instigated to disturb the peace and property of border residents. Equally unfounded is any accusation that the South desired to increase the number of African slaves by importation. Her whole history from the colonial times, when Southern colonies opposed the slave-trade, in which Old England and New England were engaged, refutes the base and baseless reflection. The Constitution of the Confederate States gave no years of grace to the slave-trade, but forbade it immediately, from any foreign country other than the slaveholding States and Territories of the United States, and gave to Congress the power to prohibit the introduction of slaves from the Federal States or Territories. No more need be said as to increase.

The next point is extension. This is based on the assertion of the equal right of all citizens in and to the territory belonging to the United States. This equality, it was contended, carried with it the right of such citizen, migrating to a territory, to take with him any kind of property lawfully held in the State from which he migrated. This was a claim reasonably deduced from the fact that the Territories belonged to the States in common, and the denial of it was resisted because of its unequality and was an offensive discrimination. There could have been little, if any, pecuniary inducement to take slaves into the Northwest Territory. Persons migrating from the Southern States would probably desire to take with them their domestics, to whom they were personally attached; but the same climatic causes which had led to the transfer of African slaves from the Northeast to the South would have prevented the permanent establishment of the institution of Slavery in the States which might arise out of its Western Territories. What, then, was the objection? The transfer from a Southern State to a Western Territory would certainly not increase the number, and dispersion could only lead to comfort and harmony. If the purpose was, as some extremists asserted, to confine the institution until, by its density, slaves should become unprofitable—that is, until their labor should no longer enable the master adequately to provide for them, and want should compel emancipation—the humane man, looking at all the progressive stages of suffering and consequent crime to which this programme inevitably would tend, might ask, Is this the feast which philanthropy has spread for us?

Chapter 2

Negro Slavery and the Slave-Trade

THE existence of African servitude gave rise to acrimonious political discussions long before the secession of the Southern States in 1861; and, owing to persistent misrepresentations and a general misunderstanding of the true nature and character of the questions growing out of the institution, the misconceptions that have been engendered not in our own country only, but, still more, abroad, have tended and still tend to mislead the judgment of the world in arriving at a correct apprehension of the causes of the war between the States and of the controversies that preceded it. It is important, therefore, at the very outset, to have a right understanding of the nature of those questions, and to show by a brief retrospect that the contest had no just application whatever to the essential merits of freedom and slavery; that no moral or sentimental considerations were really involved in either the earlier or later controversies which, after fiercely agitating, finally disrupted, the Union; that they were simply political struggles between sections with diverse institutions and conflicting interests.

At the time of the adoption of the Articles of Confederation, under which the War of Independence was waged, slavery existed in all the States that were parties to that compact. The slaves, however, were comparatively numerous in the Southern and few in the Northern States. This diversity was caused by differences of climate, soil, and industrial interests. Slave labor was profitable in the South and unprofitable in the North. No ethical consideration contributed to this diversity, for at that period moral scruples had not appeared as a factor in the problem. The same industrial interests that had checked the introduction of slave labor in the North and fostered it in the South, impelled the Northern States gradually to abolish slavery; although, at the same time, they did not inhibit Northern merchants from prosecuting the slave-trade in Northern ships between Africa and Southern ports until the traffic was forever prohibited by the Southern States themselves.

The Constitution forbade any Federal interference with the slave-trade prior to 1808. But, during the intervening period of more than twenty years, every Southern State had enacted laws prohibiting the importation of slaves. Virginia was the first of all the States of the Union to prohibit the slave-trade, and Georgia the first to abolish it by constitutional enactment.

In 1807, availing itself of the earliest moment at which the constitutional restriction ceased to be operative, Congress, with great unanimity—by a vote of 113 yeas to 5 nays—passed an act prohibiting the future importation.[96]

The slave-trade was thus finally abolished, and has never since had any legal existence in any of the States.

The question of the maintenance or extinction of the system of negro slavery in any State was one exclusively belonging to such State. It follows that no subsequent question, legitimately arising in Federal legislation, could properly have any reference to the merits or the policy of the institution itself. A few zealots in the North afterward created much agitation by demands for the abolition of slavery within the States by Federal intervention, and by their activity and perseverance finally became a recognized party, which, holding the balance of power between the two great political organizations in the North, gradually obtained the control of one, and to no small degree corrupted the other. The dominant purpose, however—the object at least of the absorbed party—was sectional aggrandizement looking to absolute control.

Theirs, therefore, is the responsibility for the war that resulted.

---

96. It is noteworthy, as showing the absence of any sectional division of sentiment at that period, that these five dissentients were divided as nearly as possible between the two sections; two of them were from New England and three from the South.

CHAPTER 3
THE EXTENSION OF SLAVERY

THE fervid phraseology of the period is essentially deceptive, and has done much to confuse the perceptions and mislead the sympathies of the world with the struggles of the South for equality of rights within the Union, and for security with independence by secession. No charge was more unjust, for example, than the accusation that the South sought the "extension of slavery" when it insisted on equal rights in the Territories. The question was merely whether the slave-holder should be permitted to go with his slaves into territory (the common property of all) into which the non-slave-holder could go with his property of any sort. It was simply a question of the dispersion of slaves rather than of the "extension of slavery." Removal is not extension.

This distinction between the two policies—essentially different although so generally confounded—was early and clearly drawn during the progress of the settlement of the Northwestern Territory.

Virginia, in 1784, ceded to the United States the vast territory out of which the great States of Ohio, Indiana, Michigan, Illinois, Wisconsin, and part of Minnesota were subsequently formed. In 1787, at the express instance of Virginia, Congress adopted the celebrated ordinance for the government of this vast domain. Its sixth article ordains that "there shall be neither slavery nor involuntary servitude in the said Territory, otherwise than in the punishment of crime whereof the party shall have been convicted."

In December, 1805, a petition of the Legislative Council and House of Representatives of the Indiana Territory—then comprising all the area now occupied by the States of Indiana, Illinois, Michigan, and Wisconsin—was presented to Congress, asking for a suspension of the sixth article, so as to permit the introduction of slaves. Similar petitions from inhabitants of the Territory, endorsed by a letter from Governor William Henry Harrison (afterward President of the United States), had been received and referred two years before. The Select Committee of seven members—representing Virginia, Ohio, Pennsylvania, South Carolina, Kentucky, and New York, with the delegate from the Territory—reported in February, 1806, in favor of the petitioners, and recommended a suspension of the prohibitory article for ten years. They reported that the suspension was "almost universally desired in the Territory," and recorded it as their opinion that "the suspension would be a measure alike in the interests of the Territory, the slave-holders, and the slaves," and that it was "a question entirely different from that between slavery and freedom, as it would merely occasion the removal of persons already slaves from one part of the country to another."

It is noteworthy that these dispassionate utterances of representatives of every part of the Union, by men contemporary with the origin of the Constitution, when repeated fifty years later, came to be denounced and repudiated as partisan and sectional.

At the next session of Congress the subject was again introduced in a more imposing form—by a letter laid before the House from Governor Harrison, indorsing resolutions unanimously adopted by the Legislature of the Indiana Territory in favor of the suspension of the prohibitory article—a measure, they stated, that would meet "the approbation of at least nine-tenths of the good citizens" of the Territory. These resolutions again disclaimed the desire to "extend slavery," as, by the suspension asked for, "the number of slaves in the United States would not be augmented," and they reiterated that the suspension would tend to be advantageous to the negroes themselves as well as to the Territory and to the States from which the slaves would be brought.

A committee again reported in favor of the petition; a resolution to suspend the prohibitory article was adopted, but it failed to pass the Senate, and there the matter seems to have been dropped.

Chapter 4

The Missouri Compromise

IT seems proper here to notice the argument that the ordinance for the government of the Northwestern Territory afforded a precedent in support of the claim of a power in Congress to determine the question of the admission of slaves into the Territories, and in a justification of the prohibiting clause applied, in 1820, to a portion of the Louisiana Territory.

The difference between the Congress of the Confederation and that of the Federal Union is so broad that the action of the former can, in no just sense, be taken as a precedent for the latter. The Congress of the Confederation was, in fact, a Convention of Sovereign States, each delegation having one vote only, so that all the States were of equal weight in the decision of any question. It had legislative, executive, and, in some degree, judicial powers thus combining all departments of government in itself. During its recess a committee, known as the Committee of the States, exercised the power of the Congress, which was, in spirit, an assemblage of the States.

On the other hand, the Congress of the United States is only the legislative department of the General Government, with legislative powers strictly defined and expressly limited to those delegated by the States. It is further held in check by an executive and a judiciary, and consists of two branches, each having peculiar and specified functions.

If, then, it be admitted—which at least is very questionable—that the Congress of the Confederation had rightfully the power to exclude slave property from the Northwest Territory, that power must have been derived from its character as an assemblage of the sovereign States, not from the Articles of Confederation, in which no indication of the grant of authority to exercise such a function can be found. The Congress of the Union is expressly prohibited from the assumption of any power not distinctly and specially delegated to it. What was questionable in the former case, therefore, becomes clearly inadmissible in the latter.

There is another material distinction. The States that owned the Northwest Territory were members of the Congress which adopted the ordinance, and gave it their full and free consent. The balance, therefore, may be regarded as a treaty between the ceding and the receiving States. But Missouri, and the entire region affected by the Missouri Compromise, were part of the territory acquired from France under the name of Louisiana; and, as it requires two parties to make or amend a treaty, France and the United States should have co-operated in any amendment of the treaty by which Louisiana had been acquired, and which guaranteed to the inhabitants of the ceded territory all the rights and advantages and immunities of citizens of the United States, and the free enjoyment of their liberty, property, and the religion they professed.

For these reasons it seems to me conclusive that the action of the Congress of the Confederation, in 1787, could not constitute a precedent to justify the action of the Congress of the United States, in 1820, and that the prohibiting clause of the Missouri Compromise was without constitutional authority, in violation of the rights of a part of the joint owners of the territory, and in disregard of the obligations of the treaty with France.

The origin of the sectional controversy was the question of the balance of political power. In its earlier manifestations this was undisguised. The purchase of the Louisiana Territory from France, in 1803, and the subsequent admission of a portion of the territory into the Union as a State, afforded one of the earliest occasions for the manifestation of sectional jealousy and gave rise to the first threats or warnings (which proceeded from New England) of a dissolution of the Union. Yet, although negro slavery existed in Louisiana, no pretext was made of that as an objection to the acquisition. The cause of opposition is frankly stated in a letter of that period from one Massachusetts statesman to another, "that the influence of our part of the Union must be diminished by the acquisition of more weight at the other extremity."[97]

---

97. Cabot to Pickering. See *Life and Letters of George Cabot*, by C. H. Lodge, p. 134.

Some years afterward (in 1819-20) occurred the memorable contest with regard to the admission into the Union of Missouri, the second State carved out of the Louisiana Territory. The controversy arose out of a proposition to attach to the admission of the new State a proviso prohibiting slavery or involuntary servitude therein. The vehement discussion that ensued was continued into the first session of the subsequent Congress, and agitated the whole country during the interval between the two. It was the first question that ever seriously threatened the stability of the Union, and the first in which the sentiment of opposition to slavery was introduced as an element of sectional controversy. It was clearly shown in debate that such considerations were irrelevant; that the number of existing slaves would not be affected by their removal from the older States to Missouri; and that the proposed restriction would be contrary to the spirit, if not to the letter, of the Constitution. Yet the restriction was adopted in the House of Representatives by a vote almost strictly sectional. It failed in the Senate through the firm resistance of the Southern, aided by a few patriotic and conservative Northern, members of that body.

The admission of the new State, without any restriction, was finally accomplished by the addition to the bill of a section forever prohibiting slavery, except as to Missouri, in all that portion of the Louisiana Territory north of 36° 30' north latitude; by implication leaving the portion south of that line open to settlement either with or without slaves.

Then and thus, as at a later period, it will be seen that the conflicts between South and North involved no ethical question as to slavery; that they were essentially struggles for sectional equality on the one side, and for sectional ascendency on the other; for the maintenance or destruction of that balance of power or equipoise between South and North which was early recognized as a cardinal principle in our federal system. It does not follow that either party to this contest was wholly right or wholly wrong. The determination of the question of right or wrong must be left to the candid inquirer after examination of the evidence.

The object of these preliminary investigations has been to clear the subject of the obscurity produced by irrelevant issues and the glamour of ethical illusions.

Chapter 5

The Compromise Measures

THE period from the first session of the Thirty-first Congress (1849–50) to the passage of the Kansas-Nebraska Bill, although marked by important controversies and measures that had a . noteworthy influence on the future of the country, can be referred to here in the briefest outline only.

The acquisition of the territory of California and New Mexico, from Mexico, required Congressional legislation. From the deliberations of the committee of which Henry Clay was chairman emanated the bills generally known as the Compromise Measures of 1850.

With some others I advocated the division of the newly acquired territory by the extension, to the Pacific Ocean, of the Missouri Compromise line of 36° 30', not because of any inherent merit or fitness in that line, but because, having been accepted as a settlement of a threatening controversy thirty years before, it had acquired a popular respect which it seemed unwise to ignore. This compromise was rejected by the majority, composed almost exclusively of Northern representatives. The tree whose first-fruits had been peace was thus recklessly hewn down and cast into the fire. History shows that the South was not responsible for this action, which proved to be the opening of Pandora's box.

By this refusal to extend the Missouri line to the Pacific, California was admitted into the Union as a free State. The compensation offered to the South was a more effective law for the rendition of fugitive slaves. The obligation to return such fugitives was a duty that had been assumed in the adoption of the compact of Union. Yet in defiance of this plain constitutional obligation the legislatures of fourteen of the States had enacted what were termed "Personal Liberty Bills," which prohibited the co-operation of all State officials in the rendition of fugitives. Hence the necessity of Federal intervention in aid of the execution of State obligations, it was argued, in forgetfulness of the obvious fact that whatever tended to lead the people of any of the States to feel that they could be relieved of their constitutional obligations by transferring them to the General Government, or that they might thus or otherwise evade or resist them, could not fail to be like the tares which the enemy sowed among the wheat. The bill was passed, but was made the pretext for the most hostile denunciations of the South from the press, platforms, and pulpits of the North, in which all guise of friendship was thrown away, constitutional obligations and respect for law alike were derided, and resistance to the execution of these laws of the land was recommended in obedience to the dictates of "the higher law."

It was during the progress of these memorable controversies that the South lost its most trusted leader, John C. Calhoun. He was taken from us,

> "Like a summer-dried fountain,
> When our need was the sorest;"

when his intellectual power, his administrative talent, his love of peace, and his devotion to the Constitution might have averted collision; or, failing in that, when he might have been to the South the Palinurus to steer the bark in safety over the perilous sea.

CHAPTER 6

POLITICS IN MISSISSIPPI

I WAS re-elected by the Legislature of Mississippi as my own successor as United States Senator, and entered on my second term on March 4, 1851.

After traversing the State I returned from my tour at the time appointed for the convention of the Democratic (or State-rights) party. During the previous year the Governor of Mississippi, General John A. Quitman, had been compelled to resign to answer an indictment against him for complicity with a recent "filibustering" expedition against Cuba. The charge was not sustained, and the Democratic party recognized an obligation to renominate him, if he should be a candidate. But when the party met in convention it was deemed expedient, in order to defeat an attempt to fix on the Democracy the reputation of a purpose of disunion, which some of General Quitman's antecedents might have seemed to encourage, to invite me to become a candidate, with the understanding, if General Quitman should be appointed my successor to the seat in the United States Senate, that I should be under the necessity of resigning. My own devotion to the Union of our fathers had been so often and so fully declared; my services to the Union, civil and military, were so extended and so well known, that it was believed that my nomination would remove the danger of defeat which the candidacy of a less pronounced advocate of the Union might provoke. Then, as afterward, I regarded the separation of the States as a great, though not the greatest, evil.

I left the decision to General Quitman. He declined to withdraw. A canvass for candidates to a State Convention, simultaneously conducted, resulted, in September, in the defeat of the Democratic candidate by about seven thousand five hundred votes. Foreseeing the inevitable defeat of the Democracy, General Quitman withdrew, and I was named to take his place six weeks before the day of election. Having been broken down in health by travelling and speaking during the summer, I was not expected to take an active part in the pending canvass. Nevertheless, I soon took the field in person, after resigning as United States Senator, and remained in active service till the close of the election. I was defeated, but the adverse majority of seven thousand five hundred was reduced to less than one thousand.

Throughout all this canvass no argument or appeal of mine was directed against the perpetuity of the Union. Believing, however, that the signs of the times portended danger to the South, I counselled that Mississippi should take part in the proposed meeting of the people of the Southern States to consider what should be done to insure our future safety from the usurpation, by the General Government, of undelegated powers, frankly stating my conviction that, unless some action were taken, sectional policy would engender greater evils in the future, and that, if the adjustment of the controversy were postponed, the last opportunity for a peaceful solution would be lost, and the issue would have to be settled by blood.

CHAPTER 7

THE KANSAS-NEBRASKA TROUBLES

RETIRING from public life and occupied with the peaceful pursuits of a planter, I was recalled by an invitation to accept a seat in the cabinet of General Franklin Pierce, who had been elected President of the United States in November, 1852. I was offered and accepted the office of Secretary of War.

As a history of my administration as Secretary of War, during this period, may easily be found in the various annual reports and in published estimates of works of defence prosecuted or recommended, arsenals of construction and depots of arms maintained or suggested, and foundries employed, during the Presidency of Mr. Pierce (1853-57), it will suffice to refer to these documents, and to add that, having been elected by the Legislature of Mississippi, I passed from the cabinet of President Pierce, on the last day of his term (March 4, 1857), to take a seat once more in the Senate of the United States.

The organization of Kansas as a Territory was the first great question that gave rise to exciting debate after my return to public life.

In May, 1854, the Kansas-Nebraska Bill was passed. Its principle was declared, in the bill itself, to be to carry into practical operation the propositions and principles established by the compromise measures of 1850. The Missouri Compromise was not, by this bill, repealed; its virtual repeal by the legislation of 1850 was recognized as an existing fact, and it was declared to be "unoperative and void." From the terms of the bill, as well as from the arguments that were used in its behalf, it is evident that its purpose was to leave the Territories equally open to the people of all the States, with every species of property recognized by any of them; to permit climate and soil to determine the current of immigration, and to secure to the people themselves the right to form their own institutions, according to their own will, as soon as they should acquire the right of self-government; that is to say, as soon as their numbers entitled them to organize themselves into a State prepared to take its place as an equal, sovereign member of the Federal Union. The claim, afterward advocated by Mr. Douglas and others, that this declaration was intended to assert the right of the first settlers of a Territory, in its inchoate, rudimental, dependent, and transitory condition, to determine the character of its institutions, constituted the doctrine popularly known as "squatter sovereignty." Its assertion led to the dissensions which ultimately resulted in a rupture of the Democratic party.

Sectional rivalry now interposed, with gigantic efforts, to prevent that free migration which had been promised, and attempted, by force and fraud, to predetermine the institutions to be established by these embryo States, instead of leaving to climate and the developed interests of the inhabitants the decision of their internal polity when the Territory should become a State. Societies were formed in the North to supply money and send emigrants into the new Territories; and a famous preacher, addressing a body of these emigrants, charged them to carry with them to Kansas "The Bible and Sharpe's rifles." The rifles were, of course, to be levelled against the bosoms of their Southern brethren who might emigrate to the same Territory; but the use to be made of the Bible, in the same fraternal enterprise, was left unexplained by the reverend gentleman.

The war-cry employed to train the Northern mind for the deeds contemplated by the agitators was "No extension of slavery," although, as is self-evident, the number of slaves would not have been increased by their transportation or augmented by further importation.

The success attending this artifice was remarkable. To such an extent was it made available that Northern indignation was aroused on the absurd accusation that the South had destroyed "that sacred instrument the Compromise of 1820."

The internecine war that raged in Kansas for several years was substituted for the promised peace under the operation of the natural laws regulating migration to new countries. For the fratricide which dyed the virgin soil of Kansas with the blood of those who should have stood shoulder to shoulder in subduing the wilderness; for the frauds which corrupted the ballot-box and made the name of election a misnomer, let the authors of "squatter sovereignty" and the fomenters of sectional hatred answer to the posterity for whose peace and happiness the fathers formed the Federal compact.

In these scenes of strife were trained the incendiaries who afterward invaded Virginia under the leadership of John Brown; and at this time germinated the sentiments which led men of high position to sustain with their influence and their money this murderous incursion into the South. Now was seen the lightning of that storm, the distant mutterings of which had been heard so long, and against which the wise and the patriotic had given solemn warning, regarding it as a sign which portended a dissolution of the Union.

Chapter 8
The Abolition Movement

By the cession of the Northwestern Territory and the prohibitory clause of the Ordinance; by the surrender to the North of all the region acquired from France, excepting: Missouri, north of the parallel of 36° 30'; by the addition of the northern part of Texas under the Compromise of 1850, the North, having obtained a majority in both Houses of Congress, took to itself all the domain secured from Mexico. Thus was destroyed the original equilibrium between the two sections, although, under the old Confederation, the Southern States had an excess of territory, which was greatly increased by the Louisiana Purchase.

Not satisfied with the use of the acquired preponderance, its abuse followed. Under the power of Congress to levy duties on imports, laws were enacted not merely to pay the debts and provide for the common defence and general welfare of the United States, as authorized by the Constitution, but, expressly and chiefly, for the protection of domestic manufacturers against foreign competition. These laws imposed an unequal burden of taxation on the Southern people, who were not manufacturers but consumers, not only by the enhanced price of imports, but by the consequent depreciation of the value of exports, which were chiefly the products of the South. The imposition of this grievance was unaccompanied by the consolation of knowing that the burden thus borne was to supply the public treasury; for the increase of price was designed for, and largely accrued to, the Northern manufacturers.

Nor was this all. A reference to the annual appropriations shows that the disbursements made were as unequal as the burdens borne, the inequality in both operating with the same discrimination against the minority.

These causes all combined to direct emigration to the Northern section. The equality, both in population and in the number of States, which existed when the first census was taken, disappeared; the disturbance of that equilibrium destroyed the power of self-protection against Federal aggression; while, with the increase of preponderance, appeared more and more distinctly a tendency in the Federal Government to pervert the functions delegated to it and to use them with sectional discrimination against the minority.

This policy soon brought to its support the passions that spring from man's higher nature, but which, like all passions, become hurtful and, it may be, destructive, when misdirected or perverted. The year 1835 was marked by the beginning of the public agitation for the abolition of that African servitude in the South which antedated the Union and existed in all the States of the Confederation. By a gross misconception of the rightful powers of the Federal Government and the responsibilities of citizens by the Northern States, many of them were brought, little by little, to the conclusion that slavery was a sin for which they were answerable, and that it was the duty of the Federal Government to abate it. At the date referred to the public demonstrations of the Abolitionists were violently and generally rebuked at the North. Yet, by the activity of the propagandists of abolitionism and the misuse of the sacred word "liberty," they soon reached such numbers as gave them, in many Northern States, the balance of power between the two great political parties, and they were courted by both of them, and naturally most by the Whigs, who had become the weaker party of the two. Fanaticism, to which there is usually accorded sincerity as an extenuation of its mischievous tenets, affords the best excuse to be offered for the original Abolitionists; but that cannot be conceded to the political associates who joined them, for with them it was hypocritical cant intended to deceive. Hence arose the declaration of an "irrepressible conflict" because of the domestic institutions of sovereign, self-governing States; institutions over which neither the Federal Government nor the people outside of the limits of such States had any control, and for which they could have no moral or legal responsibility.

Those who are to come after us, and who will look without prejudice or excitement at the record of events that occurred in our day, will not fail to wonder how men, proposing and proclaiming such a belief, should have so far imposed on the credulity of the world as to be able to arrogate to themselves the claim of being the special friends of a Union, contracted in order to "insure domestic tranquillity" among the people of the States united; that they were the advocates of peace, of law, and of order, who, when taking an oath to support and maintain the Constitution, did so with a mental reservation to violate one of the provisions of that Constitution—one of the conditions of the compact—without which the Union could never have been formed.

Chapter 9

The John Brown Raid

AT the period to which the narrative has now advanced, the Free-Soil party, which had now assumed the title of "Republican" party, had grown to a magnitude which threatened speedily to obtain control of the Government. Based on sectional opposition to the growth of the Southern equally with the Northern States of the Union, it had absorbed not only the avowed Abolitionists, but other diverse and heterogeneous elements of opposition to the Democratic party. Their presidential candidates (Frémont and Dayton) had received, in 1856, 114 of a total of 296 electoral votes, representing 1,341,264 in a total of 4,054,967. The elections of 1857 showed a great diminution of the Republican strength, and the Thirty-fifth Congress was decidedly Democratic in both branches. But, during the next two years, the Kansas agitation, and dissensions in the Democratic party, occasioned by the new doctrine of squatter sovereignty, had so augmented the ranks of the Republicans that in the House of Representatives neither party had a decided majority. The contest over the election of a Speaker was kept up for more than eight weeks, and finally ended in the election of a Republican by a majority of one vote. The balance of power had been held by a few members still adhering to the virtually extinct Whig and "American," or "Know-Nothing," parties. The Senate continued Democratic, but with a decreased majority.

It seems proper to note here that the names adopted by political parties in the United States have not always been strictly significant of their principles. In general terms it may be said that the old Federal party inclined to nationalism, or consolidation, and that the Whig party, which succeeded it, although not identical with it, was favorable, in the main, to a strong Central Government. On the other hand, its opponent, the Republican, afterward known as the Democratic party, was dominated by the idea of the sovereignty of the States and the federal or confederate character of the Union. Although other elements have entered into its organization at different periods, this has been its vital, cardinal, and abiding principle. The Know-Nothing, or American party, which sprang into existence on the decadence of the Whig organization, based on opposition to the alleged overgrowth of the political influence of naturalized foreigners and of the Roman Catholic Church, had but a brief duration, and, after the presidential election of 1856, declined as rapidly as it had arisen.

The doctrine of squatter sovereignty, which soon disintegrated the Democratic party, is supposed to have been first suggested by General Cass, in 1847; but it was not until after the passage of the Kansas-Nebraska Bill, in 1854, that it was fully developed under the plastic and constructive genius of Hon. Stephen A. Douglas, of Illinois. Logically carried out, the theory of "squatter" or "popular sovereignty" bestowed on territorial legislatures, the creatures of Congress, a power not vested in Congress itself, or in any legislature in the fully organized and sovereign States, as their authority is limited both by the State and the Federal Constitutions.

Strange as it may seem, a theory founded on fallacies so transparent and leading to conclusions so paradoxical was advocated by many eminent and experienced politicians both in the North and in the South, chiefly, perhaps, under the delusive hope that it would afford a satisfactory settlement of that "irrepressible conflict" which had been declared.

The raid into Virginia under John Brown—already notorious as a fanatical leader in Kansas—occurred in October, 1859, a few weeks before the meeting of the Thirty-sixth Congress. Insignificant in itself and in its immediate results, it afforded a startling revelation of the extent to which sectional hatred and political fanaticism had blinded the conscience of a class of persons in certain States of the Union, forming a party steadily growing stronger in numbers as well as in activity. Sympathy with its purposes and methods was earnestly disclaimed by all parties in Congress; but, in the country, the raid of John Brown intensified the spirit of domination in the North, and crystallized the spirit of resistance against further aggression in the South.

Chapter 10

A Retrospect

THE grievances that led to the War of Independence were directly inflicted on the Northern colonies. The Southern colonies had no serious cause of complaint; but, moved by sympathy for their Northern brethren and devotion to the principles of civil liberty and community independence, they made common cause with their neighbors and did their full share in the war that ensued.

At the close of the war each of the thirteen colonies was acknowledged by Great Britain to be a free and independent State. The Confederation of these States embraced an area so extensive, with climate and products so various, that rivalries and conflicts of interest soon began to be manifested. It required all the power of wisdom and patriotism, animated by the affection engendered by common sufferings and dangers, to keep these rivalries under restraint, and to effect those compromises which it was fondly hoped would insure harmony and union. Inspired by this spirit of patriotism, and confident of the continuance of good-will between the States, Virginia ceded to the confederated States all that vast Northwestern Territory out of which five States and part of a sixth have since been organized. These States increased the preponderance of the Northern section over that of the section which made the gift, and thereby destroyed the equilibrium existing at the close of the War of Independence.

By the operation of the Missouri Compromise, and the appropriation of all land obtained from Mexico, it may be stated, with approximate accuracy, the North monopolized more than three-fourths of all the territory acquired by the United States since the Declaration of Independence.

Nor was this all. By a perversion of the constitutional provision for imposing taxes on imports, the agricultural South was heavily burdened for the benefit of the manufacturing North; while the power of the majority was used to appropriate to the Northern States an unequal share of the public disbursements. These combined causes—more land, more money, more work for special industries—all served to attract immigration to the North, and, with increasing population, the greed grew by what it fed on.

This was clearly shown at the first Republican Convention, held at Chicago, May 16, 1860, to nominate a candidate for the Presidency. It was a purely sectional body. Not a single delegate represented any constituency south of the famous political line of 36° 30'. Contrary to all precedent, both candidates were selected from the North. Mr. Lincoln, the candidate for the Presidency, had publicly announced that the Union "could not permanently remain half slave and half free." A fictitious issue was presented. The most fanatical foes of the Constitution were satisfied that their ideas would be the rule and guide of the party.

Meanwhile the Democratic Convention, which had met at Charleston on April 23rd, had found it impossible to agree on a platform, and hence no nomination was possible. The Convention was adjourned, to reassemble at Baltimore, where, again, the two wings of the party disagreed and held separate Conventions—the conservative (or State-rights) wing nominating John C. Breckinridge, of Kentucky, then Vice-President of the United States, for President; and Senator Joseph Lane, of Oregon, for Vice-President: and the advocates of the doctrine of "popular sovereignty" nominating Stephen A. Douglas, of Illinois, for President; and Herschel V. Johnson, of Georgia, for Vice-President. Still another Convention, held at Baltimore on May 19th, nominated John Bell, of Tennessee, for President, and Edward Everett, of Massachusetts, for Vice-President. This third Convention was composed of delegates from all the States, representing those who still adhered to the Whig party and the "American" organization. It repudiated all sectional and geographical issues, and pledged itself to "maintain, protect, and defend those great principles of public liberty and national safety against all enemies." It declared it to be the part of patriotism and of duty to recognize no political principle other than the Constitution of the country, the Union of the States, and the enforcement of the laws. It totally ignored the territorial question.

Thus, four distinct parties presented rival tickets and platforms to the people of the United States:

Briefly, the Constitutional-Union, or Bell-Everett, party advocated, in general terms, adherence to the Constitution, the Union, and the enforcement of the laws.

The Democratic-Conservative, or Breckinridge-Lane party asserted the right of a people of a Territory, on emerging from a territorial condition to that of a State, then to determine what should be the nature of their domestic institutions.

The party of popular sovereignty, or Douglas-Johnson party affirmed the right of the people of a Territory, in their territorial condition, to determine their organic institutions, independently of the consent of Congress, and denied the power or duty of Congress to protect the persons or property of minorities in such territories against the action of majorities.

The Republican, or Lincoln-Hamlin party insisted that "slavery can exist only by virtue of municipal law;" that there was no law for it in the Territories, and that "Congress was bound to prohibit it or exclude it from any and every Federal Territory." In other words, it asserted the right and duty of Congress to exclude the citizens of half the States of the Union from territory belonging in common to all, unless on condition of the abandonment or sacrifice of property distinctly and specifically recognized as such by the compact of Union.

The conservative power of the country was thus divided into three parts, while the aggressive was held in solid column. The result was foreseen by all careful observers, and attempts were made to unite the friends of the Constitution by the withdrawal of two of the candidates, but Mr. Douglas declared that the scheme was impracticable, and declined to cooperate.

The result was the election—by a minority—of a President whose avowed principles were considered fatal to the harmony of the Union. Of the 303 electoral votes, Mr. Lincoln received 180; but of the popular suffrages—4,676,853 votes, which the electors represented—he received only 1,866,352, or a little over one-third. This discrepancy was owing to the system of casting the State votes as a unit, without regard to the popular majorities. Thus, in New York, the total popular vote was 675,156, of which 362,646 were cast for the Lincoln electors and 312,510 against them. New York was entitled to 35 electoral votes. On the basis of the popular vote, 19 of these would have been cast for Mr. Lincoln and 16 against him. But, under the State unit system, the entire 35 votes were cast for the Republican candidates, thus giving them not only the full strength of the majority, but of the great minority opposed to them also. So of other Northern States, in which the small majorities on one side operated with the weight of entire unanimity; while the virtual unanimity in the Southern States counted nothing more than a mere majority might have done.

The announcement of these results caused the smouldering fire in a majority of the Southern States to burst into flame; but it was still controlled by that love of the Union which the South had illustrated on every battle-field from Boston to Mexico. Few, if any, doubted the right of a State to withdraw its grant delegated to the Federal Government, or, in other words, to secede from the Union; but this was generally regarded as the remedy of the last resort, to be applied only when ruin or dishonor was the alternative. It was still hoped against hope that some adjustment might be made, some means be found to avert the calamities of a practical application of the theory of an "irrepressible conflict."

Chapter 11

Preliminary Preparations for Defence

THE indignation with which the result of the Presidential election was received in the Southern States proceeded from no personal hostility to the President-elect, nor from chagrin at the defeat of the Democratic candidates, but from the fact that the people of the South recognized in Mr. Lincoln the representative of a party professing principles destructive to "their peace, their prosperity, and their domestic tranquillity."

No rash or revolutionary action was taken by the Southern States. The measures for defence adopted were considerate, and were executed deliberately. The Presidential election occurred in November, 1860. Most of the State legislatures assembled soon afterward in regular session; although, in some cases, special sessions were convoked for the purpose of calling State Conventions to be elected expressly for taking such action as should be deemed expedient in the existing circumstances.

It had always been held that such Conventions possessed all the power of the people assembled in mass; it was through such Conventions that the consent of the several States to the formation of the Union had been conveyed; and by such Conventions, therefore, could that assent be revoked. The time required for the deliberate and final process also precluded the danger of precipitate or premature action, and gave opportunity for due reflection by the Federal Government and the people of the Northern States.

The character of the President in power now became an important factor in the situation. Mr. Buchanan's freedom from sectional asperity, his long life in the public service, his conciliatory disposition, his love of peace, and his reverence for the Constitution, were guarantees that he would not precipitate a conflict with any of the States. But it soon became evident that in the closing months of his administration he had little power to mould the policy of the future. Like all intelligent and impartial students of constitutional history, the President held that the Federal Government had no rightful power to coerce a State. Like his wise and patriotic predecessors in office, he believed that "our Union rests upon public opinion, and can never be cemented by the blood of its citizens shed in civil war; that if it could not live in the affections of the people it must one day perish;" and that although "Congress may possess many means of preserving it by conciliation, the sword was not placed in their hand to preserve it by force" (Message of December 3, 1860).

Ten years before the date of this message, Mr. Calhoun had uttered similar sentiments in the Senate. But, in the intervening years, the progress of sectional discord and the tendency of the stronger section to unconstitutional aggression had been frightfully rapid. With very rare exceptions, in 1850, there were none who claimed the right of the Federal Government to coerce a State. In 1860, men had grown familiar with the threat of driving the South into submission to any act that the Government might perform. During the canvass of that year demonstrations by great military organizations in the North pointed unmistakably to the employment of means not authorized by the powers delegated to the Federal Government by the States.

It was still recalled that a proposition to authorize the use of force against a delinquent State, introduced into the Convention that framed the Constitution, had been defeated, because, as Mr. Madison urged, "the use of force against a State would look more like a declaration of war, and would probably be considered by the party attacked as a dissolution of all former compacts by which it might be bound." Although the appeals to passion, preparing the Northern people to support a war against the Southern States, in the event of secession, were general and vehement, there were not wanting protests against this policy even in the ranks of the Republicans. But the strident roar of prejudice and passion drowned the still small voice of constitutional duty.

That signs of coming danger so visible, evidences of hostility so unmistakable, disregard of constitutional obligations so wanton, taunts and jeers so bitter and insulting should serve to increase excitement in the South was a consequence flowing as much from reason and patriotism as from sentiment. He must have been ignorant of human nature who did not expect such a tree to bear fruits of discord and division.

CHAPTER 12

THE CLOSE OF 1860

SHORTLY after the election in November, the Senators and Representatives of Mississippi were invited by the Governor to meet him for consultation as to the character of the message he should send to the special session of the legislature he had called to consider the propriety of assembling a convention.

While holding, with my political associates, that the right of a State to secede was unquestionable, the knowledge I had gained, as Chairman of the Military Committee of the United States Senate and as Secretary of War, had made me familiar with the entire lack of preparation for war in the South; and as, unlike most of my associates, I did not believe that secession would be peaceably accomplished, but that war would surely ensue between the sections, and that the odds against us would be far greater than what were due merely to our numerical inferiority, I was slower and more reluctant than others, who held a different opinion, to resort to that remedy. I soon learned that I was regarded as "too slow;" and my critics were probably correct in their assertions that I was behind the general opinion of the people of my State as to the propriety of prompt secession. While engaged in consultation, I received a telegraphic message from two members of President Buchanan's Cabinet urging me to proceed immediately to Washington. Advised by my associates to comply, I hastened to the capital and called on the President, who offered to read to me his forthcoming Message. I made certain suggestions for its modification, all of which he kindly accepted, but some of which he subsequently changed.

The popular movement in the South was tending rapidly toward the secession of the planting States; yet they were all represented in the House and Senate, except South Carolina, when Congress assembled, on December 3, 1860. Hopes were still cherished that the Northern leaders would appreciate the impending peril and devise means of allaying the apprehension of the South. But this hope was soon dispelled by the Congressional debates, which showed an arrogant determination to reap to the uttermost the full fell harvest of a sectional victory.

Senator Crittenden, of Kentucky, introduced a joint resolution, known afterward as "the Crittenden Compromise," proposing, in the interest of peace and Union, certain amendments to the Constitution—among them the incorporation, into the Constitution, of the Missouri Compromise line. The proposed olive branch was contemptuously rejected. Action was delayed from time to time, on various pretences, until the last day of the session, when it was defeated by seven votes.

Meanwhile, before the final vote was taken, seven States had withdrawn from the Union and established a Confederacy of their own.

Other resolutions, with a similar purpose, met practically a similar fate. In the debates on these resolutions I argued that our Government is an agency of delegated and strictly limited powers; that its founders did not look to its preservation by force; that the chain they wove to bind these States together was one of love and mutual good offices. "They had broken the fetters of despotic power; they had separated themselves from the mother country upon the question of community independence; and their sons will be degenerate indeed if, clinging to the mere name and form of free government, they forge and rivet on their posterity the fetters which their ancestors broke. . . . I cling not merely to the name and form, but to the spirit and purpose of the Union which our fathers made."

In these debates one Whig (Mr. Crittenden), and the Northern Democrats generally, co-operated with the States rights Democrats of the South; but the so-called Republican Senators of the North rejected every proposition which it was hoped might satisfy the Southern people and check the progress of the secession movement.

Similar efforts for an adjustment met a similar fate in the House of Representatives. No wonder, then, that, under the shadow of the failure of every effort in Congress to find any common ground to restore amity between the sections, the close of the year should have been darkened by a cloud in the firmament, which had lost even the silver lining so long seen, or thought to be seen, by the hopeful.

Chapter 13

Secession of South Carolina

SOUTH CAROLINA, by unanimous vote of her Convention, on December 20, 1860, passed an Ordinance revoking her delegated powers and withdrawing from the Union. The other planting States also made preparations for secession, but delayed final action for some time in the hope that Congress might avert the necessity by measures of conciliation. Seeing the hopelessness of delay, by the failure of all overtures during the first month of the session, they hastened to exercise what was generally admitted to be an undoubted right appertaining to their sovereignty as States, and the only peaceful remedy that remained for the evils already felt and the dangers feared.

Many instances and precedents are found in the previous history of the country of the assertion of this right, and of a purpose to enforce it; notably in the history of the New England States, and in the utterances of distinguished representative men who were contemporaries of the fathers of the Constitution, or who took part in the Convention that framed it. The report of the celebrated Hartford Convention, of 1814, asserts the right of secession; and its theoretical plan of separation corresponds very nearly with that actually adopted by the Southern States fifty years afterward. Again, in 1844, the annexation of Texas evoked threats of dissolution from the Northeastern States, and were formulated into a resolution, passed by the Legislature of Massachusetts, and again, in the following year, by another resolution, transmitted to Congress, declaring the act admitting Texas into the Union to be of "no binding force whatever on the people of Massachusetts."

Seven or eight States were preparing to follow the example of South Carolina, and still others were anxiously contemplating the probable necessity of joining them. Before recording the acts that led to further withdrawals from the Union and the formation of the Confederate States, it is expedient that a brief recapitulation should be made of the causes which led to this action, and a fuller exposition given of some of the constitutional questions involved in their action.

The Southern States have been persistently represented as the propagandists of slavery, and the Northern States as the defenders and champions of universal freedom. It has been dogmatically asserted that the war between the States was caused by efforts on the one side to extend and perpetuate human slavery, and on the other to resist it and establish human liberty. Neither allegation is true.

To whatever extent the question of slavery may have served as an occasion, it was far from being the cause of the war.

As an historical fact, negro slavery existed in all the original thirteen States. It was recognized by the Constitution. Owing to climatic, industrial, and economical—not moral or sentimental—reasons, it had gradually disappeared in the Northern States, while it had persisted in the Southern States. The slave-trade was never conducted by the people of the South. It had been monopolized by Northern merchants and carried on in Northern ships. Men differed in their views as to the abstract question of the right or wrong of slavery; but, for two generations after the Revolution, there was no geographical line of such differences. It was during the controversy over the Missouri question that the subject first took a sectional aspect; but long after that period Abolitionists were mobbed and assaulted in the North. Lovejoy, for example, was killed in Illinois in 1837.

These facts prove that the sectional hostility which first appeared in 1820, in the Missouri controversy, and again broke out on the proposition to annex Texas, in 1844, and reappeared after the Mexican war, never again to be suppressed until its fell results had been fully accomplished, was not the consequence of any differences on the abstract question of slavery. It was the offspring of sectional rivalry and political ambition.

In 1803 and 1811, when the Louisiana Purchase, and afterward the admission of the State of Louisiana, created threats of disunion from the representatives of New England, it is not pretended that the existence of slavery was the ground of opposition. The complaint then was not of slavery, but of the "acquisition of more weight at the other extremity of the Union." It was not slavery that threatened a rupture in 1832, but an unjust and unequal tariff.

Of course, the diversity of institutions contributed to the conflict of interests. I am stating general principles, not defining modifications and exceptions with the precision of a mathematical proposition. The truth remains, intact and incontrovertible, that the existence of African servitude was in nowise the cause of the conflict, but only an incident of it. In the later controversies, however, its effect as a lever in operating on the passions, prejudices, and sympathies of men was so potent that it has darkened the whole horizon of historic truth.

I have not attempted, therefore, and shall not permit myself to be drawn into any discussion of the merits or demerits of slavery as an ethical or even as a political question. Such discussion would only serve to divert attention from the genuine issue involved.

As to the institution of negro slavery, it was entirely subject to the control of the States. No power was given to the General Government to interfere with it; but an obligation was imposed to protect it. Its existence and validity were distinctly recognized by the Constitution in the apportionment of direct taxation and representation, in the provision for extinguishing the slave-trade, and in the article providing for the rendition of fugitives from service and labor.

All Federal and State officials were required to take an oath to support the Constitution; yet the halls of Congress were utilized as breastworks from which assaults were made upon these guarantees. The legislatures of various Northern States enacted laws to hinder the execution of the provisions made for the rendition of fugitives from service; State officials lent their aid to the work of thwarting them; and city mobs assailed the officers engaged in the duty of enforcing them. The preamble to the Constitution declared the object of its founders to be "to insure domestic tranquillity;" but now (in 1860) the people of a portion of the States had assumed an attitude of avowed hostility, not only to the provisions of the Constitution itself, but to the "domestic tranquillity" of the people of other States. Long before the formation of the Constitution one of the charges preferred against the Government of Great Britain, as justifying the separation of the colonies from that country, was that of having "excited domestic insurrection among us." Now the mails are burdened with incendiary publications; secret emissaries have been sent, and, in one case, an armed invasion of one of the States has taken place for the very purpose of exciting "domestic insurrection."

It was not the passage of the " Personal Liberty Laws," it was not the circulation of incendiary documents, it was not the raid of John Brown, it was not the operation of unjust and unequal tariff laws, that constituted the intolerable grievance; but it was also the systematic and persistent struggle to deprive the Southern States of equality in the Union, and generally to discriminate against the interests of their people, culminating in their exclusion from the Territories, the common property of the States, as well as by the infraction of their compact to promote domestic tranquillity.

The argument with regard to the Territories need not be repeated. Yet one feature of it has not been specially noticed, although it occupied a large share of public attention at the time and constituted an important element in the case. This was the manner in which the action of the Federal judiciary thereon was received in the Northern States.

In 1854 the well-known "Dred Scott Case" came before the Supreme Court. It involved the question of the status of the African race and the rights of citizens of the Southern States to migrate to the Territories, temporarily or permanently, with their slave property, on a footing of equality with the citizens of other States with their property. The long discussion of this question had been without any satisfactory conclusion; but all parties had united in declaring that a decision by the highest judicial authority in the land would be accepted as final.

After long and patient consideration of the case the decision of the Supreme Court was pronounced by Chief Justice Taney, seven of the nine Judges who composed the Court concurring in it. The salient points established by the decision were, that persons of the African race were not and could not be acknowledged as "part of the people," or citizens under the Constitution; that Congress had no right to exclude citizens of the South from taking their negro servants or any other property into any part of the common territory, and that they were entitled to its protection therein; and, finally, as a consequence of this principle, that the Missouri Compromise of 1820, in so far as it prohibited the existence of African servitude north of a designated line, was unconstitutional and void.

Instead of accepting the decision of this then august tribunal as conclusive of a controversy that had long disturbed the peace and was threatening the perpetuity of the Union, it was flouted, denounced, and utterly disregarded by the Northern agitators, and served only to stimulate the intensity of their sectional hostility.

What resource for justice, what assurance of tranquillity, what guarantee of safety, now remained for the South? No alternative remained except to seek, out of the Union, that security which they had vainly endeavored to obtain within it. The hope of our people may be stated in a sentence: it was to escape from injury and strife within the Union; to find prosperity and peace out of it.

Officers of the Confederate Army and Navy.

Chapter 14

General Principles

WHILE the limits assigned to this volume do not permit a full presentation of the arguments, or an adequate exposition of the historical facts that justified the secession of the Southern States, and entitled them to be regarded not as "rebels" or "traitors," but as defenders of the original principles on which the fathers founded our system of government, or a full demonstration of the fact that the essential truths which they declared "unalienable" are the foundation-stones on which rests the vindication of the Confederate cause, yet, before proceeding with the narrative of the events of the war between the States, it is essential that the candid student should know and bear in mind that the intelligent people of the South were practically unanimous in the belief:

That the States of which the American Union was formed, from the moment when they emerged from their colonial or provincial condition, became, severally, sovereign, free, and independent States—not one State or Nation;

That the Union formed under the Articles of Confederation was a compact between the States in which these attributes of sovereignty, freedom, and independence were expressly asserted and guaranteed;

That in forming "the more perfect Union" of the Constitution afterward adopted, the same contracting powers formed an amended compact, without any surrender of these attributes, either expressed or implied; but, on the contrary, by the Tenth Amendment to the Constitution, limiting the authority of the Federal Government to its express grants, with a distinct provision against the presumption of a surrender of anything by implication;

That political sovereignty, in contradistinction to the natural rights of man, resides neither in the individual citizen, nor in unorganized masses, nor in fractional subdivisions of a community, but in the people of an organized political body;

That no "republican form of government," in the sense in which that expression is used in the Constitution, and was generally understood by the founders of the Union—whether it be the government of a State or of a Confederation of States—is possessed of any sovereignty whatever, but merely exercises certain powers delegated by the sovereign authority of the people, and subject to recall and resumption by the same authority that conferred them;

That the "people" who organized the first Confederation, the people who dissolved it, the people who ordained and established the Constitution which succeeded it—the only people known or referred to in the phraseology of that period—were the people of the respective States, each acting separately and with absolute independence of the others;

That, in forming and adopting the Constitution, the States, or the people of the States, formed a new Government but no new People, and that, consequently, no new sovereignty was created; for sovereignty, in an American republic, can belong only to a People, never to a Government; and that the Federal Government is entitled to exercise only the powers delegated to it by the people of the several States;

That the term People in the preamble to the Constitution and in the Tenth Amendment, is used distributively; that the only "People of the United States" known to the Constitution are the people of each State in the Union; that no such political community or corporate unit as one people of the United States then existed, has ever been organized, or yet exists; and that no political action by the people of the United States in the aggregate has ever taken place, or ever can take place under the Constitution.

These principles, although they had come to be considered as peculiarly Southern, were not sectional in their origin. In the beginning and earlier years of our history they were cherished as faithfully and guarded as jealously in Massachusetts and New Hampshire as in Virginia and South Carolina.

It was in these principles that I was nurtured.

Chapter 15
The Right of Secession

THE right of a State to secede from the Union—that is, to withdraw the powers it had granted by virtue of a sovereignty which it had never delegated—was a right never disputed by the generation that established the Constitution. To resume delegated powers, and to judge of the propriety and sufficiency of the causes for doing so, are alike inseparable from the possession of sovereignty. In founding the Federal Constitution, in "forming a more perfect Union," there was not the slightest intimation of so radical a revolution as the surrender of the sovereignty of the contracting parties would have been. It was merely the institution of a new agent, who, however enlarged his powers might be, would still remain subordinate and responsible to the source from which they were derived—that of the sovereign people of each State. It was an amended Union, not a Consolidation.

The present Union owes its very existence to the dissolution, by separate secession, of its members, from the former Union, which, in its organic principles, rested upon precisely the same foundation.

These facts and principles can easily be established by abundance of contemporary evidence. But the right of the people of the several States to resume the power delegated by them to the common agency was not left without positive and ample official assertion. Even at a period when it had never been denied, Virginia, New York, and Rhode Island, in ratifying the Constitution, solemnly and formally declared that the instrument recognized the right of secession. By accepting these ratifications, with this declaration incorporated, the other States as distinctly accepted the principles thus asserted.

The alternative to secession is coercion. That is to say, if no right of secession exists—if it is forbidden by the Constitution or hostile to it—then it is a wrong for which a remedy must lawfully be provided;

which, in such a case, could only be the use of force against the State attempting to withdraw.

Early in the session of the Convention it was proposed to invest the Congress with this power of coercion. It was opposed by Madison, who offered a motion to postpone it; which was adopted *nem. con.*

Mr. Hamilton, in the New York Convention, said that "to coerce the States is one of the maddest projects that was ever devised."

Edmund Randolph, Governor of Virginia, in the State Convention, eloquently protested against the idea of coercing any delinquent State. The idea of even judicial coercion was repudiated by Hamilton, Marshall, and others; and the suggestion of military coercion was treated with still more abhorrence. No principle was more fully and firmly settled, on the highest authority, than that, under our system, there could be no coercion of a State.

Among other objections that have been advanced against the right of secession is one based on obscure and indefinite ideas with regard to allegiance.

In the light of the principles on which the Constitution was founded there can be no doubt that the primary and paramount allegiance of the citizen is due to the sovereign only; that this sovereign, under our system, is the people of the State to which he belongs—the people who created the State Government which he obeys and which protects him in the enjoyment of his personal rights; the people who alone, as far as he is concerned, ordained and established the Federal Constitution and Federal Government; the people who have reserved to themselves sovereignty, which involves the power to revoke all agencies created by them. The obligation to support the State or Federal Constitution, and the obedience due to either State or Federal Government, are alike derived from the allegiance due to the sovereign, and dependent on it. If the sovereign abolishes the State Government and establishes a new one, the obligation of allegiance requires him to transfer his obedience accordingly. If the sovereign withdraws from its association, with its confederates in the Union, the allegiance of the citizen requires him to follow the sovereign. Any other course is rebellion or treason; for his relation to the Union arises from the membership of the State of which he is a citizen, and ceases whenever his State withdraws from it. He cannot owe obedience—much less allegiance—to an association from which his sovereign has separated and thereby withdrawn him.

A little consideration of these plain and irrefutable truths will show how utterly unworthy and false are the vulgar taunts which attribute "treason" to those who, in the late secession of the Southern States, were loyal to the only sovereign entitled to their allegiance; and which still more absurdly prate of the violation of oaths to support "the Government," an oath which no citizen could have been lawfully required to take, and which must have been ignorantly confounded with the prescribed oath to support the Constitution.

To term the action of a sovereign a "rebellion" is a grave abuse of language.

So, also, is the flippant phrase which speaks of it as an appeal to the "arbitrament of the sword." In the late contest there was no appeal by the seceding States to the arbitrament of arms. They neither invited nor provoked war. They stood in an attitude of self-defence, and were attacked for merely exercising a right alienated neither by the terms of the compact nor otherwise. The man who defends his house against attack cannot with any propriety be said to have submitted the question of his right to it to the arbitrament of arms.

Two moral obligations rested on the seceding States—not to break up the partnership without good and sufficient cause; and to make an equitable settlement with former associates, and, as far as may be, avoid the infliction of loss or damage upon any of them.

Neither of these obligations was violated or neglected by the Southern States in their secession.

Part 2
Secession and Confederation

Chapter 16

Early Days of Secession

THE year 1861 was ushered in with the manifestation of a general belief among the people of the planting States in the necessity of an early secession as the only possible alternative left them. This condition of public opinion was in no measure due, as has been sometimes charged, to the "influence of a few ambitious politicians." With rare exceptions the officials were neither agitators nor leaders in the popular movement; the people everywhere were in advance of them; and the influence of the officials, as a rule, was employed to allay rather than to stimulate excitement, to restrain rather than to accelerate action. These statements apply especially to the Southern Senators and Representatives in Congress, to whose imaginary "cabals" and "conspiracies" in Washington the rapid growth of the secession movement has been attributed in certain histories of the war published in the North and in Europe. The truth is, that the movements that culminated in secession were inaugurated before the meeting of Congress, and were conducted with a dignity and formality that precluded the theory of conspiracy or of passion. These acts were the deliberate results of convictions slowly and reluctantly adopted, and due wholly to the belief that by no other policy could this relief be obtained. The acts of secession were not intended as war measures. The opinion generally prevailed that secession would be peacefully accomplished; an opinion from which I publicly dissented, with the result, as already stated, that I was regarded as "too slow," and as being behind the public sentiment of my own State.

Another fallacy should be noted here. It has been often asserted that the troops of the United States army were so disposed, by a collusion between the Southern leaders and Mr. Floyd, the Secretary of War, that the seizure of forts, arsenals, and custom-houses in the South was rendered possible and easy. No such conspiracy existed. The military forts were in their usual condition. There were no fewer troops at the time of their seizure by the States than there had been for many years, nor than there is, generally, even to this day (1889).

Still another imputation on the honor of Southern Senators should be repelled here before entering on the narrative of the ensuing events. It was alleged—and the Comte de Paris has specially singled out my name in connection with this disgraceful charge—that we held our seats as a vantage ground for plotting for the dismemberment of the Union. It is a charge which no accuser ever made in my presence, although I have in public debate more than once challenged its assertion and denounced its falsehood. It will suffice to say that I always held, and often avowed, the principle that a Senator in Congress occupied the position of an ambassador from the State he represented to the Federal Government, as well as being, also, in some sense a member of the Government; and that, in either capacity, it would be dishonorable to use his powers and privileges for the dismemberment of the Government to which he was accredited. Acting on this principle, as long as I held a seat in the Senate my best efforts were directed to the maintenance of the Constitution and the Union resulting from it, and to make the Government an effective agent of the States for its prescribed purposes. As soon as the paramount allegiance due to Mississippi forbade a continuance of these efforts I withdrew from the United States Senate. To say that, during this period, I did nothing secretly in conflict with what was done or proposed openly; would be merely to assert my own integrity, an assertion which would be worthless to those who doubt it, and superfluous to those who believe in it. What is here said on the subject for myself, I believe to be also true of my associates in Congress. Further explanation of my own position on these questions more properly belongs to biography than to history, and may therefore be passed over here.

Without at this time entering into a discussion of the legal questions involved, it is proper to add that the sites of forts, arsenals, navy-yards, and other public property of the Federal Government were ceded by the States within whose boundaries they were situated, subject to the condition that they should be used solely and exclusively for the purposes for which they were granted. By accepting such grants, under such conditions, sometimes expressed, always implied, the Federal Government assented to their propriety; and it follows that a State withdrawing from the Union would consequently resume the control over all public defences and other public property within its limits; providing, however, for adequate compensation to the other members of the partnership, or their common agent, for the value of the work or loss incurred. Such equitable settlement the seceding States were desirous to make and prompt to propose to the Federal authorities.

Chapter 17

Fort Sumter

ON the secession of South Carolina, the conditions of the defences of Charleston Harbor became a subject of general anxiety. Of the three forts of the harbor, one only—Fort Moultrie—was occupied, and that was held by a garrison of less than a hundred effective men, under the command of Major Robert Anderson.

About two weeks before the passage of the Ordinance of Secession the congressional representatives of South Carolina called on President Buchanan, to assure him, in anticipation of that event, that the State authorities had no immediate intention of attacking or molesting the Federal forts, provided that no reinforcements should be sent and that the military situation should remain unchanged. While he declined to make any formal pledge, the delegation understood the President as approving this suggestion. Subsequent developments have shown, however, that, both before and after the secession of South Carolina, preparations were secretly made for reinforcing Major Anderson.

Immediately after the secession of the State the Convention of South Carolina deputed three commissioners to "treat with the Government of the United States for the delivery of the forts, magazines, lighthouses, and other real estate, with their appurtenances, within the limits of South Carolina, and also for an apportionment of the public debt, and for a division of all other property held by the Government of the United States, as agent of the confederated States of which South Carolina was recently a member, and generally to negotiate as to all other measures and arrangements proper to be made and adopted in the existing relation of the parties, and for the continuance of peace and amity between this commonwealth and the Government at Washington."

Before these commissioners could communicate with the President an event occurred which changed the whole aspect of affairs. On

December 26th, the whole country was electrified by the news that, during the previous night, Major Anderson had "dismantled Fort Moultrie, spiked his guns, burned his gun-carriages, and removed his command to Fort Sumter," which occupied a more commanding position in the harbor.

This action was regarded by the Government and people of South Carolina as a violation of the implied pledge of a maintenance of the *status quo*. The remaining forts and other "public property were at once taken possession of by the State, and the condition of public opinion became greatly exacerbated. An interview between the President and the commissioners was followed by a sharp correspondence, and negotiations were soon abruptly broken off.

In the meantime Mr. Cass, Secretary of State, had resigned because, it was said, the President had refused to send reinforcements to Charleston; and on the occupation of Fort Sumter, which he regarded as a violation of the pledge given or implied by the Government, Mr. Floyd resigned, because the President refused to withdraw the garrison from the harbor.

Personally, I urged the President to withdraw this garrison, as it only served as a menace—for it was utterly incapable of holding the fort if attacked; while nothing would have operated more powerfully to quiet the apprehensions and allay the resentment of the people of South Carolina than the withdrawal of the impotent menace. Mr. Buchanan's abiding hope was to avert a collision, or at least to postpone it beyond the close of his official term. The management of the whole affair was what Talleyrand described as something worse than a crime—a blunder. Whatever treatment the case demanded should have been prompt. To wait was fatuity.

The ill-advised attempt to reinforce and provision Fort Sumter by the steamer *Star of the West* resulted in the repulse of that vessel at the mouth of the harbor. On January 9th, on her refusal to heave to, she was fired upon, and she put back to sea with her supplies and concealed recruits. Again I called on the President and urged such prompt measures as were now evidently necessary to avert impending calamity; but the result was even more unsatisfactory than similar previous efforts.

Another commissioner was sent by South Carolina to negotiate with the Federal Government for the peaceful transfer of the fort; but he was put off with evasive and unsatisfactory answers, and finally returned without having effected anything.

During the remainder of Mr. Buchanan's administration things went rapidly from bad to worse, and the veteran statesman, at the expiration of his term of office, retired to private life, having effected nothing to allay the storm that had been steadily gathering during his administration.

Then timid vacillation was succeeded by unscrupulous cunning, and for futile efforts, without hostile collision, to impose a claim of authority upon people who repudiated it were substituted measures which could be sustained only by force and bloodshed.

Chapter 18

Progress of Secession

MEANWHILE the popular movement in the planting States resulted in the secession of Mississippi on the 9th of January, 1861; of Florida on the 10th; of Alabama on the 11th; of Georgia on the 18th; and of Louisiana on the 26th. The Conventions of these States united with South Carolina in naming the 4th of February as the date, and Montgomery, Ala., as the place, for the assembly of a Congress of the seceded States. Each State Convention appointed delegates to it.

As soon as we received official information of the secession of our States, on January 21st, the Senators of Florida and Alabama, and myself, announced the withdrawal of our respective States and took formal leave of the Senate.

The course which events were likely to take was now shrouded in the greatest uncertainty. The common opinion in the Southern States was that the separation would be final but peaceful. For my own part, while believing that secession was a right and properly a peaceful remedy, I had never believed that it would be permitted to be peacefully exercised; I had predicted a long and desperate struggle, and advised preparations to be made therefor. Very few in the South agreed with me at that time, and my opinions were as unwelcome as they were unexpected. Let us do credit to that generous credulity, which could not understand how, in violation of the compact of Union, a war could be waged against the seceding States, or why they should be invaded because their people had deemed it necessary to withdraw from an association which had failed to fulfil the end for which they had entered into it, and which, having been broken by the other parties, to the injury of the seceding States, had ceased to be binding on them.

It is satisfactory to know that the calamities which have befallen the Southern States were the result of their credulous reliance on the power of the Constitution, that, if it had failed to protect their rights, it would at least suffice to prevent an attempt at coercion, if, in the last resort, they peacefully withdrew from the Union.

The Congress of Delegates from the seceding States met at Montgomery on the day appointed, and soon prepared a Provisional Constitution for the new Confederacy, to be formed of the States that had withdrawn from the Union, under the style of the Confederate States of America. The Constitution was adopted on the 8th of February, to continue in force for one year, unless superseded at an earlier date by a permanent organization.

On the 9th of February the Congress proceeded to vote for officers of the Provisional Government. It resulted in my election to the Presidency, with Hon. Alexander Stephens, of Georgia, as Vice-President.

I was engaged at the time in the peaceful pursuits of a planter at my home at Briarfield, Miss., when I was notified of my election, accompanied by an urgent request to proceed immediately to Montgomery.

As my election had been spoken of as a probable event, and as I did not desire that position or any civil office, but preferred to remain in the post to which I had been elected, and still held, at the head of the army of Mississippi, I had taken what seemed to me ample precautions to prevent my nomination to the Presidency. I accepted the position because I could not decline it, but with the expectation and intention of soon returning to the field.

On my way to Montgomery brief addresses were made by me at various places, which were grossly misrepresented at the North as invoking war and threatening devastation. Not deemed worthy of contradiction at the time, when problems of vital public interest were constantly presented, these false and malicious reports have since been adopted by partisan writers as authentic history. It is sufficient here to say that no utterance of mine, private or public, differed in tone and spirit from my farewell address to the Senate, or my inaugural address at Montgomery; the one a short time before, the other a short time after, the date of these fictitious addresses.

Chapter 19

The Confederate Cabinet and Congress

IMMEDIATELY after being inaugurated, I proceeded to the formation of a Cabinet, and selected, as Secretary of State, Mr. Toombs, of Georgia; as Secretary of the Treasury, Mr. Memminger, of South Carolina; as Secretary of War, Mr. Walker, of Alabama; as Secretary of the Navy, Mr. Mallory, of Florida; as Attorney-General, Mr. Benjamin, of Louisiana; as Postmaster-General, Mr. Reagan, of Texas. In making these selections I was governed by considerations of the public welfare only. Not even a single member of the Cabinet bore to me the relation of close personal friendship, and, indeed, with two of them I had had no previous acquaintance.

The first act of the Confederate Congress was to continue in force all the laws of the United States not inconsistent with the Constitution of the Confederate States, and to continue in power all officials connected with the collection of customs, and the assistant treasurers entrusted with the keeping of the moneys arising therefrom.

On the 25th of February the Congress passed an act, which the President approved, declaring the peaceful navigation of the Mississippi River free to the citizens of any of the States upon its borders, or upon the borders of its navigable tributaries, without any duty or hindrance, except light money, portage, and other like charges. Another act repealed the laws forbidding the employment in the coasting trade of vessels not enrolled or licensed, and of all laws imposing discriminating rates on foreign vessels or goods imported in them. These and similar acts indicated the wish of the people of the Confederacy to preserve the peace and encourage the freest commerce with all nations, and not least with their late associates the United States. Indeed, all the laws passed by the Provisional Congress show how consistent were the purposes and actions of its members with their original avowal of a desire peacefully to separate from those with whom they could not live in tranquillity.

In accordance with a resolution of the Congress, which was in entire accord with my own views and inclinations, I was next required to appoint commissioners to negotiate friendly relations with the United States, and an equitable and peaceable settlement of all questions pending between the two Governments. Messrs. A. R. Roman, of Louisiana; Martin J. Crawford, of Georgia; and John Forsythe, of Alabama—three discreet, well-informed, and distinguished citizens—were appointed as commissioners to proceed to Washington to negotiate for an amicable settlement of the questions consequent on separation. But as I did not hold the common opinion that we should be allowed to depart in peace, I regarded it as an imperative duty to make all possible preparations for the contingency of war.

While these events were occurring, the last noteworthy effort, within the Union, was made to arrest the progress of the usurpation that was driving the Southern States into secession. This effort was made by the General Assembly of Virginia, which invited all States which desired to unite with her in arresting disunion by an equitable adjustment of the existing controversies, to appoint commissioners to meet in Washington on the 4th of February, "to consider, and if practicable to agree upon, some suitable arrangement."

Ex-President Tyler, Messrs. Rives, Brockenburgh, Summers, and Seddon—five of the most distinguished citizens of the State—were appointed commissioners for Virginia, with instructions, if they should agree on any plan of settlement with the commissioners of other States regarding amendments to the Federal Constitution, to communicate them to Congress with a view to their submission to the several States for ratification.

The Border States promptly acceded to the proposal of Virginia; other States followed; so that, when the conference, or "Peace Congress," as it was called, assembled, on the 4th of February, it was found that twenty-one States were represented. Of this number fourteen were Northern non-slaveholding, and seven Southern and slave-holding, States. Three of the Northwestern and the two Pacific States, the six States that had seceded, and Texas and Arkansas—whose secession was inevitable—held aloof from the conference.

It is needless to recall the deliberations of this conference. A plan of settlement was finally adopted by a majority of the States represented, and the amendments deemed essential to put an end to further contention were agreed on and presented to the Senate. The plan thus formulated resembled in its chief features the plan of Mr. Crittenden, then still pending. The distinguished Senator promptly accepted it as a substitute for his own proposition, and eloquently urged its adoption. But the arrogance of a sectional majority, inflated by recent triumph, was too powerful to be allayed by the appeals of patriotism or the counsels of wisdom. The plan of the Peace Congress was treated with the same contemptuous indifference shown to every other movement for conciliation.

These efforts occurred on the eve of the inauguration of Mr. Lincoln, and the accession to power of a party founded on a basis of sectional aggression, and now thoroughly committed to its prosecution and perpetuation. With the failure of these efforts expired the last hope of reconciliation and fraternal union.

Chapter 20

Some Northern Protests

IT should be noted that the Southern States did not stand alone at this period in the assertion of the right of secession and the wrong of coercion. Leading journals of the North and many prominent politicians—such conspicuous supporters of the predominant party, for example, as the New York Tribune and New York Herald, and such political leaders as Horatio Seymour, ex-Governor of New York, James S. Thayer, ex-Chancellor Walworth, and Horace Greeley—that is to say, many influential representatives of the Republican party and a still larger portion of the Democratic party of the North—distinctly asserted the right of secession and repudiated the claim of right to restrain or coerce a State in the exercise of its free choice, and in language as distinct and emphatic as that uttered in other times by Hamilton, or Madison, or Marshall, or John Quincy Adams. One Northern journal, of great influence, even went so far as to declare that "if troops should be raised in the North to march against the people of the South, a fire in the rear would be opened on such troops, which would either stop their march altogether or wonderfully accelerate it."

Even Mr. Lincoln, in his inaugural address on the 4th of March, 1861, while arguing against the right to secede, and asserting his intention to repossess the places and property belonging to the Government, declared that "beyond what may be necessary for these objects there will be no invasion, no using of force against or among the people anywhere."

Such utterances kept alive in the hearts of the Southern people the hope that separation would be as peaceable in fact as it was on their part in purpose; that the conservative and patriotic feeling still existing in the North would control the elements of sectional hatred and bloodthirsty fanaticism, and that there would be really no war.

Chapter 21

The Confederate Constitution

ONE week after the inauguration of the Federal President at Washington, the Confederate Congress at Montgomery completed the permanent Constitution, which was forthwith submitted to the people of the respective States and duly ratified by them.

The Confederate Constitution was modelled on the Constitution of the United States, with only such changes as experience had suggested for better practical working or greater perspicuity. The chief changes are easily noted. In accordance with the original draft of the Constitution of 1787, the official term of the President was fixed at six instead of four years, and it was provided that he should not be eligible for re-election. The President was empowered to remove his cabinet officers or diplomatic agents; but, in all other cases, removals from office could be made only for cause, and the cause was to be reported to the Senate.

Congress was authorized to provide for the admission of cabinet officers to a seat in either house, with the privilege of participating in debates pertaining to their departments. Unfortunately, this wise and judicious provision remained inoperative, owing to the failure of Congress to provide the appropriate legislation.

Protective tariff-duties, bounties, and extra compensation for services of Government officials were altogether prohibited.

The President was vested with the power to veto any appropriation in a bill without thereby disapproving any other appropriation in the same bill.

Any two or more States were authorized to enter into compact for the improvement of navigable rivers flowing through or between them.

A vote of two-thirds of each house—the Senate voting by

States—was required for the admission of a new State.

The impeachment of Confederate officers was entrusted, as under the old Constitution, to the discretion of the House of Representatives; with the additional provision that, in the case of any judicial or other officer, exercising his functions within the limits of a particular State, impeachment might be made by the Legislature of such State; the trial, in all cases, to be by the Senate of the Confederate States.

With regard to amendments to the Constitution, it was made obligatory on Congress, on the demand of any three States concurring in the proposed amendment or amendments, to summon a convention of all the States to consider and act upon them, voting by States, but restricted in its action to the particular proposition thus submitted. If approved by such convention, the amendments were to be subject to final ratification by two-thirds of the States.

With regard to slavery and the slave-trade the provisions of the Constitution furnished an effective answer to the assertion, so often made, that the Confederacy was founded on slavery and intended to perpetuate and extend it. Property in slaves, already existing, was recognized and guaranteed, just as it was by the Constitution of the United States; and the rights of such property in the common Territories were protected against any such hostile discrimination as had been attempted in the Union. But the extension of slavery, in the only practical sense of that phrase, was more distinctly and effectively precluded by the Confederate than by the Federal Constitution. The further importation of negroes from any country, other than the slave-holding States and Territories of the United States, was peremptorily prohibited, and Congress was further endowed with the power to prohibit the introduction of slaves from any State or Territory not belonging to the Confederacy.

Having had no direct part in the preparation of the Confederate Constitution, no consideration of delicacy restrains me in declaring my belief that it was a model of wise, temperate, and liberal statesmanship, or from adopting the language of the Hon. Alexander H. Stephens in saying that

> "The whole document negatives the idea, which so many have been active in endeavoring to put in the enduring form of history, that the Convention at Montgomery was nothing but a set of

conspirators, whose object was the overthrow of the principles of the Constitution of the United States and the creation of a great 'slave oligarchy,' instead of the free institutions thereby secured and guaranteed. The work of the Montgomery Convention, with that of the Convention for a Provisional Government, will ever remain not only as a monument of the wisdom, forecast, and statesmanship of the men who constituted it, but an everlasting refutation of the charges which have been brought against them. These Constitutions, provisional and permanent, together, show clearly that the only leading object of their framers was to sustain, uphold, and perpetuate the fundamental principles of the Constitution of the United States."

CHAPTER 22

NEGOTIATIONS WITH THE FEDERAL GOVERNMENT

HAVING received from Mr. Buchanan, through a distinguished Senator, an intimation that he would be pleased to receive a commission or commissioners from the Confederate States, and would be willing to transmit to the Senate any communication received from them, I hastened the departure of Mr. Martin J. Crawford, one of the three gentlemen previously appointed, and authorized him to act as Special Commissioner of the Confederate States to the Government of the United States. Mr. Crawford reached Washington two or three days before the expiration of Mr. Buchanan's term of office. He found that the President had become so panic-stricken between the time that he gave his promise to receive a Confederate Commissioner and the actual arrival of the Commissioner that he declined either to receive him or to send any message to the Senate relating to his mission. He said that he had only three days of official life left, and could incur no further dangers and reproaches than he had already borne from the press and public speakers of the North.

On the arrival of Mr. Forsythe, the two Commissioners renewed their intercourse with the Federal authorities, and requested the appointment of a day for presentation to the President. Instead of being received in the friendly spirit and desire for peace which had inspired their appointment, they were kept waiting, and were deceived by false assurances and by pledges which were broken without scruple or explanation.

The purpose of this evasive and deceptive policy was to get time to reinforce the forts in the harbor of Charleston; the pledge to evacuate Sumter, for example, having been solemnly renewed even at the time when a special messenger from the State Department was on his way to

South Carolina to arrange with the Federal officers in command a plan for revictualling and reinforcing the forts.

A naval expedition for the relief of Fort Sumter was sent out from New York, and it was expected to reach Charleston Harbor on the 9th of April. Yet the Confederate Commissioners were detained at Washington under the assurance that due notice would be given of any military movement. The notice was given not to the Commissioners but to the Governor of South Carolina, and only on the eve of the day on which the fleet was expected to arrive. The history of the negotiations with the General Government is the narration of a protracted course of fraud and prevarication practised by Mr. Lincoln's administration. Every pledge made was broken, and every assurance of good faith was followed by an act of perfidy. The remonstrances, the patient and reiterated attempts of the South Carolina and Confederate Commissioners to open negotiations had been met by evasion and prevarication. It was evident that no confidence could be placed in any pledge or promise of the Federal Government. Yet no resistance other than that of pacific protest and appeals for an equitable settlement was made until after the public avowal of a purpose of coercion, and when it was known that a hostile fleet was on the way to support and enforce it.

The forbearance of the Confederate Government in the circumstances is held up as unexampled in history. It was carried to the verge of disregard of the safety of the people who had entrusted to that government the duty of their defence.

To have waited further strengthening of the enemy by land and vessel forces, with hostile purpose, now declared, for the sake of having them "fire the first gun," would have been as unwise as it would be to hesitate to strike down an assailant who levels a deadly weapon at one's heart until he has actually fired. He who makes the assault is not necessarily he who strikes the first blow or fires the first gun.

After the assault was made by the hostile descent of the fleet, the reduction of Fort Sumter was a measure of defence rendered absolutely and immediately necessary. Even Mr. Horace Greeley, with all his extreme partisan feeling, is obliged to admit that "whether the bombardment and reduction of Fort Sumter shall or shall not be justified by posterity, it is clear that the Confederacy had no alternative but its own dissolution."[98]

---

[98]. *American Conflict*, Vol. 1, Chap. 24, p. 449.

Chapter 23

Bombardment of Fort Sumter

As soon as the Confederate Government at Montgomery had received official information of the intention of the Federal Government at Washington, in violation of its pledges, to provision Fort Sumter, by force if necessary, it directed General Beauregard to demand its evacuation, and to proceed to reduce it if Major Anderson, its commander, should refuse to surrender.

After a fruitless effort to avoid the effusion of blood by arranging for a definitive and peaceful evacuation, General Beauregard opened the fire of his batteries on Fort Sumter at daylight on the morning of April 13, 1861. The bombardment continued for nearly thirty-four hours, when the fort, which had been partly destroyed by shot, was set on fire; and Major Anderson, after a gallant defence, was forced to surrender.

It is a remarkable fact that, notwithstanding the extent and magnitude of the engagement, the number and calibre of the guns, and the enormous damage done to inanimate material on both sides, especially to Fort Sumter, not a single man was killed or wounded in either of the contending forces.

The Federal garrison was generously permitted to retire with the honors of war. The event, however, was seized upon to inflame the minds of the Northern people. The disguise which had been worn in the communications with the Confederate Commissioners was now torn off, and it was craftily attempted to show that the South, which had been pleading for peace and still stood on the defensive, had, by this bombardment, inaugurated a war against the United States.

But it should be remembered that the threats implied in the declaration that the Union could not exist part slave and part free, and the denial of the right of a State peacefully to withdraw, and the sending of an army and navy to attack, were virtually declarations of war.

PART 3
THE WAR

Chapter 24

South Carolina, Maryland, and Virginia

THE fall of Sumter was quickly followed by a succession of great events, all tending to a separation of the States. Two days after the evacuation Mr. Lincoln made a call for 75,000 men, on the extraordinary pretext of overcoming "combinations too powerful to be suppressed by the ordinary course of judicial proceedings," and, by proclamation, commanded "the persons composing the combinations to disperse." That this proclamation and this action were unconstitutional and illegal it needs but the slightest acquaintance with the history of the Union to perceive. The "persons" thus characterized as "composing combinations" were States of the Union, the sovereign creators of the Federal Government. Yet they were thus commanded by their agent to "disperse." Again, the levying of so large a force could only mean war; and the power to declare war is vested by the Constitution in Congress only. But even if the acts of the seceding States had constituted a "riotous combination," it could only have been against the State; and the President had no lawful power to aid in suppressing it, except upon application from the State for that purpose; it could neither precede that application nor be exerted against the will of the State. Under any view of constitutional law the calling for an army to invade the Southern States, which were asserted to be still in the Union, was a palpable violation of the Constitution, and the usurpation of undelegated powers which had been sacredly "reserved to the State or to the people."

The first response in the South to this unconstitutional action of the Federal Executive, which occurred two days after the publication of the Proclamation, was the secession of Virginia from the Union. Two days later the unorganized citizens of Baltimore resisted the passage through their State of troops then on their way to make war on the Southern

States.

The Virginia Ordinance of Secession was subject to ratification by the people at an election to be held on the fourth Tuesday of May. In the meantime her authorities, anticipating the inevitable result of that election, formed an alliance with the Confederate States, a wise action, which was promptly approved by the Convention.

By this time South Carolina had sent a brigade to Richmond to sustain the popular movement; and, throughout the entire South there was a prevalent desire to rush to Virginia, where it was seen that the first great battles of the war were to be fought. The universal feeling was that of a common cause and common destiny; the universal desire was to sustain that broad principle of constitutional liberty, the right of self-government.

The hope which was entertained at an early date of a peaceful solution of the issues pending between the Confederate States and the United States rapidly diminished; so that, on the 6th of March, the Congress at Montgomery passed an act establishing and authorizing the President to employ the militia, and to ask for and accept the services of any number of volunteers not exceeding 100,000. On the same day an act was passed establishing and organizing the Army of the Confederate States of America, this being in contradistinction to the provisional army of troops tendered by the States, as in the first act, and volunteers received, as in the second act, to constitute a provisional army.

Chapter 25

Confederate Preparations for Defence

THREE days after my inauguration, at Montgomery, Captain (afterward Admiral) Sémmes was sent to the North to make purchases of arms, ammunition, and machinery; and, soon afterward, another officer was sent to Europe to buy in market as far as possible, and, furthermore, to make contracts for arms and ammunition to be manufactured. The subsequent intervention of the civil authorities prevented the delivery of many valuable articles contracted for by Captain Semmes in the Northern States.

Major Huse, who was sent to Europe, found few serviceable arms in the market; but, being in advance of the agents of the Federal Government, succeeded in making contracts for the manufacture of arms in large quantities. Captain Semmes had also instructions to seek for vessels that would serve for naval purposes, but could find none that were, or could be made, available for that purpose.

By the action of the Southern naval officers, in taking their vessels into Northern ports before they resigned from the Federal navy, and bringing only their swords to the Confederacy (under an idea more creditable to their sentiment than to their knowledge of the nature of our Constitutional Union), we were doubly bereft, by losing our share of the navy we had contributed to build, and by having it all employed to assail us.

As the construction of vessels had been monopolized by the North, we found ourselves, on the opening of hostilities, without a navy, and without the machinery and accessories for building one.

The general belief in the North that the South had long prepared for war, although mistaken, and the general belief in the South that there would be no war, and the fact that few realized how totally deficient we were in all which was necessary to the active operations of an army, resulted in undue caution at the North and overweening confidence at the South. This same confidence prevented our people from turning their attention at once to the production of food-supplies. The condition of the railroads in the South—insufficient in number and deficient in rolling stock—contributed, also, to prevent the rapid transportation of supplies in cases of pressing emergency. Even the skilled railroad operatives were generally Northern men, and their desertion followed fast after every disaster to the Confederate arms.

Thus hampered—without a supply of powder, without nitre, or saltpetre, without powder-mills to use the material if obtained—the new Government found great and difficult problems confronting it on every hand. Colonel Northrop, with equal ability and zeal, organized the commissariat department; prompt measures were taken to procure the materials for the manufacture of powder; and, under the well-directed skill of General Rains, we were enabled, before the close of the war, to boast of the best powder-mill in the world.

Meanwhile, the Federal Government set fire to the United States armory at Harper's Ferry, the only establishment of the kind in the Southern States. After the Federal troops evacuated the place the citizens rallied and extinguished the fire, and saved from the flames a large part of the material and machinery, which was subsequently sent to the Confederate arsenals at Richmond and Fayetteville, thus supplying, to some extent, the existing want of means for the alteration and repair of arms, and contributing to the increase of the very scanty supply of arms with which the Confederacy was furnished when the war began.

Chapter 26

Organization of Our Resources

THE first difficulty that confronted the Confederate Government was how to supply arms and munitions of war; for, of men eager to defend their country there were many more than we could arm.

The next problem was how to sustain our armies in the field. To support them it would require that the habits of our planters should be changed from the cultivation of staples for export, which had been their chief reliance in the past, to the production of supplies for home consumption. Hitherto a large proportion of our food-supplies had been imported from the West. Yet, even under the embarrassment of the war, it was expected that, without preconcerted action, the planters would conform to the new conditions imposed by the existing situation; and, extraordinary as it must appear, when viewed by comparison with the action of other people subjected to a like ordeal, the result, for a long time, justified the general expectation.

Much of our success in solving this problem of subsistence was due to the existence of the much-maligned institution of African servitude, which enabled the whites to enlist in the army and to leave the cultivation of their fields and the care of their stock to those who, in the language of the Constitution, were "held to service or labor."

It may be said, in passing, that an irrefutable answer was given to the clamor about the "horrors of slavery" by the action of the owners of the slaves and by the conduct of the slaves during the long war between the States. Had these Africans been a cruelly oppressed people, restlessly struggling to be freed from their bonds, would their masters have dared to leave them, as was everywhere done, in charge of plantations on which their wives and children lived, and would the slaves have remained, as they did remain, continuing their usual duties; or could the Proclamation of Emancipation have been issued on the plea of military necessity if the fact had been that the negroes were forced to serve, and desired only an opportunity to rise against their masters? It will be remembered that when the Proclamation was issued it was confessed by President Lincoln to be a nullity beyond the limit within which it could be enforced by the Federal troops.

As soon as the Confederate authorities were assured of an army as large as the population of the country could furnish and maintain, the next pressing problem that demanded their attention was the organization, instruction, and equipment of the army.

Owing to the prevailing belief that there would be no war, or, if any, that it would be of very short duration, the first bill prepared by the Provisional Congress provided for receiving troops for sixty days. I desired it to be changed to a term of years. But the utmost efforts of Colonel Bartow and others procured only the modification of an extension of the term of service to twelve months "unless sooner discharged."

The armies and munitions within the limits of the several States were regarded as entirely belonging to them; the forces which were to constitute the provisional army could only be drawn from the several States with their consent, and these were to be organized under the State authority and to be received with their officers so appointed; the lowest organization was to be that of a company, and the highest that of a regiment, and the appointment of general officers to command these forces was confided to the Government of the Confederate States, should the assembling of large bodies of troops require organization above that of a regiment. Thus is clearly seen two facts: how little was anticipated a war of the vast proportions and great duration that ensued; and how tenaciously the sovereignty and self-government of the States were adhered to.

Further progress in the organization of measures for the public defence was made by the enactment of a law providing for the appointment to their relative rank, in the Confederacy, of officers who had resigned or should within six months resign from the Federal army; and by the assignment under this act of Samuel Cooper to the duties of Adjutant-General of the Confederate States; of Colonel L. P. Moore as

Surgeon-General; of General Gorgas as Chief of Ordnance, and of Colonel L. B. Northrop as Commissary-General.

It is worthy of note that Samuel Cooper, A. Sidney Johnston, and R. E. Lee, the three officers highest in rank, and whose fame stands unchallenged for efficiency and zeal, were all so indifferent to any considerations of personal interest that each of them received notice of his appointment before he was aware it had been or was to be conferred.

Chapter 27

Federal Oppressions in Maryland

MARYLAND, although, for the time, she elected to remain neutral in the impending war, denied, at an early date, the right of way across her soil to Northern troops marching to invade the Southern States. On the 18th of April, three days after the requisition of the Secretary of War on States that had not seceded for their quota of troops to serve in the Federal army, Governor Hicks issued a proclamation in which he said, "I assure the people that no troops will be sent from Maryland, unless it may be for the defence of the National capital." On the following day (April 19, 1861) a body of Massachusetts troops arrived at the railroad depot. They were on their way South. The citizens assembled in large numbers, and, although unarmed and undisciplined, disputed their passage through the city. They attacked the troops with loose paving-stones and wounded several of them. The troops were ordered to fire on the multitude, and did so, killing a few and wounding others. The Baltimore police did their utmost to preserve peace, and rescued the baggage and munitions of the troops, which the citizens had secured. By order of Governor Hicks the rear portion of the troops were sent back to the borders of the State; those who had got through the city passed on to Washington.

President Lincoln, at an interview next day with the Mayor, promised that no more troops would be sent through Baltimore, unless obstructed in their transit in other directions. On the 5th of May the Relay House, at the junction of the Washington and Baltimore & Ohio Railroads, was occupied by United States troops under General B. F. Butler. On the 13th he moved a portion of the troops to Baltimore and took position on Federal Hill. Thus was consummated the military occupation of Baltimore. On the next day reinforcements were received;

and, at the same time, the commanding general issued a proclamation to the citizens in which he announced to them his purpose and authority to discriminate between citizens, those who agreed with him being denominated "well-disposed," and the others described with many offensive epithets. This was soon followed by a demand for the surrender of the arms stored by the city authorities in a warehouse. The police commissioners surrendered the arms under protest, and they were removed to Fort McHenry. Baltimore was now disarmed. There was no longer necessity to regard the remonstrance of Baltimore against sending troops through the city, and it was thereafter disregarded, despite the pledges previously given by the President. Under the pretext that he was believed to be cognizant of combinations of men waiting for an opportunity to unite with those in rebellion against the United States Government, Marshal Kane was arrested, without legal warrant and without proof, and superseded by a provost-marshal appointed by General Banks, who had succeeded to the command. Thus began a reign of terror and unbridled despotism. The Provost-Marshal instituted a system of search and seizure, in private houses, of ammunition and arms of every description. On the 1st of July General Banks, "in pursuance of orders issued from the head-quarters at Washington," arrested the members of the Board of Police, men respected, honored, and beloved by the people. Thenceforward arrests of the most illustrious citizens became the rule. Freedom of speech ceased to exist, and men were incarcerated for opinion's sake.

In the Maryland Legislature the Hon. S. Teackle Wallis, from a committee to which was referred the memorial of the Police Commissioners arrested in Baltimore, made a report on the unconstitutionality of the act, and appealed in the most earnest manner to the whole people of the country, of all parties, sections, and opinions, to take warning by the usurpation mentioned, and come to the rescue of the free institutions of the country.

For no better reason, so far as the public were informed, than a vote, General Banks sent the Provost-Marshal to Frederick, where the Legislature was in session, and placed a cordon of pickets around the town to prevent anyone from leaving it without a written permit from a member of his staff. Baltimore detectives then went into the town and arrested some twelve or fifteen members of the Legislature and several officers; an act of violence which resulted in preventing an organization of the Legislature. There was no lawful government left. Mr. Wallis, the author of the report, was among the members arrested and imprisoned; and so also was Henry May, a member of Congress who had introduced a resolution which he hoped would be promotive of peace.

Henceforth the story of Maryland was sad to the last degree, only relieved by the valor of the gallant men who left their homes to fight the battle of State-rights, when Maryland no longer furnished them a field on which they could maintain the rights their fathers bequeathed to them. Though Maryland did not become one of the Confederate States, she was endeared to the people thereof by many most endearing ties. Last in order, but first in cordiality, were the tender ministrations of her noble daughters to the sick and wounded prisoners who were carried through the streets of Baltimore; and it is with shame we remember that brutal guards inflicted wounds upon gentlewomen who approached to offer to prisoners the relief of which they so evidently stood in need.

Cabinet of the Confederacy.

Chapter 28

The Battle of Manassas

THE Provisional Congress adjourned in May, "to meet again on the 20th of July, at Richmond," the President being authorized to select some other place "if any public emergency should render it impolitic to meet at Richmond." Shortly after the adjournment of Congress the hostile demonstrations of the Federal Government against Virginia caused the President to proceed to Richmond, and to order the removal thither of the Executive Departments and their archives as soon as could be conveniently done. Richmond was the place best adapted for the execution of all necessary measures for the defence and protection of Virginia, which the accumulation of hostile forces on the Potomac sufficiently demonstrated to be destined to an early aggressive movement.

At Richmond, the forces that had assembled there from other States of the Confederacy were divided into three armies, which occupied the most important positions threatened: one, at Harper's Ferry, covering the valley of the Shenandoah, under General J. E. Johnston; another, under General Beauregard, at Manassas, covering the direct approach from Washington to Richmond; and the third, under Generals Huger and Magruder, at Norfolk and on the peninsula between the James and York Rivers, covering the approach from the seaboard.

The armies of Johnston and Beauregard, although both were confronted by forces greatly superior in numbers to their own, and although separated by the Blue Ridge, yet had such practicable communication with each other as to render their junction possible when the necessity should be foreseen.

General R. E. Lee, as commander of the army of Virginia, had established his head-quarters in Richmond. He possessed my unqualified confidence both as a soldier and a patriot, and the command he had exercised over the army Virginia, before her accession to the Confederacy, gave him that special knowledge which at the time was most needful.

Various skirmishes between Confederate and Federal troops demonstrated the fact that the individuality, self-reliance, and habitual use of small arms by the people of the South was, to some extent, a substitute for military training; and that the want of such training made the Northern new levies inferior to the same kind of Southern troops.

Military reasons rendered it desirable to hold Harper's Ferry as long as was consistent with safety, especially to secure the removal of the valuable machinery and material in the armory there which the enemy had failed to destroy. General Johnston earnestly insisted on being allowed to retire to a position near Winchester, and was authorized by the War Department to exercise his own discretion in doing so.

Meanwhile, the massing of troops in Washington indicated the intention of an invasion of Virginia at an early date. As soon as I became satisfied that Manassas was the objective point of the intended movement, I urged General Johnston to make preparations for a junction with General Beauregard; and on the 17th of July he was notified by telegraph that General Beauregard had been attacked, and that, to strike an effective blow, a junction of all of his effective force was needed.

In order to avert any possible complication and misunderstanding between the two generals, which I had some reasons to fear, I decided to go to the army in person at the earliest moment.

I delivered my message to Congress on Saturday, July 20th, and on the following morning I left for Manassas. As we approached Manassas Railroad Junction I found a large number of men bearing the usual evidence of those who leave the field of battle under a panic. They crowded around the train with fearful stories of a defeat of our army. The coolest man among them repeated that our line was broken, that all was in confusion, that the army and the battle were lost. Proceeding onward, by detaching a locomotive, we soon reached head-quarters, and, procuring horses, started to the field. The stragglers soon became numerous, and we were earnestly warned not to proceed. As we advanced, the storm of the battle was rolling westward and its fury became more faint. When I met General Johnston he informed me that we had won the battle. I left him, and rode still farther to the west. In riding over the ground it seemed quite possible to mark the line of a fugitive's flight— there was a musket, there a cartridge box, there a blanket or overcoat or haversack, as if the runner had stripped himself as he ran of all impediments to speed.

As we approached toward the left of our line the signs of an utter rout of the enemy were unmistakable, and justified the conclusion that the watchword of "On to Richmond" had been changed to "Off for Washington."

On the extreme left of our field of operations I found the troops whose opportune arrival had averted impending disaster or had so materially contributed to our victory. Some of them, under General E. K. Smith, after arriving at the Manassas Railroad Junction, hastened to our left; others, under General (then Colonel) Early, made a rapid march, under the pressing necessity, from the extreme right of our line to and beyond our left, so as to attack the enemy in flank, thus inflicting on them the discomfiture by oblique movement they designed to inflict on us. All these troops and the others near them had gone into action without supplies and camp equipage. Weary, hungry, and without shelter, night closed around them where they stood, the blood-stained victors on a hard-fought field.

It is not my purpose in this volume to describe the battles of the war. To the reports of officers serving in the field with the armies of both governments the student of history must turn for knowledge of the details. My sole object is to vindicate the rightful action of the Southern people in maintaining the sovereignty of their States against wrongful and unconstitutional usurpation of power by their common agent, the Federal Government, and to defend them from the aspersions of unscrupulous partisans who have maligned as rebels and traitors men true to their allegiance and defenders of the Constitution. The military operations of the Confederate States need no defence; the bravery of our armies and the genius of their commanders were displayed on many battlefields, and the results, which could neither be misrepresented nor ignored, have made it impossible even for the most partisan zeal to withhold the admiration always, however reluctantly, awarded to devotion to country, backed by self-sacrificing courage and fortitude. The limits of this volume will permit little more than a passing reference to the battles of the Confederacy—a bald statement of the numbers engaged, the names of their commanders, and the result of the more important engagements.

The battle of Manassas—as it was called by the South—or of Bull Run—as it was called by the North—had an important influence on the subsequent conduct of the war. It produced a panic in the North, and taught the enemy that the policy of subjugation could only be successful by the employment of all its resources of money and men. In the South, if the great victory excited intense feeling and inspired an overweening confidence, it also removed all doubt as to the intent to wage war upon us, and begat an increased desire to enter the military service. But for our want of arms and ammunition we could have enrolled an army little short of the number of able-bodied men in the Confederate States.

When the smoke of battle had lifted from the field of Manassas, and the rejoicing over the victory had spread over the land and spent its exuberance, some who, like Job's warhorse, sniffed the battle from afar, but in whom the likeness there ceased, asked why the fruits of this victory had not been gathered by the capture of Washington City, and promulgated the allegation that the President had prevented the generals from making an immediate and vigorous pursuit of the routed enemy. This slanderous accusation was afterward refuted by the generals in command: it did not rest on any semblance of truth. I had in no way interfered with the plans or action of the officers in charge, and only note the slander now because it has been repeated, since the war, by writers who have never seen, or have chosen to ignore, the official refutation of the calumny.

Chapter 29

Neutrality of Kentucky

EARLY in the controversy between the Federal Government and the seceding States, Kentucky, without deciding against the right of secession, declared that she would hold a position of neutrality in the impending war. With a view to pursue this policy, unmolested by the forces of either party, the Governor entered into a correspondence with Mr. Lincoln, as President of the United States, and with myself, as President of the Confederate States, explaining the policy of neutrality, asking for the removal of the Federal forces from the State, and an assurance that no Confederate forces should be permitted to invade the State. President Lincoln declined to comply with the request, and intimated that he believed the presence of Federal troops was desired by "a majority of the Union-loving people of Kentucky." On behalf of the Confederate Government I gave the assurance that we "neither desired nor intended to disturb the neutrality of Kentucky," and added, "but neutrality, to be entitled to respect, must be strictly maintained between both parties; for if the door be opened on the one side for the aggression of one of the belligerent parties upon the other, it ought not to be shut to the assailed when they seek to enter it for purposes of self-defence."

During the following month the movements of the Federal forces in Southwestern Kentucky, threatening two Confederate States, rendered it absolutely necessary for General Polk, the Confederate commander, to occupy the town of Columbus, Ky., a most important strategic point. General Grant, baffled by this movement, then seized Paducah and occupied it in force.

To the request of the Governor of Kentucky for the withdrawal of the Confederate troops, General Polk, after courteously explaining that the threatening attitude of the Federal commander had made the occupation of Columbus essential to the protection of Southeastern

Missouri and Western Tennessee, offered to evacuate his position and pledge his Government to refrain from any subsequent invasion of the territory of Kentucky, provided that the Governor should secure a simultaneous withdrawal of the Federal forces and a similar pledge from the Federal Government. However willing the Governor of Kentucky might have been to accede to the proposition of General Polk, the State of Kentucky had no power to prevent the United States Government from using her soil as best might suit its purposes in the war it was waging for the subjugation of the seceded States. President Lincoln, in his message of the previous July, had distinctly and reproachfully spoken of the idea of neutrality. He said:

> "To prevent the Union forces passing one way or the disunion the other, over their soil, would be disunion completed. At a stroke it would take all the trouble off the hands of secession, except only what proceeds from the external blockade."

The acts of the Federal Government corresponded with the views announced by its President. Briefly, but conclusively, General Polk showed that the United States Government paid no respect to the neutral position which Kentucky wished to maintain; that the State was armed, but not neutral, for the arms and the troops assembled on her soil were for the invasion of the South; and that he occupied Columbus to prevent the enemy from taking possession of it.

When our troops first entered Columbus they found that the inhabitants had been in alarm from demonstrations of the United States forces, but that they felt no dread of the Confederate troops. As far as the truth could be ascertained, a decided majority of the people of Kentucky, especially its southwestern portion, if left to a free choice, would have joined the Confederacy in preference to remaining in the Union. Could they have foreseen what in a short time was revealed to them there can be little doubt that mule-contracts and other forms of bribery would have proved unavailing to make her the passive observer of usurpations destructive of the personal and political rights of which she had been always a most earnest advocate. With the slow and sinuous approach of a serpent, the General Government, little by little, gained power over Kentucky, and then, throwing off the mask, proceeded to outrages so regardless of law and the usages of English-speaking peoples as could not have been anticipated, and can only be remembered with shame by those who honor the constitutional government created by the States. While artfully urging the maintenance of the Union as a duty of patriotism, the Constitution which gave the Union birth was trampled under foot, and the excesses of the Reign of Terror which followed the French Revolution were re-enacted in our land, once the vaunted home of law and liberty. Men who had been most honored by the State, and who had reflected back most honor upon it, were seized without warrant and condemned without trial, because they had exercised the privilege of free speech, and for adhering to the principles which were the bed-rock on which our fathers builded our political temple. Members of the Legislature vacated their seats and left the State to avoid arrest, the penalty hanging over them for opinion's sake. The venerable Judge Monroe, who had presided over the United States District Court for more than a generation, driven from the land of his birth, the State he had served so long and so well, with feeble step but a bright conscience and indomitable will, sought a resting-place among those who did not regard it as a crime to adhere to the principles of 1776 and 1789, and the declaratory affirmation of them in the resolutions of 1798 and 1799. About the same time others of great worth and distinction left the land violated by despotic usurpation to join the Confederacy in its struggle to maintain the personal and political liberties which the men of the Revolution had left as an inheritance to their prosperity—such men as J. C. Breckinridge, late Vice-President of the United States; William Preston, George W. Johnston, S. B. Buckner, John H. Morgan, and a host of others, alike meritorious and gratefully remembered for their great and conspicuous services to the Confederacy.

When the passions of the hour shall have subsided, and the past shall be reviewed with discrimination and justice, the question must arise in any reflecting mind, Why did such men as these expatriate themselves, and surrender all the advantages which they had won by a life of honorable effort in the land of their nativity? To such an inquiry the answer must be, that the usurpation of the General Government foretold to them the wreck of constitutional liberty.

CHAPTER 30
THE CONTEST IN MISSOURI

MISSOURI, like Kentucky, desired to preserve peaceful relations in the impending conflict between the Northern and Southern States. When the General Government denied her the right of choice, and she was driven to the necessity of deciding whether or not her citizens should be forced to aid in the subjugation of the South, her people and their representatives—the State Government—repelled the arbitrary assumption of authority to control by military force her Government and her people.

Among other acts of invasion, the Federal troops had gone to Belmont, a Missouri village opposite Columbus, and threatened the inhabitants of that town with artillery. After the occupation of Columbus, under these circumstances of full justification, a small Confederate force was thrown across the Mississippi to hold and occupy Belmont. On the 6th of November, 1861, General Polk, divining the real purpose of General Grant in landing a force at Paducah, in Kentucky, sent General Pillow, with about 2,000 men, to reinforce the garrison at Belmont. Very soon after their arrival the enemy began an assault, which was steadily resisted, and with varying fortune, for several hours. The enemy's front so far exceeded the length of our line as to enable her to attack on both flanks. Our troops were finally driven back to the bank of the river with the loss of their battery, which had been gallantly and efficiently served until nearly all the horses had been killed and the ammunition had been expended. The enemy advanced to the bank of the river, below the point to which our men had retreated, and opened an artillery fire on the town of Columbus, to which our guns from the commanding height responded with such effect as to drive them from the river bank. In the meantime General Polk had sent three regiments to reinforce General Pillow. On the arrival of the first of these three regiments, General Pillow led it to a favorable position, where, for some time, it steadily resisted and checked the advance of the enemy. General Pillow, with great energy and gallantry, rallied his repulsed troops and brought them again into action. General Polk now proceeded in person with two other regiments. The enemy commenced a retreat.

General Polk reported: "We pursued them to their boats, seven miles, and then drove their boats before us. The road was strewn with their dead and wounded, guns, ammunition, and equipments. The number of prisoners taken by the enemy, as shown by their list furnished, was over one hundred and six, all of whom have been returned by exchange. After making a liberal allowance to the enemy, a hundred of their prisoners still remain in my hands, one stand of colors, and a fraction over 1,000 stand of arms, with knapsacks, ammunition, and other military stores. Our loss in killed, wounded, and missing is 642; that of the enemy was probably not less than 1,200."

Though the forces engaged in this battle were small in comparison with those engaged in subsequent battles of the war, yet six hours of incessant combat, with repeated bayonet charges, must place this in the list of the most stubborn engagements, and victors must accord to the vanquished the meed of having fought like Americans. One of the results of the battle, which is at least significant, is the fact that General Grant, who had superciliously refused to recognize General Polk as one with whom he could exchange prisoners, did, after the battle, send a flag of truce to get such privileges as are recognized between armies acknowledging each other to be "foemen worthy of their steel."

Chapter 31

General Albert Sidney Johnston

In the meantime General Albert Sidney Johnston, having resigned from the United States Army and tendered his services to the Confederate States, had been assigned to command our army of the West, which included the States of Tennessee, Mississippi, Louisiana, Missouri, Arkansas, Texas, and the Indian country west of the Mississippi River. On assuming command he found that he lacked not only men, but munitions of war. There were men enough ready and eager to enlist, but the arms and equipments had been nearly exhausted in fitting out the first levies.

General Johnston located his line of defence from Columbus on the west to the Cumberland Mountains on the east, with his centre resting at Bowling Green, which he occupied on October 28th, with 12,000 troops, and intrenched. It was a good basis for military operations, a proper depot for supplies, and, when fortified, could be held against large and superior forces.

By the end of November the enemy's force had increased to 50,000, and continued to be reinforced until it numbered between 75,000 and 100,000 strong; while the Confederate force numbered never more than about 22,000.

General Johnston sent earnest and urgent appeals for arms to the Governors of Alabama and Georgia, to General Bragg, in command at Pensacola, and to the Confederate Government; but, although he stated that 30,000 stand of arms were a necessity to his command, only one thousand stand could be sent to him. During the autumn of 1861 fully one-half of General Johnston's troops were imperfectly armed, and whole brigades remained without weapons for months. These details illustrate the deficiencies existing in every department of the military service during the first year of the war.

Meanwhile, despite the failure to obtain arms or to increase his force so as to render it adequate to the services that were expected of it, General Johnston, by the masterly concentration of his troops, and by frequent and rapid expeditions through the sparsely settled country, kept the enemy in constant expectation of an attack, and under the apprehension that he commanded a large army.

Chapter 32

Federal Outrages in Missouri

MISSOURI, when a requisition was made to her by President Lincoln to contribute a quota of troops to be employed against the States that had seceded, replied, in the words of her Governor, that "the requisition is illegal, unconstitutional, revolutionary, inhuman, diabolical, and cannot be complied with."

Like Kentucky, Missouri sought to occupy a neutral position in the war between the States; and, like Kentucky, offered guarantees of peace and order throughout her territory if left free to control her own affairs. Both refused to furnish troops for the unconstitutional purpose of coercing the Southern States. Both, because of their stronger affinity to the South than to the North, were the objects of suspicion, and consequent military occupation by Federal troops.

During a temporary absence of General Harney, Captain (afterward General) Nathaniel Lyons initiated hostilities against the State of Missouri, under the following circumstances.

In obedience to the militia laws of the State, an annual encampment was directed by the Governor for instruction in tactics. Camp Jackson, near St. Louis, was designated for the encampment of the militia of the country in 1861. Here, for some days, companies of State militia, numbering about eight hundred men, under the command of Brigadier-General Frost, were exercised as is usual on such occasions. They presented no appearance of a hostile camp. Visitors were freely admitted; it was the pleasure-ground for the ladies of the city.

Suddenly Captain Lyon appeared with an overwhelming force of Federal troops, surrounded this holiday encampment, and demanded an unconditional surrender. Resistance was impracticable, and none was attempted. The militia surrendered, and were confined as prisoners.

There was no war, and no warrant for their arrest as offenders against the law. It is left for the usurpers to frame a vocabulary suited to their act.

General Frost, in a letter to General Harney, on his return, thus described the further proceedings of the Federal troops:

> "My command was deprived of their arms, and surrendered into the hands of Captain Lyon, after which, while thus disarmed and surrounded, a fire was opened on a portion of it by his troops and a number of my men put to death, with several innocent lookers-on—men, women, and children."

"A large crowd of citizens," says Bevier,[99] "were gathered around, gazing curiously at those strange proceedings, when a volley was fired into them, killing ten and wounding twenty non-combatants—mostly women and children. A reign of terror was at once established, and the most severe measures were adopted by the Federals to overcome the rage of the people."

This massacre produced intense excitement throughout the State. The State Legislature forthwith passed a law for the enrolment and organization of the militia, and conferring special power on the Governor.

General Price, appointed under these laws, at the urgent solicitations of leading citizens, conferred with General Harney. The result was that General Harney, on behalf of the Government of the United States, and General Price, on behalf of Missouri, promulgated an agreement that did much to allay excitement. General Price agreed to wield the entire force of the State to suppress all unlawful proceedings; and General Harney, that he would have no occasion, as he had no wish, to make military movements that might otherwise create excitement and jealousy. The distinct position of General Harney, that the military force of the United States should not be used in Missouri, except in case of necessity, and the emphatic declaration of General Price, that he had the power, and would use it, to preserve peace and order in Missouri, seemed to remove all danger of collision in that State between the Federal and State forces.

General Price at once disbanded and sent home the forces that had

---

99. See *Confederate First and Second Brigades*, pp. 24-26.

assembled to defend the capital of the State against an anticipated attack of United States troops. But, while this prospect of peace gave ground for satisfaction, a doubt of the good faith of the Government was soon aroused by the removal of General Harney from command, because, as many believed, of his successful efforts to allay excitement and avoid war.

The principal United States arsenal at the West was at St. Louis, and to it there had been transferred so large a number of the altered muskets sent from Springfield, Mass., that, in 1861, the arms in that arsenal were numerically second only to those at Springfield. These arms, by a conjunction of bold and deceptive measures, were removed and transported to Illinois.

Not satisfied with removing the public arms from the limits of Missouri, the next step was, that, in total disrespect of the constitutional right of the citizens to bear arms for their own defence, and to be free from searches and seizures, except by warrants duly issued, the officers of the General Government proceeded to search the houses of citizens in St. Louis and to seize arms wherever they were found. Missouri had refused to engage in war against her sister States of the South; therefore she was the first to be disarmed and then to be made a victim of an invasion characterized by such barbarous atrocities as shame the civilization of the age. The wrongs she suffered, the brave efforts of her unarmed people to defend their hearthstones and their liberties against the desecration and destruction of both, form a melancholy chapter in the history of the United States, which all who would cherish their fair fame must wish could be obliterated.

Chapter 33

Missouri Disarmed

THESE acts of usurpation and outrage on the political and personal rights of the people of Missouri aroused an intense feeling in that State.

The position of Missouri in 1860-61 was unquestionably that of opposition to the secession of the State. Not a single secessionist was elected to the State Convention, and General Price, an avowed "Union man," was chosen as its President. Hence the general satisfaction at the agreement between General Harney and General Price.

After the removal of General Harney reports were rife of a purpose of the Administration at Washington to disarm the citizens of Missouri who did not sympathize with the policy of the General Government, and to put arms into the hands of those who could be relied on to enforce it. Referring to these reports in an address to the people, on the 4th of June, General Price declared that "the purpose of such a movement could not be misunderstood, and it would not only be a palpable violation of the agreement referred to [his agreement with General Harney], and an equally plain violation of constitutional rights, but a gross indignity to the citizens of the State that should be resisted to the last extremity."

After the call of President Lincoln for seventy-five thousand volunteers had dispelled all doubt of the intention of the Federal authorities to coerce any State that should claim to assert its right of sovereignty, General Jackson issued a call for fifty thousand volunteers to protect the State against any attempt to interfere with her right to exercise supreme control over her own domestic affairs. General Price took the field in command. After the removal of General Harney, the Governor, in the interest of peace, proposed to the General's successor to disband the State guard and break up its organization; to disarm all companies that had been armed by the State; to pledge himself not to organize the militia under the military bill; that no arms or munitions of war should be brought into the State; that he would protect the citizens equally in all their rights, regardless of their political opinions; that he would repress all insurrectionary movements within the State; would repel all attempts to invade it, from whatever quarter and by whomsoever made; and would maintain a strict neutrality, and preserve the peace of the State. And further, if necessary, he would invoke the assistance of the United States troops to carry out the pledges. The only conditions to these propositions made by the Governor were that the United States Government should undertake to disarm the "Home Guard," which it had illegally organized and armed throughout the State, and pledge itself not to occupy with its troops any localities in the State not held by them at that time.

"Nothing," said the Governor, "but the most earnest desire to avert the horrors of cruel war from our beloved State could have tempted me to propose these humiliating terms. They were rejected by the Federal officers."

They demanded not only the disarming and disorganization of the State militia and the nullification of the military bill, but they refused to disarm their own "Home Guard," and insisted that the Government of the United States should enjoy an unrestricted right to move and station its troops whenever and wherever it might, in the opinion of its officers, be necessary either for the protection of its "loyal subjects" or for the repelling of invasion; and they plainly announced that it was the intention of the Administration to take military occupation of the whole State, and to reduce it, as avowed by General Lyon, to "the exact condition of Maryland."

The United States Government had therein adopted a policy that involved the subjugation of every State, either by voluntary submission or conquest. However much a State might desire peace and neutrality, its own will could not elect. The scheme demanded the absolute sovereignty of the General Government, the extinguishment of the independence and sovereignty of the State. Such a policy was revolutionary in the extreme. It involved the entire subversion of those principles on which the American Union was founded, and of the compact or constitution of that Union. The Constitution of the United States, in the hands of those who now wielded its authority, was made the bloody instrument to establish these usurpations on the ruins of the crushed hopes of mankind for federative strength with community freedom under constitutional government. For the justness and truthfulness of these allegations I appeal to the impartial and sober judgment of posterity.

CHAPTER 34

MILITARY OPERATIONS IN MISSOURI

THE volunteers who assembled under General Jackson's proclamation of June 13th had few arms except their squirrel rifles and shot-guns, and could hardly be said to have any military equipments.

On the 20th of June, 1861, General Lyon and Colonel Frank P. Blair, with an estimated force of 7,000 well-armed troops, having 8 pieces of artillery, ascended the Missouri River and debarked five miles below Boonville. To oppose them the Missourians had then about 800 men, poorly armed, without a piece of artillery, and with but little ammunition. With a courage that must be commended at the expense of their discretion, they resolved to engage the enemy, and after a combat of an hour and a half, or more, retired, having inflicted heavy loss and suffered but little themselves. This first skirmish of the Missouri militia inspired confidence in their fellow-citizens, and taught the enemy to respect a force which they had hitherto affected to despise, a double effect which was increased by another victory by a small force, commanded by Colonel O'Kane, over a much superior force of the enemy, at Cole Camp, in which 206 Federal soldiers were killed and wounded, and over 100 taken prisoners, and 360 muskets with bayonets were captured. The Missourians lost 4 killed and from 15 to 20 wounded.

General Price, with a view to draw his army from the base line of the enemy—the Missouri—ordered his troops to the southeastern portion of the State. The column from Lexington marched without transportation, without tents or blankets, and relied for subsistence on the country through which it passed, being, in the meantime, closely pursued by the enemy. The movement was successfully made, and a junction effected in Cedar County with the forces there present under Governor Jackson. The united force numbered about 3,600 men.

"This, then, was the patriot army of Missouri. It was a heterogeneous mass, representing every condition of Western life. There were the young and old, the rich and poor, the grave and gay, the planter and laborer, the farmer and clerk, the hunter and boatman, the merchant and woodsman. At least 500 of these men were entirely unarmed. Many had only the common rifle and shot-gun. None were provided with cartridges and canteens. They had 8 pieces of cannon, but no shells, and very few solid shot or rounds of grape and canister.

"Rude and almost incredible devices were made to supply these wants. Trace-chains, iron rods, hard pebbles, and smooth stones were substituted for shot."

Continuing his march toward Southern Missouri, Governor Jackson found that he was threatened in his rear by a force nearly equal to his own, while immediately in front, at the town of Carthage, a large hostile force awaited his coming, to dispute his passage. These undisciplined, poorly-armed Missourians were now in a position that might well have appalled less heroic men.

Nothing daunted, they moved forward, attacked the enemy in position, and, after a severe engagement, routed him; pursued him to a second position, from which he was again driven, falling back on Carthage, where he made his last stand, on being driven from which, as was subsequently ascertained, he continued his retreat all night. The dead and wounded of the enemy, during this retreat, were estimated at from 150 to 200 killed and from 300 to 400 wounded. Several hundred muskets were captured, and thus the Missourians were better prepared for future conflict. Our loss was between 40 and 50 killed and from 125 to 150 wounded.

Such heroism and self-sacrifice as these undisciplined and unequipped men displayed claims special mention as bearing evidence not only of the valor of the men, but the sanctity of the cause that could so inspire them. Unsupported, save by the consciousness of a just cause, without other sympathy than that which the Confederate States fully gave, despising the plea of helplessness, and defying the threats of a powerful Government to crush her, Missouri, without arms or other military preparations, took up the gauntlet thrown at her feet, and dared to make war in defence of the laws and liberties of her people.

If any shall ask why I have entered into such details of engagements where the forces were comparatively so small and the results so little affected the general results of the war, the reply is, that such heroism and self-sacrifice as these undisciplined, partially armed, unequipped men displayed against superior numbers, possessed of all the appliances of war, claim special notice as bearing evidence not only of the virtue of the men, but of the sanctity of the cause that could so inspire them. Unsupported, save by the consciousness of a just cause, without other sympathy than that which the Confederate States freely gave, despising the plea of helplessness, and defying the threats of a powerful Government to crush her, Missouri, without arms or other military preparation, took up the gauntlet thrown at her feet, and dared to make war in defence of the laws and liberties of her people.

CHAPTER 35

CONFEDERATE AID TO MISSOURI

IN the next battle after Carthage Missourians were no longer to be alone. The Confederate States, themselves engaged in an unequal struggle for existence, by act of Congress declared that, if Missouri was engaged in repelling a lawless invasion of her territory by armed force, it was their right and duty to aid the people and government of that State; and, on the 6th of August, appropriated one million dollars "to aid the people of the State of Missouri in the effort to maintain, within their own limits, the constitutional liberty which it is the purpose of the Confederate States in the existing war to vindicate." General McCullough, with a brigade of Confederate troops, marched from Arkansas to make a junction with General Price, then threatened with an attack by a large force of the enemy under General Lyon, which was concentrated near Springfield, Mo. The battle was fiercely contested, but finally won by our troops. In this action General Lyon was killed while gallantly trying to rally his discomfited troops.

After this battle General McCullough with his brigade returned to Arkansas. General John C. Frémont was assigned to the command made vacant by General Lyon's death. He signalized his entrance on the duty by a proclamation confiscating the estates and slave-property of "rebels."

On the 10th of September, when General Price was about to go into camp, he learned that a detachment of Federal troops were marching to Warrensburg to seize the funds of the bank there and to arrest and plunder the citizens of Johnson County in accordance with General Frémont's proclamation and instructions. General Price, with his mounted men, pressed forward to Warrensburg, where he found that the enemy had hastily fled. With his whole force he followed them to Lexington. There he found the enemy in strong intrenchments and well supplied with artillery. The place was stubbornly defended. On the morning of the 20th General Price ordered a number of bales of hemp to be transported to the point from which the advance of his troops had been repeatedly repulsed. They were ranged in a line for a breast-work, and when rolled before the men as they advanced formed a moving rampart which was proof against shot, and could only be overcome by a sortie in force, which the enemy did not dare to make. On came the hempen breastwork, while Price's artillery continued an effective fire. In the afternoon of the 20th the enemy hung out a white flag. The Federal forces, to the number of 3,500, surrendered as prisoners of war; also 7 pieces of artillery, over 3,000 stand of muskets, an innumerable number of slaves, a large supply of ammunition and commissary stores, a number of horses and other property, including the great seal of the State and the public records, and about $9,000, of which the bank of Lexington had been robbed, and which was promptly returned to it.

After the first day of the siege of Lexington General Price sent General D. R. Atchison to join General Sturgis, who, with 1,500 cavalry, was coming to the aid of General Price, against whose little army it was learned that Lane and Montgomery, from Kansas, with 4,000 men, were rapidly advancing along the north side of the Missouri River. When General Atchison had joined the forces of General Sturgis, after two-thirds of them had been passed over the river, the remaining 500 were unexpectedly attacked by the vastly superior force from Kansas. The Missourians, led and cheered by General Atchison, whom they had so long and deservedly honored, met the assault with such determination that, fighting with the skill of woodsmen and hunters, they put the enemy to rout, pursuing them for a distance of ten miles and inflicting heavy loss upon them, while that of the Missourians was but 5 killed and 20 wounded.

These victories, which so far exceeded what might have been expected from the small forces by which they were achieved, had caused an augmentation of the enemy's troops to an estimated number of 70,000. As General Price could not hope successfully to contend against such an army, he retired toward the southwestern part of the State. The want of supplies and transportation forced him to disband a portion of his troops. With the rest he continued his retreat to Neosha.

Here Governor Jackson had convened the Legislature, and it had passed the ordinance of secession.

If other evidence were wanting, the fact that, without governmental aid, without a military chest, without munitions of war, the campaign in Missouri had so far been carried on by the voluntary service of its citizens and the free-will offerings of its people must be conclusive proof that the ordinance of secession was the true expression of the will of the people of the State.

CHAPTER 36

OPERATIONS OF GENERALS WISE, FLOYD, AND LEE

IN June, 1861, Brigadier-General Henry A. Wise offered his services to the Confederacy to resist the threatened invasion of the Kanawha Valley. He was sent there, with a small force, which was to serve as a nucleus to the force he hoped to raise. After the small but brilliant affair of Stony Creek he prepared to give battle to the enemy, then advancing up the valley under General Cox; but, the defeat of our forces at Laurel Hill uncovering his right and endangering his rear, he was compelled to fall back on Lewisburg.

Meanwhile Brigadier-General John B. Floyd had raised a brigade in Southwestern Virginia and advanced to the support of General Wise. General Floyd engaged the enemy in several brilliant skirmishes, and subsequently intrenched himself on the Gauley, where he was attacked by General Rosecrans with greatly superior numbers. The attack was a failure; the enemy suffered heavily and withdrew after nightfall. General Floyd then joined the forces under General Wise, and they fell back toward Sewell's Mountain; but the want of concert between these two officers, which had been displayed in the past, again prevented their entire cooperation and destroyed all hopes of future harmony.

General Loring had succeeded General Garnett, and was in command of the remnant of the force defeated at Laurel Hill. General R. E. Lee was now ordered to proceed to Western Virginia. It was hoped that he would be able to retrieve the disaster we had suffered at Laurel Hill, and, by combining all our forces in Western Virginia in one plan of operations, give protection to that portion of our country. Reinforcements had been sent to Valley Mountain, the head-quarters of General Loring. Thither General Lee promptly proceeded.

The season had been one of extraordinary rains, rendering the mountain-roads, ordinarily difficult, almost impassable. With unfaltering purpose and energy General Lee crossed the Alleghany Mountains, and learning that the main encampment of the enemy was in the valley of Tygart River and Elk Run, Randolph County, he directed his march toward that position. The troops of General H. R. Jackson, with those under General Loring, were about 3,500 men. The force of the enemy was very much greater. At the detached work at Cheat Mountain Pass we learned that there were 3,000 men, being but a fraction less than our whole force. After a careful reconnaissance General Lee decided to attack the main encampment of the enemy by a movement of his troops converging upon the valley from three directions. The colonel of one of his regiments, who had reconnoitred the position of the works at Cheat Mountain Pass, reported that it was feasible to turn it and carry it by assault, and he was assigned to make the attack. General Lee ordered other portions of his force to take position on the spurs overlooking the enemy's main encampment, while he led three regiments to the height below and nearest to the position of the enemy. The instructions were that the officers sent to turn the position at Cheat Mountain Pass should approach it at early dawn, and immediately open fire, which was to be the signal for the concerted attack by the rest of the force. It rained heavily during the day, and, after a toilsome night march, the force led by General Lee—wet, weary, hungry, and cold—gained their position close to and overlooking the enemy's encampment. In their march they had surprised and captured the picket, without a gun being fired, so that no notice had been given of their approach.

The officer who had been sent to attack the work at Cheat Mountain Pass found, on closer examination, that he had been mistaken as to the practicability of taking it by assault, and that the heavy abatis which covered it was advanced beyond the range of his rifles. Not having understood that his firing was to be the signal for the general attack, and should therefore be opened whether it would be effective or not, he withdrew without firing a musket.

The height occupied by General Lee was shrouded in fog, and as morning had dawned without the expected signal, he concluded that some mishap had befallen the force which was to make it. By a tortuous path he went down the side of the mountain low enough to have a distinct view of the camp. He saw the men, unconscious of the near presence of an enemy, engaged in cleaning their arms, cooking, and other morning occupations; then, returning to his command, he explained to his senior officers what he had seen, and expressed his belief that though the plan of attack had failed, the troops there with him could surprise and capture the camp. The officers withdrew, conferred with their men, and reported to the General that the troops were not, from exposure, in condition for the enterprise. As the fog was then lifting, and they would soon be revealed to the enemy below, whose numbers were vastly superior to his own, he withdrew his command and returned to his camp.

The report that Rosecrans and Cox had united their commands and were advancing upon Wise and Floyd, caused General Lee to move at once to their support. He found General Floyd at Meadow Bluff, and General Wise at Sewell Mountain. The latter position being very favorable for defence, the troops were concentrated there to await the threatened attack by Rosecrans, who advanced and took position in sight of General Lee's intrenched camp, and, having remained there for more than a week, withdrew in the night without attempting the expected attack.

The weak condition of his artillery horses and the bad state of the roads prevented General Lee from attempting to pursue; and the approach of winter, always rigorous in that mountain region, closed the campaign with a small but brilliant action in which General H. R. Jackson repelled an attack of a greatly superior force, inflicting severe loss on the assailants, and losing but six of his own command.

After the withdrawal of the Confederate army from Fairfax Court-House, a movement was made by the enemy to cross the Potomac near Leesburg, where we had four regiments of infantry, a small detachment of cavalry, and seven pieces of artillery, under the command of Brigadier-General N. S. Evans, of South Carolina. On the 21st of October the enemy commenced crossing the river at Edwards' Ferry. A brigade thrown over was met and held in check at the point of crossing. In the meantime another brigade was thrown over at Ball's Bluff, and as troops continued to cross there, where the Eighth Virginia had engaged them, General Evans ordered up the Seventeenth and Eighteenth Mississippi, and the three regiments made such an impetuous attack as to drive back the enemy to the Bluff. Colonel Baker, their leader, having fallen, a panic seemed to seize the command, so that they rushed headlong down the Bluff and crowded into the flat-boats, which were their only means of transportation, in such numbers that they were sunk, and many of the foe were drowned in their attempt to swim across the river. The loss of the enemy, prisoners included, exceeded the number of our troops in the action. The Confederate loss was reported to be 36 killed, 117 wounded, and 2 captured; total, 155.

Chapter 37

Arrest of Mason and Slidell

IT soon became evident to all that the South had gone to war without counting the cost. Our chief difficulty was the want of arms and munitions of war. Lamentable cries came to us from the West for the supplies which would enable patriotic citizens to defend their homes. The resources on which our people had relied—the private arms in the hands of citizens—had proved a sad delusion; and the Confederacy was not only deficient in ammunition but in the material for making it.

Undue elation over our victory at Manassas was followed by dissatisfaction at what was termed the failure to reap the fruits of victory; and rumors were circulated that the heroes of the hour were prevented from reaping the fruits of the victory by interference from the President. Naturally there followed another rumor, equally false, that the inaction of the victorious army was due to the policy of the President. Unjust criticisms based on these slanderous accusations weakened the power of the Government to meet its pending and provide for its coming necessities; but I bore them in silence, lest to vindicate myself should injure the public service by turning public censure on the generals on whom the hopes of the country rested. That motive no longer exists, and it is due to the truth that I should record that no executive interference prevented active operations by the generals in command, and that neither the President nor any other civil officer was responsible for the dilatory execution of the law of Congress providing for a reorganization of the armies.

In November, 1861, reports became current that the enemy was concentrating troops west of the valley of the Shenandoah with a view to a descent on it. Late in November General T. J. Jackson (better known as "Stonewall" Jackson) proposed an expedition to Romney in order to frustrate this movement.

The War Department adopted the proposition and strengthened General Jackson's forces by transferring to his command his old brigade, then attached to the Army of the Potomac.

After General Jackson began his march, the cold became unexpectedly severe; and as he ascended into the mountain region the slopes were covered with ice, which impeded his progress the more because his horses were smooth-shod; but his tenacity of purpose, fidelity, and daring triumphed over every obstacle, and he drove the enemy from Romney and its surroundings, took possession of the place, and prevented the threatened concentration.

The development of the enemy's plans in Eastern Virginia showed that he had decided to move down the Potomac for a campaign against Richmond, from the Peninsula as a base. The principal portion of our army was consequently ordered to the Peninsula between the York River and the James. Thus the northern portion of Virginia, which in the first year of the war had been the main field for skirmishes, combats, and battles, of advance and retreat, and the occupation and evacuation of fortified positions, ceased for a time to tremble beneath the tread of contending armies.

On the 8th of November, 1861, an outrage was perpetrated by an armed vessel of the United States in the forcible detention on the high seas of a British mail-steamer, the *Trent*, making one of her regular trips from one British port to another, and the seizure, on that unarmed vessel, of the Confederate Commissioners, Mason and Slidell, who, accompanied by their secretaries, were bound for Europe on diplomatic service. The seizure was made by an armed force, against the protests of the captain of the vessel and of Commander Williams, R. N., the latter protesting as the representative of Her Majesty's Government. The Commissioners yielded only when force which they could not resist was used to remove them from the mail-steamer and carry them to the United States vessel-of-war.

The outrage was the more marked because the United States had been foremost in resisting the right of "visit and search," and had made it the cause of the war of 1812 with Great Britain.

The commissioners and their secretaries were transported to the harbor of Boston and imprisoned in its main fortress.

The British Government demanded the immediate and unconditional release of the commissioners, "in order that they may again be placed under British protection," and a suitable apology for the aggression which had been committed.

In the meantime Captain Wilkes, commander of the vessel which had made the visit and search of the *Trent*, returned to the United States and was received with general plaudits both by the people and the Government. The House of Representatives passed a vote of thanks.

In the midst of this exultation came the demand for the restoration of the imprisoned commissioners to British protection. As it was little to be expected, after such explicit and general commendation of the act, that the Government of the United States would accede to the demand, the War and Navy Departments of the British Government made active and extensive preparations to enforce it. The haughty temper displayed toward the four gentlemen arrested on an unarmed ship subsided in view of a demand to be enforced by the army and navy of Great Britain, and the United States Secretary of State, after a wordy and ingenious reply to the British Minister at Washington, wrote: "The four persons in question . . . will be cheerfully liberated." There was a time when the Government and the people of the United States would not have sanctioned such aggression on the rights of friendly ships to pass unquestioned on the highway of nations and on the right of a neutral flag to protect everything not contraband of war; but that was a time when arrogance and duplicity had not led them into false positions, and when the roar of the British lion could not make Americans retract what they had deliberately avowed.

Chapter 38

Our Deficient Ordnance Supplies

AT the beginning of the war there were within the limits of the Confederacy 15,000 rifles and 120,000 muskets. There were at Richmond about 60,000 old flint-muskets, and at Baton Rouge about 10,000 old Hall's rifles and carbines. At Little Rock, Ark., there were a few thousand stands, and a few at the Texas arsenal; increasing the aggregate of serviceable arms to about 143,000. Add to these the arms owned by the several States and by military organizations, and it would make a total of 150,000 for the use of the armies of the Confederacy. There were a few boxes of sabres at each arsenal, and some short artillery swords. A few hundred holster pistols were scattered about. There were no revolvers.

Before the war little powder or ammunition of any kind was stored in the Southern States, and that little was a relic of the war with Mexico. It is doubtful if there were a million rounds of small-arm cartridges. The chief store of powder was that captured at Norfolk; there was, besides, a small quantity at each of the Southern arsenals, in all, 60,000 pounds, chiefly old cannon powder. The percussion-caps did not exceed one-quarter of a million; and there was no lead on hand. There were no batteries of serviceable field-artillery at the arsenals, but there were a few old iron guns mounted on Gribeauval carriages fabricated about 1812. The States and the volunteer companies did, however, possess some serviceable batteries. But there were neither harness, saddles, bridles, blankets, nor other artillery or cavalry equipments.

To furnish 150,000 men, on both sides of the Mississippi, in May, 1861, there were no infantry accoutrements, no cavalry arms or equipments, no artillery, and, above all, no ammunition; nothing save small arms, and these almost wholly the old pattern smooth-bore muskets, altered from flint locks to percussion.

Within the limits of the Confederate States the arsenals had been used only as depots, and only one of them had a single machine above the grade of a foot-lathe.

Except at Harper's Ferry Armory, all the work of preparation of material had been carried on at the North; not an arm, not a gun, not a gun-carriage, and, except during the Mexican War, scarcely a round of ammunition, had for fifty years been prepared in the Confederate States. There were consequently no workmen, or very few, skilled in those arts. Powder, save perhaps for blasting, had not been made at the South. No saltpetre was in store at any Southern point. It was stored wholly at the North. There were no worked mines of lead except in Virginia, and the situation of those made them a precarious dependence. The only cannon-foundry existing was at Richmond. Copper, so necessary for field artillery and for percussion-caps, was just being obtained in East Tennessee. There was no rolling-mill for bar-iron south of Richmond, and but few blast-furnaces, and these, with trifling exceptions, were in the border States of Virginia and Tennessee.

The first efforts made to obtain powder were by orders sent to the North, which had been early done both by the Confederate Government and by some of the States. These were being rapidly filled when the attack was made on Fort Sumter. The shipments then ceased. Nitre was sought for in the caves of North Alabama and Tennessee. Between four and five hundred tons of sulphur were obtained in New Orleans, where it had been imported for use in the manufacture of sugar. Preparations for the construction of a large powder-mill were promptly commenced by the Government, and two small private mills in East Tennessee were supervised and improved. On June 1, 1861, there were probably 250,000 pounds, chiefly of cannon-powder, and about as much nitre, which had been imported by Georgia. There were the two powder-mills above mentioned, but we had had no experience in making powder, or in extracting nitre from natural deposits, or in obtaining it from artificial beds.

For the supply of arms an agent was sent to Europe, who made contracts to the extent of nearly half a million dollars. Some small-arms had been obtained from the North, and also important machinery. The machinery at Harper's Ferry Armory was partially saved from the flames by the heroic conduct of the operatives; that for making rifle-muskets was transported to Richmond, and that for rifles with sword-bayonets to Fayetteville, N. C. In addition to the injuries suffered by the machinery, the lack of skilled workmen caused much embarrassment. In the meantime the manufacture of small-arms was undertaken at New Orleans, and prosecuted with energy, though with limited success.

In field-artillery the manufacture was confined almost entirely to the Tredegar Works in Richmond. Some castings were made in New Orleans, and attention was turned to the manufacture of field and siege artillery at Nashville. A small foundry at Rome, Ga., was induced to undertake the casting of the 3-inch iron rifle, but the progress was very slow.

The State of Virginia possessed a number of old 4-pounder iron guns, which were reamed out to get a good bore, and rifled with three grooves after the manner of Parrott. The army at Harper's Ferry and that at Manassas were supplied with old batteries of 6-pounder guns and 12-pounder howitzers. A few Parrott guns, purchased by the State of Virginia, were with General Magruder at Big Bethel.

For the ammunition and equipment required for the infantry and artillery, a good laboratory and workshop had been established at Richmond. The arsenals were making preparations for furnishing ammunition and knapsacks; but generally what little was done in this regard was for local purposes.

Such was the general condition of ordnance and ordnance supplies in May, 1861.

But the progress of development was steady. A refinery of saltpetre was established near Nashville during the summer, which received the nitre from that vicinity, and from the caves in East and Middle Tennessee. Some inferior powder was made at two small mills in South Carolina. North Carolina established a mill near Raleigh. A stamping-mill was put up near New Orleans, and powder was made there before the fall of the city. Small quantities were also received through the blockade. It is estimated that, on the 1st of January, 1862, there were 150 sea-coast guns, of various calibre, in position, from Evansport, on the Potomac, to Fort Brown, on the Rio Grande. If their calibre was averaged at thirty-two pounders, and the charge at five pounds, it would require, at 40 rounds per gun, 600,000 pounds of powder for them. The field artillery—say, 300 guns, with 200 rounds to the piece—would require 125,000 pounds; and the small-arm cartridges—say ten million—would consume 125,000 pounds; making, in all, 850,000 pounds. Deducting 250,000 pounds, supposed to be on hand in various shapes, and the increment is 600,000 pounds for the year 1861. Of this, perhaps 200,000 pounds had been made at the Tennessee and other mills, leaving 400,000 pounds to be supplied through the blockade, or by purchase before the beginning of active hostilities.

The impossibility of procuring powder that would not deteriorate in our climate, and the uncertainty of the supply, rendered it necessary for the Confederate Government to construct a great powder-mill, which was soon accomplished, under the experience and skill of General G. W. Rains, of South Carolina; and thus this pressing problem was solved, and the Confederacy guaranteed not only a full supply of powder, but powder that would not deteriorate. All the machinery was made in the Confederate States. Contracts were made for the delivery of nitre through the blockade; and to obtain it for immediate use we resorted to caves, cellars, tobacco-houses, etc. The supply thus obtained, however, was quite inadequate to our need. Lead was obtained from the Wytheville mines, and from the gleanings of the battle-field of Manassas. By the close of 1861, eight arsenals and four depots had been supplied with materials and machinery, so as to be serviceable in producing the various munitions and equipments, the want of which had caused early embarrassment.

The troops, however, were still very poorly armed and equipped. The old smooth-bore musket was the principal weapon of the infantry; the artillery had mostly the 6-pound gun, and the 12-pound howitzer; the cavalry were armed with such various arms as they could get—sabres, horse-pistols, revolvers, Sharpe's carbines, musketoons, short Enfield rifles, Hall's carbines, muskets cut off, etc. But, poor as the arms were, enough of them could not be obtained to arm the troops pressing forward to defend their homes and their political rights.

In December, 1861, arms purchased abroad had come in, and a good many Enfield rifles were in the hands of the troops at the battle of Shiloh. The winter of 1862 was the period when our ordnance deficiencies were most keenly felt, and the equipments most needed were those we were the least able to supply. The abandonment of the line of the Potomac and the Upper Mississippi from Columbus to Memphis reduced the pressure for heavy artillery; and, after the fall of 1862, when the powder-mills at Augusta had got into full operation, there was no further inability to meet all requisitions for powder.

On the recommendation of General Gorgas, a nitre and mining bureau was organized, charged with the duty of obtaining the material from which ammunition, arms, and equipments were to be manufactured.

Under the able direction of Colonel St. John the bureau was soon aiding or managing some twenty to thirty furnaces, with a total annual yield of 50,000 tons or more of pig-iron; lead and copper smelting-works were erected sufficient for all wants, and the smelting of zinc of good quality had been achieved. Nitre-beds were formed at Richmond, Columbus, Charleston, Savannah, Mobile, Selma, and other points, and nitre was also obtained from caves and other like sources. In the course of a year the nitre production was brought up to something like half of the total consumption. The supervision of the production of iron, lead, copper, and all the minerals which needed development, as well as the manufacture of sulphuric and nitric acid (the latter required for the supply of the fulminate of mercury for percussion-caps), without which the fire-arms of our day would have been useless, was added to the other important duties of the bureau.

In equipping the armies first sent into the field the supply of accessories was embarrassingly scant. There were arms, such as they were, for over one hundred thousand men, but no accoutrements or equipments, and only a meagre supply of ammunition. In time, the knapsacks were supplanted by haversacks, which the women could make. But soldiers' shoes and cartridge boxes must be had; leather was also needed for artillery-harness and for cavalry saddles; and, as the amount of leather which the country could furnish was quite insufficient for all these purposes, it was, perforce, apportioned among them. Soldiers' shoes were the prime necessity. Therefore a scale was established by which, first, shoes and then cartridge-boxes had the preference; after these, artillery-harness, and then saddles and bridles. To economize leather, the waist and cartridge box belts were made of prepared cotton cloth, stitched in three or four thicknesses. Bridle-reins were likewise so made, and then cartridge-boxes were thus covered except the flap.

Saddle-skirts, too, were made of heavy cotton cloth strongly stitched. To get leather, each department procured its quota of hides, made contracts with the tanners, obtained hands for them by exemptions from the army, and got transportation over the railroads for the hides and for supplies. To the varied functions of this bureau was finally added that of assisting the tanners to procure the necessary supplies for the tanneries. A fishery, even, was established on Cape Fear River to get oil for mechanical purposes, and, at the same time, food for the workmen. In cavalry equipments the main thing was to get a good saddle which would not hurt the back of the horse. For this purpose various patterns were tried, and reasonable success was obtained. One of the most difficult wants to supply in this branch of the service was the horseshoe for cavalry and artillery. The want of iron and of skilled labor was strongly felt. Every wayside blacksmith-shop accessible, especially those in and near the theatre of operations, was employed. These, again, had to be supplied with material, and the employees exempted from service.

It early became manifest that great reliance must be placed on the introduction of articles of prime necessity through the blockaded ports. A vessel, capable of stowing six hundred and fifty bales of cotton, was purchased by the agent in England, and kept running between Bermuda and Wilmington. Some fifteen to eighteen trips were made before she was captured. Another was added, which was equally successful. These vessels were long, low, rather narrow, and built for speed. They were mostly of pale sky-color, and, with their lights out, and with fuel that made little smoke, they ran to and from Wilmington with considerable regularity. Several others were added, and devoted to bringing in ordnance and, finally, general supplies. Depots of stores were likewise made at Nassau and Havana. Another organization was also necessary, that the vessels coming in through the blockade might have their return cargoes promptly on their arrival. These resources were also supplemented by contracts for supplies brought through Texas from Mexico.

The arsenal in Richmond soon grew to very large dimensions, and, except cannon and small-arms, produced all the ordnance stores that the army required, in quantities sufficient to supply the forces in the field. The arsenal at Augusta was very advantageous to the armies serving in the South and West, and furnished for them much field-artillery complete. The Government powder-mills were entirely successful. The arsenal and workshops at Charleston were enlarged, steam was introduced, and good work done in various departments. The arsenal at Mount Vernon, Ala., was moved to Selma in that State, where it grew into a large and well-ordered establishment of the first class.

The chief armories were at Richmond, and Fayetteville, N. C. The Richmond armory turned out about 1,500 stand per month; the Fayetteville armory, owing to the want of operatives, only 400 per month.

Factories for Sharpe's carbines and rifle-carbines were established at Richmond, Asheville, and Tallahassee. A great part of the work of these factories consisted in the repair of arms. In this way the gleanings of the battle-field were utilized. Nearly 10,000 stand were saved from the field of Manassas, and from those about Richmond, in 1862, we obtained about 25,000 excellent arms.

All the stock of inferior arms disappeared from the armories during the first two years of the war, and were replaced by a better class of arms, rifled and percussioned. Placing the good arms lost previous to July, 1863, at 100,000, there must have been received, from various sources, 400,000 stand of infantry arms in the first two years of the war.

"We began, in April, 1861," truly writes General Gorgas, "without an arsenal, laboratory, or powder-mill of any capacity, and with no foundry or rolling-mill, except in Richmond; and before the close of 1863—or within a little over two years—we supplied them. During the harassments of war, while holding our own in the field, defiantly and successfully, against a powerful enemy; crippled by a depreciated currency; cramped by a blockade that deprived us of nearly all the means of getting material or workmen; obliged to send almost every able-bodied man to the field; unable to use the slave-labor with which we were abundantly supplied, except in the most unskilful departments of production; hampered by want of transportation even of the commonest supply of food; with no stock on hand, even of articles such as steel, copper, leather, iron, which we must have to build up our establishments—against all these obstacles, in spite of all these deficiencies, we persevered at home, as determinedly as did our troops in the field against a more inspiring opposition; and, in that short period, created, almost literally out of the ground, foundries and rolling-mills at

Selma, Richmond, Atlanta, and Macon; smelting works at Petersburg; chemical works at Charlotte, N. C.; a powder-mill far superior to any in the United States, and unsurpassed by any across the ocean; and a chain of arsenals, armories, and laboratories equal in their capacity and their approved appointments to the best of those in the United States, stretching, link by link, from Virginia to Alabama."

Cabinet of the Confederacy.

CHAPTER 39

THE CONFEDERATE FINANCIAL SYSTEM

THE Confederate Government began its existence not only without the munitions of war, but without a treasury; and, thus defenceless against hostile movements, in less than two months was called on to defend its territory from invasion on every side by an implacable and well-equipped enemy. Its ways and means consisted of loans and taxes; and to these it resorted. The financial system thus adopted from necessity proved adequate, during the early part of the war, to supply all the wants of the Government and people; so that, notwithstanding an unexpected and very large increase of expenditure had resulted from the great enlargement of the necessary means of defence, the Government entered on its second year without a floating debt and with its credit unimpaired. The total expenditure of the first year, ending February 1, 1862, amounted to $170,000,000. From the organization of the Government to August 1, 1862—the first eighteen months of the Confederacy—the total expenditure amounted to $328,748,830.70, of which, in round numbers, $298,000,000 were expended for the army and $14,600,000 for the navy. The total receipts were $302,503,096.60. Received from customs, about a million and a half; war tax, $10,539,910.70; bonds (February, 1886), $15,000,000; bonds (August), $22,600,000; call certificates, $37,515,200; Treasury and demand notes, $209,930,000; and one and two dollar notes, $846,900; bank loans, $2,645,000.

A brief review of the legislation of the Confederate Congress will clearly present the financial system of the Government. The first action of the Provisional Congress was confined to the adoption of a tariff law and an act authorizing a loan of fifteen million dollars, with the pledge of a small export duty on cotton to provide for the redemption of the debt.

At the next session, after the commencement of the war, provision was made for the issue of twenty million dollars in Treasury notes, and for borrowing thirty million dollars in bonds. At the same time the tax was revised, and preparatory measures were taken for the levy of internal taxes. After the purpose of subjugation became manifest by the action of the Federal Congress, early in July, 1861, and the certainty of a long war was demonstrated, there arose the necessity that a financial system should be devised on a basis sufficiently large for the vast proportions of the approaching contest. The plan then adopted was founded on the theory of issuing Treasury notes, convertible, at the pleasure of the holder, into eight per cent bonds, with the interest payable in coin. It was assumed that any tendency to depreciation which might arise from the over-issue of the currency would be checked by the constant exercise of the holders' right to fund the notes at a liberal interest payable in specie. The success of this system depended on the ability of the Government constantly to pay the interest in specie. The measures, therefore, adopted to secure that payment consisted in the levy of an internal tax and the appropriation of the revenue from imports.

The first operation of the plan was quite successful. The interest was paid from the revenue of coin existing in the country, and experience sustained the expectations of those who devised the system. Wheat and other agricultural products were selling, in the beginning of 1862, at very moderate prices—little exceeding the average price in times of peace, while the premium on coin had reached about twenty per cent.

But, when it became evident that, by the policy of neutral nations in treating our invasion by a special agent having only delegated powers as though it were the attempt of a sovereign to suppress a rebellion against lawful authority, the commerce of our country was threatened with permanent suspension, the premium on specie rose, because the situation indicated the coming exhaustion of our reserve without the possibility of renewing the supply.

The measures adopted to promote voluntary funding, in order to decrease the volume of notes in circulation, were but partially successful. In December, 1863, the currency in circulation amounted to over $600,000,000, or more than threefold the amount required by the business of the country. The evils of this financial condition soon became apparent in a constant increase of prices, in stimulating the spirit of speculation, and in discouraging legitimate commerce.

I therefore recommended to Congress (in December, 1863) the compulsory reduction of the currency to the volume required to carry on the business of the country, to be accompanied by a pledge that in no strain of circumstances would the amount be increased.

The recommendation was incorporated in the act of February, 1864; one of the features of which was a tax levied on the circulation. After the law had been in operation for one year, it was manifest that it had produced the desired effect of withdrawing from circulation the large excess of Treasury notes which had been issued. On July 1, 1864, the outstanding amount was estimated at $230,000,000. The estimate of the amount funded under the act about this time was $300,000,000, while new notes were authorized to be issued to the extent of two-thirds the sum received under its provisions.

The chief difficulty apprehended in connection with our finances up to the close of the war resulted from the depreciation of our Treasury notes, the inevitable consequence of their increasing redundancy and the diminishing confidence in their ultimate redemption.

Chapter 40

Reforms in the Military Legislation

During the first year of the war the authority granted to the President to call for volunteers in the army for a short period was sufficient to secure all the military force we could equip and use advantageously. As it became evident that the contest would be long and severe, better measures of preparation were enacted. I was authorized to call out and enroll in the military service, for three years, unless the war should sooner end, all white men, residents of the Confederate States, between the ages of eighteen and thirty-five years, and to continue those already in the field until three years from the date of their enlistment. Those under eighteen and over thirty-five were required to remain ninety days. The terms of service being lengthened, the changes by discharge and by receiving recruits were diminished, so that, while additions were made to the forces already in the field, the discipline was greatly improved.

At the same time, on March 13, 1862, General Robert E. Lee was "charged with the conduct of the military operations of the armies of the Confederacy," under my direction.

The good effects of these measures were soon seen in the increased strength and efficiency of our armies. On September 27, 1862, all white men between the ages of thirty-five and forty-five were placed in the military service for three years. On February 11, 1864, it was enacted that all white men between the ages of eighteen and forty-five should be in the military service for the war, and that all then in service, of the same age and class, should be retained during the war. On February 17th all male free negroes between the ages of eighteen and fifty years were made liable to perform duties with the army, or in connection with the defensive and manufacturing works, or the hospital departments. The

Secretary of War was also authorized to employ, for the same duties, any number of negro slaves not exceeding 20,000. The exemptions hitherto accorded by law to persons engaged in specified pursuits and professions were also abandoned.

The act authorizing the employment of slaves produced less important results than were anticipated, but it brought to the front the question of the employment of negroes as soldiers, which was ardently advocated by some and as zealously opposed by others.

Subsequent events convinced me of the expediency of enrolling negroes as soldiers, and I urged that policy with members of Congress when they called on me. General Lee was summoned before a Congressional Committee to give his opinion of the probable efficiency of negroes as soldiers. Contrary, as it is believed, to the expectations of those who called him, General Lee gave his unqualified adherence to the proposed measure.

After much discussion a bill passed the House of Representatives authorizing the President to accept from their owners such a number of negroes as he might deem expedient; but the bill failed to become a law, by a single vote, in the Confederate Senate. The Virginia senators strongly opposed it. The Virginia Legislature thereupon instructed them to vote for it, and they so voted. Finally the bill passed, with an amendment that not more than twenty-five per cent of the male slaves between the ages of eighteen and forty-five should be called out. But ere the law was thus enacted the opportunity had passed. It came too late.

CHAPTER 41

FEDERAL HOSTILITIES AND USURPATIONS

BEFORE entering on the narrative of those terrible scenes of wrong and blood, in which the Government of the United States, driven to desperation by our successful resistance to its outrages, broke through every restraint of the Constitution, of national law, of justice, and of humanity, it is proper that we should sum up the hostile acts and usurpations committed during the first year.

Our people had been declared to be combinations of insurrectionists, and more than 150,000 men had been called to arms to invade our territory. Our forts were blockaded for the destruction of our regular commerce. We had been threatened with denunciation as pirates if we molested a vessel of the United States, and some of our citizens had been confined in cells to await the punishment of piracy. One of our States was rent asunder, and a new State constructed out of one of the fragments. Every proposition for a peaceful solution of pending issues had been spurned. An inhuman warfare had been waged against our peaceful citizens; their dwellings had been burned, and their crops destroyed. A law had been passed imposing a penalty of forfeiture on the owner of any faithful slave who gave military and naval service to the Confederacy, and forbidding military commanders to interfere for the restoration of fugitives. The United States Government had refused to agree to an exchange of prisoners, and suffered those we had captured to languish in captivity. They had maligned us in every court in Europe to defeat our efforts to obtain a recognition from foreign powers. The Federal Government had seized a portion of the members of the Legislature of one State and confined them in a distant military prison, merely because they were thought to sympathize with us, although they had not committed any overt act. It had refused all the propositions of another State for a peaceful neutrality, invaded her soil, and seized important positions where not even a disturbance of the peace had occurred, and perpetrated the most horrible outrages on her people. It had rejected the most conciliatory terms offered for the sake of peace by the Governor of another State, and claimed for itself an unrestricted right to move and station its troops whenever and wherever its officers might think it to be desirable; and it persisted in its aggressions until the people were involved in conflicts, and a provisional government became necessary for their protection.

Within the Northern States, which professed to be struggling to maintain the Union, the Constitution, its only bond, and the laws made in pursuance of it, were in peaceful, undisputed existence; yet even there the Government ruled with a tyrant's hand, and the provisions for the freedom of speech, freedom of the press, and the personal liberty of the citizen were daily violated, and these sacred rights of man suppressed by military force.

The extent of armed resistance of our part the people of the North were slow to comprehend. They would not realize that their purpose of subjugation would be so resolutely resisted, or that, if persisted in, it must be carried to the extent of bloodshed in sectional war. With them the lust of dominion was stronger than the sense of justice, or of the fraternity of equal rights of the States, which the Union was formed to secure. They were blind, therefore, to palpable results. The division of sentiment in the South on the question of the expediency of immediate secession was mistaken for the existence of a submission party; whereas the division was confined to expediency, and wholly disappeared when our territory was invaded. Then was revealed to all the necessity of defending their homes and liberties against the ruthless assault on both, and then extraordinary unanimity prevailed. Then, as Hamilton and Madison had foreseen, war against the States had effected the deprecated dissolution of the Union.

The policy of subjugation, adopted without provocation, was pressed with a ferocity that disregarded all the laws of civilized warfare. The Government waged war not only with those who bore arms, but with the entire population of the Confederate States. Private houses in isolated retreats were bombarded and burned; grain crops in the field were consumed by the torch; and, when the torch was not applied, careful labor was bestowed to render complete the destruction of every article of use or ornament remaining in the private dwellings after their female inhabitants had fled from the insults of brutal soldiers. A petty war was made on the sick, including women and children, by carefully devised measures to prevent them from obtaining the necessary medicines. Were these the appropriate means by which to execute the law and preserve a voluntary union? Was this a government resting on the consent of the governed?

We could not compensate for our lack of a navy by the usual resort to privateers, as the common incentive to such ventures, the hope of gain, was lacking, from the fact that all foreign ports were closed against our prizes and our own ports blockaded. Nevertheless, as the only alternatives thus left in the circumstances were the burning or bonding of captures, the Confederate Government received applications for letters of marque, and issued them, and there was soon a little fleet afloat composed partly of vessels for which letters of marque had been issued, and partly of vessels that had been bought and fitted out by the Navy Department. They hovered on the coast of the Northern States, capturing and destroying their vessels and filling the enemy with consternation. The President of the United States had declared, by proclamation dated April 19th, 1861, that any person who under the pretended authority of the said (Confederate) States should molest a vessel of the United States, or the persons or cargo aboard, "should be held amenable to the laws of the United States for the crime of piracy." Happily for the United States the threat was not executed; but the failure to carry out the declared purpose was coupled with humiliation, because it was the result of a notice to retaliate as fully as there might need be, to stop such a barbarous practice.

On June 3, 1861, the little schooner *Savannah*, an old pilot-boat, sailing under a Confederate commission, was captured by the United States brig *Perry*. The crew were placed in irons and sent to New York. As soon as it was ascertained in Richmond that they were not treated as prisoners of war, I addressed a letter to President Lincoln, dated July 6th, in which it was explicitly stated that, "Painful as will be the necessity, this Government will deal out to the prisoners held by it the same treatment and the same fate as shall be experienced by those captured on the *Savannah*; and if driven to the terrible necessity of retaliation by your execution of any of the officers or crew of the *Savannah*, that retaliation will be extended so far as shall be requisite to secure the abandonment of a practice unknown to the warfare of civilized man, and so barbarous as to disgrace the nation which shall be guilty of inaugurating it." Still later in the year the privateer *Jefferson Davis* was captured, the captain and crew were brought into Philadelphia, and the captain was tried, found guilty of piracy, and threatened with death. Immediately I instructed General Winder, at Richmond, to select one Federal prisoner of the highest rank, to be confined in a cell appropriate to convicted felons, and treated in all respects as if convicted, and to be held for execution in the same manner as might be adopted for the execution of the prisoner of war in Philadelphia. He was further instructed to select thirteen other prisoners, of the highest rank, to be held in the same manner as hostages for the thirteen prisoners held in New York for trial as pirates. By this course the infamous attempt made by the United States Government to inflict judicial murder was arrested.

The appearance of this little fleet on the ocean made it necessary for the powers of Europe to define their position in relation to the contending powers. Great Britain, adopting a position of neutrality and recognizing both as belligerents, interdicted the armed ships and privateers of both from carrying prizes into the waters of the United Kingdom or its colonies. All the other powers also recognized the Confederate States to be belligerent, and closed their ports against the admission of prizes captured by either belligerent.

Up to the close of 1861 the war enlarged its proportions so as to include new fields, until it then extended from the shores of the Chesapeake to the boundaries of Missouri and Arizona. Sudden calls from the remotest points for military aid were met with promptness enough not only to arrest disaster in the face of superior numbers, but to roll back the tide of invasion on the border.

At the beginning of the war the enemy were possessed of certain strategic points and strong places within the Confederate States. They greatly exceeded us in numbers, in available resources, and in the supplies of war. Their military establishments had been long organized and were complete; the army and navy, once common to both, were in their exclusive possession. To meet all this we had to create not only an army in the face of war itself, but also the military establishment necessary to equip it and place it in the field. The spirit of the volunteers and the patriotism of the people enabled us, under Providence, to grapple successfully with these difficulties. A succession of glorious victories at Bethel, Manassas, Springfield, Lexington, Leesburg, and Belmont checked the invasion of our soil. After seven months of war the enemy had not only failed to extend their occupancy of the soil, but new States and Territories had been added to our Confederacy. Instead of their threatened march of unchecked conquest, the enemy were driven, at more than one point, to assume the defensive, and the Confederate States were relatively much stronger at the end of the year than when the struggle began.

The necessities of the times called into existence new branches of manufacture and stimulated the activity of those previously in operation; and gradually we were becoming independent of the rest of the world for the supply of such military stores and munitions as were indispensable for war.

At an election on November 6, 1861, the chief executive officers of the Provisional Government were unanimously chosen to similar positions in the permanent Government to be inaugurated on the ensuing 22nd of February, 1862.

Chapter 42

Forts Henry and Donelson Surrendered

IMPORTANT changes were made about this time in the military arrangements of the enemy. General Scott was retired, and General McClellan was assigned to the chief command of the Federal army. General Halleck superseded General Frémont in command of the Department of the West. The States of Ohio, Michigan, Indiana, and Kentucky, east of the Cumberland and Tennessee Rivers, were constituted into the Department of the Ohio, and General Buell was assigned to its command. General W. T. Sherman was ordered to report to General Halleck.

General A. S. Johnston was now confronted by General Halleck in the West, and by General Buell in Kentucky. Halleck, with armies at Cairo and Paducah under Generals Grant and C. F. Smith, threatened equally Columbus, the bay of the Lower Mississippi River, and the water-lines of the Cumberland and the Tennessee, with other defences at Fort Donelson and Henry; while his centre was directed against General Zollicoffer, at Mill Spring, on the Upper Cumberland. At the northeast corner of Kentucky there was a force under Colonel (afterward President) Garfield of Ohio, opposed to the Confederate force under General Humphrey Marshall.

The strength of Marshall's force was about 1,600 effective men. Knowing that Colonel Garfield was advancing to meet him, and that a small force was moving to his rear, he fell back some fifteen miles and took position on Middle Creek, near Prestonburg. On January 10, 1862, Garfield attacked him. The firing was kept up, with some intervals, about four hours, and was occasionally very spirited. Marshall reported: "The enemy came up to attack, yet came so cautiously that my left wing never fired a shot, and he never came up sufficiently to engage my centre or left wing. Garfield was said to have fallen back fifteen miles to Paintsville, and Marshall seven miles, where he remained two days, and then slowly pursued his retreat."

At Mill Springs, on the upper waters of the Cumberland, a small but gallant army had been collected for the defence of the mountains. This force was under the command of General Crittenden, who had recently joined General Zollicoffer.

On the 18th it was decided to attack General Thomas, who was marching on the Confederate position, before he should be reinforced by a brigade which was moving to unite with him. The enemy were attacked at Fishing Creek early in the morning, and the battle raged fiercely. The action was progressing successfully, when the news of the death of General Zollicoffer, commanding the advance, threw the line of battle into confusion and made a retreat unavoidable, despite the gallant efforts of General Crittenden to rally his men.

The enemy did not follow up by a vigorous pursuit the advantage he had gained. He halted in front of the Confederate intrenchments. As General Crittenden was without supplies, and therefore could not hold the position, he successfully, during the night, moved his men across the Cumberland River, but had not the transportation to save his camp equipage, baggage, horses, wagons, or artillery, which had to be abandoned.

Although not specially memorable for the number of its killed and wounded, this battle was the most serious defeat that we had hitherto met. It broke the right of our defensive line and involved the loss of Eastern Kentucky. Yet the strategy and heroism displayed entitles the affair to be ranked as one of the most brilliant conceptions and most heroic incidents of the war.

When Tennessee seceded, measures were immediately adopted to occupy and fortify all the strong strategic points on the Mississippi, such as Memphis and Randolph, Fort Pillow and Island Number Ten. As it was not our purpose to enter Kentucky, these defensive works were located within the boundaries of Tennessee, and as near the Kentucky line as suitable sites could be found. On these were begun the construction of Fort Donelson, on the west side of the Cumberland, and Fort Henry on the east side of the Tennessee, and about twelve miles apart.

Fort Henry stood on the low lands adjacent to the river, about high-water mark, and being just below a bend of the river, and at the head of a straight stretch of two miles, it commanded the river for that distance. It was also commanded by high ground on the opposite bank of the river, which it was intended should be occupied by our troops in case of a land attack. The power of iron-clad gunboats against land defences had not yet been shown, and the low position of the fort brought the battery to the water level and secured the advantage of ricochet firing, the most effective against wooden ships.

Fort Donelson was placed on high ground, and with the plunging fire of its batteries was thereby more effective against the ironclads brought to attack it on the water side. But on the land side it required extensive outworks and a considerable force to resist an attack in that quarter.

General Polk, just before the battle of Shiloh, reported to General Johnston that the principal difficulty in the way of a successful defence of the river was the want of an adequate force of infantry and of experienced artillerists. This tells only half of the story. To match the vessels of the enemy—floating forts—we needed vessels like theirs, or the means of constructing them. We had neither.

The efforts put forth to resist the operations on the Western rivers, for which the United States made such vast preparations, were, therefore, necessarily very limited. There was a lack of skilled labor, of ship-yards, and of materials for constructing ironclads, which could not be readily obtained or prepared in a beset and blockaded country. Proposals were considered both for building gunboats, and for converting the ordinary side-wheel, high-pressure steamboats into gunboats. The Engineer Department decided that it was not feasible. There was not plate iron with which to armor a single vessel; and even railroad iron could not be spared from its uses for transportation. Unless a fleet could have been built to match the enemy's, we had to rely on land batteries, torpedoes, and marching forces. It was thought best to concentrate the resources on what seemed practicable. One ironclad gunboat, however, the *Eastport*, was undertaken on the Tennessee River, but under so many difficulties that, after the surrender of Fort Henry, while still unfinished, it was destroyed lest it should fall into the hands of the enemy.

The fleet of gunboats prepared by the United States for the

Mississippi and its tributaries consisted of twelve, seven of which were iron-clad, and able to resist all except the heaviest solid shot. Their unusual breadth gave them, in the smooth river waters, the steadiness of land batteries when discharging their heavy guns. This flotilla carried 142 guns—some 64-pounders, some 32-pounders, and some French rifled guns carrying 8-pound shells.

On February 2nd General Grant started for Cairo with 17,000 men on transports, accompanied by Commodore Foote with seven gunboats. On the 4th the landing of the troops commenced three or four miles below Fort Henry. General Grant took command on the east bank, with the main column, while General Charles F. Smith, with some 5,000 or 6,000 men, landed on the left bank, with orders to take the earthwork known as Fort Hindman, opposite Fort Henry. General Tilghman held Fort Henry with 3,400 men. On the 6th, before the attack by the gunboats, he abandoned his purpose to dispute Grant's advance by land, and, regarding a successful defence as hopeless, made arrangements for the escape of his main body to Fort Donelson, while he, by heroic devotion, would insure the delay necessary for the movement by use of the battery, and by standing a bombardment in Fort Henry. For this purpose he retained seventy-five men to work the guns, a number unequal to the strain of labor of the defence,

Noon was fixed as the hour of the attack; but Grant, impeded by the overflow of water, and unwilling to expose his men to the heavy guns of the fort, held them back to await the result of the gunboat attack. In the meantime the Confederate troops were in retreat. Four ironclads, mounting 48 heavy guns, approached, firing as they advanced, and took position within 600 yards of the fort. About half a mile behind these came three unarmored vessels, mounting 27 heavy guns, which kept up a bombardment of shells, which fell within the fort. Some 400 of the formidable missiles of the iron-clad boats were also thrown into the fort. This bombardment was rapidly responded to, and no fewer than 59 shots were seen to strike the gunboats, some of them inflicting serious damage.

Five minutes after the fight began the 24-pounder rifled gun, one of the most formidable in the fort, burst, disabling every man at the piece. Then a shell exploded at the muzzle of one of the 32-pounders, ruining the gun, and killing or wounding all the men who served it. About the same moment a premature discharge occurred at one of the 42-pounder guns, killing three men and dangerously wounding several others. The ten-inch columbiad, the only gun able to match the artillery of the enemy, was next rendered useless by an accident.

The men became exhausted and lost confidence, and Tilghman, seeing this, in person served a 32-pounder for fifteen minutes. Though but four of his guns were disabled, six stood idle for want of artillerists, and but two were replying to the enemy. After an engagement of two hours and ten minutes he ceased firing and lowered his flag. Our casualties were 5 killed and 16 wounded; those of the enemy were 63 of all kinds. Twelve officers and 63 non-commissioned officers and privates were surrendered with the fort. The Tennessee River was thus open, and a base by short lines was established against Fort Donelson.

The next movement was a combined attack, by land and water, upon Fort Donelson. The fort consisted of two water batteries on the hillside, protected by a bastioned earthwork of irregular outline on the summit, inclosing about 100 acres.

The water batteries were admirably placed to sweep the river approaches, with an armament of 13 guns—8 32-pounders, 3 32-pound carronades, 1 10-inch columbiad, and 1 rifled gun of 32-pound calibre. The field-work, which was intended for infantry supports, occupied a plateau about one hundred feet above the river, commanding and protecting the water batteries at close musket-range. These works afforded a fair defence against gunboats; but they were not designed or adapted for resistance to a land attack or investment by an enemy.

The Confederate forces under Generals Floyd, Pillow, and Buckner, in Fort Donelson, during the siege, numbered between 14,500 and 15,000 men. On February 13th, the fire of the enemy's artillery was incessant throughout the day, but was responded to by a well-directed fire from the intrenchments, which inflicted a considerable loss on the assailants, and almost silenced their fire in the afternoon. The artillery fire was continued at intervals during the night. Nearly every Confederate regiment reported a few casualties from shot and shell, which fell frequently within the works. Meanwhile a gunboat of 13 guns arrived in the morning, and, taking a position behind a headland, fired 138 shots, when a shot from our one 128-pounder crashed through one of her ports, injuring her machinery and crippling her. The enemy's fire did not damage the fort.

The weather became cold during the night, and a driving snow-storm prevailed, so that some of the soldiers were frozen, and the wounded between the lines suffered extremely. The fleet of gunboats under Commodore Foote arrived with reinforcements to the enemy. They were landed and put in position, but no assault was made, although a rambling and ineffectual fire was kept up. About three o'clock in the afternoon the commander of the naval force brought his four ironclads, followed by two gunboats, up to the attack. He expected an easy victory, like that at Fort Henry. Each of the ironclads mounted thirteen guns, and the gunboats nine. Any one of them was more than a match for the guns of the forts. Their guns were 8-, 9-, and 10-inch—three in the bow of each. One columbiad and the rifled gun were our only two pieces effective against the ironclads. The enemy moved directly against the water battery, firing with great weight of metal. It was Commodore Foote's intention to silence these batteries, pass them, and enfilade the fort with broadsides. The shot and shell of the fleet tore up the earthwork, but did no further injury. But the Confederate guns, aimed from an elevation of not less than thirty feet, by cool and courageous hands, sent their shot with destructive power, and overcame all the enemy's advantages in number and weight of guns. The bolts of our two heavy guns went crashing through iron and massive timbers with resistless force, scattering slaughter and destruction through the fleet.

According to the report of the enemy, the four ironclads received no less than one hundred and forty-two wounds. "The fleet, therefore," it is added, "gathering itself together and rendering mutual help to its disabled members, proceeded to Cairo to repair damages." 54 men were killed or wounded.

Major Gilmer, who laid out the works, reported: "Our batteries were uninjured, and not a man in them killed. The repulse of the gunboats closed the operations of the day, except a few scattering shots along the land defences."

A conference of the Confederate Generals at midnight determined the operations for the next day. The enemy had been largely reinforced, and the great disproportion in numbers that had marked the opening of the struggle for Fort Donelson was hourly increasing to our disadvantage. It was determined that the whole of the left wing of the army, except eight regiments, should move out of the trenches, attack, turn, and drive the enemy's right, until the Wynn's Ferry road, which led to Charlotte through a good country, was cleared, and an exit thus secured. Moving in the small hours of the night, over icy and broken roads, which wound through the obstructed area of defence, our troops made slow progress, and delayed the projected operations. At four o'clock in the morning Pillow's troops were ready; two hours later the bloody contest of the day had begun. At one o'clock the enemy's right was doubled back and the Wynn's Ferry road cleared.

The conflict on the left soon ended; 300 prisoners, 5,000 stand of small arms, 6 guns, and other spoils of victory had been won by our forces. But the enemy, cautiously advancing, gradually recovered most of his lost ground. It was about 4 P.M. when the assault on the right was made by General C. F. Smith. The enemy succeeded in carrying the advanced work, which General Buckner considered the key to his position. The loss of the enemy during the siege was 400 killed, 1,785 wounded, and 300 prisoners. Our losses were about 325 killed, 1,097 wounded; including missing, they were estimated at 1,500.

After nightfall, at a conference of the commanding officers, it was decided that a surrender was inevitable, and that to accomplish its objects it must be made before the assault, which was expected at daylight.

General Buckner wrote: "I regarded the position of the army as desperate, and that the attempt to extricate it by another battle, in the suffering and exhausted condition of the troops, was almost hopeless. The troops had been worn down with watching, with labor, with fighting. Many of them were frosted by the cold; all of them were suffering and exhausted by their incessant labors. There had been no regular issue of rations for several days, and scarcely any means of cooking. The ammunition was nearly expended. We were completely invested by a force fully four times the strength of our own."

The decision to surrender having been made, it was allotted to General Buckner, who opened negotiations with General Grant, and surrendered the Fort on the following morning. Only two roads were open to the retreat of the garrison. By the upper road they would have been forced to cut through the main body of the enemy, which, it was estimated, would have involved the loss of three-fourths of the command; while a retreat by the lower road would have compelled the retreating force to wade through water three feet deep, which, on account of their physical exhaustion and the severity of the weather, would have been death to half of the command in the opinion of the medical director.

CHAPTER 43

TRANS-MISSISSIPPI MILITARY OPERATIONS

THE loss of Forts Donelson and Henry, opening the river routes to Nashville and Alabama, and turning the positions at Bowling Green and Columbus, rendered it expedient to remove our army to Nashville, in rear of the Cumberland River, a strong point some miles below that city being fortified to defend the river against the passage of gunboats and transports. The retreat was made as soon as it was determined that Fort Donelson was untenable. Hardly had the retreat to Nashville been accomplished than the news of the fall of Fort Donelson was received. The news created general and profound excitement.

"Dissatisfaction was general. Its mutterings, already heard, began to break out in denunciations. The demagogues took up the cry and hounded on one another and the people in hunting down a victim. The public press was loaded with abuse. The Government was denounced for intrusting the public safety to hands so feeble."[100]

The senators and representatives of Tennessee, with one exception, waited on the confederate President and demanded the removal of General Johnston.

The fall of Fort Donelson made it necessary for General Johnston to evacuate Nashville or sacrifice the army. Not more than 11,000 effective men were left to him with which to oppose General Buell, with not less than 40,000 men, moving by Bowling Green; while another superior force, under General Thomas, was on the eastern flank; and the armies from Fort Donelson, with the gunboats and transports, had it in their power to ascend the Cumberland so as to interrupt all communication

---

100. Colonel Munford's speech at Memphis.

with the South.

On the 17th and 18th of February, 1862, the main body of the army was moved to Murfreesboro. By the junction of the command of General Crittenden and the fugitives from Donelson, the force of General Johnston was increased to 17,000 men. On February 28th the march was commenced for Decatur, through Shelbyville and Fayetteville. Halting at those points, he saved his provisions and stores, removed his depots and machine-shops, obtained new arms, and finally, at the close of March, joined Beauregard at Corinth with 20,000 men—making their aggregate force 50,000.

In view of the great advantage which the means of transportation upon the Tennessee and Cumberland afforded the enemy, and the peculiar topography of the State, General Johnston found that he was compelled to select whether the enemy should be permitted to occupy Middle Tennessee or turn Columbus, take Memphis, and open the valley of the Mississippi. Deciding that the defence of the valley was of immeasurable importance he crossed the Tennessee and united with Beauregard.

The evacuation of Nashville, and the evident intention of General Johnston to retreat still farther, created a panic which spread over the whole State. He was accused of imbecility, cowardice, and treason. An appeal from every class was made to the President demanding his removal. Congress took the matter in hand; great feeling was shown in the debates; a committee of inquiry was appointed; but it was evident that the case was prejudged.

A candid review of the situation at that period will show that, with the forces at his command, General Johnston achieved everything that was possible, and showed great capacity as a soldier—that in all he did sound judgment and soldierly daring went hand in hand.

Meanwhile west of the Mississippi some active operations had taken place. Detached conflicts with the enemy had been fought by the small forces under Generals Price and McCulloch, but without definite results.

General Earl Van Dorn assumed command on January 29, 1862. General Curtis was then in command of the enemy's forces, numbering about 12,000 men. Van Dorn immediately determined to attack him.

The battle of Elkhorn, or Pea Ridge, was fought on the morning of March 5th, Van Dorn reported his force to be 14,000, and Curtis put his force at about 10,000. Van Dorn, with Price's division, encountered Carr's division, which had already advanced, and drove it back with heavy loss. Meanwhile McCulloch's command met a division under Osterhaus, and after a sharp, quick struggle, swept it away. Pushing forward through stunted oak, his widely extended line met Sigel's, Astroth's, and Davis's divisions, and here, on the ragged spurs of the hills, a fearful combat ensued. In the crisis of the struggle McCulloch, dashing forward to reconnoitre, fell a victim to a sharpshooter, and McIntosh, his second in command, fell in charging a battery of the enemy with a regiment of Texas cavalry. Without leader or direction, the shattered lines of our forces left the field, to rally, after a wide circuit, on Price's division. When Van Dorn heard of this misfortune he urged his attack, pressing back the enemy until night closed the bloody combat. Van Dorn's head-quarters were then at Elkhorn Tavern, where the enemy's head-quarters had been in the morning. Each army was now in its opponent's line of communication. Van Dorn found his troops much disorganized and exhausted, short of ammunition, and without food. He made his arrangements to retreat. The battle was renewed at 7 A.M., and raged three hours. The retreat then began. There was no real pursuit. The attack had failed. The object had been to effect a diversion in behalf of General Johnston. This failed; but the enemy was badly crippled, and soon fell back to Missouri, of which he still retained possession.

General Van Dorn was now ordered to join General Johnston by the quickest route.

The movement of the enemy up the Tennessee River began on March 10th. The ultimate design was to mass the forces of Grant and Buell against our army at Corinth. Buell was still in the occupation of Nashville. On the 16th Sherman disembarked at Pittsburg Landing. On the next day General Grant took command. Two more divisions were added, and he assembled his army near Pittsburg Landing, the most advantageous base for a movement against Corinth. There it lay inactive until the battle of Shiloh.

Pittsburg Landing, containing three or four log cabins, is situated about midway between the mouths of Owl and Lick Creeks, tributaries of the Tennessee. The mouths of these creeks are bordered by swamps filled with back water, and impassable except where the roads crossed them. The position of the enemy was naturally strong. With few and difficult approaches, guarded on either side by impassable streams and morasses, protected by a succession of ravines and acclivities, commanded by eminences in the rear, it seemed safe against attack and easy to defend. No defensive works were constructed.

Chapter 44

The Battle of Shiloh

GENERAL JOHNSTON, after falling back from Nashville, sought to concentrate his army at Corinth, and to fight the enemy in detail—Grant first and Buell afterward. General Polk's army was driven back from Columbus. General Lovell brought a brigade from Louisiana; and General Bragg, with his well-disciplined army, was ordered from Florida to the aid of Johnston. In a period of four weeks fragments of commands from Kentucky, Alabama, and Louisiana, with such new levies as could be hastily raised, all badly armed and equipped, were united at and near Corinth and organized as an army. "It was a heterogeneous mass," wrote General Bragg, "in which there was more enthusiasm than discipline, more capacity than knowledge, more valor than instruction. Rifles, rifled and smooth-bore muskets—some of them originally percussion, others hastily altered from flint-locks by contractors—many with the old flint-and-steel, and shot-guns of all sizes and patterns held place in the same regiments. The task of organizing such a command in four weeks, and supplying it, especially with ammunition suitable for action, was simply appalling."

This force, about 40,000 men of all arms, was divided into four corps, commanded respectively by Generals Polk, Bragg, Hardee, and Breckinridge. General Beauregard was second in command under Johnston.

The plan to attack the Federal forces before Buell should unite with Grant was frustrated by the arrival of Buell two days earlier than he was expected. His advance reached Savannah on April 5, 1862: next day we attacked Grant.

At one o'clock on the morning of April 3rd preliminary orders were issued to move at a moment's notice. General Hardee led the advance, and next morning reached Mickey's, a position about eighteen miles from Corinth and four or five miles from Pittsburg Landing. The second corps, under Bragg, bivouacked in the rear of Hardee's on the night of the 4th. The first corps, under General Polk, consisted of two divisions, under Cheatham and Clarke. Clarke was ordered to follow Hardee at an interval of half an hour, and to halt near Mickey's, so as to allow Bragg's corps to fall in behind Hardee, at a thousand yards' interval, and form a second line of battle. Polk's corps was to form the left wing of the third line of battle, and Breckinridge's reserve the right wing. The other division of Polk was on outpost duty near Bethel; Cheatham, commanding it, was ordered to assemble his forces at Purdy and pursue the route to Monterey. He effected his junction on the 5th, and took position on the left wing of Polk's corps. Breckinridge's corps, delayed by rains, did not effect its junction with the other corps until late in the afternoon of the 5th.

Owing to their delay in the march it was about four o'clock when the lines were completely formed—too late to begin the battle on that day. General Johnston, therefore, determined to attack early on the following morning.

The results of the first day of the famous battle are very concisely presented in the following brief report of General Beauregard:

> "At 5 A.M., on the 6th instant, a reconnoitring party of the enemy having become engaged with an advance picket, the commander of the forces gave orders to begin the movement and attack as determined upon. . . . Thirty minutes after 5 A.M. our lines and columns were in motion, all animated, evidently, with a promising spirit. The front line was engaged at once, but advanced steadily, followed, in due order, with equal resolution and steadiness, by the other lines, which were brought successively into action with rare skill, judgment, and gallantry by the several corps commanders, as the enemy made a stand, with his masses rallied, for the struggle for his encampments. Like an Alpine avalanche our troops moved forward, despite the desperate resistance of the enemy, until after 6 A.M., when we were in possession of all his encampments between Owl and Lick Creeks but one, nearly all of his field artillery, about 30 flags, colors, and standards, over 3,000 prisoners—including a division commander and several brigade commanders—thousands of small arms, an immense supply of subsistence, forage, and munitions of war, and a large amount of means of transportation, all the substantial fruits of a complete victory, such, indeed, as rarely have followed the most successful

battles; for never was an army so well provided as that of our enemy.

"The remnant of this army had been driven, in utter disorder, to the immediate vicinity of Pittsburg, under the shelter of the heavy guns of his iron-clad gunboats, and we remained undisputed masters of his well-selected, admirably provided cantonments, after our twelve hours of obstinate conflict with his forces, who had been beaten from them and the contiguous covert, but only by the sustained onset of all the men we could bring into action."

Alas! it was that one uncaptured encampment that deprived us of "the substantial fruits of a complete victory;" that furnished a foothold for all the subsequent reinforcements sent by Buell, and gave occasion for the final withdrawal of our troops; whereas, if it had been captured, and the waters of the Tennessee reached, as General Johnston designed, it was not too much to expect that Grant would have surrendered; that, with a skilful commander like Johnston to lead our troops, the enemy would have sought safety on the north bank of the Ohio; that Tennessee, Kentucky, and Missouri would have been recovered, the Northwest disaffected, and our armies filled with the men of the Southwest, and perhaps of the Northwest also.

But a terrible and unforeseen calamity robbed the South of the great results that would have followed the complete victory impending at Shiloh. General Johnston was killed on the field of battle, just as the Confederate army was so fully victorious that, had the attack been vigorously pressed, General Grant and his army would have been prisoners or fugitives before the setting of the sun. Such, at least, is the belief founded on the abundant and trustworthy evidence.

"On the death of General Johnston," reported General Hardee, "the command having devolved upon General Beauregard, the conflict was continued until near sunset, and the advance divisions were within a few hundred yards of Pittsburg, where the enemy were hurled in confusion, when the order to withdraw was received."

General Polk said: "We had an hour or more of daylight still left, were within one hundred and fifty to four hundred yards of the enemy's position, and nothing seemed wanting to complete the most brilliant victory of the war but to press forward and make a vigorous assault on the demoralized remnant of his forces."

General Gilmer, the chief engineer of the Confederate States Army, in a letter dated September 17, 1872, to the son of General Johnston, writes:

> "It is my well-considered opinion that, if your father had survived the day, he would have crushed and captured General Grant's army before the setting of the sun of the 6th. In fact, at the time your father received the mortal wound the day was ours. The enemy having lost all the strong positions on that memorable field, his troops fell back in great disorder on the banks of the Tennessee. To cover the confusion rapid fires were opened from the gunboats the enemy had placed in the river, but the shots passed entirely over our devoted men, who were exultant and eager to be led forward to the final assault, which must have resulted in a complete victory, owing to the confusion and general disorganization of the Federal troops. I knew the condition of General Grant's army at the moment, as I had reached a high projecting point on the bank of the river, about a mile above Pittsburg Landing, and could see the hurried movements to get the disordered troops across to the right bank. Several thousand had already passed, and a confused mass of men crowded to the landing to get on the boats that were employed in crossing. I rode rapidly to General Bragg's position to report what I had seen, and suggested that if he would suspend the fire of his artillery and marshal his infantry for a general advance the enemy must surrender. General Bragg decided to advance, and authorized me and other officers to direct the commanders of the batteries to cease firing.
>
> "In the midst of the preparations orders reached General Bragg from General Beauregard directing the troops to be withdrawn and placed in camp for the night—the intention being to resume the contest in the morning. This decision was fatal, as the delay enabled General Buell and General Wallace to arrive on the field, That is, they came up in the course of the night."

Sidney Johnston fell in sight of victory. The hour he had waited for, the event he had planned for, had arrived. His fame was vindicated; but far dearer than this to his patriotic spirit was it with his dying eyes to see his country's flag, so lately drooping in disaster, triumphantly advancing. In his fall the great pillar of the Southern Confederacy was crushed.

Grant's army being beaten, the next step of General Johnston's programme would have been followed—the defeat of Buell's and Wallace's forces, as they successively came up, and a return by our victorious army through Tennessee to Kentucky. The great embarrassment had been the want of good military weapons. These would have been largely supplied by the victory hoped for, and, in the light of what occurred, not unreasonably anticipated. I believe that again, in the history of war, the, fate of an army depended on one man; and more, that the fortunes of a country hung by the single thread of the life that was yielded on the field of Shiloh.

Chapter 45

Further Military Events in the West

THE condition of the Federal army, on the cessation of hostilities on the evening of the 6th, is thus described by General Buell:

> "Of the army of not less than 50,000 effective men, which Grant held on the west bank of the Tennessee River, not more than 5,000 were in ranks and available on the battle-field at nightfall on the 6th, exclusive of Lew Wallace's division (say 8,500 men), that only came up during the night. The rest were either killed, wounded, captured, or scattered in inextricable and hopeless confusion for miles along the banks of the river."

Reinforced by the divisions of Wallace, Nelson, Crittenden, and McCook, and other forces, the enemy, on the morning of the 7th, advanced and opened a heavy fire of musketry and artillery. A series of combats ensued, in which the Confederates showed their usual valor; but after the junction of Grant and Buell, which Johnston's movement was made to prevent, our force was unequal to resist the combined armies, and retreat was a necessity.

Before the battle of Shiloh the Confederate forces aggregated 40,335 men; after the battle, 29,636, showing a loss of 10,699 effective men; of whom 1,728 were killed, 8,012 wounded, and 959 were missing. Before the battle General Grant's effective force was 49,314; of whom he lost, in killed, wounded, and missing, 11,220. But Buell's reinforcements numbered 21,579, thus leaving ready for duty on the 7th 59,673 men.

On April 9th Major-General Halleck assumed command of the Federal armies at Pittsburg Landing. A reorganization was made with Grant's divisions for the right wing; those of Buell for the centre; and those of General Pope for the left wing. An advance on Corinth was commenced.

Corinth is a small village in the northeast corner of the State of Mississippi, ninety miles east of Memphis, and twenty miles west of the Tennessee River. The Memphis & Charleston Railroad, from east to west, and the Mobile and Ohio Railroads, from south to north, ran through it. Thus it served admirably for the concentration of our forces. Corinth was a strategic point of importance, and it was intended to hold it as long as possible; but it was untenable in the face of a largely superior force, owing to the ease with which railroad communications in the rear could be cut by the enemy's cavalry. The defences were slight rifle-pits, and earthworks of little elevation or strength.

Against this position General Halleck began a movement from Pittsburg Landing, on April 28th, with a force of 85,000 effective men. He made slow progress. He had only reached within eight miles of Corinth on the 3rd of May; on the 21st his batteries were within three miles. He continued his approaches with extreme caution; every night his army lay in an intrenched camp.

The effective force of General Beauregard was less than 45,000 men. He estimated the Federal force at between 85,000 and 90,000 men. General Beauregard's opinion was that no general attack was to be hazarded; but on May 3rd an advance was made to attack the corps of General Pope, when only one of his divisions was in position. It gave way so rapidly that it could not be overtaken. Six days afterward another attempt to surprise the enemy was made, but it failed through the mistake of a guide. On May 26th, therefore, General Beauregard began his preparations for an evacuation, which, on the 29th, he succeeded in accomplishing without the loss of life or stores.

On June 14th General Beauregard retired on surgeon's certificate of physical incapacity, and General Bragg was assigned to the command.

Meanwhile other noteworthy events had occurred in the Western Department. The strategy of the enemy in flanking some of our positions on the Mississippi River, by advancing up the Tennessee River, was followed by his fitting out a naval fleet to move down the Mississippi. The fleet consisted of seven ironclads and one gunboat, ten mortar-boats (each carrying a 13-inch mortar), a coal-barge, two ordnance steamers, and two transports with troops. This fleet left Cairo on March 14th, and, after staying overnight at Hickman, continued its course down to Island Number Ten, an island situated in that bend of the river which touches the border of Tennessee, a few miles farther up than New Madrid.

In the latter part of February a large force of the enemy, under General Pope, left Missouri and moved to New Madrid, with the view of capturing it. Aided by the gunboats of Commander Hollins, our small force repulsed the assaults of the enemy three times; but the disparity of numbers soon demonstrated that the position was untenable. It was evacuated on the night of March 13th. Its defence consisted of two earthworks, in which about twenty guns were mounted. They were spiked and rendered useless.

The bombardment of Island Number Ten began on March 15th, and was kept up night and day. On March 17th a general attack, with five gunboats and four mortar-boats, was made, and continued nine hours without serious results. Up to the 1st of April several thousand 13-inch- and rifle-shells were fired by the enemy. Finally, the Federal forces were greatly increased, and began to occupy both banks of the river, and also the river both above and below the island, when a portion of our force retired, and about April 7th the remainder surrendered.

A week afterward the Federal fleet proceeded to Fort Pillow, about one hundred and eighty miles below Island Number Ten, and a bombardment was begun next day. It was continued without effect until the night of June 4th, when both Fort Pillow and Fort Randolph, some twelve miles below it, were evacuated, these positions having become untenable in consequence of the withdrawal of our forces from Corinth and the adjoining district of Tennessee.

Nothing more remained to oppose the enemy's fleet but our gunboats at Memphis, some seventy miles farther down the river. The gallantry and efficiency displayed by our improvised river navy at New Madrid and Island Number Ten gave rise to hopes hardly justified by the number of our vessels or their armament. Our boats had fewer guns than those of the enemy, and they were less substantially constructed. But their officers and crews took counsel of their country's need rather than of their own strength; they manfully engaged the enemy and disabled one of his rams; but, after an hour's conflict, were compelled to retire.

The possession of Memphis being no longer disputed, its occupation by the enemy promptly followed.

CHAPTER 46

NAVAL OPERATIONS IN THE EAST

COMBINED naval and military expeditions were organized at an early period by the United States Government to capture our harbors and hold them, and to seize a portion of our cotton crop. The first of these expeditions—a fleet of naval vessels and transports—appeared off Hatteras Inlet on August 27, 1861. This inlet is a gap in the sandy barrier that lines the coast of North Carolina about eighteen miles southwest of Cape Hatteras. It is the principal entrance to Pamlico Sound. The channel was protected by two small forts constructed on the sand. After a short bombardment, which developed the greatly superior strength of the enemy, our forces, under the command of Captain Barron, capitulated.

A much larger fleet, carrying 15,000 men, appeared off the harbor of Port Royal, S. C., on November 4, 1861. This harbor is situated midway between the cities of Charleston and Savannah. It is a broad estuary, and contains a group of numerous islands, on which grow rice, and the famous sea-island cotton. It is the richest agricultural region of the State. Its principal defences were Fort Walker, a strong earthwork on Hilton Head, and Fort Beauregard on Phillip's Island. The assault was made by the enemy on the 7th. The attacking fleet consisted of eight steamers and a sloop-of-war. The conflict continued for four hours, when the forts, becoming untenable, were abandoned.

It seems proper here briefly to refer to the system of coast defences adopted to resist the aggressions of the enemy. Immediately after the bombardment of Fort Sumter the work of improving the sea-coast defence was begun, and carried forward as rapidly as the limited means of the Government would permit. In the words of General A. L. Long, a distinguished officer of artillery:

"Roanoke Island and other points on Albemarle and Pamlico Sounds were fortified. Batteries were established on the southeast entrance of Cape Fear River, and the works on the southwest entrance strengthened. Defences were constructed at Georgetown and at all available points on the northeast coast of South Carolina. The works of Charleston Harbor were greatly strengthened by earthworks and floating batteries. The defences from Charleston down the coast of South Carolina and Georgia were confined chiefly to the islands and salient points bearing upon the channels leading inland. Defensive works were erected at all important points along the coast. Many of the defences, being injudiciously located and hastily erected, offered but little resistance to the enemy when attacked. As soon as a sufficient naval force had been collected, an expedition, under the command of General B. F. Butler, was sent to the coast of North Carolina, and it captured several important points. A second expedition, under Admiral Du Pont and General Thomas W. Sherman, was sent to make a descent on the coast of South Carolina. On the 7th of November Du Pont attacked the batteries that were designed to defend Port Royal Harbor, and almost without resistance carried them and gained possession of Port Royal. This is the best harbor on South Carolina, and is the strategic key to all the South Atlantic coast. Later, Burnside captured Roanoke Island and established himself in eastern North Carolina without resistance. The rapid fall of Roanoke Island and Port Royal Harbor struck consternation into the hearts of the inhabitants along the entire coast. The capture of Port Royal gave to the Federals the entire possession of Beaufort Island, which afforded a secure place of rest for the army, while the harbor gave a safe anchorage for the fleet. The evacuation of Hilton Head followed the capture of Port Royal. This exposed Savannah, only about twenty-five miles distant, to an attack from that direction. At the same time, the Federals having possession of Helena Bay, Charleston was liable to be assailed from North Edisto or Stone Inlet, could the railroad have been reached without opposition by the route from Port Royal to Pocotaligo.

"Such was the condition of affairs when General Robert E. Lee reached Charleston, about December 1, 1861, to assume the command of the Department of North Carolina, Georgia, and Florida. Directing fortifications to be constructed on the Stone, the Edisto, and the Combahee, he fixed his headquarters at Coosawhatchie, the point most threatened, and ordered the erection of defences opposite Hilton Head and on the Broad and Salkehatchie, to cover Savannah. He superintended in person the works overlooking the approach to the railroad from Port Royal, and soon infused into the troops a part of his own energy. The works rose with magical rapidity. A few days after his arrival Du Pont and Sherman sent their first reconnaissance in the direction of Coosawhatchie. They were met and repulsed by shots from the newly created batteries; and now, whether the Federals advanced toward the railroad or turned in the direction of Charleston or Savannah, they were arrested by our batteries. The people, seeing the Federals repulsed at every point, regained their confidence, and with it their energy.

"General Lee next proceeded to organize a new system of sea-coast defence. After a careful reconnaissance of the coast, he designated, as the most important positions that he considered it necessary to fortify, Charleston, Pocotaligo, Coosawhatchie, and Savannah. These detached and supporting works covered a most important agricultural country, and sufficed to defend it from the smaller expeditions made against that district.

"About March 1st the gunboats of the enemy entered the Savannah River by way of the channel leading from Hilton Head. Our naval force was too weak to dispute the possession with them, and they thus cut off the communications of Fort Pulaski with the city. Soon after, the enemy landed a force, under General Gillmore, on the opposite side of the fort. By April 1st they had powerful batteries in position, and on that day opened fire on the fort. Having no hopes of succor, Fort Pulaski, after striking a blow for honor, surrendered with about 500 men."[101]

---

101. General A. L. Long, in *Historical Society Papers*.

Chapter 47

Opening of the Peninsular Campaign

EARLY in the year 1862 the Federal Government, by the advice of Major-General McClellan and twelve other Federal commanders, abandoned the line of operations against Richmond, and decided in favor of the movement by the way of Annapolis, and thence to the Rappahannock.

As soon as we ascertained that the enemy was concentrating his forces at Fortress Monroe, to advance upon our capital by that line of approach, all our disposable force was ordered to the peninsula between the James and York Rivers, to the support of General John B. Magruder, who, with a force of 7,000 or 8,000 men, had constructed an intrenched line across the peninsula, and had thus far successfully checked every attempt to break it, though the enemy was vastly superior in numbers to the troops under his command. The greater part of our army, under General Joseph E. Johnston, was sent to strengthen them in counteracting the new plan of the enemy.

Early in April McClellan had landed about 100,000 men in and near Fortress Monroe. At that time Magruder occupied the lower peninsula with his force of 7,000 or 8,000 men. Marshes, creeks, and dense wood gave to the position of the Confederate commander such advantage that he expressed the belief that with 20,000 or 25,000 men he could hold it against any supposable attack. When McClellan advanced with his immense army, Magruder fell back to the line of the Warwick River, and there checked the enemy. Repulsed in regular assaults by the heroic conduct of our troops, the vast army of invasion commenced a siege by regular approaches. By reinforcements from the army of Northern Virginia General Magruder's force was increased to about 20,000 men. McClellan's force numbered 85,000.

Various conflicts ensued soon after the landing of the enemy, and a vigorous attempt was made to break our line at Lee's Mills, where there were some newly constructed defences. The enemy was signally repulsed. Another serious attempt was made soon afterward to break the line of the Warwick, at Dam No. 1, about the centre of the line, and its weakest point. Opening at nine o'clock in the morning with a heavy bombardment, which continued until three o'clock in the afternoon, heavy masses of infantry then commenced to deploy, and, with musketry fire, were thrown forward to storm our 6-pounder battery, which had been effectively used, and was the only artillery we had in position. A portion of the column charged across the dam, but General Howell Cobb met the attack with great firmness, and the enemy was driven by the bayonet from some of our rifle-pits, of which he had gained possession, and the assaulting column recoiled with severe loss from the well-directed fire of our troops.

The enemy's skirmishers pressed closely in front of the redoubts on the left of our line, and with their long-range rifles had a decided advantage over our men, armed with smooth-bore muskets. In addition to the rifle-pits which they dug, they were covered by a dwelling-house and a large peach orchard, which extended to within a few hundred yards of our works. On the 11th of April General Magruder ordered sorties to be made from all the main points of his line. General Wilcox's detachment encountered the advance of the enemy in his front and drove it back to the main line. Later in the day Colonel Taylor, with a Florida regiment and the Second Mississippi Battalion, drove the sharpshooters from their rifle-pits and pursued them to the main road from Warwick Courthouse, encountered a battery posted at an earthwork, and compelled it precipitately to retire. On the approach of a large force of the enemy's infantry, Colonel Ward, commanding the Florida regiment, returned to our works, after having set fire to the dwelling-house above mentioned. On the next night Colonel Terry's Virginia regiment was sent out to cut down the peach orchard and burn down the rest of the houses that had afforded shelter to the assailants; and on the succeeding day Colonel McRae, with his North Carolina regiment, went still farther to the front and felled the cedars along the main road, which partially hid the enemy's movements. Subsequently our men were not annoyed by the sharpshooters.

About the middle of April a further reinforcement of two divisions from the army of Northern Virginia was added to our forces on the peninsula, which amounted, when General Johnston assumed command, to something over 50,000.

The work of strengthening the defences was still continued. On the 16th of April an assault was made on our line to the right of Yorktown. It was repulsed with heavy loss to the enemy. So serious was his discomfiture that henceforward he seemed to rely on bombardment, for which numerous batteries were prepared.

Meanwhile, the brilliant movements of the intrepid Jackson created such apprehensions of an attack on Washington City by the army of the Shenandoah, that President Lincoln refused the repeated requests of General McClellan to send him McDowell's corps to operate on the north side of the York River against our battery at Gloucester Point.

The month of April was cold and rainy, and our men were poorly provided with shelter, and with only the plainest rations; still, they labored steadily to perfect the defences, and, when they were not on the front line, were constantly employed in making traverses and epaulments in the rear. Yet the great superiority of the enemy in men and materials of war caused our commanding general to abandon the Warwick; and the permanent occupation of Norfolk, after our army should withdraw from the lower peninsula, was clearly impossible. Notified by General Johnston that he would withdraw on the 21st of April, I ordered the abandonment of the navy-yard and the removal of public property both from Norfolk and the peninsula. The order for the withdrawal of the army from the line of the Warwick River, delayed until the night of the 3rd, was so successfully carried out that the enemy were surprised next morning to find our lines unoccupied.

The entire Federal army was at once put in motion to pursue the retreating Confederate army. At Williamsburg, about twelve miles from Yorktown, General Magruder had constructed a line of detached works. Fort Magruder, the largest of these works, was constructed at a point a short distance beyond where the Lee's Mill and the Yorktown roads united.

On the morning of the 5th of May General Hooker's division came up, near Williamsburg, with the Confederate rear-guard under General Longstreet. Hooker's forces were massed in a forest. As soon as they were brought into open ground they were gallantly attacked, and they retired with the loss of five guns. Hooker was reinforced until nine brigades were engaged with Longstreet. During the entire day the Federal army was held in check, and next morning the Confederate forces continued their retreat without further molestation.

McClellan's army at this time numbered 112,392. The Confederate force did not exceed 50,000, and was probably less.

General McClellan's official report, dated from "Bivouac in front of Williamsburg," says:

> "General Hancock had taken two redoubts and repulsed Early's rebel brigade by a real charge of the bayonet, taking one colonel and 150 other prisoners."

From General Early's report only the briefest extract can be given:

> "In an open field in view of Fort Magruder, at the end farthest from the fort, the enemy had taken position with a battery of six pieces, supported by a brigade of infantry under command of Brigadier-General Hancock. In this field were two or three redoubts, previously built by our troops, of one, at least, of which the enemy had taken possession, his artillery being posted in front of it, near some farm-houses, and supported by a body of infantry, the balance of the infantry being in the redoubt and in the edge of the woods close by. The Twenty-fourth Virginia regiment came directly upon this battery, and, without pausing or wavering, charged upon the enemy under heavy fire and drove back his guns, and the infantry supporting them, to the cover of the redoubt. I sent orders to the other regiments to advance. These orders were anticipated by Colonel McRae of the Fifth North Carolina regiment, who marched down to the support of the Twenty-fourth, traversing the whole front that should have been occupied by the other two regiments."

General Early, severely wounded, was obliged to leave the field just as the North Carolinans charged on the enemy's artillery. He witnessed the charge and said of it, "Its gallantry is unsurpassed in the annals of warfare."

The claim of the enemy to have achieved a victory at Williamsburg is refuted by the fact that our troops remained in possession of the field overnight, and resumed their march without molestation next morning, carrying with them nine pieces of Federal artillery that they had captured. The loss of the enemy greatly exceeded our own, which was about 1,200; while General Hooker stated the loss in his division to have been 1,700. Here, for the first time, subterra shells were employed to check a marching column. The event is thus described by General Rains, the inventor:

> "On the day we left Williamsburg, after the battle, we worked hard to get our artillery, and some we had captured, over the sloughs about four miles distant. On account of the tortuous course of the road we could not bring a single gun to bear upon the enemy, who were pursuing us and shelling the road as they advanced. Fortunately we found in a mud-hole a broken-down ammunition wagon containing five loaded shells. Four of these, armed with a sensitive fuse-primer were planted in our rear, near some trees cut down as obstructions on the road. A body of the enemy's cavalry came upon these subterra shells and they exploded with terrific effect.
>
> "The force behind halted for three days, and finally turned off from the road, doubtless under the apprehension that it was mined throughout. Thus our rear was relieved of the enemy."

The retreat was successfully accomplished.

Madison House.

Chapter 48

Jackson's Shenandoah Campaign

THE withdrawal of our army to the Chickahominy, the abandonment of Norfolk, the destruction of the *Virginia*, and the opening of the lower James River, together with the fact that McClellan's army, by changing his base to the head of York River, was in a position to cover the approach to Washington, and thus be joined by the large forces hitherto specially retained for the protection of the Federal capital—all combined to give a new phase to our military problem. Attempts to utilize the James River for transportation, so as to approach directly to Richmond, soon followed. We had no defences in the James River below Drury's Bluff, about seven miles from Richmond. There an earthwork had been constructed and provided with an armament of four guns. Rifle-pits had been made in front of the fort, and obstructions had been placed in the river by driving piles and sinking some vessels. The fort was in charge of Commander Farrand of the Confederate navy.

On the morning of the 15th of April the enemy's fleet of five ships of war—among them the *Monitor*—opened fire on the fort. The *Monitor* and the ironclad *Galena* steamed up to about six hundred yards' distance; the wooden vessels were kept at long range. The armor of the flag-ship, *Galena*, was badly injured, and thirty of her men were killed and wounded. The *Monitor* was struck repeatedly, but the shots only bent her plates. After an engagement of four hours the fleet withdrew, discomfited. The result of the action was the adoption of a policy by the enemy, founded on the belief that a land force was necessary to co-operate with the fleet in reducing earthworks, and that without such a co-operating force the water approach to Richmond was impracticable.

The relative strength of the contending armies should be noted here.

On the 30th of April, 1862, McClellan's army had present for duty 112,392 men; on the 20th of June—omitting the army corps of General Dix at Fortress Monroe—105,825. The strength of the army under General Johnston, on the 21st of May, was 53,688 of all arms; subsequently, on the 21st of May, 62,096. McClellan had been constantly demanding reinforcements. They were not furnished to the extent called for, because the movements of "Stonewall" Jackson had created an alarm in Washington, which amounted to a panic, for the safety of the capital.

On May 23rd General Jackson, with whose force that of General Ewell had united, moved with such rapidity as to surprise the enemy. Ewell, who was in advance, captured most of the troops at Front Royal, and pressed directly on toward Winchester, while Jackson, returning across, struck the main column of the enemy in flank and drove it back to Strasburg. The pursuit was continued to Winchester, and the enemy, under General Banks, filed across the Potomac into Maryland. Two thousand prisoners were taken in the pursuit.

When the news of the attack on Front Royal, on May 23rd, reached General Geary, charged with the protection of the Manassas Gap Railroad, he immediately moved to Manassas Junction. At the same time his troops, hearing the most extravagant stories, burned their tents and destroyed a quantity of arms. General Duryea, at Catlett's station, becoming alarmed at hearing of the withdrawal of Geary, took his three New York regiments, leaving a Pennsylvania one behind, hastened back to Centreville, and telegraphed back to Washington for aid. He left behind a large quantity of army stores. The alarm spread to Washington, and Stanton, the Secretary of War, issued a call to the governors of the "loyal" States for militia to defend that city.

The alarm at Washington, and the call for more troops for its defence, produced an indescribable panic in the cities of the North on the following Sunday, the 25th of May. Governors and mayors issued frantic appeals to induce further enlistments.

While this panic in the head-quarters of the enemy had disseminated itself through the military and social ramifications of Northern society, the excitement was tumultuous. Meanwhile General Jackson, knowing nothing of the panic he had caused, after driving the enemy out of Winchester, pressed eagerly on, not pausing to accept the congratulations of the overjoyed people at the sight of their own friends again among them; for he had learned that the enemy had garrisons at Charlestown and Harper's Ferry, and he was resolved they should not rest on Virginia soil. General Winder's brigade, in the advance, found the enemy drawn up in line of battle at Charlestown. He engaged them and drove them in disorder toward the Potomac. The main column then moved on near to Harper's Ferry, where General Jackson received information that Frémont was moving from the west, and the whole, or a part, of McDowell's corps from the east, to make a junction in his rear and thus cut off his retreat. At this time General Jackson's effective force was about 15,000 men—much less than either of the two armies which were marching to form a junction against him. General Jackson had captured, in his campaign down the Valley, a very large amount of valuable stores, over 9,000 small-arms, 2 pieces of artillery, many horses, and, besides the sick and wounded who had been released on parole, was said to have 2,300 prisoners. The amount of captured stores and other property which he was anxious to preserve required a wagon train twelve miles long. This, under escort of a regiment, was sent forward in advance of the army, which promptly retired up the Valley.

On his retreat General Jackson received information of the defeat of a small force he had left at Front Royal in charge of prisoners and captured stores. The stores, however, had been destroyed by the garrison before retreating. Strasburg being Jackson's objective point, he had farther to march to reach that position than either of the columns operating against him. The rapidity of movement which marked General Jackson's operations had given to his command the appellation of "foot cavalry" and never had they more need to prove themselves entitled to the name of "Stonewall."

On the night of the 31st of May, by a forced march, General Jackson arrived with the head of his column at Strasburg, and learned that General Frémont's advance was in the immediate vicinity. To gain time for the rest of his army to arrive, General Jackson decided to check Frémont's march by an attack in the morning. The movement was assigned to Ewell, General Jackson personally giving his attention to preserving his immense train filled with captured stores. The repulse of Frémont's advance was so easy that General Taylor described it as offering a temptation to go beyond Jackson's orders and make a serious attack upon Frémont's army; but recognizing the justice of the restraint imposed by the order, as "we could not waste time chasing Frémont," for it was reported that General Shields was at Front Royal with troops of a different character from those of Fremont's army, which had been encountered near Strasburg, *id est*, the corps commanded by General O. O. Howard, and called by both sides "the flying Dutchman." This more formidable command of General Shields therefore required immediate attention.

On the evening of the 1st of June General Jackson continued his march up the Valley. Frémont followed in pursuit, while Shields moved slowly up the Valley, *via* Luray, for the purpose of reaching New Market in advance of Jackson.

On the morning of the 5th Jackson reached Harrisonburg and turned toward the east in the direction of Port Republic. General Ashby had destroyed all the bridges between Front Royal and Port Republic to prevent Shields from crossing the Shenandoah to join Frémont. The troops were now permitted to make shorter marches, and were allowed some halts to refresh themselves after their forced marches and frequent combats.

Early on the 6th of June Frémont's reinforced cavalry attacked our cavalry rear-guard under General Ashby. A sharp conflict ensued, which resulted in the repulse of the enemy and the capture of Colonel Percy Wyndham, commanding the brigade, and of 63 others. Seeing indications of a more serious attack, General Ashby sent a message to Ewell, informing him of the situations and two regiments—the Fifty-eighth Virginia and the First Maryland—were sent to his support. An attack on the enemy was made, and he was driven from the field with heavy loss. Our own loss was 17 killed, 50 wounded, and 3 missing. But we suffered a great loss in the death of that stainless, fearless hero, General Turner Ashby, of whom General Jackson truly said, "As a partisan officer I never knew his superior."

The main body of General Jackson's command had now reached Port Republic, a village situated in the angle formed by the junction of the North and South Rivers, tributaries of the south fork of the Shenandoah. Over the North River was a wooden bridge, connecting the town with Harrisonburg. Over the South River there was a ford. Jackson's immediate command was encamped on the high ground north of the village, and about a mile from the river. Ewell was four miles distant, near the road leading from Harrisonburg to Port Republic. General Frémont had arrived with his forces in the vicinity of Harrisonburg, and General Shields was moving up the east side of the Shenandoah and had reached Conrad's Store. Each was about fifteen miles distant from Jackson's position. To prevent a junction, the bridge over the river near Shields' position had been destroyed.

As the advance of General Shields approached on the 8th, the brigades of Taliaferro and Winder were ordered to occupy positions immediately north of the bridge. The enemy's cavalry, accompanied by artillery, then appeared, and, after directing a few shots into the village, planted one of their pieces at the southern entrance of the bridge. Meanwhile our batteries were placed in position, and Taliaferro's brigade, having approached the bridge, was ordered to dash across, capture the piece, and occupy the town. This was gallantly done, and the enemy's cavalry were dispersed and driven back, abandoning another gun. A considerable body of cavalry was now seen advancing, when our batteries opened with such effect that in a short time the infantry followed the cavalry, falling back three miles. They were pursued about a mile by our batteries on the opposite side, but they disappeared in a wood.

Hardly had the attack of Shields been repulsed when Ewell became seriously engaged with Frémont, moving on the opposite side of the river. The enemy pushed forward, driving in the pickets, which by gallant resistance checked their advance until Ewell had time to select his position on a commanding ridge, with a rivulet and open ground in front, woods on both flanks, and the road at Port Republic intersecting his line. Trimble's brigade was posted on the right, four batteries in the centre, Stuart's brigade on the left, and Elzey's in rear of the centre. Both wings were in the woods. About ten o'clock the enemy posted his artillery opposite our batteries, and a fire was kept up for several hours, with great spirit, on both sides. Meanwhile a brigade of the enemy advanced under cover upon General Trimble, who reserved his fire until they reached within range, when he poured forth a deadly fire, under which they fell back. Trimble, supported by two regiments of Elzey's reserve, now advanced with spirit, skirmishing more than a mile from his original line, driving the opposing force back to its former position. Ewell, finding that no attack on his left was designed by the enemy, advanced and drove in their skirmishers, and at night was in the position previously occupied by the foe.

This engagement has generally been known as the battle of Cross Keys.

As Shields made no movement to renew the action of the 8th, Jackson determined to attack him on the 9th. Ewell's forces were moved at an early hour toward Port Republic, and Trimble was left to hold Frémont in check, or, if hard pressed, to retire across the river and burn the bridge.

Meanwhile the enemy had taken position about two miles from Port Republic, their right on the river bank, their left on the top of the mountain, which here threw out a spur, between which and the river was a smooth plain about one thousand yards wide. On an elevated plateau of the mountain was placed a battery of long-range guns to sweep the plain over which our forces must pass to attack. In front of that plateau was a deep gorge, through which flowed a small stream bending to the southern part of the promontory, so as to leave its northern point in advance of the southern. The mountain side was covered with dense wood.

Such was the position which Jackson must assail or lose the opportunity to fight his foe in detail, the object for which his forced marches had been made, and on which his best hopes depended.

General Winder's brigade moved down the river to attack, when the enemy's battery upon the plateau opened, and it was found to rake the plain over which we must advance for a considerable distance in front of Shields' position. Our guns were brought forward and an attempt was made to dislodge the battery of the enemy, but our fire proved unequal to theirs; whereupon General Winder, having been reinforced, attempted by a rapid charge to capture it, but encountered such a heavy fire of artillery and small-arms as to compel his command, composed of his own and another brigade, with a light battery, to fall back in disorder. The enemy advanced steadily, and in such numbers as to drive back our infantry supports and render it necessary to withdraw our guns. Ewell was hurrying his men over the bridge, and there was no fear, if human effort would avail, that he would come too late. But the condition was truly critical. General Taylor describes his chief at that moment thus:

> "Jackson was on the road, a little in advance of his line, where the fire was hottest, with the reins on his horse's neck, seemingly in

prayer. Attracted by my appearance, he said in his usual voice, 'Delightful excitement.'"

He then briefly gave Taylor instructions to move against the battery on the plateau, and sent a young officer from his staff as guide.

The advance of the enemy was checked by an attack on his flank by two of our regiments under Colonel Scott. But this was only a temporary relief, for this small company was soon afterward driven back to the woods with severe loss. Our batteries during the attack were all safely withdrawn except one 6-pounder gun.

In this critical condition of Winder's command, General Taylor made a successful attack on the left and rear of the enemy, which diverted his attention and led to a consolidation of his force upon Taylor. Moving to the right along the mountain acclivity, he was unseen before he emerged from the wood, just as the loud cheers of the enemy proclaimed their success in front. Although opposed by a superior force in front and flank, and with their guns in position, with a rush and shout the gorge was passed, impetuously the charge was made, and the battery of six guns fell into our hands. Three times was the battery lost and won in the desperate and determined efforts to capture and recover it, and the enemy finally succeeded in carrying off one of the guns, leaving both caisson and limber. Thus occupied with Taylor, the enemy halted in his advance and formed a line facing to the mountain. Winder succeeded in rallying his command, and our batteries were replaced in their former positions. At the same time reinforcements were brought by Ewell to Taylor, who pushed forward with them, assisted by the well-directed fire of our artillery.

Of this period in the battle General Taylor gives a graphic description:

> "The fighting in and around the battery was hand to hand, and many fell from bayonet wounds. Even the artillerymen used their rammers in a way not laid down in the manual, and died at the guns. . . . With a desperate rally, in which I believe the drummer-boys shared, we carried the battery for the third time, and held it. Infantry and riflemen had been driven off, and we began to feel a little comfortable, when the enemy, arrested in his advance by our attack, appeared. He had countermarched, and, with left near the river, came into full view of our situation.

Wheeling to the right, with colors advanced, like a solid wall he marched straight upon us. There seemed nothing left but to set our backs to the mountain and die hard. At the instant, crashing through the underwood, came Ewell, outriding staff and escort. He produced the effect of a reinforcement, and was welcomed with cheers. The line before us halted and threw out skirmishers. A moment later a shell came shrieking along it, loud Confederate cheers reached our delighted ears, and Jackson, freed from his toils, rushed up like a whirlwind."[102]

The enemy, in his advance, had gone in front of the plateau where his battery, was placed, the elevation being sufficient to enable the guns, without hazard, to be fired over the advancing line; so when he commenced retreating he had to pass by the position of this battery, and the captured guns were effectively used against him, that dashing old soldier, "Ewell, serving as a gunner." Although the retreat of the enemy was so precipitate as to cause him to leave his killed and wounded on the field, it was never converted into a rout. The pursuit was continued some five miles beyond the battlefield. We captured 450 prisoners, some wagons, one piece of abandoned artillery, and about 800 muskets. Some 275 wounded were paroled in the hospitals near Port Republic. On the next day Frémont withdrew his forces and retreated down the Valley. The rapid movements of Jackson, the eagle-like swoop with which he descended upon each army of the enemy, and the terror which his name had come to inspire, created a general alarm at Washington, where it was believed that he must have an immense army, and that he was about to come down like an avalanche upon the Federal capital. Milroy, Banks, Frémont, and Shields were all moved in that direction, and peace again reigned in the valley of the Shenandoah.

During this remarkable campaign "Jackson had marched six hundred miles, fought four pitched battles, seven minor engagements, and daily skirmishes; had defeated four armies, captured 7 pieces of artillery, 10,000 stand of arms, 4,000 prisoners, and a very large amount of stores, inflicting upon his adversaries a known loss of 2,000 men, with a loss on his part comparatively small."[103]

The general effect upon the affairs of the Confederacy was even

---

102. See *Destruction and Reconstruction*, pp. 75, 76.
103. *Stonewall Jackson, a Military Biography*, by John Esten Cooke, p. 191.

more important, and the motives which influenced Jackson presented him in a grander light than any military success could have done. Thus, on the 26th of March, 1862, he learned that a large body of the enemy, before which he had retired, was returning down the Valley; and, divining the object to be to send forces to the east side of the mountain to co-operate in the attack on Richmond, General Jackson, with a small force of about 3,000 infantry and 290 cavalry, moved with his usual celerity in pursuit. He overtook the rear column at Kernstown, attacked a very superior force he found there, and fought with such desperation as to impress the enemy with the idea that he had a large army. The detachments, therefore, which had already started for Manassas, were recalled and additional forces were sent into the Valley. Nor was this all. McDowell's corps, under orders to join McClellan, was detached for the defence of the Federal capital.

Jackson's bold strategy having effected its object he slowly withdrew to the south bank of the Shenandoah, where he was undisturbed and had time to recruit his forces, which now (in April) amounted to 6,000 or 7,000 men.

General Banks held Harrisonburg, fifteen miles from Jackson's position, and Frémont, with a force estimated at 15,000, was preparing to join him. Jackson left Ewell at Gordonville, to hold Banks in check, and marched to unite with the brigade of Edward Johnson. The united forces attacked Milroy and Schenck, who after a severe conflict retreated in the night to join Frémont.

Jackson then returned toward Harrisonburg and attacked and defeated Banks, inflicting great loss and driving him across the Potomac.

In all these operations there conspicuously appears the self-abnegation of a devoted patriot. Jackson was not seeking by great victories to acquire fame for himself. He heroically strove to do what was possible for the general welfare of the cause he maintained. His whole heart was his country's, and his whole country's heart became his.

Chapter 49

The Battle of Seven Pines

AS early as the 20th of May, finding the crossing at Bottom's Bridge unobstructed, the enemy threw a brigade across the Chickahominy, and on the 23rd and 25th he sent additional forces and commenced fortifying a line near to Seven Pines. In the afternoon of the 31st of May, riding out on the New Bridge road, I heard firing in the direction of the Seven Pines. As we could not find out from any of our officers what the firing meant, General Lee and myself rode to the field of battle, which may be briefly described as follows:

The Chickahominy, flowing in front, is a deep, sluggish, and narrow river, bordered by marshes and covered with tangled wood. The line of battle extended along the Nine-mile road, across the York River Railroad and Williamsburg stage-road. The enemy had constructed redoubts, with long lines of rifle-pits covered by abatis, from below Bottom's Bridge to within less than two miles of New Bridge, and had constructed bridges to connect his forces on the north and south sides of the Chickahominy. The left of his forces, on the south side, was thrown forward from the river; the right was on its bank, and covered by its slope. Our main force was on the right flank of our position, extending on both sides of the Williamsburg road, near to its intersection with the Nine-mile road. This wing consisted of Hill's, Huger's, and Longstreet's divisions, with light batteries and a small force of cavalry; the division of General G. W. Smith, less Hood's brigade, ordered to the right, formed the left wing, and its position was on the Nine-mile road. There were small tracts of cleared land, but most of the ground was wooded, and much of it so covered with water as to seriously embarrass the movements of troops.

When General Lee and I, riding down the Nine-mile road, reached the left of our line, we found the troops hotly engaged. Our men had driven the enemy from his advanced encampment, and he had fallen back behind an open field to the bank of the river, where, in a dense wood, was concealed an infantry line, with artillery in position. Soon after our arrival, General Johnston, who had gone farther to the right, where the conflict was expected, and whither reinforcements from the left were marching, was brought back severely wounded, and as soon as an ambulance could be obtained, was removed from the field.

Our troops on the left made vigorous assaults under most disadvantageous circumstances. They made several gallant attempts to carry the enemy's position, but were each time repulsed with heavy loss.

After a personal reconnaissance on the left of the open in our front, I sent one, then another, and another courier to General Magruder. When I met the third courier he said he had not found General Magruder, but had delivered the message to Brigadier-General Griffith, who was moving by the path designated to make the attack.

On returning to the field I found that the attack in front had ceased; it was, therefore, too late for a single brigade to effect anything against the large force of the enemy, and messengers were sent through the woods to direct General Griffith to go back.

The heavy rain during the night of the 30th had swollen the Chickahominy; it was rising when the battle of Seven Pines was fought, but had not reached such height as to prevent the enemy from using his bridges; consequently, General Sumner, during the engagement, brought over his corps as a reinforcement. He was on the north side of the river, had built two bridges to connect with the south side, and, though their coverings were loosened by the upward pressure of the rising water, they were not yet quite impassable. With the true instinct of the soldier to march upon fire when the sound of the battle reached him, he formed his corps and stood under arms waiting for an order to advance. He came too soon for us, and, but for his forethought and promptitude, would have arrived too late for his friends. It may be granted that his presence saved the left wing of the Federal army from defeat.

As we had permitted the enemy to fortify before our attack, it would have been better to have waited another day, until the bridges should have been rendered impassable by the rise of the river.

General Lee, at nightfall, gave instructions to General Smith, the senior officer on that part of the battle-field, and left with me to return to Richmond.

Thus far I have only attempted to describe events on the extreme left of the battle-field, being that part of which I had personal observation; but the larger force, and consequently the more serious conflict, were upon the right of the line. To these I will now refer. Our force there consisted of the divisions of Major-Generals D. H. Hill, Huger, and Longstreet, the last in chief command. In his report, first published in the "Southern Historical Society Papers," vol. iii., pp. 277, 278, he writes:

> "Agreeably to verbal instructions from the commanding general, the division of Major-General D. H. Hill was, on the morning of the 31st ultimo, formed at an early hour on the Williamsburg road as the column of attack upon the enemy's front on that road. The division of Major-General Huger was intended to make a strong flank movement around the left of the enemy's position, and attack him in rear of that flank. After waiting some six hours for these troops to get into position, I determined to move forward without regard to them, and gave orders to that effect to Major-General D. H. Hill. The forward movement began about two o'clock, and our skirmishers soon became engaged with those of the enemy. The entire division of General Hill became engaged about three o'clock, and drove the enemy steadily back, gaining possession of his abatis and part of his intrenched camp; General Rodes, by a movement to the right, driving in the enemy's left. The only reinforcements on the field in hand were my own brigades, of which Anderson's, Wilcox's, and Kemper's were put in by the front on the Williamsburg road, and Colston's and Pryor's by my right flank. At the same time the decided and gallant attack made by the other brigades gained entire possession of the enemy's position, with his artillery, camp-equipage, etc. Anderson's brigade, under Colonel Jenkins, pressing forward rapidly, continued to drive the enemy till nightfall. The conduct of the attack was left entirely to Major-General Hill. The entire success of the affair is sufficient evidence of his ability, courage, and skill."

On the next day, the 1st of June, General Longstreet states that a serious attack was made on our position, and that it was repulsed. This refers to the works which Hill's division had captured the day before, and which the enemy endeavored to retake.

From the final report of General Longstreet, already cited, it appears that he was ordered to attack on the morning of the 31st, and he explains why the attack was postponed for six hours; then he states that it was commenced by the division of General D. H. Hill, which drove the enemy steadily back, pressing forward until nightfall. The movement of Rodes' brigade on the right flank is credited with having contributed much to the dislodgement of the enemy from their abatis and first intrenchments. As just stated, General Longstreet reported a delay of some six hours in making this attack, because he was waiting for General Huger; and he then made it successfully with Hill's division and some brigades from his own.

By the official reports our aggregate loss was, "killed, wounded, and missing," 6,084, of which 4,851 were in Longstreet's command on the right, and 1,233 in Smith's command on the left.

The enemy, reported his aggregate loss at 5,739. It may have been less that ours, for we stormed his successive defences.

Our success upon the right was proved by our possession of the enemy's works, as well as by the capture of ten pieces of artillery, four flags, a large amount of camp-equipage, and more than one thousand prisoners.

Our aggregate of both wings was about 40,500. The force of the enemy confronting us may be approximated by taking his returns for the 20th of June and adding thereto his casualties on the 31st of May and 1st of June, because between the last-named date and the 20th of June no action occurred to create any material change in the number present. From these data, viz., the strength of Heintzelman's corps, 18,810, and of Keyes' corps, 14,610, on June 20th, by adding their casualties of the 31st of May and 1st of June—4,516—we deduce the strength of these two corps on the 31st of May to have been 37,936 as the aggregate present for duty.

It thus appears that, at the commencement of the action on the 31st of May, we had a numerical superiority of about 2,500. Adopting the same method to calculate the strength of Sumner's corps, we find it to have been 18,724, which would give the enemy, in round numbers, a force of 16,000 in excess of ours after General Sumner crossed the Chickahominy. Both combatants claimed the victory.

General Lee was now in immediate command and thenceforward directed the movements of the army in front of Richmond. Laborious and exact in details as he was vigilant and comprehensive in grand strategy, a power, with which the public had not credited him, soon became manifest in all that makes an army a rapid, accurate, compact machine with responsive action in all its parts.

Chapter 50

The Battle of New Cold Harbor

WHEN riding from the field of the battle of Seven Pines with General R. E. Lee on the previous day, I informed him that he would be assigned to the command of the army, *vice* General Johnston, wounded, and that he could make his preparations as soon as he reached his quarters, as I should send the order to him as soon as I arrived at mine. On the next morning he took command. During the night our forces on the left had fallen back from their position at the close of the battle, but those on the right remained in the one they had gained, and some combats occurred there between the opposing forces. The enemy proceeded further to fortify his position on the Chickahominy, covering his communication with his base of supplies on York River. His left was on the south side of the Chickahominy, between White-Oak Swamp and New Bridge, and was covered by a strong intrenchment, with heavy guns, and with abatis in front. His right wing was north of the Chickahominy, extending to Mechanicsville, the approaches being defended by strong works.

Our army was in line in front of Richmond, but without intrenchments. General Lee immediately commenced the construction of an earthwork for a battery on our left flank, and a line of intrenchment to the right, necessarily feeble because of our deficiency in tools. It seemed to be the intention of the enemy to assail Richmond by regular approaches, which our numerical inferiority and want of engineer troops, as well as the deficiency of proper utensils, made it improbable that we should be able to resist. The day after General Lee assumed command, I was riding out to the army. I found him in consultation with a number of his general officers. The tone of the conversation was quite despondent. I rode to the front, where, after a short time, General Lee joined me, and entered into conversation as to what, under the circumstances, I thought it most advisable to do. I then said to him, substantially, that I knew of nothing better than the plan he had previously explained to me, which was to have been executed by General Johnston, but which was not carried out; that the change of circumstances would make one modification necessary—that, instead of bringing General A. P. Hill, with his division, on the rear flank of the enemy, it would now be necessary to bring the stronger force of General T. J. Jackson from the Valley of the Shenandoah. So far as we were then informed, Jackson was hotly engaged with a force superior to his own, and, before he could be withdrawn, it was necessary that the enemy should be driven out of the Valley. For this purpose, as well as to mask the design of bringing Jackson's forces to make a junction with those of Lee, a strong division under Whiting was detached to go by rail to the Valley to join General Jackson, and, by a vigorous assault, to drive the enemy across the Potomac. As soon as he commenced a retreat which unmistakably showed that his flight would not stop within the limits of Virginia, Jackson was instructed to move rapidly, with his whole force, on the right flank of the enemy north of the Chickahominy. The manner in which the division was detached to reinforce Jackson was so open that it was not doubted McClellan would soon be apprised of it, and would probably attribute it to any other than the real motive, and would confirm him in his exaggerated estimate of our strength.

By the rapidity of movement and skill with which Jackson handled his troops, he, after several severe engagements, finally routed the enemy before the reinforcement of Whiting arrived; and then, on the 17th of June, proceeded, with that celerity which gave to his infantry its wonderful fame and efficiency, to execute the orders of General Lee.

Preparatory to this campaign, a light intrenchment for infantry cover, with some works for field-guns, was constructed on the south side of the Chickahominy, and Whiting, with two brigades, was sent to reinforce Jackson in the Valley, so as to hasten the expulsion of the enemy, after which Jackson was to move rapidly so as to arrive in the vicinity of Ashland by the 24th of June, and, by striking the enemy on his right flank, to aid in the proposed attack. The better to insure the success of this movement, Lawton, who was coming with a brigade from Georgia to join General Lee, was directed to change his line of march and unite with General Jackson in the Valley.

To observe the enemy, as well as to prevent him from learning of the approach of Jackson, J. E. B. Stuart was sent with a cavalry force, on June 8th, to cover the route by which the former was to march, and to ascertain whether the enemy had any defensive works or troops in position to interfere with the advance of those forces. He reported favorably on both these points, as well as with regard to the natural features of the country.

Our order of battle directed Jackson to march from Ashland on the 25th toward Slash Church, encamping for the night west of the Central Railroad; to advance at 3 A.M. on the 26th, and to turn Beaver-Dam Creek. General A. P. Hill was to cross the Chickahominy at Meadow Bridge when Jackson advanced beyond that point, and to move directly upon Mechanicsville. As soon as the bridge there should be uncovered, Longstreet and D. H. Hill were to cross, the former to proceed to the support of A. P. Hill and the latter to that of Jackson.

The four commands were directed to sweep down the north side of the Chickahominy toward the York River Railroad—Jackson on the left and in advance; Longstreet nearest the river and in the rear. Huger, McLaws, and Magruder, remaining on the south side of the Chickahominy, were ordered to hold their positions as long as possible against any assault of the enemy; to observe his movements, and to follow him closely if he should retreat. Stuart, with the cavalry, was thrown out on Jackson's left to guard his flank and give notice of the enemy's movements. Pendleton was directed to employ the reserve artillery so as to resist any advance toward Richmond, to superintend that portion of it posted to aid in the operations on the north bank, and to hold the remainder for use when needed. The whole of Jackson's command did not arrive in time to reach the point designated on the 25th. He had, therefore, more distance to move on the 26th, and he was retarded by the enemy.

Not until 3 P.M. did A. P. Hill begin to move. Then he crossed the river and advanced upon Mechanicsville. After a sharp conflict he drove the enemy from his intrenchments, and forced him to take refuge in his works, on the left bank of Beaver Dam, about a mile distant. This position was naturally strong, the banks of the creek in front being high and almost perpendicular, and the approach to it being over open fields commanded by the fire of artillery and infantry under cover on the opposite side. The difficulty of crossing the stream had been increased by felling the fringe of woods on its banks and destroying the bridges. Jackson was expected to pass Beaver Dam above, and turn the enemy's right, so Hill made no direct attack. Longstreet and D. H. Hill crossed the Mechanicsville bridge as soon as it was uncovered and could be repaired, but it was late before they reached the north bank of the Chickahominy. An effort was made by two brigades to turn the enemy's left, but the troops were unable in the growing darkness to overcome the obstructions, and were withdrawn. The engagement ceased about 9 P.M. Our troops retained the ground from which the foe had been driven.

McClellan's position was regarded at this time as extremely critical. If he concentrated on the left bank of the Chickahominy, he abandoned the attempt to capture Richmond, and risked a retreat upon the White House and Yorktown, where he had no reserves or reason to expect further support. If he moved to the right bank of the river, he risked the loss of his communications with the White House, whence his supplies were drawn by railroad. He would then have to attempt the capture of Richmond by assault, or be forced to open new communications by the James River, and move at once in that direction. There he would receive the support of the enemy's navy. This latter movement, it appears, had been thought of previously, and transports had been sent to the James River. During the night, after the close of the contest last mentioned, the whole of Porter's baggage was sent over to the right bank of the river, and united with the train that set out on the evening of the 27th for the James River.

It would almost seem as if the Federal Government anticipated, at this period, the failure of McClellan's expedition. On June 27th President Lincoln issued an order creating the "Army of Virginia," to consist of the forces of Frémont, in their Mountain Department; of Banks, in their Shenandoah Department; and of McDowell, at Fredericksburg. The command of this army was assigned to Major-General John Pope. This cut off all reinforcements from McDowell to McClellan.

In expectation of Jackson's arrival on the enemy's right, the battle was renewed at dawn, and continued with animation about two hours, during which the passage of the creek was attempted, and our troops forced their way to its banks, where their progress was arrested by the nature of the stream and the resistance encountered. They maintained their position while preparations were being made to cross at another point nearer the Chickahominy. Before these were completed, Jackson crossed Beaver Dam, and the enemy, abandoned his intrenchments, and retired rapidly down the river, destroying a great deal of property, but leaving much in his deserted camps.

After repairing the bridges over Beaver Dam, the several columns resumed their advance. Jackson, with whom D. H. Hill had united, bore to the left, in order to cut off reinforcements to the enemy or intercept his retreat in that direction. Longstreet and A. P. Hill moved nearer the Chickahominy. Many prisoners were taken in their progress; and the conflagration of wagons and stores marked the course of the retreating army. Longstreet and Hill reached the vicinity of New Bridge about noon. It was ascertained that the enemy had taken a position behind Powhite Creek, prepared to dispute our progress. He occupied a range of hills, with his right resting in the vicinity of McGhee's house, and his left near that of Dr. Gaines, on a wooded bluff, which rose abruptly from a deep ravine. The ravine, was filled with sharpshooters, to whom its banks gave protection. A second line of infantry was stationed on the side of the hill, overlooking the first, and protected by a breastwork of logs. A third occupied the crest, strengthened with rifle-trenches and crowned with artillery. The approach to this position was over an open plain about a quarter of a mile wide, commanded by a triple line of fire, and swept by the heavy batteries south of the Chickahominy. In front of his centre and right the ground was generally open, bounded on the side of our approach by a wood, with dense and tangled undergrowth, and traversed by a sluggish stream, which converted the soil into a deep morass. The woods on the further side of the swamp were occupied by sharpshooters, and trees had been felled to increase the difficulty of its passage, and detain our advancing columns under the fire of infantry massed on the slopes of the opposite hills and of the batteries on their crests.

Pressing on toward the York River Railroad, A. P. Hill, who was in advance, reached the vicinity of New Cold Harbor about 2 P.M., where he encountered the foe. He immediately formed his line nearly parallel to the road leading from that place toward McGhee's house, and soon became hotly engaged. The arrival of Jackson on our left was momentarily expected, and it was supposed that his approach would cause the extension of the opposing line in that direction. Under this impression Longstreet was held back until this movement should commence. The principal part of the enemy's army was now on the north side of the Chickahominy. "Till's single, division met this large force with the impetuous courage for which that officer and his troops were distinguished. They drove it back, and assailed it in its strong position on the ridge. The battle raged fiercely, with varying fortune, more than two hours. Three regiments pierced the enemy's line, and forced their way to the crest of the hill on his left, but were compelled to fall back before overwhelming numbers. This superior force, assisted by the fire of the batteries south of the Chickahominy, which played incessantly on our columns as they pressed through the difficulties that obstructed their way, caused them to recoil. Though most of the men had never been under fire until the day before, they were rallied, and in turn repelled the advance of our assailant. Some brigades were broken, others stubbornly maintained their positions, but it became apparent that the enemy was gradually gaining ground. The attack on our left being delayed by the length of Jackson's march and the obstacles he encountered, Longstreet was ordered to make a diversion in Hill's favor by a feint on the enemy's left. In making this demonstration, the great strength of the position already described was discovered, and General Longstreet perceived that, to render the diversion effectual, the feint must be converted into an attack. He resolved to carry the heights by assault. His column was quickly formed near the open ground, and, as his preparations were completed, Jackson arrived, and his right division—that of Whiting—took position on the left of Longstreet. At the same time, D. H. Hill formed on our extreme left, and, after a short but bloody conflict, forced his way through the morass and obstructions, and drove the foe from the woods on the opposite side. Ewell advanced on Hill's right, and became hotly engaged. The arrival of these fresh troops enabled A. P. Hill to withdraw some of his brigades, wearied and reduced by their long and arduous conflict. The lines being now complete, a general advance from right to left was ordered. On the right, the troops moved forward with steadiness, un-checked by the terrible fire from the triple lines of infantry on the hill, and the cannon on both sides of the river, which burst upon them as they emerged upon the plain. The dead and wounded marked the line of their intrepid advance, the brave Texans leading, closely followed by their no less daring comrades. The enemy were driven from the ravine to the first line of breastworks, over which our impetuous column dashed up to the intrenchments on the crest. These were quickly stormed, fourteen pieces of artillery captured, and the foe driven into the field beyond. Fresh troops came to his support, and he endeavored repeatedly to rally, but in vain. He was forced back with great slaughter until he reached the woods on the banks of the Chickahominy, and night put an end to the pursuit. Long lines of dead and wounded marked each stand made by the enemy in his stubborn resistance, and the field over which he retreated was strewed with the slain.

On the left, the attack was no less vigorous and successful. D. H. Hill charged across the open ground in front, one of his regiments having first bravely carried a battery whose fire enfiladed his advance. Gallantly supported by the troops on his right, who pressed forward with unfaltering resolution, he reached the crest of the ridge, and, after a sanguinary struggle, broke the enemy's line, captured several of his batteries, and drove him in confusion toward the Chickahominy, until darkness rendered further pursuit impossible.

Our troops remained in undisturbed possession of the field, covered with the dead and wounded of our opponent; and his broken forces fled to the river or wandered through the woods. Owing to the nature of the country, the cavalry was unable to participate in the general engagement. It, however, rendered valuable service in guarding Jackson's flank, and took a large number of prisoners.

On the morning of the 28th none of the enemy remained in our front, north of the Chickahominy. As he might yet intend to give battle to preserve his communications, the Ninth Cavalry, supported by Ewell's division, was ordered to seize the York River Railroad, and General Stuart with his main body to co-operate. When the cavalry reached Dispatch Station, the enemy retreated to the south bank of the Chickahominy, and burned the railroad bridge. During the forenoon columns of dust south of the river showed that he was in motion. The abandonment of the railroad and destruction of the bridge proved that no further attempt would be made to hold that line. But, from the position the enemy occupied, the roads which led toward the James

River would also enable him to reach the lower bridges over the Chickahominy, and retreat down the peninsula. In the latter event, it was necessary that our troops should continue on the north bank of the river, and, until the intention of General McClellan was discovered, it was deemed injudicious to change their disposition. Ewell was ordered to proceed to Bottom's Bridge, to guard that point, and the cavalry to watch the bridges below. No certain indications of a retreat to the James River were discovered by our forces on the south side of the Chickahominy, and late in the afternoon the enemy's works were reported to be fully manned. The strength of these fortifications prevented Generals Huger and Magruder from discovering what was passing in their front. Below the enemy's works the country was densely wooded and intersected by swamps, concealing his movements and precluding reconnaissances except by the regular roads, all of which were strongly guarded. The bridges over the Chickahominy in rear of the enemy were destroyed, and their reconstruction by us was impracticable in the presence of his whole army and powerful batteries. We were, therefore, compelled to wait until his purpose should be developed. Generals Huger and Magruder were again directed to pursue the foe vigorously should they discover that he was retreating. During the afternoon of the 28th the signs were suggestive of a general movement, and, no indications of his approach to the lower bridges of the Chickahominy having been discovered by the pickets in observation at those points, it became inferable that General McClellan was about to retreat to the James River.

Chapter 51

The Battles of Frazier's Farm and Malvern Hill

DURING the night I visited the several commands along the intrenchment on the south side of the Chickahominy. General Huger's was on the right, General McLaws' in the centre, and General Magruder's on the left. The enemy did move before morning, and the fact of the works having been evacuated was first learned by an officer on the north side of the river, who, the next morning, the 29th, about sunrise, was examining their works by the aid of a field-glass.

Longstreet and A. P. Hill were promptly ordered to recross the Chickahominy at New Bridge, and move by the Darbytown and Long Bridge roads. General Lee, having sent his engineer, Captain Meade, to examine the condition of the abandoned works, came to the south side of the Chickahominy to unite his command and direct its movements.

Magruder and Huger found the whole line of works deserted, and large quantities of military stores of every description abandoned or destroyed. They were immediately ordered in pursuit. Jackson was directed to cross the "Grapevine" Bridge, and move down the south side of the Chickahominy. Magruder reached the vicinity of Savage Station, where he came upon the rear-guard of the retreating army. Being informed that it was advancing, he halted and sent for reinforcements. Two brigades of Huger's division were ordered to his support, but were subsequently withdrawn, it having been ascertained that the force in Magruder's front was merely covering the retreat of the main body.

Jackson's route led to the flank and rear of Savage Station, but he was delayed by the necessity of reconstructing the "Grapevine" Bridge.

Late in the afternoon Magruder attacked the enemy. A severe action ensued, and continued about two hours, when night put an end to the conflict. The troops displayed great gallantry, and inflicted heavy loss; but, owing to the lateness of the hour and the small force engaged, the result was not decisive, and the enemy continued his retreat under cover of night, leaving several hundred prisoners, with his dead and wounded, in our hands. Our loss was small in numbers but great in value.

At Savage Station were found about 2,500 men in hospital, and a large amount of property. Stores of much value had been destroyed, including the necessary medical supplies for the sick and wounded. The night was so dark that, before the battle ended, it was only by challenging that on several occasions it was determined whether the troops in front were friends or foes. It was therefore deemed unadvisable to attempt immediate pursuit.

Our troops slept upon their arms, and in the morning it was found that the enemy had retreated during the night; and, by the time thus gained, he was enabled to cross the White-Oak Creek, and destroy the bridge.

Early on the 30th Jackson reached Savage Station. As he advanced he captured so many prisoners and collected so large a number of arms, that two regiments had to be detached for their security. His progress at White-Oak Swamp was checked by the enemy, who occupied the opposite side, and obstinately resisted the rebuilding of the bridge.

Longstreet and A. P. Hill, continuing their advance, on the 30th came upon the foe strongly posted near the intersection of the Long Bridge and Charles City roads, at the place known in the military reports as Frazier's Farm.

Huger's route led to the right of this position, Jackson's to the rear, and the arrival of their commands was awaited to begin the attack.

On the 29th General Holmes had crossed from the south side of the James River, and, on the 30th, was reinforced by a detachment of General Wise's brigade. He moved down the river road, with a view to gain, near to Malvern Hill, a position which would command the supposed route of the retreating army.

The enemy, instead of being a straggling mass moving toward the James River, as had been reported, were found halted between West's house and Malvern Hill on ground commanding Holmes' position, with an open field between them.

Holmes ordered his chief of artillery to commence firing upon the enemy's infantry, which immediately gave way; but a heavy fire of twenty-five or thirty guns promptly replied to our battery, and formed, with the gunboats, a cross-fire upon General Holmes' command. The numerical superiority of the opposing force, both in infantry and artillery, would have made it worse than useless to attempt an assault unless previously reinforced, and, as no reinforcements arrived, Holmes, about an hour after nightfall, withdrew to a point somewhat in advance of the one he held in the morning.

General Huger reported that his progress was delayed by trees which his opponent had felled across the Williamsburg road. In the afternoon, after passing the obstructions and driving off the men who were still cutting down trees, they came upon an open field (P. Williams'), where they were assailed by a battery of rifled guns. The artillery was brought up, and replied to the fire. In the meantime a column of infantry was moved to the right, so as to turn the battery, and the combat was ended. The report of this firing was heard at Frazier's Farm, and erroneously supposed to indicate the near approach of Huger's column, and, it has been frequently stated, induced Longstreet to open fire with some of his batteries as notice to General Huger where our troops were, and that thus the engagement was brought on. General A. P. Hill, who was in front, and had made the dispositions of our troops while hopefully waiting for the arrival of Jackson and Huger, states that the fight commenced by fire from the enemy's artillery, which swept down the road.

The detention of Huger, and the failure of Jackson to force a passage of the White-Oak Swamp, left Longstreet and Hill, without the expected support, to maintain the unequal conflict as best they might. The superiority of numbers and the advantage of position were on the side of the enemy. The battle raged furiously until 9 P.M. By that time the enemy had been driven with great slaughter from every position but one, which he maintained until he was enabled to withdraw under cover of darkness. At the close of the struggle nearly the entire field remained in our possession, covered with the enemy's dead and wounded. Many prisoners, including a general of division, were captured, and several batteries and some thousands of small-arms were taken.

After this engagement, Magruder, who had been ordered to go to the support of Holmes, was recalled, to relieve the troops of Longstreet and Hill. He arrived during the night, with the troops of his command much fatigued by the long, hot march.

In the battle of Frazier's Farm the troops of Longstreet and Hill, though disappointed in the expectation of support, and contending against superior numbers advantageously posted, made their attack successful by the most heroic courage and unfaltering determination.

The current of the battle, which was then setting against us, was reversed. That more important consequences would have followed had Huger and Jackson, or either of them, arrived in time to take part in the conflict, is unquestionable; and there is little hazard in saying that the army of McClellan would have been riven in twain, beaten in detail, and could never, as an organized body, have reached the James River.

Our troops slept on the battle-field they had that day won, and couriers were sent in the night with instructions to hasten the march of the troops who had been expected during the day.

Valor less true or devotion to their cause less sincere than that which pervaded our army and sustained its commanders would, in this hour of thinned ranks and physical exhaustion, have thought of the expedient of retreat; but no such resort was contemplated. To bring up reinforcements and attack again was alike the expectation and the wish.

This battle was in many respects one of the most remarkable of the war. Here occurred on several occasions the capture of batteries by the impetuous charge of our infantry, defying the canister and grape which ploughed through their ranks, and many hand-to-hand conflicts, where bayonet wounds were freely given and received, and men fought with clubbed muskets in the life-and-death encounter.

The estimated strength of the enemy was double our own, and he had the advantage of being in position. From both causes it necessarily resulted that our loss was very heavy.

During the night those who fought us at Frazier's Farm fell back to the stronger position of Malvern Hill, and by a night march the force which had detained Jackson at White-Oak Swamp effected a junction with the other portion of the enemy.

Early on the 1st of July Jackson reached the battle-field of the previous day, having forced the passage of White-Oak Swamp, where he captured some artillery and a number of prisoners. He was directed to follow the route of the enemy's retreat, but soon found him in position on a high ridge in front of Malvern Hill. Here, on a line of great natural strength, he had posted his powerful artillery, supported by his large force of infantry, covered by hastily constructed intrenchments. His left rested near Crew's house and his right near Binford's. Immediately in his front the ground was open, varying in width from a quarter to half a mile, and, sloping gradually from the crest, was completely swept by the fire of his infantry and artillery. To reach this open ground our troops had to advance through a broken and thickly wooded country, traversed nearly throughout its whole extent by a swamp passable at only a few places, and difficult at these. The whole was within range of the batteries on the heights and the gunboats in the river, under whose incessant fire our movements had to be executed.

Jackson formed his line with Whiting's division on his left and D. H. Hill's on his right, one of Ewell's brigades occupying the interval. The rest of Ewell's and Jackson's own division were held in reserve. Magruder was directed to take position on Jackson's right, but before his arrival two of Huger's brigades came up, and were placed next to Hill. Magruder subsequently formed on the right of these brigades, which, with a third of Huger's, were placed under his command. Longstreet and A. P. Hill were held in reserve, and took no part in the engagement. Owing to ignorance of the country, the dense forests impeding necessary communications, and the extreme difficulty of the ground, the whole line was not formed until a late hour in the afternoon. The obstacles presented by the woods and swamp made it impracticable to bring up a sufficient amount of artillery to oppose successfully the extraordinary force of that arm employed by the enemy, while the field itself afforded us few positions favorable for its use, and none for its proper concentration.

Orders were issued for a general advance at a given signal, but the causes referred to prevented a proper concert of action among the troops. D. H. Hill pressed forward across the open field, and engaged the enemy gallantly, breaking and driving back his first line; but, a simultaneous advance of the other troops not taking place, he found himself unable to maintain the ground he had gained against the overwhelming numbers and numerous batteries opposed to him. Jackson sent to his support his own division and that part of Ewell's which was in reserve; but, owing to the increasing darkness and intricacy of the forest and swamp, they did not arrive in time to render the desired assistance. Hill was therefore compelled to abandon part of the ground he had gained, after suffering severe loss and inflicting heavy damage.

On the right the attack was gallantly made by Huger's and Magruder's commands. Two brigades of the former commenced the action, the other two were subsequently sent to the support of Magruder and Hill. Several determined efforts were made to storm the hill at Crew's house. The brigade advanced bravely across the open field, raked by the fire of a hundred cannon and the musketry of large bodies of infantry. Some were broken and gave way; others approached close to the guns, driving back the infantry, compelling the advance batteries to retire to escape capture, and mingling their dead with those of the enemy. For want of co-operation by the attacking columns, their assaults were too weak to break the enemy's line; and, after struggling gallantly, sustaining and inflicting great loss, they were compelled successively to retire. Night was approaching when the attack began, and it soon became difficult to distinguish friend from foe. The firing continued until after 9 P.M., but no decided result was gained.

Part of our troops were withdrawn to their original positions; others remained in the open field; and some rested within a hundred yards of the batteries that had been so bravely but vainly assailed. The lateness of the hour at which the attack necessarily began gave the foe the full advantage of his superior position, and augmented the natural difficulties of our own.

At the cessation of firing, several fragments of different commands were lying down and holding their ground within a short distance of the enemy's line, and, as soon as the fighting ceased, an informal truce was established by common consent. Numerous parties from both armies, with lanterns and litters, wandered over the field seeking for the wounded, whose groans and calls on all sides could not fail to move with pity the hearts of friend and foe.

The morning dawned with heavy rain, and the enemy's position was seen to have been entirely deserted. The ground was covered with his dead and wounded, and his route exhibited evidence of a precipitate retreat. To the fatigue of hard marches and successive battles, enough to have disqualified our troops for rapid pursuit, was added the discomfort of being thoroughly wet and chilled by rain.

The foe had silently withdrawn in the night by a route which had been unknown to us, but which was the most direct road to Harrison's Landing, and he had so many hours the start, that, among the general officers who expressed to me their opinion, there was but one who thought it was possible to pursue effectively. That was General T. J. Jackson, who quietly said, "They have not all got away if we go immediately after them."

During the pursuit, which has just been described, the cavalry of our army had been absent, having been detached on a service which was reported as follows: After seizing the York River Railroad, on June 28th, and driving the enemy across the Chickahominy, the force under General Stuart proceeded down the railroad to ascertain if there was any movement of the enemy in that direction. He encountered but little opposition, and reached the vicinity of the White House on the 29th. On his approach the enemy destroyed the greater part of the immense stores accumulated at that depot, and retreated toward Fortress Monroe. With one gun and some dismounted men General Stuart drove off a gunboat, which lay near the White House, and rescued a large amount of property, including more than ten thousand stand of small-arms, partially burned. General Stuart describes his march down the enemy's line of communication with the York River as one in which he was but feebly resisted. He says:

> "We advanced until, coming in view of the White House (a former plantation residence of General George Washington), at a distance of a quarter of a mile, a large gunboat was discovered lying at the landing. I was convinced that a few bold sharpshooters could compel the gunboat to leave. I accordingly ordered down about seventy-five, partly of the First and Fourth Virginia Cavalry, and partly of the Jeff Davis Legion, armed with the rifled carbines. They advanced on this monster, so terrible to our fancy, and a body of sharpshooters was sent ashore from the boat to meet them. To save time I ordered up the howitzer, a few shells from which, fired with great accuracy, and bursting directly over her decks, caused an instantaneous withdrawal of the sharpshooters, and a precipitous flight under headway of steam down the river.... An opportunity was here offered for observing the deceitfulness of the enemy's pretended reverence for everything associated with the name of Washington—for the dwelling-house was burned to the ground,

not a vestige left except what told of desolation and vandalism.

" Nine large barges, laden with stores, were on fire as we approached; immense numbers of tents, wagons, and cars in long trains, loaded, and five locomotives; a number of forges; quantities of every species of quartermaster's stores and property, making a total of many millions of dollars—all more or less destroyed."

Leaving one squadron at the White House, he returned to guard the lower bridges of the Chickahominy. On the 30th he was directed to recross and co-operate with Jackson. After a long march he reached the rear of the enemy, at Malvern Hill, on the night of July 1st, at the close of the engagement.

On the 2nd of July the pursuit was commenced, the cavalry under Stuart in advance. It appears, from the testimony taken before the United States Congressional Committee on the Conduct of the War, that it was not until July 3rd that the heights which overlooked the encampment of the retreating army were occupied; and, from the manuscript notes on the war by General J. E. B. Stuart, we learn that he easily gained and took possession of the heights, and with his light howitzer opened fire upon the enemy's camp, producing great commotion. This was described by the veteran soldier, General Casey, of the United States Army, thus:

"The enemy had come down with some artillery upon our army massed together on the river, the heights commanding the position not being in our possession. Had the enemy come down and taken possession of those heights with a force of twenty or thirty thousand men, they would, in my opinion, have taken the whole of our army except that small portion of it that might have got off on the transports."

General Lee was not a man of hesitation. Longstreet and Jackson were ordered to advance, but a violent storm which prevailed throughout the day greatly retarded their progress. The enemy, harassed and closely followed by the cavalry, succeeded in gaining Westover, on the James River, and the protection of his gunboats. His position was one of great natural and artificial strength, after the heights were occupied and intrenched. It was flanked on each side by a creek, and the approach in front was commanded by the heavy guns of his shipping, as well as by those mounted in his intrenchments. Under these circumstances it was deemed inexpedient to attack him; and, in view of the condition of our troops, who had been marching and fighting almost incessantly for seven days, under the most trying circumstances, it was determined to withdraw, in order to afford to them the repose of which they stood so much in need.

Several days were spent in collecting arms and other property abandoned by the enemy, and, in the meantime, some artillery and cavalry were sent below Westover to annoy his transports. On July 8th our army returned to the vicinity of Richmond.

The siege of Richmond was raised, and the object of a campaign which had been prosecuted after months of preparation, at an enormous expenditure of men and money, was completely frustrated.[104]

More than ten thousand prisoners, including officers of rank, fifty-two pieces of artillery, and upward of thirty-five thousand stand of small-arms were captured. The stores and supplies of every description which fell into our hands were great in amount and value, but small in comparison with those destroyed by the enemy. His losses in the battle exceeded our own, as attested by the thousands of dead and wounded left on every field, while his subsequent inaction shows in what condition the survivors reached the protection of the gunboats.

In the archive office of the War Department in Washington there are on file some of the field and monthly returns of the strength of the Army of Northern Virginia. These are the original papers which were taken from Richmond. They furnish an accurate statement of the number of men in that army at the periods named. They were not made public at the time, as I did not think it judicious to inform the enemy of the numerical weakness of our forces. The following statements have been taken from those papers by Major Walter H. Taylor, of the staff of General Lee, who supervised for several years the preparation of the original returns.

A statement of the strength of the troops under General Johnston shows that on May 21, 1862, he had present for duty 53,688 effective men.

---

[104]. Reports of Generals Robert E. Lee, Pendleton, A. P. Hill, Huger, Alexander, and Major W. H. Taylor, in his *Four Years With General Lee*, have been drawn upon for the foregoing.

Major Taylor, in his work,[105] states:

> "In addition to the troops above enumerated as the strength of General Johnston on May 21, 1862, there were two brigades subject to his orders then stationed in the vicinity of Hanover Junction, one under the command of General J. R. Anderson, and the other under the command of General Branch; they were subsequently incorporated into the division of General A. P. Hill, and participated in the battles around Richmond."

He had no official data by which to determine their numbers, but, from careful estimates and conference with General Anderson, he estimated the strength of the two at 4,000 effectives.

Subsequent to the date of the return of the army around Richmond, heretofore given, but previous to the battle of Seven Pines, General Johnston was reinforced by General Huger's division of three brigades. The total strength of these three brigades, according to the "Reports of the Operations of the Army of Northern Virginia," was 5,008 effectives. Taylor says:

> "If the strength of these five be added to the return of May 21st, we shall have sixty-two thousand six hundred and ninety-six (62,696) as the effective strength of the army under General Johnston on May 31, 1862.
>
> "Deduct the losses sustained in the battle of Seven Pines as shown by the official reports of casualties, say 6,084, and we have 56,612 as the effective strength of the army when General Lee assumed command."

It appears from the official returns of the Army of the Potomac that on June 20th General McClellan had present for duty 115,102 men. It is stated that McClellan reached the James River with "between 85,000 and 90,000 men," and that his loss in the seven days' battles was 15,249; this would make his army 105,000 strong at the commencement of the battles.[106] Probably General Dix's corps of 9,277 men, stationed at Fortress Monroe, is not included in this last statement.

---

105. *Four Years With General Lee.*
106. Swinton's *History of the Army of the Potomac.*

Chapter 52

Federal Legislative Usurpations

AT the beginning of 1862 it became evident that it was the purpose of the United States Government to assail us in every manner, at every point, and with every engine of destruction. While the Executive was preparing immense armies, iron-clad fleets, and huge instruments of war with which to invade our territory and destroy our citizens, the aid of Congress was invoked by usurpation to legislate the subversion of our social institutions and to give the form of legality to the plunder of a frenzied soldiery.

Congress had no sooner assembled than it brought forward the doctrine that the Government of the United States was engaged in a struggle for its existence, and could therefore resort to any measure which a case of self-defence could justify. It next declared that our institution of slavery was the cause of all the troubles of the country, and that therefore the whole power of the Government must be so directed as to remove the cause.

The authors of the aggressions which had disturbed the harmony of the Union had lately acquired power on a sectional basis, and were eager for the spoils of their sectional victory. To conceal their real motive and artfully to appeal to the prejudice of foreigners, they declared that slavery was the cause of the troubles of the country and of the "rebellion" which they were engaged in suppressing. In his inaugural address President Lincoln said:

> "I have no purpose, directly or indirectly, to interfere with the institution of slavery in States where it exists. I believe I have no lawful right to do so, and I have no inclination to do so."

The leader of the Abolition party in Congress, Senator Sumner, in February, 1861, said:

> "I take this occasion to declare most explicitly that I do not think that Congress has any right to interfere with slavery in a State."

This principle had regulated all the legislation of Congress from the first session in 1789 down to the session of the 37th Congress, beginning July 4, 1861.

Yet, a few months after the inaugural address above quoted, Congress began to legislate for the abolition of slavery. No change had been made in the Constitution; not a word or letter of that instrument had been changed since the possession of the power was disclaimed; yet, after July 4, 1861, it was asserted by the majority in Congress that the Government had power to interfere with slavery in the States. Whence came the change? It was wrought by the same plea that tyranny has ever employed against liberty and justice, the time-worn excuse of usurpation—necessity; an excuse quite sure to be valid, as the usurper claims to be the sole judge of the necessity.

Under this plea a system of legislation was devised which embraced the following usurpations: confiscation of private property; prohibition of the extension of slavery in the Territories; emancipation of slaves in all places under the exclusive control of the Government of the United States; emancipation with compensation in the border States and in the District of Columbia; practical emancipation to follow the progress of the armies; all restraints to be removed from the slaves, so that they could go free whenever they pleased, and be fed and clothed, when destitute, at the expense of the United States—literally, to become the wards of the Government.

For none of these exercises of power was there the least warrant in the Constitution, while some of the laws passed were in direct violation of the explicit text of that instrument.

Perhaps it may be urged that the Confederate States were out of the Union and beyond the protection of the provisions of the Constitution. This objection cannot be admitted in extenuation of the usurpations of Congress and the Executive; for there was, thus far, no act of Congress or proclamation of the President in existence showing that either of them regarded the Confederate States in any other position than as States within the Union, whose citizens were subject to all the penalties contained in the Constitution, and therefore entitled to the benefit of all its provisions for their protection. Unhesitatingly it may be said that all the conduct of the Confederate States pertaining to the war consisted in just efforts to preserve to themselves and their posterity rights and protections guaranteed to them in the Constitution of the United States, and that the actions of the Federal Government consisted in efforts to suppress those rights, destroy those protections, and subjugate us into compliance with its arbitrary will; and that this conduct on their part involved the subversion of the Constitution and the destruction of the fundamental principles of liberty. Who is the criminal? Let posterity answer.

Chapter 53

Federal Executive Usurpations

SIMULTANEOUSLY with the Federal legislative usurpations just noted there was a series of usurpations in which the President of the United States was the principal actor. On March 2, 1862, he began a direct and unconstitutional interference with slavery by sending a message to Congress recommending the adoption of a resolution which should declare that the United States ought to co-operate with any State which might adopt the gradual abolition of slavery by giving pecuniary aid to such State. It was an artful scheme to create dissensions in the Slave States. In every previous declaration the President had said that he did not contemplate any interference with slavery within the States. The resolution, although unconstitutional, was passed by large majorities.

Fortified by Congressional and public approval of the plea of necessity, which superseded all theories of constitutional obligation, the wheels of revolution were soon made to move with accelerated velocity in their destructive work.

On the 25th of April, 1862, Major-General Hunter issued an order declaring the States of Georgia, Florida, and South Carolina under martial law. On the 9th of May the same officer issued another order declaring "the persons held as slaves in those States to be forever free."

President Lincoln, ten days afterward, issued a proclamation declaring the order to be void, and reserving to himself the decision of the question whether it be competent for the President, as commander-in-chief, to declare the slaves of any State free.

Meanwhile the education of the people of the North up to the point of making the abolition of slavery by force of arms for the sake of the Union steadily progressed. The so-called pressure upon the President was organized for a final onset. The governors of fifteen States united in a request that 300,000 more men should be called out to fill up the reduced ranks of the Federal army; and it was done. The anti-slavery press then entered the arena, and severely criticised the policy of the President with regard to the slaves of rebels.

Another call for 300,000 men was made; but enlistments were slow, so that most liberal bounties and threats of a draft were required. The champions of emancipation asserted that the reluctance of the people to enter the army was caused by the policy of the Government in not adopting bold emancipation measures. They insisted that slavery in the seceded States should be treated as a military question; that it constituted nearly all the subsistence which supported the Southern men in arms, dug their trenches, and built their fortifications.

At last, on September 22, 1862, the President yielded to the "pressure," and issued a preliminary proclamation of emancipation. It declared that, at the next session of Congress, the proposition for emancipation in the border slaveholding States would be again recommended; and that, on January 1, 1863, "all persons held as slaves within any State or designated part of a State, the people whereof shall then be in rebellion against the United States, shall be then, henceforward, and forever free."

On January 1st another proclamation was issued by the President of the United States, declaring the emancipation to be absolute within the Confederate States, with the exception of a few districts. Both before and during the war between the States Mr. Lincoln and his advisers had solemnly and repeatedly disavowed their intention or desire to interfere with slavery in the States, and asserted that the Constitution gave them no power to interfere with it. The same principle was avowed in the diplomatic correspondence of the United States. Whence, then, was authority found to do an act for which not only was there no authority to be found in the Constitution, but which the Constitution expressly forbids? Mr. Lincoln's proclamation closed with these words:

> "And upon this act, sincerely believed to be an act of justice, warranted by the Constitution upon military necessity, I invoke the considerate judgment of mankind and the gracious favor of Almighty God."

Let us test the existence of the military necessity here spoken of by a few facts.

The white male population of the Northern States was then 13,690,364. The white male population of the Confederate States was 5,449,463. The United States had called into the field a force exceeding one million men. The number of troops which the Confederate Government had then under arms was less than four hundred thousand. The United States Government had a navy that was only third in rank in the world. The Confederate Government had a navy which at that time consisted of a single small ship on the ocean. The people of the United States had a commerce afloat all over the world. The people of the Confederate States had not a single port open to commerce. The people of the United States were the rivals of the greatest nations in all kinds of manufactures. The people of the Confederate States had few manufactures, and those were of articles of inferior importance. The Government of the United States possessed the treasury of a Union of eighty years, with its vast resources. The Confederate States had to create a treasury by the development of financial resources. The representatives and ambassadors of the United States were welcomed at every port of the world. The representatives of the Confederate States were not recognized anywhere.

Thus the consummation of the original anti-slavery purposes was now reached; but even that achievement was attended with disunion, bloodshed, and internecine war, followed by such foul progeny as usurpation breeds.

Officers of the Confederate Army and Navy.

Chapter 54

Confederate Naval Operations

THE grades of officers in the Confederate navy consisted of admirals, captains, commanders, surgeons, lieutenants, and midshipmen. Of officers at the close of the first year there were one admiral, twelve captains, thirty commanders, and one hundred and twelve first and second lieutenants.

All the principal officers had belonged to the United States navy. Owing to the limited number of vessels afloat, many of these officers were employed on shore duties.

The vessels of the navy may be reduced to two classes: those intended for river and harbor defence, as ironclads, rams, floating batteries, or river steamboats transformed into gunboats; and sea-going steamers of moderate size, some of them of great speed, but, not having been designed for war purposes, all unsuited for a powerful armament that could contend successfully with ships of war.

After Virginia had seceded from the United States, but before she acceded to the Confederate States—viz., on the 19th of April, 1861—General Taliaferro, in command of Virginia's forces, arrived at Norfolk. Commander McCauley, United States navy, and commandant of the navy-yard, held a conference with General Taliaferro, the result of which was an agreement "that none of the vessels should be removed, nor a shot fired except in self-defence." The excitement which had existed in the town was quieted by the announcement of this arrangement; but it was soon ascertained that the *Germantown* and *Merrimac*, frigates in the port, had been scuttled, and the former otherwise injured. About midnight a fire was started in the navy-yard, which continued to increase, involving the destruction of the ship-houses, a ship of the line, and the unfinished frame of another.

Several frigates, in addition to those mentioned, had been scuttled and sunk, and other property destroyed to an amount estimated at several million dollars. The *Pawnee*, which arrived on the 19th, had been kept under steam, and, taking the *Cumberland* in tow, retired down the harbor, freighted with a great portion of valuable munitions, and the commandant and other officers of the yard. In the haste and secrecy of the conflagration a large amount of material remained uninjured. The *Merrimac*, a beautiful frigate, in the yard for repairs, was raised by the Virginians, and the work immediately commenced to convert her hull into an iron-clad vessel. Two-inch plates were prepared, and she was covered with a double-inclined roof of four inches thickness. This armor, though not sufficiently thick to resist direct shot, sufficed to protect against a glancing ball, and was as heavy as was consistent with the handling of the ship.

Her armament consisted of ten guns, four single-banded Brooke rifles, and six 9-inch Dahlgren shell-guns. Two of the rifles, bow and stern pivots, were 7-inch; the other two were $6^{4/10}$-inch, one on each broadside. The 9-inch gun on each side nearest the furnaces was fitted for firing hot shot. The work of construction was prosecuted with all haste, the armament and crew were put on board, and the vessel started on her trial trip. She was our first ironclad; her model was an experiment, and many doubted its success. Her commander, Captain (afterward Admiral) Franklin Buchanan, with the wisdom of age and the experience of sea-service from his boyhood, combined the daring and enterprise of youth; and with him was Lieutenant Catesby Ap R. Jones, who had been specially in charge of the battery, and otherwise thoroughly acquainted with the ship. His high qualifications as an ordnance officer were well known in the "old navy," and he was soon to exhibit a like ability as a seaman in battle.

Now that the first Confederate ironclad was afloat the stars and bars were given to the breeze, and she was new-christened the *Virginia*. She was joined by the *Patrick Henry*, six guns; the *Jamestown*, two guns; the *Beaufort*, one gun; the *Raleigh*, one gun; and the *Teaser*, one gun.

The enemy's fleet in Hampton Roads consisted of the *Cumberland*, twenty-four guns; *Congress*, fifty guns; *St. Lawrence*, fifty guns; steam-frigates *Minnesota* and *Roanoke*, forty guns each. The relative force was as twenty-one guns to two hundred and four, not counting the small steamers of the enemy, though they had heavier armament than the small vessels of our fleet which have been enumerated. The *Cumberland* and the *Congress* lay off Newport News; the other vessels were anchored about nine miles eastward, near Fortress Monroe. Strong shore batteries and several small steamers, armed with heavy rifled guns, protected the frigates *Cumberland* and *Congress*.

Buchanan no doubt felt the inspiration of a sailor when his vessel bears him from the land, and the excitement of a hero at the prospect of battle, and thus we may understand why the trial trip was at once converted into a determined attack upon the enemy. After the plan of the *Virginia* had been decided upon, the work of her construction was pushed with all possible haste. Her armament was on board, and she was taken out of the dock while the workmen were still employed upon her—indeed, the last of them were put ashore after she was started on her experimental trip. Few men conscious, as flag-officer Buchanan was, of the defects of his vessel would have dared such unequal conflict. Slowly—about five knots an hour—he steamed down to the Roads. The *Cumberland* and *Congress*, seeing the *Virginia* approach, prepared for action, and from the flag-ship *Roanoke* signals were given to the *Minnesota* and *St. Lawrence* to advance. The *Cumberland* had swung so as to give her full broadside to the *Virginia*, which silently and without any exhibition of her crew, moved steadily forward. The shot from the *Cumberland* fell thick upon her plated roof, but rebounded, harmless as hailstones. At last the prow of the *Virginia* struck the *Cumberland* just forward of her starboard fore-chains. A dull, heavy thud was heard, but so little force was given to the *Virginia* that the engineer hesitated about backing her. It was soon seen, however, that a gaping breach had been made in the *Cumberland*, and that the sea was rushing madly in. She reeled; and while the waves ingulfed her, her crew gallantly stood to their guns and vainly continued their fire. She went down in nine fathoms of water, with at least one hundred of her gallant crew, her pennant still flying from her mast-head.

The *Virginia* then ran up stream a short distance, in order to turn and have sufficient space to get headway, and come down on the *Congress*. The enemy, both ashore and afloat, supposing that she had retired at the sight of the vessels approaching to attack her, cheered loudly. But when she turned to descend upon the *Congress*, as she had on the *Cumberland*, the *Congress* slipped her cables and ran ashore, bows on. The *Virginia* took position as near as the depth of water would permit, and opened upon her a raking fire. The *Minnesota* was fast aground about a mile and a half below. The *Roanoke* and *St. Lawrence* retired toward the fort. The shore batteries kept up their fire on the *Virginia*, as did also the *Minnesota*, at long range, and quite ineffectually. The *Congress*, being aground, could but feebly reply. Several of our smaller vessels came up and joined the *Virginia*, and the combined fire was fearfully destructive to the *Congress*. Her commander was killed, and soon her colors were struck, and the white flag appeared both at the main and spanker gaff. The *Beaufort* and the *Raleigh*, tugs which had accompanied the *Virginia*, were ordered to the *Congress* to receive the surrender. The flag of the ship and the sword of its then commander were delivered to Lieutenant Parker, by whom they were subsequently sent to the Navy Department at Richmond. Other officers delivered their swords in token of surrender, and entreated that they might return to assist in getting their wounded out of the ship. The permission was granted to the officers, and they then took advantage of the clemency shown them to make their escape. In the meantime the shore batteries fired upon the tugs, and compelled them to retire. By this fire five of their own men, our prisoners, were wounded. Flag-officer Buchanan had stopped the firing upon the *Congress* when she struck her flag and ran up the white flag. Lieutenant Jones, referring to the *Congress*, wrote: "But she fired upon us with the white flag flying, wounding Lieutenant Minor and several of our men. We again opened fire upon her, and she is now in flames." The crews of the *Congress* and *Cumberland* escaped by boats, or by swimming, and our men generously abstained from firing on them while so exposed. Flag-officer Buchanan was wounded by a rifle-ball, and had to be carried below. His intrepid conduct won the admiration of all. The executive and ordnance officer, Lieutenant Catesby Ap R. Jones, succeeded to the command. It was now so near night and the change of the tide that nothing further could be attempted on that day. The *Virginia*, with the smaller vessels attending her, withdrew and anchored off Sewell's Point. She had sunk the *Cumberland*, left the *Congress* on fire, blown up a transport steamer, sunk one schooner, and captured another. Her casualties were two killed and eight wounded. The prow of the *Virginia* was somewhat damaged, her anchor and all her flag-staffs were shot away, and her smoke-stack and steam-pipe were riddled; otherwise the vessel was uninjured, and ready for action next morning. The prisoners and wounded were immediately sent up to the hospital at Norfolk.

During the night the *Monitor*, an iron-clad turret-steamer, of an entirely new model, came in and anchored near the *Minnesota*. Like our *Virginia*, she was an invention, and her merits and demerits were yet untested in the crucible of war. She was of light draught; very little save the revolving turret was visible above the water; she was readily handled, and had good speed; but, like the *Virginia*, was not supposed by nautical men to be capable of braving rough weather at sea.

The *Virginia* was the hull of a frigate modified into an iron-clad vessel. She was only suited to smooth water, and it had not been practicable to obtain for her such engines as would have given her the requisite speed. Her draught—twenty-two feet—was too great for the shoal water in the Roads. Her great length, depth, and want of power, caused difficulty in handling to be anticipated. In many respects she was an experiment, and, had we possessed the means to build a new vessel, no doubt a better model could have been devised.

In the morning the *Virginia*, with the *Patrick Henry*, the *Jamestown*, and the three little tugs, jestingly called the "mosquito fleet," returned to the scene of the previous day's combat, and to the completion of the work—the destruction of the *Minnesota*—which, the evening before, had been interrupted by the change of tide and the coming of night. The *Monitor*, which had been seen by the light of the burning *Congress*, opened fire on the *Virginia* when about the third of a mile distant. The *Virginia* sought to close with her, but the greater speed of the *Monitor*, and the celerity with which she was handled, made this impracticable. The ships passed and repassed very near each other, and the *Virginia* frequently delivered her broadside at close quarters, but with no perceptible effect. The *Monitor* fired rapidly from her revolving turret, but not with such aim as to strike successively in the same place, and the armor of the *Virginia* therefore remained unbroken. Lieutenant-commanding Catesby Jones soon discovered that the *Monitor* was invulnerable to his shells. He determined, therefore, to run her down, and got all the headway he could obtain for that purpose, but the speed was so small that it merely pushed her out of the way. It was then decided to board her, and all hands were piped for that object. Then the *Monitor* slipped away into shoal water, where the *Virginia* could not approach her; and Commander Jones, after waiting a due time, and giving the usual signals of invitation to combat, without receiving any manifestation on the part of the *Monitor* of an intention to return to deep water, withdrew to the navy-yard.

In the two days of conflict our only casualties were from the *Cumberland*, as she went down, valiantly fighting to the last; from the men on shore when the tugs went to the *Congress* to receive her surrender; and from the perfidious fire from the *Congress* while her white flags were flying. None was killed or wounded in the fight with the *Monitor*.

As this was the first combat between two iron-clad vessels, it attracted great attention and provoked much speculation. Some assumed that wooden ships were henceforth to be of no use, and much has been done by the addition of armor to protect sea-going vessels; but certainly neither of the two which provoked the speculation could be regarded as seaworthy or suited to other than harbor defence.

A new prow was put on the *Virginia*, she was furnished with bolts and solid shot, and the slight repairs needed were promptly made. The distinguished veteran, Commodore Josiah Tatnall, was assigned to the command of the *Virginia*, vice Admiral Buchanan, temporarily disabled. The *Virginia* was prepared for battle and for cruising in the Roads, and on the 11th of April Commodore Tatnall moved down to invite the *Monitor* to combat. But her officers kept the *Monitor* close to the shore, with her steam up, and under the guns of Fortress Monroe. To provoke her to come out, the little *Jamestown* was sent in and pluckily captured many prizes; but the *Monitor* lay safe in the shoal water under the guns of the formidable fortress. An English man-of-war, which was lying in the channel, witnessed this effort to draw the *Monitor* out into deep water in defence of her weaker countrymen, and as Barney, on the *Jamestown*, passed with his prizes, cut out in full view of the enemy's fleet, the Englishmen, with their national admiration of genuine "game," as a spectator described it, "unable to restrain their generous impulses, from the captain to the side-boy, cheered our gunboat to the very echo." I quote further from the same witness: "Early in May a magnificent Federal fleet, the *Virginia* being concealed behind the land, had ventured across the channel, and some of them, expressly fitted to destroy our ship, were furiously bombarding our batteries at Sewell's Point. Dashing down comes old Tatnall on the instant, as light-stepping and blithe as a boy. But the *Virginia* no sooner draws into range than the whole fleet, like a flushed covey of birds, flutters off into shoal water and under the guns of the forts"—where they remained. After some delay, and there being no prospect of active service, the commodore. ordered the executive officer to fire a gun to windward and take the ship back to her buoy. Here, waiting for an enemy to engage her, but never having the opportunity, she remained until the 10th of the ensuing month.

Notwithstanding the injury done to it by conflagration, the Norfolk navy-yard was yet the most available and best equipped yard in the Confederacy. A land force under General Huger had been placed there for its protection, and defensive works had been constructed with a view to hold it, as well for naval construction and repair as for its strategic importance in connection with the defence of Richmond. On the opposite side of the lower James, on the peninsula between the James and York Rivers, we occupied an intrenched position of much natural strength. The two positions—Norfolk and the peninsula—were necessary to each other, and the command of the channel between them was essential to both. As long as the *Virginia* closed the entrance to the James River, and the intrenchment on the peninsula was held, it was deemed possible to keep possession of Norfolk.

On the 1st of May General Johnston, commanding on the peninsula, having decided to retreat, sent an order to General Huger to evacuate Norfolk. The Secretary of War—General Randolph—having arrived just at that time in Norfolk, assumed the authority of postponing the execution of the order "until General Huger could remove such stores, munitions, and arms as could be carried off." The Secretary of the Navy—Mr. Mallory—gave like instructions to the commandant of the yard. To the system and energy with which General Huger conducted the removal of heavy guns, machinery, stores, and munitions we were greatly indebted in our future operations, both of construction and defence. A week was thus employed in the removal of machinery, etc.; and the enemy, occupied with the retreating army on the peninsula, did not cross the James River above, either to interrupt the transportation or to obstruct the retreat of the garrisons of the forts at Norfolk and its surroundings.

When our army had been withdrawn from the peninsula, and

Norfolk had been evacuated, and the James River did not furnish depth of channel sufficient for the *Virginia* to ascend it more than a few miles, her mission was ended. It is not surprising that her brilliant career created a great desire to preserve her, and that it was contemplated to lighten her, and thus try to take her up the river; but the pilots declared this to be impracticable, and the court which subsequently investigated the matter sustained their opinion that "the only alternative was then and there to abandon and burn the ship." She could not ascend the river, was unseaworthy, and was uncovered by the retreat of the troops with whom she had co-operated. So, on the 10th of May, the *Virginia* was taken to Craney Island, one mile above, and there her crew landed. They fell in and formed on the beach, and, in the language of an eye-witness, "then and there, on the very field of her fame, within sight of the *Cumberland's* top-gallant masts, within sight of that magnificent fleet still cowering on the shoal, with her laurels all fresh and green, we hauled down her drooping colors, and, with mingled pride and grief, we gave her to the flames."

At Wilmington, N. C., the Southwest bar was defended by Fort Caswell, and New Inlet bar by Fort Fisher. The naval defences consisted of two ironclads, the *North Carolina* and the *Raleigh*. The *North Carolina* could not cross any of the bars in consequence of her draught of water. Her steam-power hardly gave propulsion. She sank, during the war, off Smithville. The *Raleigh's* services were almost valueless in consequence of her deep draught and her feeble steam-power. She made one futile trip out of New Inlet, and, after a few hours, attempted to return, but was wrecked upon the bar.

The brave and invincible defence of Fort Sumter gave to the city of Charleston, S. C., additional lustre. For nearly four years that fort covered its harbor, defying the army and navy of the United States.

When the city was about to be abandoned to the army of General Sherman, the forts defending the harbor were embraced in General Hardee's plan of evacuation.

On the 17th of February, 1865, Captain Huguenin, with about 300 war-worn soldiers, retired, in obedience to the order of their commanding general. Then, after its brave defenders had been withdrawn, Fort Sumter, left alone with its record of glory, passed into the possession of the enemy, its battle-scarred walls showing how faithfully it had served the purpose for which South Carolina had granted the site.

In 1863, or 1864, the gallant commander of that fort, Colonel Stephen Elliott, Jr., had been under continuous bombardment, day and night, for so long a period that it was supposed he might be exhausted, and he was invited to retire temporarily for rest. With unyielding fortitude he declined, and remained at his post until he was promoted and transferred to duty more appropriate to the higher grade.

The naval force of the Confederacy in Charleston Harbor consisted of three ironclads. Their steam-power was totally inadequate for the effective use of the vessels. In fact, when the wind and tide were moving in the same direction it was impossible for the vessels to advance against them, light though the wind might be. Under such circumstances it was necessary to come to an anchor. On one occasion the ironclads *Palmetto State* and *Chicora* ran out of Charleston under favorable circumstances. The *Palmetto State* assaulted the *Mercidata*, commanded by Captain Stellwagen, who unconditionally surrendered. But the ironclad was under orders to follow her consort in chase of the enemy, and, having no boats in which to transfer her prisoners, the parole of the officers and men was accepted, with their promise to observe the same until its return. The surrender was accepted, an honest parole being the consideration for not being sunk on the spot. Captain Stellwagen abided but a short time, when, getting up steam, he broke his plighted word and ran off with the captured vessel. The deficiency of speed on the part of the Confederate ironclads frustrated their efforts to relieve the city of Charleston from continued blockade.

The harbor defences of Savannah were intrusted to Commodore Tatnall, who defended the approach to the city with a small steamer of one gun, an inefficient floating battery, and an ironclad, which had been constructed from a blockade-runner. Several attempts were made to attack the enemy's vessels with the ironclad, but these were frustrated by the delay in opening a passage through the obstructions in the river when tide and opportunity offered. Her draught was too great for the depth of water, except at high tides, and these were at long intervals. The ironclad was armed with a battery of four guns—two 7-inch and two 6-inch. Her force consisted of some twenty-one officers and twenty-four men, when she was fully furnished. Another vessel was under construction and nearly completed, and Commodore Tatnall, notwithstanding his well-known combative instincts, was understood to be unwilling to send the *Atlanta* alone against the enemy's blockading vessels. Lieutenant Webb, who had been lately placed in command of the *Atlanta*, took her to Warsaw Sound to deliver battle singly to the two ironclads *Weehawken* and *Nahant*, which awaited her approach. The *Atlanta* got twice aground—the second time inextricably so. In this situation she was attacked, and, though hopelessly, was bravely defended, but was finally forced to surrender.

Mobile Harbor was thought to be adequately provided for, as torpedoes obstructed the approach, and Forts Morgan and Gaines commanded the entrance, aided by the improvised fleet of Admiral Buchanan, which consisted of the wooden gunboats *Morgan* and *Gaines*, each carrying six guns, and *Selma*, four guns, with the ram *Tennessee* of six guns—in all, twenty-two guns and four hundred and seventy men. On August 4, 1864, Fort Gaines was assaulted by the United States force from the sea side of the beach. The resistance made was feeble, and the fort was soon surrendered. On the next day Admiral Farragut stood into the bay with a force consisting of four monitors, or ironclads, and fourteen steamers, carrying one hundred and ninety-nine guns and twenty-seven hundred men. One ironclad was sunk by a torpedo. Admiral Buchanan advanced to meet this force, and sought to run into the larger vessels with the *Tennessee*, but they avoided him by their superior speed. Meanwhile the gunboats became closely engaged with the enemy, but were soon dispersed by his overwhelming force. The *Tennessee* again stood for the enemy, and renewed the attack with the hope of sinking some of them with her prow, but she was again foiled by their superior speed in avoiding her. The engagement with the whole fleet soon became general, and lasted an hour. Frequently the *Tennessee* was surrounded by the enemy, and all her guns were in action almost at the same moment. Four of their heaviest vessels ran into her, under full steam, with the view of sinking her. While surrounded by six of these heavy vessels, which were suffering fearfully from her heavy battery, the steering-gear of the *Tennessee* was shot away, and her ability to manœuvre was completely destroyed, leaving the formidable Confederate entirely at the disposal of the enemy. This misfortune, it was believed, saved the greater part of Farragut's fleet. Further resistance becoming unavailable, the wounded Admiral was under the painful necessity of ordering a surrender. His little fleet became a prey to the enemy, except the *Morgan*, which made good her escape to Mobile.

This unequal contest was decidedly creditable to the Confederacy. The entire loss of the enemy, most of which was ascribed to the *Tennessee*, amounted to quite three hundred in killed and wounded, exclusive of one hundred lost on the sunken ironclad, making a number almost as large as the entire Confederate force. On August 22nd Fort Morgan was bombarded from the land, also by ironclads at sea, and by the fleet inside. Thus Forts Powel, Morgan, and Gaines shared the fate of the Confederate fleet, and the enemy became masters of the bay. On this as on other occasions, the want of engines of sufficient power constituted a main obstacle to the success which the gallantry and skill of the seamen so richly deserved.

The system of torpedoes adopted by us was probably more effective than any other means of naval defence. The destructiveness of these little weapons had long been known, but no successful modes for their application to the destruction of the most powerful vessels of war and ironclads had been devised. It remained for the skill and ingenuity of our officers to bring the use of this terrible instrument to perfection. The success of their efforts is very frankly stated by one of the most distinguished of the enemy's commanders—Admiral Porter.[107] He says:

> "Most of the Southern seaports fell into our possession with comparative facility, and the difficulty of capturing Charleston, Savannah, Wilmington, and Mobile was in a measure owing to the fact that the approaches to these places were filled with various kinds of torpedoes, laid in groups, and fired by electricity. The introduction of this means of defence on the side of the Confederates was for a time a severe check to our naval forces, for the commanders of squadrons felt it their duty to be careful when dealing with an element of warfare of which they knew so little, and the character and disposition of which it was so difficult to discover. In this system of defence, therefore, the enemy found their greatest security; and, notwithstanding all the efforts of Du Pont and Dahlgren, Charleston, Wilmington, and Savannah remained closed to our forces until near the close of the war."

---

107. See "Torpedo Warfare," in *North American Review*, September, October, 1878.

In 1862, while General McClellan was in command of the enemy's forces below Richmond, it was observed that they had more than a hundred vessels in the James River, as if they were about to make an advance by that way upon the city. This led to an order placing General G. J. Rains in charge of the submarine defences; and, on the James River, opposite Drewry's Bluff, the first submarine torpedo was made. The secret of all his future success consisted in the sensitive primer, which is unrivalled by any other means to explode torpedoes or subterra shells on undefended lines of approach.

The torpedoes were made of the most ordinary materials generally, such as beer-barrels fixed with conical heads, coated within and without with rosin dissolved in coal-tar; some were made of cast-iron, copper, or tin; and glass demijohns were used. There were three essentials to success, viz., the sensitive fuse-primer, a charge of sixty pounds of gunpowder, and actual contact between the torpedo and the bottom of the vessel.

There were 123 marine torpedoes placed in Charleston Harbor and Stono River. It was blockaded by 13 large ships and ironclads, with 6 or 7 store-ships, and some 20 other vessels. The position of each one was known, and they could be approached within a half-mile, which made it easy to attack, destroy, or disperse them at night by floating torpedoes, connected together by twos by a rope 130 yards long, buoyed up and stretched across the current by two boats, which were to be dropped during ebbing tide, to float down among the vessels.

One hundred and one torpedoes were planted in Roanoke River, N. C., after a flotilla of twelve vessels had started up to capture Fort Branch. The torpedoes destroyed six of the vessels and frustrated the attack.

Every avenue to the outworks or to the city of Mobile was guarded by submarine torpedoes, so that it was impossible for any vessel drawing three feet of water to get within effective cannon-range of the defences. Two ironclads attempted to get near enough to Spanish Fort to take part in the bombardment. They both struck torpedoes, and went to the bottom on Apalachie bar; thenceforward the fleet made no further attempt to encounter the almost certain destruction they saw awaited any vessel which might attempt to enter the torpedo-guarded waters. But many were sunk when least expecting it. Some went down long after the Confederate forces had evacuated Mobile. The *Tecumseh* was probably sunk, says Major-General D. H. Maury, on her own torpedo. While steaming in lead of Farragut's fleet she carried a torpedo affixed to a spar, which projected some twenty feet from her bows; she proposed to use this torpedo against the *Tennessee*, our only formidable ship; but, while passing Fort Morgan, a shot from that fort cut away the stays by which the torpedo was secured; it then doubled under her, and, exploding fairly under the bottom of the ill-fated ship, she careened and sank instantly in ten fathoms of water. Only six or eight of her crew of a hundred or more were saved.

The total number of vessels sunk by torpedoes in Mobile Bay was twelve, viz., three ironclads, two tinclads, and seven transports. Fifty-eight vessels were destroyed in Southern waters by torpedoes during the war; these included ironclads and others of no mean celebrity.

Chapter 55

Confederate Naval Operations in the West

NEW ORLEANS was the most important commercial port in the Confederacy, being the natural outlet of the Mississippi Valley, as well to the ports of Europe as to those of Central and Southern America. It had become before 1861 the chief cotton-mart of the United States, and its defence attracted the early attention of the Confederate Government. The approaches for an attacking party were numerous. They could through several channels enter Lake Pontchartrain, to approach the city in rear for land attack, could ascend the Mississippi from the Gulf or descend it from the northwest, where it was known that the enemy was preparing a formidable fleet of iron-clad gunboats,

At the mouth of the Mississippi there is a bar, the greatest depth of water on which seldom exceeded eighteen feet, and it was supposed that heavy vessels of war, with their armament and supplies, would not be able to cross it. Such proved to be the fact, and the vessels of that class had to be lightened to enable them to enter the river. In that condition of affairs an inferior fleet might have engaged them with a prospect of success. Captain Hollins, who was in command of the squadron at New Orleans, had been sent with the greater part of his fleet up the river to join in the defence there being made. Two powerful vessels were under construction—the *Louisiana* and the *Mississippi*—but neither of them was finished. A volunteer fleet of transport-vessels had been fitted up by some river men, but it was in the unfortunate condition of not being placed under the orders of the naval commander. A number of fire-rafts had been also provided, which were to serve the double purpose of lighting up the river in the event of the hostile fleet attempting to pass the forts under cover of the night, and of setting fire to any vessel with which they might come in contact.

After passing the bar there was nothing to prevent the ascent of the river until Forts Jackson and St. Philip were reached. These works were on opposite banks of the river. Their armament, December 5, 1861, consisted of—Fort Jackson: six 42-pounders, twenty-six 24-pounders, two 32-pounders (rifles), sixteen 32-pounders, three 8-inch columbiads, one 10-inch columbiad, two 8-inch mortars, one 10-inch mortar, two 40-pounder howitzers, and ten 24-pounder howitzers; Fort St. Philip: six 42-pounders, nine 32-pounders, twenty-two 24-pounders, four 8-inch columbiads, one 8-inch mortar, one 10-inch mortar, and three field-guns.

General Duncan reported that on March 27th he was informed that the enemy's fleet was crossing the bars and entering the Mississippi River in force; whereupon he repaired to Fort Jackson.

The garrisons of Forts Jackson and St. Philip were about one thousand men on December 5, 1861; afterward, so far as I know, the number was not materially changed.

The prevailing belief that vessels of war, in a straight, smooth channel, could pass batteries, led to the construction of a raft between the two forts, which, it was supposed, would detain the ships under fire of the forts long enough for the guns to sink them, or at least to compel them to retire. The power of the river when in flood, and the drift-wood it bore upon it, broke the raft; another was constructed, which, when the drift-wood accumulated upon it, met a like fate.

The general plan for the defence of New Orleans consisted of two lines of works; an exterior one, passing through the forts near the mouth of the river, and the positions taken to defend the various water approaches. Nearer to the city was the interior line, embracing New Orleans and Algiers, which was intended principally to repel an attack by land, but also, by its batteries on the river-bank, to resist approach by water. The total length of the intrenchments on this interior line was more than eight miles. When completed, it formed, in connection with impassable swamps, a very strong line of defence. At the then high stage of the river all the land between it and the swamps was so saturated with water that regular approaches could not have been made. The city, therefore, was at the time supposed to be doubly secure from a land attack.

In the winter of 1861-62 I sent one of my aides-de-camp to New Orleans to make a general inspection, and hold free conference with the commanding general. Upon his return he reported that General Lovell was quite satisfied with the condition of the land defences.

The interior lines of defence mounted more than sixty guns of various calibre, and were surrounded by wide and deep ditches. On the various water approaches, including bays and bayous on both sides of the river, there were sixteen different forts, and these, together with those on the river, and the batteries of the interior line, had in position about three hundred guns.

One ironclad, the *Louisiana*, mounting sixteen guns of heavy calibre, though she was not quite completed, was sent down to co-operate with the forts. Her defective steam-power and imperfect steering apparatus prevented her from rendering active co-operation. The steamship *Mississippi*, then under construction at New Orleans, was in such an unfinished condition as to be wholly unavailable when the enemy arrived. There were also several small river-steamers which were lightly armed, and their bows were protected so that they could act as rams, and otherwise aid in the defence of the river; but, from the reports received, they seem, with a few honorable exceptions, to have rendered little service.

The means of defence, therefore, mainly relied on were the two heavy-armed forts, Jackson and St. Philip, with the obstruction placed between them: this was a raft consisting of cypress-trees, forty feet long, and averaging four or five feet at the larger end. They were placed longitudinally in the river, about three feet apart, and held together by gunwales on top, and strung upon two two-and-a-half-inch chain-cables fastened to their lower sides. This raft was anchored in the river, abreast of the forts.

The fleet of the enemy below the forts consisted of seven steam sloops-of-war, twelve gunboats, and several armed steamers, under Commodore Farragut; also, a mortar fleet consisting of twenty sloops and some steam-vessels. The whole force was forty-odd vessels of different kinds, with an armament of three hundred guns of heavy calibre, of improved models.

The bombardment of the forts by the mortar fleet commenced on April 18th. After six days of vigorous and constant shelling the resisting power of the forts was not diminished in any perceptible degree. On the 23rd there were manifest preparations by the enemy to attempt the passage of the forts. The sloops-of-war and the gunboats were each formed in two divisions, and, selecting the darkest hour of the night, between 3 and 4 A.M. of the 24th, moved up the river in two columns. The commanders of the forts had vainly endeavored to have the river lighted up in anticipation of an attack by the fleet.

In the meantime, while the fleet moved up the river, there was kept up from the mortars a steady bombardment on the forts, and these replied by a fire on the ascending columns of ships and gunboats; but, from the failure to send down the fire-rafts to light up the river, the fire was less effective than it otherwise would have been. The straight, deep channel enabled the vessels to move at their greatest speed, and thus the forts were passed.

Brigadier-General J. K. Duncan, commanding the coast defences, says, in his report of the passing of Forts Jackson and St. Philip by the enemy's fleet:

> "Finding that the only resistance offered to his passage was the anticipated fire of the forts—the broken and scattered raft being no obstacle—I am satisfied that he was suddenly inspired, for the first time, to run the gauntlet at all hazards, although not a part of his original design. Be that as it may, a rapid rush was made by him in columns of twos in echelon, so as not to interfere with each other's broadsides. The mortar fire was furiously increased upon Fort Jackson, and, in dashing by, each of the vessels delivered broadside after broadside, of shot, shell, grape, canister, and spherical case, to drive the men from our guns.
>
> "Both the officers and men stood up gallantly under this galling and fearful hail, and the batteries of both forts were promptly opened at their longest range, with shot, shell, hot shot, and a little grape, and most gallantly and rapidly fought until the enemy succeeded in getting above and beyond the range. The absence of light on the river, together with the smoke of the guns, made the obscurity so dense that scarcely a vessel was visible, and in consequence the gunners were obliged to govern their firing entirely by flashes of the enemy's guns. I am fully satisfied that the enemy's dash was successful mainly owing to the cover of darkness, as a frigate and several gunboats were forced to retire as day was breaking. Similar results had attended every previous attempt made by the enemy to pass or to reconnoitre when we had sufficient light

to fire with accuracy and effect."

The vessels which passed the forts anchored at the quarantine station about six miles above, and in the forenoon proceeded up the river. Batteries had been constructed where the interior line of defence touched both the right and the left bank of the river. The high stage of the river gave to its surface an elevation above that of the natural bank; but a continuous levee to protect the land from inundation existed on both sides of the river. When the ascending fleet approached these batteries, a cross fire, which drove two of the vessels back, was opened upon it, and continued until the useful ammunition was exhausted. The garrisons were then withdrawn—casualties, one killed and one wounded.

General Duncan, whose protracted, skilful, and gallant defence of the forts is above all praise, closes his official report with the following sentence: "Except for the cover afforded by the obscurity of the darkness, I shall always remain satisfied that the enemy would never have succeeded in passing Forts Jackson and St. Philip." The darkness to which he referred was not only that of night, but also the failure to utilize the means prepared to light up the river. As further proof of the intensity of the darkness, and the absence of that intelligent design and execution which had been expected, I will quote a sentence from the report of Commodore Farragut: "At length the fire slackened, the smoke cleared off, and we saw to our surprise that we were above the forts."

On the 25th of April the enemy's gunboats and ships of war anchored in front of the city and demanded its surrender. Major-General M. Lovell, in command, refused to comply, but, believing himself unable to make a successful defence, and in order to avoid a bombardment, agreed to withdraw his forces, and turn the city over to the civil authorities. It was evacuated on the same day. The forts still continued defiantly to hold their position. By assiduous exertion the damage done to the works was repaired, and the garrisons valiantly responded to the resolute determination of General Duncan and Colonel Higgins to defend the forts against the fleet still below, as well as against that which had passed and was now above.

During the 25th, 26th, and 27th there was an abatement of fire on the forts. A rumor became current that the city had surrendered, and no reply had been received to inquiries sent on the 24th and 25th. About midnight on the 27th the garrison of Fort Jackson revolted *en masse*, seized upon the guard, and commenced to spike the guns. Captain S. O. Comay's company, the Louisiana Cannoneers of St. Mary's Parish, and a few others remained true to their cause and country. The mutiny was so general that the officers were powerless to control it, and they therefore decided to let those go who wished to leave, and after daybreak to communicate with the fleet below and negotiate for the terms which had been previously offered and declined.

Under the incessant fire to which the forts had been exposed, and the rise of the water in the casemates and lower part of the works, the men had been not only deprived of sleep, but of the opportunity to prepare their food. Heroically they had braved alike dangers and discomfort; had labored constantly to repair damages; to extinguish fires caused by exploding shells; to preserve their ammunition by bailing out the water which threatened to submerge the magazine; yet, in a period of comparative repose, these men, who had been cheerful and obedient, as suddenly as unexpectedly broke out into mutiny. Under the circumstances which surrounded him, General Duncan had no alternative. It only remained for him to accept the proposition which had been made for a surrender of the forts. As this mutiny became known about midnight of the 27th, soon after daylight of the 28th a small boat was procured, and notice of the event was sent to Captain Mitchell, on the *Louisiana*, and also to Fort St. Philip. The officers of that fort concurred in the propriety of the surrender, though none of their men had openly revolted.

A flag of truce was sent to Commodore Porter to notify him of a willingness to negotiate for the surrender of the forts. The gallantry with which the defence had been conducted was recognized by the enemy, and the terms were as liberal as had been offered on former occasions.

The garrisons were paroled, the officers were to retain their side-arms, and the Confederate flags were left flying over the forts until after our forces had withdrawn. If this was done as a generous recognition of the gallantry with which the forts had been defended, it claims acknowledgment as an instance of martial courtesy—the flower that blooms fairest amid the desolations of war.

Captain Mitchell, commanding the Confederate States naval forces, had been notified by General Duncan of the mutiny in the forts, and of the fact that the enemy had passed through a channel in rear of Fort St. Philip and had landed a force at the quarantine, some six miles above, and that, under the circumstances, it was deemed necessary to surrender the forts. As the naval forces were not under the orders of the general commanding the coast defences, it was optional with the naval commander to do likewise, or not, as to his fleet. After consultation with his officers, Captain Mitchell decided to destroy his flagship, the *Louisiana*, the only formidable vessel he had, rather than allow her to fall into the hands of the enemy. The crew was accordingly withdrawn, and the vessel set on fire.

Commodore Porter, commanding the fleet below, came up under a flag of truce to Fort Jackson, and, while negotiations were progressing for the surrender, the *Louisiana*, in flames, drifted down the river, and, when close under Fort St. Philip, exploded and sank.

The confusion which prevailed in the city, when the news arrived that the forts had been passed by the enemy's fleet, shows how little it was expected. There was nothing to obstruct the ascent of the river between Forts Jackson and St. Philip, up to the batteries on the river where the interior line of defence rested on its right and left banks, about four miles below the city. The guns were not sufficiently numerous in these batteries to inspire much confidence; they were nevertheless well served until the available ammunition was exhausted, after which the garrisons withdrew, and made their way by different routes to join the forces withdrawn from New Orleans.

Under the supposition entertained by the generals nearest to the operations, the greatest danger to New Orleans was from above, not below the city; therefore, most of the troops had been sent from the city to Tennessee, and Captain Hollins, with the greater part of the river-fleet, had gone up to check the descent of the enemy's gunboats.

Batteries like those immediately below the city had been constructed where the interior line touched the river above, and armed to resist an attack from that direction. Doubtful as to the direction from which, and the manner in which, an attempt might be made to capture the city, such preparations as circumstances suggested were made against many supposable dangers by the many possible routes of approach. To defend the city from the land, against a bombardment by a powerful fleet in the river before it, had not been contemplated. All the defensive preparations were, properly, I think, directed to the prevention of a near approach by the enemy. To have subjected the city to bombardment by a direct or plunging fire, as the surface of the river was then higher than the land, would have been exceptionally destructive. Had the city been filled with soldiers whose families had been sent to a place of safety, instead of being filled with women and children whose natural protectors were generally in the army and far away, the attempt might have been justified to line the levee with all the effective guns and open fire on the fleet, at the expense of whatever property might be destroyed before the enemy should be driven away. The case was the reverse of the hypothesis, and nothing could have been more unjust than to censure the commanding general for withdrawing a force large enough to induce a bombardment, but insufficient to repel it. His answer to the demand for the surrender showed clearly enough the motives by which he was influenced. His refusal enabled him to withdraw the troops and most of the public property, and to use them, with the ordnance stores thus saved, in providing for the defence of Vicksburg; but especially it deprived the enemy of any pretext for bombarding the town and sacrificing the lives of women and children. It has been stated that General Lovell called for ten thousand volunteers from the citizens, but failed to get them.

The fall of New Orleans was a great disaster, over which there was general lamentation, mingled with no little indignation. The excited feeling demanded a victim, and the conflicting testimony of many witnesses most nearly concerned made it convenient to select for censure those most removed and least active in their own justification. Thus the naval constructors of the *Mississippi* and the Secretary of the Navy became the special objects of attack. The selection of these had little of justice in it, and could not serve to relieve others of their responsibility, as did the old-time doom of the scapegoat. New Orleans had never been a ship-building port, and when the Messrs. Tift, the agents to build the iron-clad steamer *Mississippi*, arrived there, they had to prepare a ship-yard, procure lumber from a distance, have the foundries and rolling-mills adapted to such iron-work as could be done in the city, and contract elsewhere for the balance. They were ingenious, well informed in matters of ship-building, and were held in high esteem in Georgia and Florida, where they had long resided. They submitted a proposition to the Secretary of the Navy to build a vessel on a new model. The proposition was accepted after full examination of the plan proposed, the novelty of which made it necessary that they should have full control of the work of construction. To the embarrassments above mentioned were added interruptions by calling off the workmen occasionally for exercise and instruction as militiamen, the city being threatened by the enemy. From these causes unexpected delay in the completion of the ship resulted, regret for which increased as her most formidable character was realized.

These constructors—the brothers Tift—hoped to gain much reputation by the ship which they designed, and, from this motive, agreed to give their full service and unremitted attention in its construction without compensation or other allowance than their current expenses. It would, therefore, on the face of it, seem to have been a most absurd suspicion that they willingly delayed the completion of the vessel, and at last wantonly destroyed it.

Mr. E. C. Murray, who was the contractor for building the *Louisiana*, in his testimony before a committee of the Confederate Congress, testified that he had been a practical shipbuilder for twenty years, and a contractor for the preceding eighteen years, having built about a hundred and twenty boats, steamers, and sailing-vessels. There was only a fence between his ship-yard and that where the *Mississippi* was constructed. Of this latter vessel he said: "I think the vessel was built in less time than any vessel of her tonnage, character, and requiring the same amount of work and materials, on this continent. . . . They worked on nights and Sundays upon her, as I did upon the *Louisiana*, at least for a large portion of the time."

On March 22nd the Secretary, by telegraph, directed the constructors to "strain every nerve to finish the ship," and added, "work day and night." April 5th he wrote again: "Spare neither men nor money to complete her at the earliest moment. Can you not hire night-gangs for triple wages?" April 10th the Secretary again says: "Enemy's boats have passed Island 10. Work day and night, with all the force you can command, to get the *Mississippi* ready. Spare neither men nor money." April 11th he asks, "When will you launch, and when will she be ready for action?" These inquiries indicate the prevalent opinion, at that time, that the danger to New Orleans was from the iron-clad fleet above, and not from the vessels at the mouth of the river; but the anxiety of the Secretary of the Navy, and the efforts made by him, were of a character applicable to either or both sources of danger. Thus we find, as early as the 24th of February, 1862, that he instructed Commander Mitchell to make all proper exertions to have guns and carriages ready for both the iron-clad vessels, the *Mississippi* and *Louisiana*. Reports having reached him that the work on the latter vessel was not pushed with sufficient energy, on the 15th of March he authorized Commander Mitchell to consult with General Lovell, and, if the contractors were not doing everything practicable to complete her at the earliest moment, that he should take her out of their hands, and, with the aid of General Lovell, go on to complete her himself. On the 5th of April, 1862, Secretary Mallory instructed Commander Sinclair, who had been assigned to the command of the *Mississippi*, to urge on by night and day the completion of the ship. In March, 1861, the Navy Department sent from Montgomery officers to New Orleans, with instructions to purchase steamers and fit them for war purposes. Officers were also sent to the North to purchase vessels suited to such uses, and another to Europe for like objects; and in April, 1861, contracts were made with foundries at Richmond and New Orleans to make guns for the defence of New Orleans. On the 8th of May, 1861, the Secretary of the Navy communicated at some length to the Committee on Naval Affairs of the Confederate Congress his views in favor of iron-clad vessels, arguing as well for their efficiency as the economy in building them, believing that one such vessel could successfully engage a fleet of the wooden vessels which constituted the enemy's navy.

CHAPTER 56

NAVAL AFFAIRS IN THE WEST

AFTER the troops had been withdrawn and the city restored to the administration of the civil authorities, Commodore Farragut, on April 26, 1862, addressed the Mayor, repeating his demand for the surrender of the city. In his letter he said: "It is not within the province of a naval officer to assume the duties of a military commandant," and added: "The rights of persons and property shall be secured." He proceeded then to demand "that the emblem of sovereignty of the United States be hoisted over the City Hall, Mint, and Custom-house by meridian this day. All flags and other emblems of sovereignty other than those of the United States must be removed from all the public buildings by that hour." To this the Mayor, John T. Monroe, replied, and the following extracts convey the general purport of his letter:

> "The city is without the means of defence, and is utterly destitute of the force and material that might enable it to resist an overpowering armament displayed in sight of it. . . . To surrender such a place were an idle and unmeaning ceremony. . . . As to hoisting any flag other than the flag of our own adoption and allegiance, let me say to you that the man lives not in our midst whose hand and heart would not be paralyzed at the mere thought of such an act; nor could I find in my entire constituency so wretched and desperate a renegade as would dare to profane with his hand the sacred emblem of our aspirations. . . . Peace and order may be preserved without resort to measures which I could not at this moment prevent. Your occupying the city does not transfer allegiance from the government of their choice to one which they have deliberately repudiated, and they yield the obedience which the conqueror is entitled to extort from the conquered."

On the 29th of April Admiral Farragut adopted the alternative presented by the answer of the Mayor, and sent a detachment of marines to hoist the United States flag over the Custom-house, and to pull down the Confederate flag from the staff on the City Hall. An officer and some marines remained at the Custom-house to guard the United States flag hoisted over it until the land forces under General Butler arrived.

On the 1st of May General Butler took possession of the defenceless city; then followed the reign of terror, pillage, and a long train of infamies, too disgraceful to be remembered without a sense of shame by anyone who is proud of the American name.

Had the population of New Orleans been vagrant and riotous the harsh measures adopted might have been excused, though nothing could have justified the barbarities which were practised; but, notable as the city had always been for freedom from tumult, and occupied as it then was mainly by women and children, nothing can extenuate the wanton insults and outrages heaped upon them. That those not informed of the character of the citizens may the better comprehend it, a brief reference is made to its history.

When Canada, then a French colony, was conquered by Great Britain, many of the inhabitants of greatest influence and highest cultivation, in a spirit of loyalty to their flag, migrated to the wilds of Louisiana. Some of them established themselves in and about New Orleans, and their numerous descendants formed, down to a late period, the controlling element in the body politic. Even after they had ceased, because of large immigration, to control in the commercial and political affairs of the city, their social standard was still the rule. No people were more characterized by refinement, courtesy, and chivalry. Of their keen susceptibility the Mayor informed Commodore Farragut in his correspondence with that officer.

When the needy barbarians of the upper plains of Asia descended upon the classic fields of Italy, their atrocities were such as shocked the common sense of humanity; but, if anyone shall inquire minutely into the conduct of Butler and his followers at New Orleans, he will find there a history yet more revolting. A graphic and full description of the atrocities perpetrated may be found in the "Decades of Louisiana," a work of an eye-witness, published in New Orleans by Alexander Walker.

On May 17, 1862, Captain Eagle, United States Navy, commanding the naval forces before Galveston, summoned it to surrender, "to prevent the effusion of blood and the destruction of property which would result from the bombardment of the town," adding that the land and naval forces would appear in a few days. The reply was, that "when the land and naval forces made their appearance the demand would be answered." The harbor and town of Galveston were not prepared to resist a bombardment, and, under the advice of General Hébert, the citizens remained quiet, resolved, when the enemy should attempt to penetrate the interior, to resist his march at every point. This condition remained without any material change until the 8th of the following October, when Commander Renshaw, with a fleet of gunboats consisting of the *Westfield*, *Harriet Lane*, *Owasco*, *Clifton*, and some transports, approached so near the city as to command it with his guns. Upon a signal the mayor *pro tem.* came off to the flag-ship and informed Commander Renshaw that the military and civil authorities, by a meeting of citizens, had chosen him to act as mayor, and that he had come for the purpose of learning the intentions of the naval commander. In reply he was informed that there was no purpose to interfere with the municipal affairs of the city; that Commander Renshaw did not intend to occupy it before the arrival of a military commander, but that he intended to hoist the United States flag upon the public buildings, and claim that it should be respected. The acting mayor informed him that persons over whom he had no control might take down the flag, and he could not guarantee that it should be respected. Commander Renshaw replied that, to avoid any difficulty like that which occurred in New Orleans, he would send with the flag a sufficient force to protect it, and would not keep the flag flying for more than a quarter or half an hour.

The vessels of the fleet were assigned to positions commanding the town and the bridge which connected the island with the mainland, and a battalion of Massachusetts volunteers was posted on one of the wharves.

Late in 1862 General John B. Magruder, a skilful and knightly soldier, who had at an earlier period of the year rendered distinguished service by his defence of the peninsula between the James and York Rivers, Va., was assigned to the command of the Department of Texas. On his arrival he found the enemy in possession of the principal port—Galveston—and other points on the coast. He promptly collected the scattered arms and field artillery, had a couple of ordinary high-pressure steamboats used in the transportation of cotton on Buffalo Bayou protected with cotton-bales piled from the main deck to and above the hurricane-roof; and these, under the command of Captain Leon Smith, of the Texas Navy, in co-operation with the volunteers, were relied upon to recapture the harbor and island of Galveston. Between night and morning on the 1st of January, 1863, the land forces entered the town and the steamboats came into the bay, manned by Texas cavalry and volunteer artillery. The field artillery was run down to the shore and opened fire upon the boats. The battalion of the enemy having torn up the plank of the wharf, our infantry could only approach them by wading through the water, and climbing upon the wharf. The two steamboats attacked the *Harriet Lane*, the gunboat lying farthest up the bay. They were both so frail in their construction that their only chance was to close and board. One of them was soon disabled by collision with the strong vessel, and in a sinking condition ran into shoal water. The other closed with the *Harriet Lane*, boarded and captured the vessel. The flag-ship, *Westfield*, got aground and could not be got off. General Magruder then sent a demand that the enemy's vessels should surrender except one, on which the crews of all should leave the harbor, giving until ten o'clock for compliance with his demand, to enforce which he put a crew on the *Harriet Lane*, then the most efficient vessel afloat of the enemy's fleet, and, while waiting for an answer, ceased firing. Commander Renshaw refused to accede to the proposition, directing the commander of the *Clifton* to get all the vessels, including the *Corypheus* and *Sachem*, which had recently joined, out of port as soon as possible, and stating that he would blow up the *Westfield*, and leave on the transports lying near him with his officers and crew. In attempting to execute this purpose Commander Renshaw and ten or fifteen others perished soon after leaving the ship, in consequence of the explosion being premature. The general commanding made the following preliminary report:

> "HEAD-QUARTERS, GALVESTON, TEXAS. This morning, the 1st of January, at three o'clock, I attacked the enemy's fleet and garrison at this place, captured, the latter and the steamer *Harriet Lane*, two barges, and a schooner. The rest, some four or five, escaped ignominiously under cover of a flag of truce. I have about

six hundred prisoners and a large quantity of valuable stores, arms, etc. The *Harriet Lane* is very little injured. She was carried by boarders from two high-pressure cotton steamers, manned by Texas cavalry and artillery. The line troops were gallantly commanded by Colonel Green, of Sibley's brigade, and the ships and artillery by Major Leon Smith, to whose indomitable energy and heroic daring the country is indebted for the successful execution of a plan which I had considered for the destruction of the enemy's fleet. Colonel Bagby, of Sibley's brigade, also commanded the volunteers from his regiment for the naval expedition, in which every officer and every man won for himself imperishable renown. J. BANKEAD MAGRUDER, Major-General."

The conduct of Commander Renshaw toward the inhabitants of Galveston had been marked by moderation and propriety, and the closing act of his life was one of manly courage and fidelity to the flag he bore.

Commander Wainright and Lieutenant-commanding Lea, who fell valiantly defending their ship, were buried in the cemetery with the honors of war; thus was evinced that instinctive respect which true warriors always feel for their peers. The surviving officers were paroled.

The capture of the enemy's fleet in Galveston Harbor, by means so novel as to excite surprise as well as grateful admiration, was followed by another victory on the coast of Texas, under circumstances so remarkable as properly to be considered marvellous. To those familiar with the events of that time and section, it is hardly necessary to say that I refer to the battle of Sabine Pass.

The strategic importance to the enemy of the possession of Sabine River caused the organization of a large expedition of land and naval forces to enter and ascend the river. If successful, it gave the enemy short lines for operation against the interior of Texas.

The fleet of the enemy numbered twenty-three vessels. The forces were estimated to be ten thousand men. No adequate provision had been made to resist such a force, and, under the circumstances, none might have been promptly made on which reliance could have been reasonably placed. A few miles above the entrance into the Sabine River a small earthwork had been constructed, garrisoned at the time of the action by forty-two men and two lieutenants, with an armament of six guns. The officers and men were all Irishmen, and the company was called the "Davis Guards," under the command of Lieutenant R. W. Dowling. Wishing to perpetuate the history of an affair, in which, I believe, the brave garrison did more than an equal force had ever elsewhere performed, I quote from the publications of the day the main facts, as they were then printed in the Texas newspapers.

From Captain F. H. Odlum's official report: "I have the honor to report that we had an engagement with the enemy yesterday and gained a handsome victory. We captured two of their gunboats, crippled a third, and drove the rest out of the Pass. We took eighteen fine guns, a quantity of smaller arms, ammunition, and stores, killed about fifty, wounded several, and took one hundred and fifty prisoners, without the loss or injury of anyone on our side, or serious damage to the fort."

From Commodore Leon Smith's official report: "Arriving at the Pass at 3 P.M., I found the enemy off and inside the bar, carrying, as well as I could judge, fifteen thousand men. I proceeded with Captain Odlum to the fort, and found Lieutenant Dowling and Lieutenant N. H. Smith, of the engineer corps, with forty-two men defending the fort. Until 3 P.M. our men did not open on the enemy, as the range was too distant. The officers of the fort coolly held their fire until the enemy had approached near enough to reach them. But, when the enemy arrived within good range, our batteries were opened, and gallantly replied to a galling and most terrific fire from the enemy. As I entered the fort the gunboats *Clifton*, *Arizona*, *Sachem*, and *Granite State*, with several others, came boldly up to within one thousand yards, and opened their batteries, which were gallantly and effectively replied to by the Davis Guards. For one hour and thirty minutes a most terrific bombardment of grape, canister, and shell was directed against our heroic and devoted little band within the fort. The shot struck in every direction, but, thanks be to God! not one of the noble Davis Guards was hurt. Too much credit cannot be awarded Lieutenant Dowling, who displayed the utmost heroism in the discharge of the duty assigned him and the defenders of the fort. The honor of the country was in their hands, and nobly they sustained it. Every man stood at his post, regardless of the murderous fire that was poured upon them from every direction. The result of the battle, which lasted from 3.30 to 5 P.M., was the capturing of the *Clifton* and *Sachem*, eighteen heavy guns, one hundred and fifty prisoners, and the killing and wounding of fifty men, and driving outside the bar the enemy's fleet, comprising twenty-three vessels in all."

The inquiry may naturally arise how this small number of men could take charge of so large a body of prisoners. This required that to their valor they should add stratagem. A few men were placed on the parapet as sentinels, the rest were marched out as guard to receive the prisoners and their arms. Thus was concealed the fact that the fort was empty. The report of the guns bombarding the fort had been heard, and soon after the close of the battle reinforcements arrived, which relieved the little garrison from its embarrassment.

At the commencement of the war the Confederacy was not only without a navy, all the naval vessels possessed by the States having been, as explained elsewhere, left in the hands of our late associates; but worse than this was the fact that ship-building had been almost exclusively done in the Northern States, so that we had no means of acquiring equality in naval power. The numerous deep and wide rivers traversing the Southern States gave a favorable field for the operations of gunboats suited to such circumstances. The enemy rapidly increased their supply of these by building on the Western waters, as well as elsewhere, and converting existing vessels into iron-clad gunboats. The intrepidity and devotion of our people met the necessity by new expedients and extraordinary daring. This was especially seen in the operations in Western Louisiana, where numerous bayous and rivers, with difficult land-routes, gave an advantage to the enemy. which might well have paralyzed anything less than the most resolute will.

One by one successful conflicts between river-boats and gunboats impaired the estimate which had been put upon the latter. The most illustrious example of this was the attack and capture of the *Indianola*, a heavy ironclad, with two 11-inch guns forward, and two 9-inch aft, all in iron casemates. She had passed the batteries at Vicksburg, and was in the section of the river between Vicksburg and Port Hudson, which, in February, 1863, was the only gate of communication which the Confederacy had between the east and west sides of the Mississippi. The importance of keeping open this communication, always great, became vital from the developed necessity of drawing commissary stores from the trans-Mississippi.

Major Brent, of General Taylor's staff, proposed, with the tow-boat

Webb, which had been furnished as a ram, and the *Queen of the West*, which four or five days before had been captured by the land-battery at Fort De Russy, to go to the Mississippi and attack the *Indianola*. On the 19th of February the expedition started, though mechanics were still working upon the repairs of the *Queen of the West*, which were needed because of injuries inflicted at the time of her capture.

The service was so hazardous that only volunteers formed the crews, but of these more offered than were wanted. On the 24th, while ascending the Mississippi, Major Brent learned, when about sixty miles below Vicksburg, that the *Indianola* was a short distance ahead, with a coal-barge lashed on either side. He determined to attack in the night, being assured that, if struck by a shell from one of the 11- or 9-inch guns, either of his boats would be destroyed. At 10 P.M. the *Queen*, followed by the *Webb*, was driven at full speed directly upon the *Indianola*. The momentum of the *Queen* was so great as to cut through the coal-barge, and indent the iron plates of the *Indianola*. As the *Queen* backed out, the *Webb* dashed in at full speed, and tore away the remaining coal-barge. Both the forward guns were fired at the *Webb*, but missed her. Again the *Queen* struck the *Indianola*, abaft the paddle-box, crushing her frame and loosening some plates of armor, but received the fire of the guns from the rear casemates. One shot carried away a dozen bales of cotton on the right side; the other, a shell, entered the forward port-hole and exploded, killing six men and disabling two field-pieces. Again the *Webb* followed the *Queen*, striking the same spot, pushing aside the iron plates, and crushing the timbers. Voices from the *Indianola* announced the surrender, and that she was sinking. The river here sweeps the western shore, and there was deep water up to the bank; General Grant's army was on the west side of the river; and for either or both of these reasons Major Brent towed the *Indianola* to the opposite side, where she sank on a bar, her gun-deck above water. Both boats were much shattered in the conflict, and Major Brent returned to the Red River to repair them. A tender accompanied the *Queen* and the *Webb*, and a frail river-boat, without protection for her boilers, which was met on the river, turned back and followed them, but, like the tender, could be of no service in the battle.

The ram *Arkansas*, which has been previously noticed as being under construction at Memphis, was removed before she was finished to the

Yazoo River, events on the river above having rendered this necessary for her security. After she was considered ready for service, Commander Brown, then as previously in charge of her, went down the Yazoo to enter the Mississippi and proceed to Vicksburg. The enemy's fleet of some twelve or thirteen rams, gunboats, and sloops-of-war were in the river above Vicksburg, but below the point where the Yazoo enters the Mississippi. Anticipating the descent of the *Arkansas*, a detachment had been made from this fleet to prevent her exit. The annexed letter of Commander Brown describes what occurred in the Yazoo River:

> "STEAMER *ARKANSAS*, July 15, 1862. GENERAL: The *Benton*, or whatever ironclad we disabled, was left with colors down, evidently aground to prevent sinking, about one mile and a half above the mouth of the Yazoo (in Old River), on the right-hand bank, or bank across from Vicksburg.
>
> "I wish it to be remembered that we whipped this vessel, made it run out of the fight and haul down colors, with two less guns than they had; and at the same time fought two rams, which were firing at us with great guns and small-arms; this, too, with our miscellaneous crew, who had never for the most part been on board a ship, or at big guns. . . . J. N. BROWN."

When entering the Mississippi the fleet of the enemy was found disposed as a phalanx, but the heroic commander of the *Arkansas* moved directly against it; and though, in passing through this formidable array, he was exposed to the broadsides of the whole fleet, the vessel received no other injury than from one 11-inch shot which entered the gun-room, and the perforation in many places of her smoke-stack. The casualties to the crew were five killed, four wounded; among the latter was the gallant commander. General Van Dorn, commanding the department, in a despatch from Vicksburg, July 15th, states the number of the enemy's vessels above Vicksburg, pays a high compliment to the officers and men, and adds:

> "All the enemy's transports and all the vessels of war of the lower fleet (i.e., the fleet just below Vicksburg), except a sloop-of-war, have got up steam, and are off to escape from the *Arkansas*."

A vessel inspiring such dread is entitled to a special description. She was an iron-clad steamer, one hundred feet in length, her armament ten

Parrott guns, and her crew one hundred men, who had volunteered from the land forces for the desperate service proposed. Her commander had been from his youth in the navy of the United States, and his capacity was such as could well supplement whatever was wanted of naval knowledge in his crew. The care and skill with which the vessel had been constructed were tested and proved under fire. Had her engines been equal to the hull and armor of the vessel, it is difficult to estimate the value of the service she might have performed. At this period the enemy occupied Baton Rouge, with gunboats lying in front of it to co-operate with the troops in the town. The importance of holding a section of the Mississippi, so as to keep free communication, has been heretofore noticed. To this end it was deemed needful to recover possession of Baton Rouge, and it was decided to make a land attack in co-operation with the *Arkansas*, to be sent down against the enemy's fleet.

Major-General J. C. Breckinridge was assigned to the command of the land forces. This distinguished citizen and alike distinguished soldier, surmounting difficulties which would have discouraged a less resolute spirit, approached Baton Rouge, and moved to the attack at the time indicated for the arrival of the *Arkansas*. In his address to the officers and soldiers of his command, after the battle, viz., on August 6, 1862, he complimented the troops on the fortitude with which they had borne a severe march, on the manner in which they attacked the enemy, superior in numbers and admirably posted, drove him from his positions, taking his camps, and forcing him to seek protection under cover of the guns of his fleet. Major-General Breckinridge attributed his failure to achieve entire success to the inability of the *Arkansas* to co-operate with his forces, and adds:

> "You have given the enemy a severe and salutary lesson, and now those who so lately were ravaging and plundering this region do not care to extend their pickets beyond the sight of their fleet."

The *Arkansas* in descending the river moved leisurely, having ample time to meet her appointment; but, when about fifteen miles above Baton Rouge, her starboard engine broke down. Repairs were immediately commenced, and by 8 A.M. on the 5th of August were partially completed. General Breckinridge had commenced the attack at four o'clock, and the *Arkansas*, though not in condition to engage the enemy, moved on, and when in sight of Baton Rouge her starboard engine again broke down, and the vessel was run ashore. The work of repair was resumed, and next morning the Federal fleet was seen coming up. The *Arkansas* was moored head down-stream, and cleared for action. The *Essex* approached and opened fire. At that moment the engineers reported the engines able to work half a day; the lines were cut, and the *Arkansas* started for the *Essex*, when the other—the larboard—engine suddenly stopped, and the vessel was again secured to the shore, stern-down. The *Essex* now valiantly approached, pouring a hot fire into her disabled antagonist. Lieutenant Stevens, then commanding the *Arkansas*, ordered the crew ashore, fired the vessel, and, with her flag flying, turned her adrift—a sacrificial offering to the cause she had served so valiantly in her brief but brilliant career. Lieutenant Reed, of the ram *Arkansas*, in his published account of the affair, states, "After all hands were ashore, the *Essex* fired upon the disabled vessel most furiously."

Chapter 57

The Confederate Navy on the High Seas

TO maintain the position assumed by the Confederate States, as a separate power among the nations, it was obviously necessary to have a navy, not only for the defence of their coast, but for the protection of their commerce. These States, after their secession from the Union, were, in that regard, in a destitute condition, similar to that of the United States after their Declaration of Independence.

It has been shown that, among the first acts of the Confederate Administration was the effort to buy ships which could be used for naval purposes. The policy of the United States Government being to shut up our commerce, rather than protect their own, induced the wholesale purchase of vessels found in the Northern ports—not only such as could be made fit for cruisers, but also any which would serve even for blockading purposes. There was little shipping of any kind in the Southern ports, and to that scanty supply we were, for the time, restricted.

A previous reference has been made to the *Sumter*, Commander Raphael Semmes, but a more extended notice is considered due.

Educated in the naval service of the United States, Raphael Semmes had attained the rank of commander, and was distinguished for his studious habits and varied acquirements. When Alabama passed her ordinance of secession he was on duty at Washington as a member of the Lighthouse Board. He promptly tendered his resignation, and, at the organization of the Confederate Government, repaired to Montgomery and tendered his services to it. The efforts which had been made to obtain steamers suited to cruising against the enemy's commerce had been quite unsuccessful, none being found which the naval officers charged with their selection regarded fit for the service. One of the reports described a small propeller-steamer, of five hundred tons burden, sea-going, low-pressure engine, sound, and capable of being so strengthened as to carry an ordinary battery of four or five guns; speed between nine and ten knots; but the board condemned her because she could carry but five days' fuel, and had no accommodations for the crew.

The Secretary of the Navy showed this report to Commodore Semmes, who said: "Give me that ship; I think I can make her answer the purpose." She was christened the *Sumter*, in commemoration of our first victory, and had the honor of being the first ship of war commissioned by the Confederates States, and the first to display the stars and bars of the Confederacy on the high seas. The *Sumter* was at New Orleans, to which place Commodore Semmes repaired; and, as forcibly presenting the difficulties under which we labored in all attempts to create a navy, I will quote from his "Memoirs" the account of his efforts to get the *Sumter* ready for sea:

> "I now took my ship actively in hand, and set gangs of mechanics at work to remove her upper cabins and other top hamper, preparatory to making the necessary alterations. These latter were considerable, and I soon found that I had a tedious job on my hands. It was no longer the case, as it had been in former years, when I had had occasion to fit out a ship, that I could go into a navy-yard, with well-provided workshops and skilled workmen, ready with all the requisite materials at hand to execute my orders. Everything had to be improvised, from the manufacture of a water-tank to the kids and cans of the berth-deck messes, and from a gun-carriage to a friction-primer. . . . Two long, tedious months were consumed in making alterations and additions. My battery was to consist of an 8-inch shell-gun, to be pivoted amidships, and of four light 32-pounders, of thirteen hundred weight each, in broadside."

On the 3rd of June, 1861, the *Sumter* was formally put in commission, and a muster-roll of the officers and men transmitted to the Navy Department. On the 18th of June she left New Orleans and steamed down and anchored near the mouth of the river. While lying at the head of the passes, the commander reported a blockading squadron outside, of three ships at Passe à l'Outre, and one at the Southwest Pass. The *Brooklyn*, at Passe à l'Outre, was not only a powerful vessel, but she had greater speed than the *Sumter*. The *Powhatan's* heavy armament made it very hazardous to pass her in daylight, and the absence of buoys and lights made it next to impossible to keep the channel in darkness. The *Sumter*, therefore, had been compelled to lie at the head of the passes and watch for some opportunity, in the absence of either the *Brooklyn* or the *Powhatan*, to get to sea. Fortunately neither of these vessels came up to the head of the passes, where, there being but a single channel, it would have been easy to prevent the exit of the *Sumter*.

On the 30th of June, one bright morning, a boatman reported that the *Brooklyn* had gone off in chase of a sail. Immediately the *Sumter* was got under way, when it was soon discovered that the *Brooklyn* was returning, and that the two vessels were about equally distant from the bar. By steady courage and rare seamanship the *Sumter* escaped from her swifter pursuer, and entered on her career of cutting the enemy's sinews of war by destroying his commerce.

Numerous armed vessels of the enemy were hovering on our coast, yet this one little cruiser created a general alarm, and, though a regularly commissioned vessel of the Confederacy, was habitually denounced as a "pirate."

During her cruise, up to January 17, 1862, she captured three ships, five brigs, six barks, and three schooners; but the property destroyed formed a very small part of the damage done to the enemy's commerce. Her appearance on the seas created such alarm that Northern ships were, to a large extent, put under foreign flags, and the carrying-trade, in which the United States stood second only to Great Britain, passed rapidly into other hands. The *Sumter*, while doing all this mischief, was nearly self-sustaining, her running expenses to the Confederate Government being but $28,000 when, at the close of 1861, she arrived at Gibraltar. Not being able to obtain coal, she remained there until sold.

Captain James D. Bullock, an officer of the old navy, of high ability as a seaman, and of an integrity which stood the test under which a less stern character might have given way, was our naval agent at Liverpool. In his office he disbursed millions, and, while there was no one to whom he could be required to render an account, paid out the last shilling in his hands, and confronted poverty without prospect of other reward than that which he might find in a clear conscience. He contracted with the Messrs. Laird, of Birkenhead, to build a strong steam merchant-ship—the same which was afterward christened the *Alabama* when, in a foreign port, she had received her armament and crew.

There was no secrecy about the building of the *Alabama*. She was frequently visited while under construction, and it is known that the British Government was applied to to prevent her from leaving port. It was feared that she might be delayed; but it was not considered possible that the British authorities would prevent an unarmed merchant-ship from leaving her coast, lest she might elsewhere procure an armament, and, in the service of a recognized belligerent, revive the terror in the other belligerent which the little *Sumter* had recently inspired.

When the *Alabama* was launched and ready for sea, Captain Bullock summoned Captain Semmes. The *Alabama*, then known as the 290, had proceeded a few days previously to her rendezvous, the Portuguese island Terceira, one of the group of the Azores. The story that the name 290 was given to her because she had been built by two hundred and ninety Englishmen, sympathizers in our struggle, was a mere fiction. She was built under a contract with the Confederate States, and paid for with Confederate money. She happened to be the two hundred and ninetieth ship built by the Lairds, and, not having been christened, was called 290. Captain Semmes followed her, accompanied by Captain Bullock, on the steamer *Bahama*, and found her at the place of rendezvous; also a sailing-ship which had been despatched before the *Alabama* with her battery and stores. Captain Semmes, with a sailor's enthusiasm, describes his first impression on seeing the ship which was to be his future home. The defects of the Sumter had been avoided, so that he found his new ship "a perfect steamer and a perfect sailing-ship at the same time, neither of her two modes of locomotion being at all dependent upon the other. . . . She was about nine hundred tons burden, two hundred and thirty feet in length, thirty-two feet in breadth, twenty feet in depth, and drew, when provisioned and coaled for a cruise, fifteen feet of water. Her model was of the most perfect symmetry, and she sat upon the water with the lightness and grace of a swan." She was yet only a merchant-ship, and the men on board of her, as well as those who came out with the captain on the *Bahama*, were only under articles for the voyage. She therefore had no crew for future service. When her armament and stores had been put on board, she steamed from the harbor out to the open sea, where she was to be christened and put in commission. The scantling was comparatively light, the vessel having been intended as a scourge to the enemy's commerce rather than for battle, and merely to defend herself if it became necessary. Her masts were proportioned so as to carry large canvas, and her engine was of three hundred horse-power, with an apparatus for condensing vapor to supply the crew with all the fresh water requisite. The coal, stores, and armament having been received from the supply-ships, she steamed out to sea on Sunday morning, August 24, 1862. There, more than a marine league from the shore, on the blue water over which man holds no empire, Captain Semmes read the commission of the President of the Confederacy appointing him a captain, and the order of the Secretary of the Navy assigning him to the command of the *Alabama*. There, where no government held jurisdiction, where the commission of the Confederacy was as valid as that of any power, the *Alabama* was christened; and she was thenceforth a ship of war in the navy of the Confederate States. The men who had come thus far under articles no longer binding were left to their option whether to be paid off, with a free passage to Liverpool, or to enlist in the crew of the *Alabama*. Eighty of the men who had come out in the several vessels enrolled themselves in the usual manner. Captain Semmes had a full complement of officers, and with this, though less than the authorized crew, he commenced his long and brilliant cruise. The ship's armament consisted of six 32-pounders in broadsides, and two pivot-guns amidships, one of them a smooth-bore 8-inch, the other a 100-pounder rifled Blakely.

Captain Semmes, from his varied knowledge of affairs both on sea and land, did not sail by chance in quest of adventure, but directed his course to places where the greatest number of the enemy's merchantmen were likely to be found; and to this line of action the large number of captures he made is in no small degree attributable. On board one of the ships captured they got New York papers, from which he learned that General Banks, with a large fleet of transports, was to sail on a certain day for Galveston. On this he decided to go to the rendezvous appointed for his coal-ship, and make all due preparation for a dash into the fleet when they should arrive at the harbor of Galveston, and he therefore directed his course into the Gulf of Mexico.

In the meantime General Magruder had recaptured Galveston; so, on his arrival, the lookout informed him that, instead of a fleet, there were five ships of war blockading the harbor and throwing shells into the town, from which he drew the conclusion that we had possession of the town, and that he was confronted by ships of war, not transports laden with troops. As each of the five ships observed by the lookout was supposed to be larger than his own, he had no disposition to run into that fleet. It therefore only remained to tempt one of the ships to follow him beyond supporting distance. The hope was soon realized, as a vessel was seen to come out from the fleet. The *Alabama* was under sail, and Captain Semmes says: "To carry out my design of decoying the enemy, I now wore ship as though I were fleeing from his pursuit, and lowered the propeller into the water. When about twenty miles from the fleet, the *Alabama* was prepared for action, and wheeled to meet her pursuer. To the first hail made, the answer from the *Alabama* was, 'This is her Britannic Majesty's steamer *Petrel*;' and the answer was 'This is the United States ship—,' name not heard." Captain Semmes then directed the first lieutenant to call out through his trumpet, "This is the Confederate States steamer *Alabama*." A broadside was instantly returned by the enemy. Captain Semmes describes the state of the atmosphere as highly favorable to the conduct of sound, and the wind as blowing in the direction of the enemy's fleet. The Federal Admiral, as afterward learned, immediately got under way with the *Brooklyn* and two others of his steamers to go to the rescue. The crews of both ships must have been standing at their guns, as the broadsides so instantly followed each other. In thirteen minutes after firing the first gun the enemy hoisted a light and fired an off gun as a signal that he had been beaten. Captain Semmes steamed quite close to the *Hatteras*, and asked if he had surrendered; then, if he was in want of assistance. An affirmative answer was given to both questions. The boats of the *Alabama* were lowered with such promptitude and handled with such care that, though the *Hatteras* was sunk at night, none of her crew was drowned. When her captain came on board Captain Semmes learned that he had been engaged with the United States steamer *Hatteras*, "a larger ship than the *Alabama* by one hundred tons," with an equal number of guns, and a crew numbering two less than that of the *Alabama*. There was "considerable disparity between the two ships in the weight of their pivot-guns, and the *Alabama* ought to have won the fight, which she did in thirteen minutes." The *Alabama* had received no appreciable injury, and, continuing her cruise to the island of Jamaica, entered the harbor of Port Royal, where, by the permission of the authorities, Captain Semmes landed his prisoners, putting them on parole.

As an answer to the stereotyped charges against Captain Semmes as a "pirate" and "robber," I will select from the many unarmed ships captured by him one case. He had gone to the track of the California steamers between Aspinwall and New York, in the hope of capturing a vessel homeward bound with Government treasure. On the morning before such a vessel was expected a large steamer, the *Ariel*, was seen, but unfortunately not going in the right direction. An exciting chase occurred, when she was finally brought to, but, instead of the million of dollars in her safe, she was outward bound, with a large number of women and children on board. A boarding officer was sent on her, and returned, giving an account of great alarm, especially among the ladies. Captain Semmes sent a lieutenant on board to assure them that they had "fallen into the hands of Southern gentlemen, under whose protection they were entirely safe." Among the passengers were a battalion of marines and some army and navy officers. These were all paroled, rank and file numbering one hundred and forty, and the vessel was released on ransom-bond. Captain Semmes states that there were five hundred passengers on board. It is fair to presume that each passenger had with him a purse of from three to five hundred dollars. Under the laws of war all this money would have been good prize, but not one dollar of it was touched, or so much as a passenger's baggage examined.

The *Alabama* now proceeded to run down the Spanish Main, thence bore eastward into the Indian Ocean, and, after a cruise into every sea where a blow at American commerce could be struck, came back around the Cape of Good Hope, and, sailing north, ran up to the thirtieth parallel, where so many captures had been made at a former time. Of the ship at this date Captain Semmes wrote:

> "The poor old *Alabama* was not now what she had been then. She was like the wearied fox-hound, limping back after a long chase, footsore, and longing for quiet repose.
>
> "She had, in her mission to cripple the enemy's commerce and cut his sinews of war, captured sixty-three vessels, among them one of the enemy's gunboats, the *Hatteras*, sunk in battle, had released nine under ransom-bond, and had paroled all prisoners taken."

All neutral ports being closed against her prizes, the rest of the vessels were, of necessity, burned at sea. Much complaint was made on account of the burning of these merchantmen, though very little reflection would have taught the complainants that the interest of the captor would have induced him to save the vessels, and send them into the nearest port for condemnation, as prizes; and, therefore, whatever grievance existed was the result of the blockade and of the rule which prevented the captures from being sent into a neutral port to await the decision of a prize court.

On the morning of the 11th of June, 1864, the *Alabama* entered the harbor of Cherbourg.

> "An officer was sent to call on the port-admiral and ask leave to land the prisoners from the last two ships captured; this was readily granted."

The next day Captain Semmes went on shore to consult the port-admiral "in relation to docking and repairing" the *Alabama*. As there were only government docks at Cherbourg, the application had to be referred to the Emperor. Before an answer was received, the *Kearsarge* steamed into the harbor, sent a boat ashore, and then ran out and took her station off the breakwater. Captain Semmes learned that the boat from the *Kearsarge* sent on shore had borne a request that the prisoners discharged from the *Alabama* might be delivered to the *Kearsarge*. It will be remembered that the Government of the United States, in many harsh and unjust phrases, had refused to recognize the *Alabama* as a ship of war, and held that the paroles given to her were void. This request was therefore regarded by Captain Semmes as an attempt to recruit for the *Kearsarge* from the prisoners lately landed by the *Alabama*, and he so presented the facts to the port-admiral, who rejected the application from the *Kearsarge*.

Captain Semmes sent notice to Captain Winslow, of the *Kearsarge*, whose presence in the offing was regarded as a challenge, that, if he would wait until the *Alabama* could receive some coal on board, she would come out and give him a battle.

As he had shown by extracts previously made, Captain Semmes knew that, after his long cruise, the *Alabama* needed to go into dock for repairs. It had not been possible for him, on account of the rigid enforcement of "neutrality," to replenish his ammunition. Unless nitre is more thoroughly purified than is usually, if ever, done by those who manufacture for an open market, it is sure to retain nitrate of soda, and the powder, of which it is the important ingredient, to deteriorate by long exposure to a moist atmosphere. The *Kearsarge* was superior to the *Alabama* in size and, having been built for war, in stanchness of construction; her armament was also greater, if measured, not by the number of guns, but by the amount of metal she could throw at a broadside. The crew of the *Kearsarge*, all told, was 162; that of the *Alabama*, 149. Captain Semmes says: "Still, the disparity was not so great but that I might hope to beat my enemy in a fair fight. But he did not show me a fair fight; for, as it afterward turned out, his ship was iron-clad." This expression "Iron-clad" refers to the fact that the *Kearsarge* had chains on her sides, which Captain Semmes describes as concealed by planking, the forward and after ends of which so accorded with the lines of the ship as not to be detected by telescopic observation. Many of that class of critics whose wisdom is only revealed after the event have blamed Captain Semmes for going out under the circumstances. Like most other questions, there are two sides to this one. If he had gone into dock for repairs, the time required would have resulted in the dispersion of his crew, and, from the known improvidence of sailors, it would have been more than doubtful whether they could have been reassembled. It was, moreover, probable that other vessels would have been sent to aid the *Kearsarge* in effectually blockading the port, so that, if his crew had returned, the only chance would have been to escape through the guarding fleet. Proud of his ship, and justly confiding in his crew, surely something will be conceded to the Confederate spirit so often exhibited and so often triumphant over disparity of force.

On the 19th of June, 1864, the *Alabama* left the harbor of Cherbourg to engage the *Kearsarge*, which had been lying off and on the port for several days previously. Captain Semmes in his report of the engagement writes:

> "After the lapse of about one hour and ten minutes our ship was ascertained to be in a sinking condition . . . to reach the French coast, I gave the ship all steam, and set such of the fore and aft sails as were available. The ship filled so rapidly, however, that, before we had made much progress, the fires were extinguished. I now hauled down my colors, and despatched a boat to inform the enemy

of our condition. Although we were now but four hundred yards from each other, the enemy fired upon me five times after my colors had been struck. It is charitable to suppose that a ship of war of a Christian nation could not have done this intentionally."

Captain Semmes states that, his waist-boats having been torn to pieces, he sent the wounded, and such of the boys of the ship as could not swim, in his quarter-boats, off to the enemy's ship, and as there was no appearance of any boat coming from the enemy, the crew, as previously instructed, jumped overboard, each to save himself if he could. All the wounded—twenty-one—were saved. Ten of the crew were ascertained to have been drowned. Captain Semmes stood on the quarter-deck until his ship was settling to go down, then threw his sword into the sea, there to lie buried with the ship he loved so well, and leaped from the deck just in time to avoid being drawn down into the vortex created by her sinking. He and many of his crew were picked up by a humane English gentleman in the boats of his yacht, the *Deerhound*. Others were saved by two French pilot-boats which were near the scene. The remainder, it is hoped, were picked up by the enemy. Captain Semmes states in his official report, two days after the battle, that about the time of his rescue by the *Deerhound* the "*Kearsarge* sent one, and then, tardily, another boat." The reader is invited to compare this with the conduct of Captain Semmes in his fight with the *Hatteras*, when, though it was in the night, by ranging up close to her, and promptly using all his boats, he saved her entire crew.

Mention has been made of the defective ammunition of the *Alabama*, and in that connection I quote the following passage from Captain Semmes's book:

> "I lodged a rifle percussion-shell near to her [the *Kearsarge's*] sternpost—*where there were no chains*—which failed to explode because of the defect of the cap. If the cap had performed its duty, and exploded the shell, I should have been called upon to save Captain Winslow's crew from drowning, instead of his being called upon to save mine."

As it appears by the same authority that the *Kearsarge* had greater speed than the *Alabama*, it followed that, though the captain of the *Kearsarge* might have closed with and boarded the *Alabama*, the captain of the *Alabama* could not board the *Kearsarge*, unless by consent.

The *Alabama*, built like a merchant-ship, sailed in peaceful garb from British waters, on a far-distant sea received her crew and armament, fitted for operations against the enemy's commerce. On "blue water" she was christened, and in the same she was buried. She lived the pride of her friends and the terror of her enemies. She went out to fight a wooden vessel, and was sunk by one clad in secret armor.

Those of the crew rescued by the *Deerhound* were landed at Southampton, England.

The United States Government then, through its minister, Mr. Charles Francis Adams, made the absurd demand of the English Government that they should be delivered up to her as escaped prisoners. With this demand Lord John Russell declined to comply.

The *Oreto*, which sailed from Liverpool about the 23rd of March, 1862, was, while under construction at Liverpool, the subject of diplomatic correspondence and close scrutiny by the custom officers. After her arrival off Nassau, upon representations by the United States consul at that port, she was detained and again examined; and it being found that she had none of the character of a vessel of war, she was released. Captain Maffitt, who had gone out with a cargo of cotton, here received a letter which authorized him to take charge of the *Oreto*, and get her promptly to sea. She was a steamer of two hundred and fifty horse-power, tonnage 560, bark-rigged; speed, under steam, eight to nine knots; with sail, in a fresh breeze, fourteen knots; crew 22, all told. The United States Minister, Mr. Adams, had made a report to the British Government, which, it was apprehended, would cause her seizure at once. This was soon effected, and with great difficulty the vessel was saved to the Confederacy by her commander. She arrived at Nassau on the 28th of April, and was detained until the session of the Admiralty Court in August. As soon as discharged by the proceedings therein, she sailed for the uninhabited island Green Kay, ninety miles to the southward of Providence Island, with a tender in tow having equipments provided by a Confederate merchant, where she anchored the next day, and proceeded to take on board her military armament sent out on the tender. She now became a ship of the Confederate navy, and was christened *Florida*. Her long detention in Nassau had caused the ship to be infected with yellow fever, and, as she had no surgeon on board, the vessel was directed to the island of Cuba, and ran into the harbor of Cardenas for aid. The crew was reduced to one fireman and two seamen, and eventually the captain was prostrated by the fever. The Governor of Cardenas refused to send a physician aboard, and warned the steamer that she must leave in twenty-four hours. Lieutenant Stribling, executive officer of the ship, had been sent to Havana to report her condition to the Captain-General, Marshal Serrano. That chivalrous gentleman, soldier, and statesman at once invited the ship to the hospitalities of the harbor of Havana, whither she repaired, and where she received the kindness which her forlorn situation required.

On the 1st of September, 1862, the vessel left Havana to obtain a crew and to complete her equipment, which was so imperfect that her guns could not all be used. The vessel was directed to the harbor of Mobile. On approaching that harbor she found several blockading vessels on the station, and boldly ran through them, escaping, with considerable injury to her masts and rigging, to the friendly shelter of Fort Morgan.

In the meantime the blockading squadron had been increased, with the boastful announcement that the cruiser should be "hermetically sealed" in the harbor of Mobile. After the vessel was ready for sea some impatience was manifested that she did not go out; but Captain Maffitt, with sound judgment and nautical skill, decided to wait for a winter storm and a dark night before attempting to pass through the close investment. When the opportunity offered, he steamed out into a rough sea and a fierce north wind. As he passed the blockading squadron he was for the first time discovered, when a number of vessels gave chase, and continued the pursuit throughout the next day. In the next evening all except the two fastest had hauled off, and, as night again closed in, the smoke and canvas of the *Florida* furnished their only guide. Captain Maffitt thus describes the ruse by which he finally escaped :

> "The canvas was secured in long, neat bunts to the yards, and the engines were stopped. Between high, toppling seas, clear daylight was necessary to enable them to distinguish our low hull. In eager pursuit the Federals swiftly passed us, and we jubilantly bade the enemy good-night, and steered to the northward."

She was now fairly on the high seas, and after long and vexatious delays entered on her mission to cruise against the enemy's commerce.

She commenced her captures in the Gulf of Mexico, then progressed through the Gulf of Florida to the latitude of New York, and thence to the equator, continuing to 12° south, and returned again within thirty miles of New York. When near Cape St. Roque, Captain Maffitt captured a Baltimore brig, the *Clarence*, and fitted her out as a tender. He placed on her Lieutenant C. W. Read, commander, 14 men, armed with muskets, pistols, and a 12-pound howitzer. The instructions were to proceed to the coast of America, to cruise against the enemy's commerce. Under these orders the *Clarence* destroyed many Federal vessels.

While under the command of Captain Maffitt, the *Florida*, with her tenders, captured some fifty-five vessels, many of which were of great value. The Florida being built of light timbers, her very active cruising so deranged her machinery that it was necessary to go into some friendly harbor for repairs. Captain Maffitt says: "I selected Brest, and the Government courteously consenting to the *Florida* having the facilities of the navy-yard, she was promptly docked." The effects of the yellow fever from which he had suffered, and the fatigue attending his subsequent service, had so exhausted his strength that he asked to be relieved from command of the ship. In compliance with the request, Captain C. M. Morris was ordered to relieve him.

After completing all needful repairs Captain Morris proceeded to sea and sighted the coast of Virginia, where he made a number of important captures. Turning from that locality he crossed the equator, destroying the commerce of the Northern States on his route to Bahia. Here he obtained coal, and had also some repairs done to the engines, when the United States steamship *Wachusett* entered the harbor. Not knowing what act of treachery might be attempted by her commander on the first night after his arrival, the *Florida* was kept in a watchful condition for battle.

This belligerent demonstration in the peaceful harbor of a neutral power alarmed both the governor and the admiral, who demanded assurance that the sovereignty of Brazil and its neutrality should be strictly observed by both parties. The pledge was given. In the evening, with a chivalric belief in the honor of the United States commander, Captain Morris unfortunately permitted a majority of his officers to accompany him to the opera, and also allowed two-thirds of the crew to visit the shore on leave. About one o'clock in the morning the *Wachusett* was surreptitiously got under way, and her commander, with utter disregard of his word of honor, ran into the *Florida*, discharging his battery and boarding her. The few officers on board and the small number of men were unable to resist this unexpected attack, and the *Florida* fell an easy prey to this covert and dishonorable assault. She was towed to sea amid the execrations of the Brazilian forces, army and navy, who, completely taken by surprise, fired a few ineffectual shots at the infringer upon the neutrality of the hospitable port of Bahia. The Confederate was taken to Hampton Roads.

Brazil instantly demanded her restoration intact to her late anchorage in Bahia. Mr. Lincoln was confronted by a protest from the different representatives of the courts of Europe, denouncing this extraordinary breach of national neutrality, which placed the government of the United States in a most unenviable position. Mr. Seward, with his usual diplomatic insincerity and machiavelism, characteristically prevaricated, while he plotted with a distinguished admiral as to the most adroit method of disposing of the "elephant." The result of these plottings was that an engineer was placed in charge of the stolen steamer, with positive orders to "open her sea-cock at midnight, and not to leave the engine-room until the water was up to his chin, as at sunrise *the Florida must be at the bottom.*"

The following note was sent to the Brazilian chargé d'affaires by Mr. Seward:

> "While awaiting the representations of the Brazilian Government, on the 28th of November she (the *Florida*) sank, owing to a leak, which could not be seasonably stopped. The leak was at first represented to have been caused, or at least increased, by collision with a war-transport. Orders were immediately given to ascertain the manner and circumstances of the occurrence. It seemed to affect the army and navy. A naval court of inquiry and also a military court has submitted its report, and a copy thereof is here communicated. . . . It is assumed that the loss of the *Florida* was in consequence of some unforeseen accident, which casts no responsibility on the Government of the United States."

The restitution of the ship having thus become impossible, the President expressed his regret that "the sovereignty of Brazil had been violated; dismissed the consul at Bahia, who had advised the offence; and sent the commander of the *Wachusett* before a court-martial."[108]

The commander of the *Wachusett* experienced no annoyance, and was soon made an admiral.

The *Georgia* was the next Confederate cruiser that Captain Bullock succeeded in sending forth. She was of 560 tons, and was fitted out on the coast of France. Her commander, W. L. Maury, Confederate States Navy, cruised in the North and South Atlantic with partial success. The capacity of the vessel in speed and other essentials was entirely inadequate to the service for which she was designed. She proceeded as far as the Cape of Good Hope, and returned, after having captured seven ships and two barks. Then she was laid up and sold.

The *Shenandoah*, once the *Sea-King*, was purchased by Captain Bullock, and placed under the command of Lieutenant-commanding J. J. Waddell, who fitted her for service, under many difficulties, at the barren island of Porto Santo, near Madeira. After experiencing great annoyances through the activity of the American consul at Melbourne, Australia, Captain Waddell finally departed, and commenced an active and effective cruise against American shipping in the Okhotsk Sea and Arctic Ocean. In August, 1865, hearing of the close of the war, he ceased his pursuit of United States commerce, sailed for Liverpool, England, and surrendered his ship to the English Government, which transferred it to the Government of the United States. The *Shenandoah* was a full-rigged ship of 800 tons, very fast under canvas. Her steam-power was merely auxiliary.

This was the last, but not the first appearance of the Confederate flag in Great Britain. The first vessel of the Confederate Government which unfurled it there was the swift, light steamer *Nashville*, R. B. Pegram, commander. Having been constructed as a passenger-vessel, and mainly with reference to speed and the light draught suited to the navigation of the Southern harbors, she was quite too frail for war purposes and too lightly armed for combat.

On her passage to Europe and back she destroyed two merchantmen. Nearing the harbor on her return voyage she found it blockaded, and a heavy vessel lying close on her track. Her daring commander headed directly for the vessel, and ran so close under her

---

[108]. M. Bernard's *Neutrality of Great Britain during the American Civil War*.

guns that she was not suspected in her approach, and had passed so far before the guns could be depressed to bear upon her that none of the shots took effect. Being little more than a shell, a single shot would have sunk her; and she was indebted to the address of her commander and the speed of his vessel for her escape. Wholly unsuited for naval warfare, this voyage terminated her career.

A different class of vessels than those adapted to the open sea was employed for coastwise cruising. In the month of July, 1864, a swift twin-screw propeller, called the *Atlanta*, of 600 tons burden, was purchased by the Secretary of the Navy, and fitted out in the harbor of Wilmington, N. C., for a cruise against the commerce of the Northern States. Commander J. Taylor Wood, an officer of extraordinary ability and enterprise, was ordered to command her, and her name was changed to the *Tallahassee*. This extemporaneous man-of-war ran safely through the blockade, and soon lit up the New England coast with her captures, which consisted of two ships, four brigs, four barks, and twenty schooners. Great was the consternation among Northern merchants. The construction of the *Tallahassee*, exclusively for steam, made her dependent on coal; her cruise was of course brief, but it was brilliant while it lasted.

About the same time another fast double-screw propeller of 585 tons, called the *Edith*, ran into Wilmington, N. C., and the Navy Department, requiring her services, bought her and gave to her the name of *Chickamauga*. A suitable battery was placed on board, with officers and crew, and Commander John Wilkinson, a gentleman of consummate naval ability, was ordered to command her. When ready for sea he ran the blockade under the bright rays of a full moon. Strange to say, the usually alert sentinels neither hailed nor halted her. Like the *Tallahassee*, though partially rigged for sailing, she was exclusively dependent upon steam in the chase, escape, and all important evolutions. She captured seven vessels, despite the above-noticed defects.

Confederate Generals.

Chapter 58

Federal Appeals to Europe Not to Aid "Pirates"

THE excitement produced in the North by the effective operations of our cruisers compelled the attention of the Federal Government to the subject. It might have been expected that they would have sought, by their great fleets, to protect their commerce on the high seas by capturing or driving off our light cruisers; but, instead of doing so, their ships of war were employed in blockading our ports or watching those of the West Indies, from which blockaders were expected to sail. Shameful as was this dereliction of duty, this failure to protect commerce, there was a still more humiliating feature in the conduct of the Federal Government.

While the Confederacy was regarded by the Federal State Department as an insurrection soon to be suppressed, and the cruisers regularly commissioned by the Confederate States were called "pirates," diplomatic demands were made upon Great Britain to prevent the so-called "pirates" from violating international law, as if it applied to pirates. Appeals to that Government were also made to prevent the sale of materials of war to the Confederacy, and thus indirectly aid the United States in performing what, according to its own declaration, was a mere police duty—to suppress a combination of some evil-disposed persons—gallantly claiming that they, armed cap-a-pie, should meet their adversary in the lists, he to be without helmet, shield, or lance.

To one who, from youth to age, had seen with exultant pride the flag of his country, as it unfolded, disclosing to view the stripes recordant of the original size of the family of States, and the constellation which told of that family's growth, it could be but deeply mortifying to witness such a paltry exhibition of deception and unmanliness in the representatives of a Government around which fond memories still lingered, despite the perversions of which it was the subject.

If this attempt on the part of the Government of the United States to deny the existence of war, after having, by proclamation of blockade, compelled all nations to take notice that war did exist, and to claim that munitions should not be sold to a country because there were some disorderly people in it, had been all, the attempt would have been ludicrously absurd, and the contradiction too bald to require refutation; but this would have been but half of the story. Subsequently the United States Government claimed reclamation from Great Britain for damage inflicted by vessels which had been built in her ports, and which had elsewhere been armed and equipped for purposes of war. International war recognizes the right of a neutral to sell an unarmed vessel, without reference to the use to which the purchaser might subsequently apply it. The United States Government had certainly not practised under a different rule, but had even gone further than this so much further as to transgress the prohibition against armed vessels.

At the beginning of the war the United States Government sought to contract for the construction of iron-plated vessels in the ports of England, which were to be delivered fully armed and equipped to her. To this it may be added that her armies, down to almost the last month of the war, were recruited from nearly all the countries of Europe; that a portion of their arms were of foreign manufacture, as well as the munitions of war; that a large number of the sailors of her fleets came from the seaports of Great Britain and Germany; in a word, whatever could be of service to her in the conflict was unhesitatingly sought among neutrals, regardless of the law of nations. At the same time an effort was made on her part to make Great Britain responsible for the damage done by our cruisers and for the warlike stores sold to our Government.

Lord John Russell, noting this point, in a despatch dated December 19, 1862, says:

> "If it be sought to make Her Majesty's Government responsible to that of the United States because arms and munitions of war have left this country on account of the Confederate Government, the Confederate Government, as the other belligerent, may very well maintain that it has a just cause of complaint against the British

Government because the United States arsenals have been replenished from British sources. Nor would it be possible to deny that, in defiance of the Queen's proclamation, many subjects of Her Majesty, owing allegiance to her crown, have enlisted in the armies of the United States. . . . Her Majesty's Government therefore has just ground of complaint against both of the belligerent parties, but most especially against the Government of the United States, for having systematically, and in disregard of the comity of nations, which it was their duty to observe, induced subjects of Her Majesty to violate those orders which, in conformity with her neutral position, she has enjoined all her subjects to obey."

A candid study of the duty of neutrals under international law, with regard to the construction and equipment of cruisers of either belligerent, and especially of American precedents and authorities, will demonstrate the utter groundlessness of the claims put forth by the Government of the United States, and establish the lawfulness of the acts of the Confederate Government. The complaints made by the Government of the United States against the Government of Great Britain for acts involving a breach of neutrality found no support in the letter of the law, or in its principles, and were conclusively answered by the antecedent acts of the United States Government.

It is a remarkable fact that the Government of the United States, in no one instance, from the opening to the close of the war, formally spoke of the Confederate Government or States as belligerents. Although on many occasions it acted with the Confederate Government as a belligerent, yet no official designations were ever given to them or their citizens but those of "insurgents" or "insurrectionists." Nevertheless, the United States Government, although refusing belligerent rights to the Confederate States, were very ready to take advantage of such concessions by other nations whenever an opportunity offered. The voluminous correspondence of the Secretary of State of the United States Government, relative to the Confederate cruisers and their so-called "depredations," was filled with charges of violations of international law, which could be committed only by a belligerent, and which, it was alleged, had been permitted in the ports of Great Britain. On this foundation was based the subsequent claim for damages advanced by the Government of the United States against that of Great Britain; and for the pretended lack of "due diligence" in watching the actions of the Confederate belligerents in her ports, she was mulcted in a heavy sum by the Geneva Conference, and paid it to the Government of the United States.

The party against which the Government of the United States was conducting hostilities consisted of the people within the limits of the Confederate States. Was it against them as individuals in an unorganized condition, or as organized political communities? In the former condition they might be a mob; in the latter condition they formed a state. By the actions of unorganized mobs may arise insurrections, but by the actions of organized people or states arise wars.

The Government of the United States adopted a fiction when it declared that the execution of the laws in certain States was impeded by insurrection. The people whom it designated insurrectionists were the organized people of the States. Every public act of theirs was originated with State authority and was conducted under the supervision of the State officers; the results were reported to State Government and put in operation by the State executives. Why, then, did an intelligent and powerful Government so outrage the understanding of mankind as to adopt a fiction on which to base the authority and justification of its hostile action. The United States Government was the result of a compact between the States—a written Constitution. It owed its existence simply to a delegation of certain powers by the respective States, which it was authorized to exercise for their common welfare. One of these powers was to "suppress insurrections;" but no power was delegated to subjugate States—the authors of its existence—or to make war on any of the States. If, then, without any delegated power or lawful authority for its proceedings, the Government of the United States commenced war upon some of the States of the Union, how could it be justified before the world? It became the aggressor—the Attila of the continent. Its action inflicted a wound on the principles of constitutional liberty, a crushing blow to the hopes that men had begun to repose in their latest efforts for self-government, which its friends should neither forgive nor forget. To palliate the enormity of such an offence, its authors resorted to a vehement denial that their hostile action was a war against the States, and persistently asserted the fiction that these immense armies and fleets were merely a police authority to put down insurrection. They hoped to conceal from the observation of the American people that the contest on the part of the central Government was for empire—for its absolute supremacy over the State Governments; that the Constitution was rolled up and laid away among the old archives; and that the conditions of their liberty in the future were to be decided by the sword or by "national" control of the ballot-box.

With like disregard of truth our cruisers were denounced as "pirates" by the Federal Government. By the laws of nations a pirate is the enemy of mankind, and can be destroyed by the ships of any nation. The difference between the lawful cruiser and the pirate is, that the former has behind it a government which is recognized by civilized nations as entitled to the rights of war, and from which the commander of the cruiser receives his commission or authority; but the pirate represents no government, and is not recognized by any one.

The Government of the United States well knew that after the issue of the Queen's proclamation, recognizing our Government, the application of the word pirate to our cruisers was simply an exhibition of vindictive passion. A *de facto* Government, by its commission, legalizes among nations a cruiser. That there was such a Government even its own courts decided.[109] The belligerent character of the Confederate States was fully acknowledged by the highest judicial tribunal of the United States.

During the first months of the war all the principal ports of the Confederacy were blockaded, and finally every inlet was either in the possession of the enemy or had one or more vessels watching it. The steamers were independent of wind and weather, and could hold their positions before a port day and night. At the same time the ports of neutrals had been closed against the prizes of our cruisers by proclamations and Orders in Council. Says Admiral Semmes: "During my whole career upon the sea, I had not so much as a single port into which I could send a prize."

No course was left to us but to destroy the prizes, as was done in many instances under the Government of the United States Confederation.

---

109. Vol. 2, Black, p. 635; Vol. 7, Wheaton, p. 337.

In January, 1871, the British Government proposed to the Government of the United States that a joint commission should be convened to adjust certain differences between the two nations relative to the fisheries, the Canadian boundary, etc. To the proposition the latter acceded, on condition that the so-called Alabama claims should also be considered. To this condition Great Britain assented. In the convention the American commissioners proposed an arbitration of these claims. The British commissioners replied that Her Majesty's Government could not admit that Great Britain had failed to discharge toward the United States the duties imposed on her by the rules of international law, or that she was justly liable to make good to the United States the losses occasioned by the acts of the cruisers to which the American commissioners referred.

Without following the details it may be summarily stated that the Geneva Conference ensued, which decided that "England should have fulfilled her duties as a neutral with the exercise of a diligence equal to the gravity of the danger," and that "the circumstances were of a nature to call for the exercise, on the part of Her Britannic Majesty's Government, of all possible solicitude for the observance of the rights and duties involved in the proclamations issued by Her Majesty on May 13, 1861." The Conference also added: "It cannot be denied that there were moments when its watchfulness seemed to fail, and when feebleness in certain branches of the public service resulted in great detriment to the United States."

The various claims for damage done by fourteen Confederate cruisers aggregated $26,408,170. The Conference rejected the claims founded on the damage done by the *Boston*, the *Sallie*, and the *Jefferson Davis*, and then awarded to the United States Government $15,500,000 in gold.

The indirect damages upon the commerce of the United States by these cruisers were far beyond the amount of the claims presented to the Geneva Conference. The number of ships owned by the United States at the beginning of the war, which were subsequently transferred to foreign owners by a British register, was 715; the amount of the tonnage, 480,882 tons. Such are the laws of the United States that not one of them has been allowed to resume an American register.

In the year 1860 nearly seventy per cent of the foreign commerce of the country was carried in American ships. But in consequence of the danger of capture by our cruisers to which these ships were exposed, the amount of this commerce carried by them had dwindled down in 1864 to forty-six per cent. It continued to decline after the war, and in 1872 it had fallen to twenty-eight and one-half per cent.

Before the war the amount of American tonnage was second only to that of Great Britain, and we were competing with her for the first place. At that time the tonnage of the coasting trade, which had grown from insignificance, was 1,735,863 tons. Three years later, in 1864, it had declined to about 867,931 tons.

The damage to the articles of export is illustrated by the decline in breadstuffs exported from the Northern States. In the last four months of each of the following years the value of this export was as follows: 1861, $42,500,000; 1862, $27,842,000; 1863, $8,909,042; 1864, $1,850,819. Some of this decline resulted from good crops in England; but, in other respects, it was a consequence of causes growing out of the war. The increase in the rates of marine insurance, in consequence of the danger of capture by cruisers, was variable; but the claims on this account presented to the Conference, and allowed, aggregated $6,146,219.

Chapter 59

The Military Government of States

ON the capture of Nashville, on February 25, 1862, Andrew Johnson was made military governor of Tennessee, with the rank of brigadier-general, and immediately entered on the military duties of his office. The will of the Governor was the supreme law. Public officers were required to take an oath of allegiance to the United States Government, and on refusal were expelled from office. Newspapers were suppressed and their offices closed. Subsequently the offices were sold out under the provisions of the Confiscation Act. All persons using "treasonable or seditious" language were arrested and required to take the oath of allegiance to the Government of the United States, and to give bonds for the future, or go into exile. Clergymen, on their refusal to take the oath, were confined in the prisons until they could be sent away. School-teachers and editors, and finally large numbers of private citizens, were arrested and held until they took the oath. Conflicts became frequent in the adjacent country. Murder and the violent destruction of property ensued.

On October 21, 1862, an order for an election of members of the United States Congress in the ninth and tenth State districts was issued. Every voter was required to give satisfactory evidence of "loyalty" to the Northern Government. Two persons were chosen and admitted to seats in that body.

That portion of the State in the possession of the forces of the United States continued without change until the beginning of 1864. Measures were then commenced for an organization of a State Government in sympathy with the Government of the United States. These measures were subsequently known as the process for "State reconstruction." The Governor issued his proclamation for an election of county officers on

March 5th, to be held wherever it was practicable, in the various counties of the State. "It is not expected," says the Governor, "that the enemies of the United States will propose to vote, nor is it intended that they be permitted to vote or hold office."

The election was a failure. For a time all further efforts at reconstruction were suspended. An attempt was made, at the end of 1864, to obtain a convention to amend the State Constitution, and, without any regular authority, a body assembled, which adopted amendments. These were submitted to the voters and declared to be ratified by a vote of 25,000. The vote of the State in 1860 was 145,000. Slavery was abolished, and other changes were made; so-called State officers were elected; and this body of voters was proclaimed as the reconstructed State of Tennessee.

The next attempt to guarantee "a republican form of government" to a State was commenced in Louisiana by the military occupation of New Orleans, on May 1, 1862. The Federal forces were under the command of Major-General Benjamin F. Butler; and Brigadier-General Shepley was appointed military governor of the State. Under this rule, in Louisiana, aged and peaceful citizens, unresisting captives, and non-combatants were confined at hard labor, with chains attached to their limbs, and held in dungeons and fortresses; others, for selling medicine to the sick soldiers of the Confederacy, were subjected to a similar degrading punishment. The soldiers of the invading force were incited and encouraged by general orders to insult and outrage the wives and mothers and sisters of the citizens; and helpless women were torn from their homes and subjected to solitary confinement, some in fortresses and prisons—and one, especially, on an island of barren sand, under a tropical sun-and were fed with loathsome rations and exposed to vile insults. Prisoners of war, who surrendered to the naval forces of the United States on the agreement that they should be released on parole, were seized and kept in close confinement. Repeated pretexts were sought or invented for plundering the inhabitants of the captured city, by fines levied and collected under threats of imprisonment at hard labor with ball and chain. The entire population was forced to elect between starvation by the confiscation of all their property or taking an oath against their conscience to bear allegiance to the invader. Egress from the city was refused to those whose fortitude stood the test, and even to lone and aged women and helpless children; and, after being ejected from their houses and robbed of their property, they were left to starve in the street or subsist on charity. The slaves were driven from their plantations in the neighborhood of New Orleans until their owners consented to share their crops with the commanding general, his brother, and other officers. When such consent had been extorted the slaves were restored to the plantations and compelled to work under the bayonets of a guard of United States soldiers. Where that partnership was refused, armed expeditions were sent to the plantations to rob them of everything that could be removed; and even slaves too aged and infirm for work, in spite of their entreaties, were forced from the homes provided by their owners, and driven to wander helpless on the highway. By one order (No. 91) the entire property in the part of Louisiana west of the Mississippi River was sequestered for confiscation, and officers were assigned to the duty, with orders to gather up and collect the personal property, and turn over to the proper officers, upon their receipts, such of it as might be required for the use of the United States Army; and to bring the remainder to New Orleans, and cause it to be sold at public auction to the highest bidder. The African slaves, also, were not only incited to insurrection by every license and encouragement, but numbers of them were armed for a servile war. In many instances the officers were active and zealous agents in the commission of these crimes, and no instance was known of the refusal of any one of them to participate in the outrages.

Another example was the cold blooded execution of William B. Mumford, on June 7th. He was an unresisting and non-combatant captive, and no offence was ever alleged to have been committed by him subsequent to the date of the capture of New Orleans. He was charged with aiding and abetting certain persons in hauling down a United States flag hoisted on the mint, which was left there by a boat's crew on the morning of April 26th, and five days before the military occupation of the city. He was tried before a military commission, sentenced, and afterward hanged.

On December 15, 1862, General Banks took command of the military forces, and General Butler retired. Early in August the military Governor had attempted to set on foot a judicial system for the city and State. For this purpose he appointed judges in two of the District Courts;

of which the judges were absent, and authorized a third, who held a commission dated anterior to 1861, to resume the sessions. This was an establishment of three new courts, with the jurisdiction and powers pertaining to the courts that previously bore their names, by a military officer representing the Executive of the United States. These were the only courts within the territory of the State held by the United States which claimed to have civil jurisdiction; but this jurisdiction was limited to citizens of the parish of Orleans as against defendants residing in the State. As to other residents of the State, outside of the parish of Orleans, there was no court in which they could be sued. In this condition several parishes were held by the United States forces.

It was therefore necessary to take another step to enable the military power to administer civil affairs. It involved a complete subversion of the fundamental principles of social organization. According to this advanced step—with absolute disregard of the fundamental principle that the military shall be subject to the civil authority—the military absorbs by force the civil functions, fixes at will its rules and modes of action, and determines the limit of its power.

This attempt to administer civil affairs on the basis of military authority involved the subversion of fundamental principles. The military power may remove obstacles to the exercise of the civil authority; but when these are removed it cannot enter the forum and sit in judgment on civil affairs any more than the hawk can become a dove by assuming her plumage.

However, the next step was taken, and an order from the President of the United States was published, creating a "Provisional Court," constituting it a court of record, "with authority to hear, try, and determine all causes, civil and criminal, including causes in law, equity, revenue, and admiralty, and particularly with all such powers and jurisdiction as belong to the District and Circuit Courts of the United States."

A New York lawyer was appointed judge, with power to appoint the necessary subordinate officers—"these appointments to continue during the pleasure of the President, not extending beyond the restoration of the civil authority in that city (New Orleans] and the State of Louisiana."

The Constitution of the United States says: "The judicial power of the United States shall be vested in one Supreme Court, and in such

Supreme Courts as the Congress may from time to time ordain and establish." This Provisional Court was neither ordained nor established by Congress; it had not, therefore, vested in it any of the judicial power of the United States. Neither does the Constitution give to Congress any power by which it can constitute an independent State court within the limits of any State in the Union, as Louisiana was said to be.

This court, therefore, was a mere instrument of martial law, constituted by the commander-in-chief of the United States forces, without any of the reasons by which such courts are justified; for to warrant the establishment of this court no authority was to be found either in the Constitution of the United States or outside of it.

When called upon to state any just ground for such a measure, the invader has usually replied that he had, *ex necessitate rei*, the right to establish such a tribunal. Thus said the commander-in-chief of the United States, and Congress acquiesced—indeed leading the way; for it had urged the same plea to justify the passage of the Confiscation Act. The judiciary has observed the silence of acquiescence. Thus the doctrine of necessity—the rule that in the administration of affairs, both military and civil, the necessity of the case may and does afford ample authority and power to subvert or to suspend the provisions of the Constitution, and to exercise powers and do acts unwarranted by the grants of that instrument—has apparently become incorporated as an unwritten clause in the Constitution of the United States.

Chapter 60

Progress of Centralization

ON December 3rd, under an order of the military Governor, Shepley, a so-called election was held for members of Congress in the First and Second State Districts, each composed of about half the city of New Orleans and portions of the surrounding parishes. Benjamin F. Flanders received the majority of all votes cast in the First District, and Michael Hahn the majority in the Second District. Those persons presented themselves at Washington, and their claims to seats in the House of Representatives were favored by the Committee on Elections. As the proclamation for the elections was not issued by the civil Governor, as the law explicitly required, the admission of these claimants, elected in defiance of the legal requirement, would be a recognition by Congress of the validity of a military order over a State civil law. But although all the departments of the Federal Government had acted on the theory that the Confederate States were in a state of insurrection, and that the Union was unbroken, so that they could come back to the Union with all their laws unimpaired; and although Congress, under this theory, was as much bound to uphold the laws of Louisiana as the laws of New York—yet the Louisiana claimants were admitted to seats in the House of Representatives.

Nor was this all. The work of reconstructing the State of Louisiana out of the small portion of her population and territory subjugated by the military forces of the United States still went on. The next project was to hold a State Convention to frame a new Constitution; but its advocates were so few that nothing was done during the year 1863. The object of the military power was to secure such civil authority as to enforce the abolition of slavery; and, until the way was clear to that result, every method of organization was held in abeyance.

Meanwhile, on December 8, 1863, the President of the United States issued a proclamation which contained his plan of making a Union State out of a fragment of a Confederate State, and also grant only an amnesty to the general mass of the people on taking an oath of allegiance. His plan, briefly stated, was that, whenever any number of persons in any one of the Confederate States, not less than one-tenth in number of the votes cast in such State at the Presidential election of 1860, each having taken the prescribed oath of allegiance, and having been a qualified voter by the election laws of the State existing immediately before the act of secession, should reestablish a State government, said government should be recognized as the true government of the State. The oath required was to support the Constitution, the Union, and "all acts of Congress passed during the existing rebellion with reference to slaves," and also "all proclamations of the President" issued during the same period and referring to slaves, until or unless modified and declared void by decision of the Supreme Court.

This Presidential plan to restore States to the Union did not contain a single feature to secure a republican form of government, nor a single provision authorized by the Constitution of the United States. With his usurped war-power to sustain him in the work of destruction, he found it easy to destroy; but he was powerless to create or restore.

Under the proclamation of the President, Major-General Banks issued at New Orleans, on January 11, 1864, a proclamation for an election of State officers and for members of a State Constitutional Convention. The State officers, when elected, were to constitute, according to the proclamation, "the civil government of the State under the Constitution and laws of Louisiana, except so much of the said Constitution and laws as recognize, regulate, or relate to slavery, which, being inconsistent with the present condition of public affairs, and plainly inapplicable to any class of persons now existing within its limits, must be suspended." The number of votes given for State officers was 10,270. The population of the State in 1860 was 708,902. The so-called Governor-elect was inaugurated on March 4th, and on March 11th he was invested with the powers hitherto exercised by the military Governor for the President of the United States. On the same day Major-General Banks issued an order relative to the election of delegates to a so-called State Convention. The most important provisions of it defined the qualifications of voters. The delegates were elected entirely within the army lines of the forces of the United States. The so-called Convention assembled and adopted a so-called Constitution, declaring "instantaneous, universal, uncompensated, unconditional emancipation of slaves." The meagre vote on the Constitution was, for its adoption, 6,836; for its rejection, 1,566. The vote of New Orleans was, yeas, 4,664; nays, 789. This state of affairs continued after the close of the war. Violent disputes arose as to the validity of the so-called Constitution. The so-called Legislature elected under it adopted Article XIII as an amendment to the Constitution of the United States, prohibiting the existence of slavery in the United States.

It will be seen from these facts that the State of Louisiana was not a republican State, instituted by the consent of the governed; that its Legislature was an unconstitutional body without any "just powers;" and that the vote which it gave for the amendment of the Constitution of the United States was no vote at all; for it was given by a body that had no authority to give it, because it had no "just powers" whatever. Yet this vote was counted among those necessary to secure the passage of the constitutional amendment. Was this an attempt to enforce a fiction or to establish the truth? Such are the deeds which go to make up the record of crime against the liberties of mankind.

The proceedings in Arkansas to "institute" a republican State government were inaugurated by an order from the President of the United States to Major-General Steele, commanding the Federal forces in Arkansas. At this time the regular government of the State, established by the consent of the people, was in full operation outside the lines of the United States army.

Meanwhile some persons in the northern part of Arkansas, acting under the proclamation of December 8, 1863, got together a so-called State Convention, containing the slavery prohibition, etc. This was ordered to be submitted to the popular vote, and at the same time State officers were to be elected. President Lincoln acceded to these proceedings after they had been placed under the direction of General Steele, the military commander. The election was held, the Constitution received 12,000 votes, and the State officers were declared to be elected. Then Arkansas came forth as a so-called republican State, "instituted" by military authority, and of course received the benefit of the constitutional provision which declares that "the United States shall guarantee to every State in the Union a republican form of government." It should be added that Arkansas, thus "instituted" a State, was regarded by the Government of the United State as competent to give as valid a vote as New York, Massachusetts, or any other Northern State for the ratification of Article XIII, as an amendment to the Constitution of the United States, prohibiting the existence of slavery in the United States. The vote was thus given; it was counted; and it served to make up the exact number deemed by the managers to be necessary. Thus were fraud and falsehood triumphant over popular rights and fundamental law.

The perversion of republican principles was greater in Virginia than in any other State, through the co-operation of the Government of the United States. In the winter of 1860-61 a special session of the Legislature of the State, convened at Richmond, passed an act directing the people to elect delegates to a State Convention, to be held on February 14, 1861. The Convention assembled and was occupied with the subject of Federal relations and the adjustment of difficulties until the call for troops by President Lincoln was made, when an ordinance of secession was passed. The contiguity of the northwestern counties of the State to Ohio and Pennsylvania led to the manifestation of much opposition to the withdrawal of the State from the Union, and the determination to reorganize that portion as a separate State. This resulted in the assembling of a so-called Convention of Delegates at Wheeling on June 11th. One of its first acts was to provide for a reorganization of the State government of Virginia by declaring its offices vacant and the appointment of new officers throughout. The new organization assumed to be the true representative of the State of Virginia; and, after varying fortunes, was recognized as such by President Lincoln. The next act of the Convention was "to provide for the formation of a new State out of a portion of the territory of this State." Under this act delegates were elected to a so-called Constitutional Convention, which framed a so-called Constitution for the new State of West Virginia, which was submitted to a vote of the people in April, 1862, and carried by a large majority of that section. Meanwhile the Governor of the reorganized government of Virginia issued his proclamation for an election of members, and the assembly of an extra session of the so-called Legislature. The body assembled on May 6, 1862, and assumed to be the Legislature of the State of Virginia. This body immediately passed an act giving its consent to the formation of a new State out of the territory of Virginia. The formal act of consent and the draft of the new Constitution of West Virginia were ordered by this so-called Legislature to be sent to the Congress of the United States, then in session, with the request that "the said new State be admitted into the Union." On December 31, 1862, the President approved an act for that purpose.

When the question of the admission of West Virginia was before the House of Representatives of the United States Congress, Mr. Thaddeus Stevens, of Pennsylvania, declared, with exemplary frankness, that he would not stultify himself by claiming the act to be constitutional. He said: "We know that it is not constitutional; but it is necessary."

Chapter 61

Military Operations in Virginia

AFTER the retreat of McClellan to Westover his army remained inactive about a month. His front was closely watched by a brigade of cavalry, and preparations were made to resist a renewal of his attempt upon Richmond from his new base. The main body of our army awaited the development of his intentions, and no important event took place.

Meantime another army of the enemy, under General Pope, advanced southward from Washington and crossed the Rappahannock, as if to seize Gordonsville and move thence upon Richmond. Contemporaneously the enemy appeared in front at Fredericksburg and threatened the railroad from Gordonsville to Richmond, apparently for the purpose of co-operating with the movements of General Pope. To meet the advance of Pope, and restrain as far as possible the atrocities which he threatened to perpetrate upon our defenceless citizens, General Jackson, with his own and Ewell's division, was ordered to proceed, on July 13th, toward Gordonsville.

The nature of the outrages threatened by General Pope may be inferred from his General Orders No. 5, No. 6, and No. 7.

No. 5 ordered that, as far as practicable, the troops of his command should subsist upon the country in which their operations were carried on; that, for supplies thus taken, vouchers were to be given to the owners, payable at the close of the war "upon sufficient testimony being furnished that such owners had been loyal citizens of the United States since the date of the voucher."

No. 6 ordered that "in any operation of the cavalry forces no supply- or baggage-trains of any description should be used, and that all villages and neighborhoods through which they should pass should be laid under contribution for the subsistence of men and horses."

No. 7 notified the people of the valley of the Shenandoah and other regions in which the army might operate that they would be held responsible for any injury done the track, line, or railroads; that they would be held responsible for any attacks on the trains or straggling soldiers by bands of guerillas in their neighborhood; that if a soldier or legitimate follower of the army should be fired upon from any house, the house would be razed to the ground and the inhabitants taken prisoners; that "if such an outrage occur at any place distant from settlements, the people within five miles around shall be held accountable and made to pay an indemnity sufficient for the case; and any person detected in such outrages, either during the act or at any time afterward, shall be shot, without waiting civil process."

These orders announcing a policy of pillage were followed ten days later by General Order No. 11, inaugurating a policy of expatriation.

Commanders were ordered to proceed immediately to "arrest all disloyal male citizens within their lines or within their reach in the rear of their respective stations." "Such as are willing to take the oath of allegiance to the United States, and will furnish sufficient security for its observance, shall be permitted to remain at their homes. Those who refuse shall be conducted south beyond the extreme pickets of the army, and be notified that, if found again within our lines, or at any point in the rear, they will be considered spies, and subjected to the extreme rigor of the military law."

Had the vigor of this campaign been equal to the bombastic manifesto of this disgrace to the profession of arms, the injuries inflicted would have been more permanent; the conduct could hardly have been more brutal. On receipt of General Pope's last order, I instructed General Lee to communicate to the Federal commander in his front that, until said order was revoked, the Confederate Government would not consider any officers hereafter captured from General Pope's army as prisoners of war; and that while, for the time being, we should renounce our right of retaliation on the innocent, and should continue to treat the private enlisted soldiers of General Pope's army as prisoners of war, yet, if these savage practices were continued, we should be reluctantly forced to the last resort of accepting the war on the terms chosen by the foe, until the outraged voice of a common humanity should force a respect for the recognized rules of war.

When General Jackson arrived near Gordonsville, on July 19, 1862, he was reinforced by General A. P. Hill. Receiving information that only a part of General Pope's army was at Culpeper Court-House, General Jackson, hoping to defeat it before reinforcements should arrive, moved forward the divisions of Ewell, Hill, and Jackson, on August 7th, from their intrenchments near Gordonsville. On August 9th Jackson arrived within eight miles of Culpeper Court-House, and found the foe on his front near Cedar Run. His cavalry in large force occupied a ridge to the right of the road. A battery opened on it and soon forced it to retire. Our fire was responded to by some guns beyond the ridge from which the advance had just been driven. Soon afterward the cavalry returned to the position where it was first seen, and General Early was ordered forward. General Early, forming his brigade in line of battle, moved into the open field and drove the opposing cavalry before him to the crest of a hill which overlooked the ground between his troops and the opposite hill, along which the enemy's batteries were posted, which opened upon him as soon as he reached the eminence. Early retired his troops under the protection of the hill, and a small battery of ours in advance of his right opened. Meanwhile General Winder, with Jackson's brigade, was placed on the left of the road; Campbell's brigade, Colonel Garnett commanding, being on the left; Taliaferro's, parallel to the road, supporting the batteries; and Winder's own brigade in reserve.

The battle opened with a fierce fire of artillery, which lasted about two hours.

The enemy's infantry advanced about 5 P.M., and attacked Early in front, while another body, concealed, moved upon his right. The contest soon became animated. In the meantime the main body of the opposing army gained the left of Jackson's division, General Taliaferro commanding, and poured a destructive fire into its flank and rear. Campbell's brigade fell back in confusion, exposing the flank of Taliaferro's, which gave way, as also did the left of Early's. The rest of his brigade held its ground firmly.

Winder's brigade, with Branch's, of A. P. Hill's division, on its right, advanced promptly to the support of Jackson's division, and after a sanguinary struggle the assailants were repulsed with loss. Pender's and Archer's brigades, of Hill's division, came up on the left of Winder's, and by a general charge the foe was driven back in confusion, leaving the ground covered with his dead and wounded. General Ewell, with his two brigades, on the extreme right, had been prevented from advancing by the fire of our own artillery, which swept his approach to the enemy's left. The obstacle now being removed, he pressed forward under a hot fire, and came gallantly into action. Repulsed and vigorously followed on our left and centre, and now hotly pressed on our right, the whole line of the enemy gave way, and was soon in full retreat. Night had now set in, but General Jackson, desiring to enter Culpeper Court-House before morning, determined to pursue.

Hill's division led the advance, but, owing to the darkness, was compelled to move with caution.

The enemy was found about a mile and a half in the rear of the field of battle, and information was received that reinforcements had arrived. Jackson therefore halted for the night. Next day he became satisfied that the enemy's force had been so largely increased as to render imprudent a further advance. Sending his wounded to the rear, he proceeded to bury the dead, and collect the arms from the battle-field. On the 11th the enemy asked and got permission to bury those of his dead not already interred. Jackson remained in position during the day, and at night returned to the vicinity of Gordonsville.

In this engagement—known as the battle of Cedar Run—400 prisoners were captured; and 5,300 stand of small-arms, 1 piece of artillery, several caissons, and 3 colors fell into our hands. Our killed were 229; wounded, 1,047; total loss, 1,276. The loss on the other side exceeded 1,500.

This victory effectually checked the invader for the time; but it soon became apparent that his army was receiving a large increase. Burnside's corps had moved up the Rappahannock, a few days after the battle, to unite with Pope, and for the same purpose a part of McClellan's army had left Westover.

It seemed, therefore, that the most effectual way to relieve Richmond from any danger of an attack would be to reinforce Jackson and advance on Pope.

Accordingly, on August 13th, Longstreet, Anderson, and Stuart proceeded to Gordonsville. On the 16th the troops began to move from the vicinity of Gordonsville toward the Rapidan, on the north side of which the army of invasion lay in great force. It was determined, with the cavalry, to destroy the railroad bridge over the Rappahannock in rear of the enemy, while Jackson and Longstreet crossed the Rapidan and attacked his left flank. But the enemy, becoming apprised of our design, hastily retreated beyond the Rappahannock. On the 21st our forces moved toward that river, and some sharp skirmishing ensued with our cavalry that had crossed at Beverly's Ford. As it had been determined not to attempt the passage of the river at that point with the army, the cavalry withdrew to the south side. Soon the enemy appeared in great numbers on the opposite bank, and an active fire was kept up between his artillery and Taliaferro's batteries,

But as our positions on the south bank of the Rappahannock were commanded by those on the north bank, which served to guard all the fords, General Lee determined to seek a more favorable place to cross higher up the river, and thus gain his adversary's right. Longstrect was directed to leave Kelly's Ford on the 21st, and take position in the vicinity of Beverly's Ford and the railroad bridge, then held by Jackson, in order to mask the movement of Jackson, who was instructed to ascend the river. On the 22nd Jackson proceeded up the Rappahannock, leaving Trimble's brigade to guard his train. In the afternoon Longstreet sent Hood, with two brigades, to relieve Trimble. Hood had just reached the position, when he and Trimble were attacked by a considerable force. After a short engagement the enemy was driven precipitately over the river with heavy loss. Jackson was prevented from crossing by a heavy rain, which caused the river to rise so rapidly as to be impassable for infantry and artillery, and he withdrew the troops that had reached the opposite side. General Stuart crossed the Rappahannock on the morning of the 22nd, about six miles above the Springs, with parts of two brigades, but was prevented from destroying the railroad bridge at Catlett's Station by the same storm that arrested Jackson's movements. He captured more than 300 prisoners. Apprehensive of the effects of the rain, he then recrossed the Rappahannock. The rise of the river, rendering the lower fords impassable, enabled the enemy to concentrate his main body opposite Jackson. Longstreet was ordered to his support by General Lee. Although retarded by the swollen Rappahannock and its tributaries, he reached Jeffersonton in the afternoon of the 24th. Jackson's command lay between that place and the Spring's Ford, and a warm cannonade was progressing between the batteries of General A. P. Hill's division and those in his front. The enemy was massed between Warrenton and the Springs, and guarded the fords of the Rappahannock as far above as Waterloo.

McClellan's army had left Westover, and part of it had marched to join Pope. It was reported that the rest would soon follow. For the same purpose the greater part of General Cox's army had been withdrawn from the Kanawha Valley.

Jackson crossed the Rappahannock on the 25th, and reached Bristoe Station on the evening of the 26th. At Gainesville he was joined by Stuart, with the brigades of Robertson and Fitzhugh Lee, who continued with him during his operations, and guarded both his flanks.

Jackson was now between the army of Pope and Washington City, without having met any considerable force. General Trimble volunteered to push forward in the night, with two Carolina regiments, to capture the enemy's depot at Manassas Junction, seven miles from Jackson's encampment. The offer was accepted. About midnight the place was captured with little difficulty. Eight pieces of artillery, with their horses, ammunition, and equipments were captured; more than 300 prisoners, 175 horses, besides those belonging to the artillery, 200 new tents, and immense quantities of commissary and quartermaster's stores fell into our hands.

Ewell's division was left at Bristoe Station, and the rest of the command arrived at the Junction early on the 27th. Soon a considerable force of the enemy, under General Taylor, of New Jersey, pushed forward boldly to recover the stores. After a sharp engagement he was routed and driven back, leaving his killed and wounded on the field. The troops remained at Manassas Junction during the day, and supplied themselves with everything they required. In the afternoon two brigades advanced against General Ewell, at Bristoe, from the direction of Warrenton Junction, but were broken and repulsed. Their place was soon supplied with fresh troops, and it was apparent that the commander had turned upon General Jackson with his whole force. General Ewell, perceiving the strength of the column, withdrew and rejoined General Jackson. The enemy halted at Bristoe. General Jackson, having a much inferior force to General Pope's, retired from Manassas Junction and took a position west of the turnpike road from Warrenton to Alexandria, where he could more readily unite with the approaching column of Longstreet. Having supplied the wants of his troops, he was compelled, through lack of transportation, to destroy the rest of the captured property. Many thousand pounds of bacon, a thousand barrels of corned beef, two thousand barrels of salt pork, and two thousand barrels of flour, besides other property of great value, were burned.

During the night of the 27th of August Taliaferro's division halted near the battle-field of July 21, 1861, where it was joined on the 28th by the divisions of Hill and Ewell. During the afternoon the enemy, approaching from the direction of Warrenton toward Alexandria, exposed his left flank, and General Jackson determined to attack him. A fierce and sanguinary conflict ensued, which continued until about 9 P.M., when he slowly fell back and left us in possession of the field. The loss on both sides was heavy. On the next morning the enemy had taken a position to interpose his army between Jackson and Alexandria, and about 10 A.M. opened with artillery upon the right of Jackson's line. The troops of the latter were disposed in rear of Groveton, Jackson's division, under Brigadier-General Starke, being on the right; Ewell's, under General Lawton, in the centre; and A. P. Hill's on the left. The attacking columns were evidently concentrating on Jackson with the design of overwhelming him before the arrival of Longstreet. This latter officer left his position opposite Warrenton Springs on the 26th, and marched to join Jackson. On the 28th, arriving at Thoroughfare Gap, he found the enemy prepared to dispute his progress. Holding the eastern extremity of the pass with a large force, the enemy directed a heavy fire of artillery upon the road leading to it and upon the sides of the mountain. An attempt was made to turn his right, but before our troops reached their destination he advanced to the attack, and being vigorously repulsed, withdrew to his position at the eastern end of the Gap, keeping up an active fire of artillery until dark. He then retreated. On the morning of the 29th Longstreet's command resumed its march, the sound of cannon at Manassas announcing that Jackson was already engaged. The head of the column came upon the field in rear of the enemy's left, which had already opened with artillery upon Jackson's right. Longstreet immediately placed some of his batteries in position, but, before he could complete his dispositions to attack the force before him, it withdrew to another part of the field. He then took position on the right of Jackson. The cavalry guarded our right and left flanks, that on the right being under General Stuart in person, After the arrival of Longstreet the enemy changed his position and began to concentrate opposite Jackson's left, opening a brisk artillery fire, which was responded to by some of A. P. Hill's batteries.

Soon afterward General Stuart reported the approach of a large force from the direction of Bristoe Station, threatening Longstreet's right. But no serious attack was made, and after firing a few shots that force withdrew. Meanwhile a large column advanced to assail the left of Jackson's position, occupied by the division of A. P. Hill. The attack was received by his troops with steadiness, and the battle raged with great fury. The enemy was repeatedly repulsed, but again pressed on the attack with fresh troops. Once he succeeded in penetrating an interval between General Gregg's brigade on the extreme left and that of General Thomas, but was quickly driven back with great slaughter by the Fourteenth South Carolina Regiment and the Forty-ninth Georgia. The contest was close and obstinate; the combatants sometimes delivered their fire at a few paces. Gregg had successfully and most gallantly resisted the attack until the ammunition of his brigade was exhausted and all his field-officers but two were killed or wounded. The reinforcement (Hay's brigade) was of like high-tempered steel, and together in hand-to-hand fight they held their post until they were relieved, after several hours of severe fighting, by Early's brigade and the Eighth Louisiana Regiment. General Early drove the enemy back with heavy loss, and pursued about two hundred yards beyond the line of battle, when he was recalled to the position on the railroad. While the battle was raging on Jackson's left, Hood and Evans were ordered by Longstreet to advance, but before the order could be obeyed Hood was himself attacked, and his command became at once warmly engaged. The enemy was repulsed by Hood after a severe contest, and fell back, closely followed by our troops.

The battle continued until 9 P.M., the foe retreating until he reached a strong position, which he held with a large force. Our troops remained in their advanced position until early next morning, when they were withdrawn to their first line. One piece of artillery, several stands of colors, and a number of prisoners were captured. Our loss was severe.

On the morning of the 30th the enemy again advanced, and skirmishing began along the line. The troops of Jackson and Longstreet maintained their position of the previous day. At noon the firing of the batteries ceased, and all was quiet for some hours. About 3 P.M. the enemy, having massed his troops in front of Jackson, advanced in strong force. His front line pushed forward until it was engaged at close quarters by Jackson's troops, when its progress was checked, and a fierce and bloody struggle ensued. A second and third line of great strength moved up to support the first, but in doing so came within easy range of a position a little in advance of Longstreet's left. He immediately ordered up two batteries, and, two others being thrown forward about the same time by Colonel S. D. Lee, the supporting lines were broken, and fell back in confusion under their well-directed and destructive fire. Their repeated efforts to rally were unavailing, and Jackson's troops, being thus relieved from the pressure of overwhelming numbers, began to press steadily forward, driving everything before them. The enemy retreated in confusion, suffering severely from our artillery, which advanced as he retired. Longstreet, anticipating the order for a general advance, now threw his whole command against the centre and left. The whole line swept steadily on, driving the opponents with great carnage from each successive position, until 10 P.M., when darkness put an end to the battle and the pursuit.

The obscurity of the night and the uncertainty of the fords of Bull Run rendered it necessary to suspend operations until morning, when the cavalry, being pushed forward, discovered that the retreat had continued to the strong position of Centreville, about four miles beyond Bull Run. The prevalence of a heavy rain, which began during the night, threatened to render Bull Run impassable, and to impede our movements. Longstreet remained on the battle-field to engage attention and to protect parties for the burial of the dead and the removal of the wounded, while Jackson proceeded by Sudley's Ford to the Little River turnpike to turn the enemy's right and intercept his retreat to Washington. Jackson's progress was retarded by the inclemency of the weather and the fatigue of his troops. He reached the turnpike in the evening, and the next day (September 1st) advanced by that road toward Fairfax Court-House. The enemy in the meantime was falling back rapidly toward Washington, and had thrown a strong force to Germantown, on the Little River turnpike, to cover his line of retreat from Centreville. The advance of Jackson encountered him at Ox Hill, near Germantown, about 5 P.M. Line of battle was at once formed, and two brigades were thrown forward to attack and ascertain the strength of the position. A cold and drenching rain-storm drove in the faces of our troops as they advanced and gallantly engaged. They were subsequently supported, and the conflict was obstinately maintained until dark, when the enemy retreated, having lost two general officers, one of whom—Major-General Kearney—was left dead on the field. Longstreet's command arrived after the action was over, and the next morning it was found that the retreat had been so rapid that the attempt to intercept was abandoned. The proximity of the fortifications around Alexandria and Washington was enough to prevent further pursuit. Our army rested during the 2nd near Chantilly, the retreating foe being followed only by our cavalry, which continued to harass him until he reached the shelter of his intrenchments.

In the series of engagements on the plains of Manassas more than 7,000 prisoners were taken, in addition to about 2,000 wounded left in our hands. Thirty pieces of artillery, upward of 20,000 stand of small-arms, numerous colors, and a large amount of stores, besides those taken by General Jackson at Manassas Junction, were captured.

Major-General Pope in his report says:

> "The whole force that I had at Centreville, as reported to me by the corps commanders, on the morning of the 1st of September, was as follows: McDowell's corps, 10,000 men; Sigel's corps, about 7,000; Heintzelman's corps, about 6,000; Reno's, 6,000; Banks's, 5,000; Sumner's, 11,000; Porter's, 10,000; Franklin's, 8,000—in all, 63,000 men. . . . The small fraction of 20,500 men was all of the 91,000 veteran troops from Harrison's Landing which ever drew trigger under my command."

Our losses in the engagement at Manassas Plains were considerable. The number killed was 1,090; wounded, 6,154—total, 7,244. The loss of the enemy in killed, wounded, and missing was estimated between 15,000 and 20,000.

Chapter 62

War Transferred to the Frontier

THE enemy having retired to the protection of the fortifications around Washington and Alexandria, Lee's army, on September 3rd, marched toward Leesburg. The armies of McClellan and Pope has now been brought back to the point from which they had set out on the campaign of the spring and summer. The objects of those campaigns had been frustrated, and the futile designs against the coast of North Carolina and in Western Virginia thwarted by the withdrawal of the main body of the forces from those regions.

From Northeastern Virginia the enemy had withdrawn his forces to the intrenchments of Washington. The hostile troops that had held Winchester had retired to Harper's Ferry. The war had been transferred to the frontier. The supplies of rich and fertile districts were thus made accessible to our army. Not to permit the season of active operations to pass without endeavoring to impose a further check on the enemy, the best course appeared to be the transfer of our army to Maryland. Although not properly equipped for invasion, poorly provided with clothing and shoes for the soldiers, and greatly deficient in transportation, we yet believed that we were strong enough to detain the opposing army on the northern frontier until the approach of winter should render its advance into Virginia difficult, if not impossible. The condition of Maryland encouraged the belief, also, that the presence of our army, although numerically inferior to the army of the North, would compel the Washington Government to retain all its available forces to provide against contingencies which its conduct toward the people of Maryland gave reason to apprehend. It was hoped also, that military success might give us the power to aid the people of that State in any effort they might make to recover their liberty.

Influenced by these considerations the army was put in motion. It was decided to cross the Potomac east of the Blue Ridge, in order by threatening Washington and Baltimore to force the enemy to withdraw from the south bank, where his presence endangered our communications and the safety of our men engaged in the removal of our wounded and the captured property from the late battle-field. This result accomplished, it was proposed to move the army into Western Maryland, and by threatening Pennsylvania induce the enemy to withdraw from our territory for the protection of his own.

General Hill's division crossed the Potomac, September 4 and 7, near Leesburg, and encamped near Frederick. It had been supposed that this advance would lead to the evacuation of Martinsburg and Harper's Ferry, thus opening the line of communication through the Shenandoah Valley. This not having occurred, it became necessary to dislodge the garrisons from those positions before concentrating the army west of the mountains. For this purpose Jackson, after a rapid march, crossed the Potomac, sent Hill's division to Martinsburg, and disposed of the rest of his command so as to cut off retreat to the westward. The enemy evacuated Martinsburg and retired to Harper's Ferry. Meanwhile General McLaws was ordered to seize Maryland Heights, north of the Potomac, opposite Harper's Ferry. He found the heights in possession of the enemy, with infantry and artillery, protected by intrenchments. On the 13th he assailed the works, and carried them; the enemy retreated to Harper's Ferry, and on the next day the investment was complete.

Simultaneously with the beginning of the march of these troops upon Harper's Ferry the rest of Longstreet's command and the division of D. H. Hill crossed the South Mountain and moved toward Boonsboro. Longstreet continued his march to Hagerstown, and Hill halted near Boonsboro to support the cavalry, and prevent the force invested at Harper's Ferry from escaping through Pleasant Valley. The advance of the Federal army bad been so slow as to justify the belief that we should reduce Harper's Ferry and concentrate our forces before we should be called upon to meet the foe. In that event it was intended to oppose his passage through South Mountain. But a copy of Lee's order of battle, found after the evacuation of Frederick City, having fallen into McClellan's hands, he pushed forward his forces rapidly, and was reported approaching South Mountain on the afternoon of the 13th.

General Stuart's cavalry impeded his progress, and gained us time for preparations to oppose his advance. General Hill guarded the Boonsboro Gap, and Longstreet was ordered to support him in order to prevent the passage of a force to release the garrison at Harper's Ferry. Early on the 14th a large body of the enemy attempted to force its way to the rear of Hill's position. Hill's small command, with Garland's brigade, repelled the repeated assaults, and held the enemy in check for five hours. Longstreet hurried to the assistance of Hill, and reached the scene of action between 3 and 4 P.M. The battle raged fiercely until night. On the south the enemy was driven back some distance, and his attack in the centre repulsed with loss. Darkness put an end to the contest.

Although the attempt of the enemy to force the pass had failed, it was evident that Lee could not hazard a renewal of the engagement without reinforcements, for McClellan, by his great superiority of numbers, could easily turn either flank. The news was received also that another large body of his troops had forced its way through Crampton Gap, only five miles in rear of McLaws. It was determined, therefore, to retire to Sharpsburg, where we should be on the flank and rear of the enemy should he move against McLaws, and where we could more readily unite with the rest of our army. This movement was accomplished without interruption, and skilfully and efficiently covered by the cavalry brigade of General Fitzhugh Lee. McClellan's advance did not appear on the west side of the pass at Boonsville until about 8 A.M. on the following morning.

The resistance that our troops had offered there gave Jackson time to complete the reduction of Harper's Ferry. The attack on the garrison began at dawn on the 15th. A rapid and vigorous fire was opened both by the batteries of Jackson and those on Maryland and Loudon Heights. In about two hours the garrison surrendered. Eleven thousand men, 73 pieces of artillery, about 13,000 small-arms, and a large quantity of military stores fell into our hands.

The commands of Longstreet and D. H. Hill reached Sharpsburg on the morning of the 15th, Jackson arrived early on the 16th, and General J. G. Walker came up in the after General McLaws retained his position in Crampton Gap until the 14th, when, finding that he was not to be attacked, he gradually withdrew his command toward the Potomac, crossed at Harper's Ferry, and marched by way of Shepardstown, and therefore did not reach the battle-field of Sharpsburg until some time after the engagement of the 17th began.

When his forces were approaching Frederick, General Lee, in obedience to instructions from the President, issued a proclamation to the people of Maryland, announcing the motives and purposes of his presence among them at the head of an invading army.

After briefly reciting some of the acts of tyranny perpetrated by the Washington Administration on the people of Maryland, in arresting and imprisoning citizens upon no charge and contrary to the forms of law; in usurping by armed force the government of the chief city; in dissolving its legislature by the unlawful arrest of its members; in suppressing freedom of the press and of speech; and in reducing a commonwealth, allied to the States of the South by the strongest social, commercial, and political ties, to the condition of a conquered province, General Lee added:

> "Believing that the people of Maryland possess a spirit too lofty to submit to such a government, the people of the South have long wished to aid you in throwing off this foreign yoke, to enable you again to enjoy the inalienable rights of freemen, and restore the independence and sovereignty of your State. In obedience to this wish our army has come among you, and is prepared to assist you with the power of its arms in regaining the rights of which you have been so unjustly despoiled.
>
> "This, citizens of Maryland, is our mission, so far as you are concerned. No restraint upon your free-will is intended; no intimidation will be allowed, within the limits of the army at least. Marylanders shall once more enjoy their ancient freedom of thought and speech. We know no enemies among you, and will protect all of you in every opinion."

CHAPTER 63

THE BATTLE OF ANTIETAM

ON their arrival at Sharpsburg the commands of Longstreet and D. H. Hill were placed in position along the range of hills between the town and the Antietam, nearly parallel to the course of that stream, Longstreet on the right of the road to Boonsboro, and Hill on the left. The advance of the enemy was delayed by Fitzhugh Lee's cavalry, and he did not appear on the opposite side of the Antietam until about 2 P.M. During the afternoon the batteries on each side were partially engaged. On the 16th the artillery-fire became warm, and continued throughout the day. A column crossed the Antietam beyond the reach of our batteries and menaced our left. In anticipation of this movement Hood's two brigades had been transferred from the right and posted between D. H. Hill and the Hagerstown road. General Jackson was now directed to take position on Hood's left, and formed his line with his right resting on the Hagerstown road and his left extending toward the Potomac, protected by General Stuart with the cavalry and horse-artillery. General Walker with his two brigades was stationed on Longstreet's right. As evening approached, the enemy fired more vigorously with his artillery and bore down heavily with his infantry upon Hood, but the attack was gallantly repulsed. At 10 P.M. Hood's troops were relieved by the brigades of Lawton and Trimble, of Ewell's division, commanded by General Lawton. Jackson's own division, under General J. M. Jones, was on Lawton's left, supported by the remaining brigades of Ewell.

At early dawn on the 17th his artillery opened vigorously from both sides of the Antietam, the heaviest fire being directed against our left. Under cover of this fire a large force of infantry attacked General Jackson's division. For several hours the conflict raged with intense fury and alternate success. The enemy's lines were repeatedly broken and forced to retire. Fresh troops, however, soon replaced those that were beaten, and Jackson's men were in turn compelled to fall back. Nearly all the field officers, with a large proportion of the men, were killed or wounded. Our troops slowly yielded to overwhelming numbers and fell back, obstinately disputing every point. General Early, in command of Ewell's division, was ordered to take the place of Jackson's division, most of which was withdrawn, its ammunition being nearly exhausted and its numbers much reduced. The battle now raged with great violence, the small commands under Hood and Early holding their ground against many times their own infantry force and under a tremendous fire of artillery. Hood was reinforced; then the enemy's lines were broken and driven back, but fresh numbers advanced to their support, and they began to gain ground. The desperate resistance they encountered, however, delayed their progress until the troops of McLaws arrived, and those of General J. G. Walker could be brought from the right. Hood's brigade, though it had suffered extraordinary loss, only withdrew to replenish their ammunition, their supply being entirely exhausted. They were relieved by Walker's command, who attacked vigorously, driving his combatant back with much slaughter. Upon the arrival of the reinforcements under McLaws, General Early attacked resolutely the large force opposed to him. McLaws advanced at the same time, and the forces before them were driven back in confusion, closely followed by our troops beyond the position occupied at the beginning of the engagement.

The attack on our left was speedily followed by one in heavy force on the centre. This was met by part of Walker's division and the brigades of G. B. Anderson and Rodes, of D. H. Hill's command, assisted by a few pieces of artillery. General R. H. Anderson's division came to Hill's support, and formed in rear of his line. At this time, by a mistake of orders, Rodes's brigade was withdrawn from its position. During the absence of that command a column pressed through the gap thus created, and G. B. Anderson's brigade was broken and retired. The heavy masses moved forward, being opposed only by four pieces of artillery, supported by a few hundred of our men belonging to different brigades rallied by Hill and other officers, and parts of Walker's and R. H. Anderson's commands. Colonel Cooke, with the Twenty-seventh North Carolina regiment, stood boldly in line without a cartridge. The firm front presented by this small force, and the well-directed fire of the artillery, checked the progress of the enemy, and in about an hour and a half he retired. Another attack was made soon afterward, a little farther to the right, but was repulsed by Miller's guns, of the Washington Artillery, which continued to hold the ground until the close of the engagement, supported by a part of R. H. Anderson's troops.[110]

While the attack on the centre and left was in progress, repeated efforts were made to force the passage of the bridge over the Antietam, opposite the right wing of Longstreet, commanded by General D. R. Jones. The bridge was defended by General Toombs with two regiments and the batteries of General Jones. This small command repulsed five different assaults, made by a greatly superior force. In the afternoon the enemy, in large numbers, having passed the stream, advanced against General Jones, who held the ridge with less than two thousand men. After a determined and brave resistance, he was forced to give way, and the summit was gained. General A. P. Hill, ordered to reinforce General Jones, moved to his support and attacked the force now flushed with success. Hill's batteries were thrown forward and united their fire with those of Jones, and one of D. H. Hill's also opened with good effect from the left of the Boonsboro road. The progress of the enemy was immediately arrested, and his line began to waver. At this moment General Jones ordered Toombs to charge the flank, while Archer, supported by Branch and Gregg, moved on the front of the enemy's line. After a brief resistance he broke and retreated in confusion toward the Antietam, pursued by the troops of Hill and Jones, until he reached the protection of the batteries on the opposite side of the river.

It was now nearly dark, and McClellan had massed a number of batteries to sweep the approach to the Antietam, on the opposite side of which the fresh corps of General Porter now appeared to dispute our advance. Our troops were much exhausted, and greatly reduced in numbers. Under these circumstances it was deemed injudicious to push our advantage further in the face of these fresh troops added to an army previously much exceeding the number of our own. Ours were

---

110. The corps designated the Washington Artillery was composed of Louisiana batteries, organized at New Orleans in the beginning of the war. It was distinguished by its services in the first great battle of Manassas, and in nearly every important conflict, as well of the army of Virginia as that of Tennessee, to the close of the war.

accordingly recalled. The repulse on the right ended the engagement, a protracted and sanguinary conflict in which every effort to dislodge us from our position had been defeated with severe loss.

This great battle was fought by less than forty thousand men on our side, all of whom had undergone the greatest labors and hardships in the field and on the march. Nothing could surpass the determined valor with which they met the large army of the enemy, fully supplied and equipped, and the result reflected the highest credit on the officers and men engaged.

On the 18th our forces occupied the position of the preceding day, except in the centre, where our line was drawn in about two hundred yards. Our ranks were increased by the arrival of a number of troops, who had not been engaged the day before, and, though still too weak to assume the offensive, Lee waited without apprehension a renewal of the attack. The day passed without any hostile demonstration. During the night of the 18th our army was withdrawn to the south side of the Potomac, crossing near Shepardstown, without loss or molestation. The enemy advanced on the next morning, but was held in check by General Fitzhugh Lee with his cavalry. The condition of our troops now demanded repose, and the army marched to the Opequan, near Martinsburg, where it remained several days, and then moved to the vicinity of Bunker Hill and Winchester. General McClellan seemed to be concentrating in and near Harper's Ferry, but made no forward movement.

The contest on our left in this battle was the most violent. This and the privations of our men are very forcibly shown in the following account by Major-General Hood:

> "On the morning of the 15th my forces were again in motion. My troops at this period were sorely in need of shoes, clothing, and food. We had had issued to us no meat for several days, and little or no bread; the men had been forced to subsist principally on green corn and green apples. Nevertheless they were in high spirits and defiant as we contended with the advanced guard of McClellan on the 15th and forenoon of the 16th. During the afternoon of this day I was ordered, after great fatigue and hunger endured by my soldiers, to take position near the Hagerstown turnpike, in open field in front of the Dunkard church. General Hooker's corps crossed the Antietam, swung round with its front on the pike, and

about an hour before sunset encountered my division. I had stationed one or two batteries on a hillock in a meadow, near the edge of a corn-field, and just by the pike. The Texas brigade had been disposed on the left, and that of Law on the right. We opened fire, and a spirited action ensued, which lasted till a late hour in the night. When the firing had in a great measure ceased, we were so close to the enemy that we could distinctly hear him massing his heavy bodies in our immediate front.

"The extreme suffering of my troops for want of food induced me to ride back to General Lee, and request him to send two or more brigades to our relief, in order that the soldiers might have a chance to cook their meagre rations. He said that he would cheerfully do so, but he knew of no command that could be spared for the purpose; he, however, suggested that I should see General Jackson, and endeavor to obtain assistance from him. After riding a long time in search of the latter, I finally discovered him alone, lying upon the ground asleep by the root of a tree. I aroused him, and made known the half-starved condition of my troops; he immediately ordered Lawton's, Trimble's, and Hays's brigades to our relief. He exacted of me a promise that I would come to the support of these forces the moment I was called upon. I quickly rode off in search of my wagons, that the men might prepare and cook their flour, as we were still without meat; unfortunately, the night was then far advanced, and, although every effort was made in the darkness to get the wagons forward, dawn of the morning of the 17th broke upon us before many of the men had time to do more than prepare the dough. Soon thereafter an officer of Lawton's staff dashed up to me, saying, 'General Lawton sends his compliments, with the request that you come at once to his support.' 'To arms!' was instantly sounded, and quite a large number of my brave soldiers were again obliged to march to the front, leaving their uncooked rations in camp.

"Not far distant in our front were drawn up, in close array, heavy columns of Federal infantry; not less than two corps were in sight to oppose my small command, numbering approximately two thousand effectives. However, we moved forward to the assault. Notwithstanding the overwhelming odds of over ten to one against us, we drove the enemy from the wood and corn-field back upon his reserves, and forced him to abandon his guns on our left. This most deadly combat raged till our last round of ammunition was expended. The First Texas Regiment had lost in the corn-field fully two-thirds of its number; and whole ranks of brave men were mowed down in heaps to the right and left. . . . After several ineffectual efforts to procure reinforcements, and our last shot had been fired, I ordered my troops back to Dunkard church, for the same reason which had previously compelled Lawton, Hays, and Trimble to retire (a want of cartridges). Upon the arrival of McLaws's division we marched to the rear, renewed our supply of ammunition, and returned to our position in the wood near the church, which ground we held till a late hour in the afternoon, when we moved somewhat farther to the right and bivouacked for the night. With the close of this bloody day ceased the hardest-fought battle of the war."

The following account, by Colonel Taylor, is more comprehensive:

"On the afternoon of the 16th General McClellan directed an attack by Hooker's corps on the Confederate left—Hood's two brigades—and during the whole of the 17th the battle was waged, with varying intensity, along the entire line. When the issue was first joined, on the afternoon of the 16th, General Lee had with him less than eighteen thousand men, consisting of the commands of Longstreet and D. H. Hill, the two divisions of Jackson, and two brigades under Walker. Couriers were sent to the rear to hurry up the divisions of A. P. Hill, Anderson, and McLaws, hastening from Harper's Ferry, and these several commands, as they reached the front at intervals during the day, on the 17th, were immediately deployed and put to work. Every man was engaged. We had no reserve.

"The fighting was heaviest and most continuous on the Confederate left. It is established by Federal evidence that the three corps of Hooker, Mansfield, and Sumner were completely shattered in the repeated but fruitless efforts to turn this flank, and two of these corps were rendered useless for further aggressive movements. The aggregate strength of the attacking column at this point reached forty thousand men, not counting the two divisions of Franklin's corps, sent at a late hour in the day to rescue the Federal right from the impending danger of being itself destroyed; while the Confederates, from first to last, had less than fourteen thousand men on this flank, consisting of Jackson's two divisions, McLaws's division, and the two small divisions, of two brigades each, under Hood and Walker, with which to resist their fierce and oft-repeated assaults. The disproportion in the centre and on our right was as great as, or even more decided than, on our left."

In the "Report of Committee on the Conduct of the War," General Sumner testifies as follows:

"General Hooker's corps was dispersed; there is no question about that. I sent one of my staff-officers to find where they were, and General Rickets, the only officer he could find, said that he could not raise three hundred men of the corps. There were troops lying down on the left, which I took to belong to Mansfield's command. In the meantime General Mansfield had been killed, and a portion of his corps had also been thrown into confusion."

The testimony of General McClellan, in the same "Report," is to the same effect:

"The next morning (the 18th) I found that our loss had been so great, and there was so much disorganization in some of the commands, that I did not consider it proper to renew the attack that day, especially as I was sure of the arrival that day of two fresh divisions, amounting to about fifteen thousand men. As an instance of the condition of some of the troops that morning, I happen to recollect the returns of the First Corps, General Hooker's, made on the morning of the 18th, by which there were thirty-five hundred men reported present for duty. Four days after that, the returns of the same corps showed thirteen thousand five hundred."

On the night of the 19th our forces crossed the Potomac, and some brigades of the enemy followed. In the morning General A. P. Hill, who commanded the rear-guard, was ordered to drive them back. Having disposed his forces, an attack was made, and, as the foe massed in front of General Pender's brigade and endeavored to turn his flank, General Hill says, in his report:

"A simultaneous daring charge was made, and the enemy driven pell-mell into the river. Then commenced the most terrible slaughter that this war has yet witnessed. The broad surface of the Potomac was blue with the floating bodies of our foe. But few escaped to tell the tale. By their own account they lost three thousand men killed and drowned from one brigade alone. Some two hundred prisoners were taken."

General McClellan states, in his official report, that he had in this battle, in action, 87,164 men of all arms.

The official reports of the commanding officers of our forces, made at the time, show our total effective infantry to have been 27,255. The estimate made for the cavalry and artillery, which is rather excessive, is 8,000. This would make General Lee's entire strength 35,255.

The official return of the Army of Northern Virginia on September 22, 1862, after its return to Virginia, and when the stragglers had rejoined their commands, shows present for duty 36,187 infantry and artillery. The cavalry, of which there is no return, would perhaps increase these figures to 40,000 of all arms.

The return of the United States Army of the Potomac on September 20, 1862, shows present for duty at that date, of the commands that participated in the battle of Sharpsburg, 85,930 of all arms.

The loss of the enemy at Boonsboro and Sharpsburg was 14,794.

Chapter 64

Treasury Regulations and the Cotton Famine

AS early as July 13, 1861, the Government of the United States passed the first of a series of measures, the object of which was practically and effectually to plunder us of a large portion of our cotton crop and secure its transportation to the manufacturers of Europe. The first of these measures authorized the President to issue his proclamation declaring the inhabitants of any of our States, or a portion of any one of them, to be in insurrection, and therefore all commercial intercourse became unlawful and was required to cease, and all goods and chattels, wares and merchandise, on the way to or from the State, or part of a State, were forfeited to the United States, together with the vessel or vehicle in which they were conveyed. Two effects were to follow this proclamation: first, the cessation of all commercial intercourse with the citizens of the United States; second, the forfeiture of all vessels *in transitu*. When this condition had been reached the act then authorized the President, in his discretion, to reopen the trade in such articles, and for such time, and by such persons as he might think most conducive to the public interest. The articles of trade were chiefly cotton and tobacco; the time during which the trade might be continued was evidently so long as it could be used for the purpose in view; the persons were those who would most skilfully advance the end to be accomplished; and the public interest was the collection and transportation of the cotton to the European manufacturers.

One may search the Constitution of the United States in vain to find any grant of power to Congress by which it could be authorized to pass this act, much less to find any authority conferred upon the President to approve the act or to justify him in a violation of the oath he had taken to support and maintain the provisions of the Constitution. Congress was guilty of a most flagrant violation of the Constitution by the passage of the act; and the President, instead of being a check upon the unconstitutional measure, for which object the veto power was granted to him, became, by his approval, an accomplice in the usurpation. For nothing is more evident than that it is one of the powers reserved to the States to regulate the commercial intercourse between the citizens, to the extent even of the establishment of inspectors and quarantine regulations.

Neither did a state of war authorize the Government of the United States to interfere with the commercial intercourse between the citizens of the States, although under the law of nations it might be so justified with regard to foreign enemies. But this relation it persistently refused to concede to the Confederate States or to their citizens. It constantly asserted that they were its subjects in a state of insurrection; if so, they were equally entitled to the provisions of the Constitution for their protection as well as to its penalties. Still less could the Government make an absolute forfeiture of the goods seized.

That a state of war did not enlarge the powers of the Government, as was assumed by this act, was expressly decided by Chief-Justice Taney in a case that arose under the act. One Carpenter refused or neglected to obtain the permit required, and his goods were seized. He contested the right of seizure, and the Chief-Justice gave a decision at Baltimore in May, 1863. He said:

> "Undoubtedly the United States authorities may take proper measures to prevent trade or intercourse with the enemy. But it does not by any means follow that they disregard the limits of all their own powers as prescribed by the Constitution or the rights and powers reserved to the States or to the people.
>
> "A civil war, or any other, does not enlarge the powers of the Federal Government over the States or the people beyond what the compact has given to it in time of war. A state of war does not annul the Tenth Article of the Amendment of the Constitution, which declares that 'the powers not delegated to the United States by the Constitution, nor prohibited by it to the States, are reserved to the States respectively or to the people.' Nor does a civil war, or any other war, absolve the judicial department from the duty of maintaining with an even and firm hand the rights and powers of the Federal Government, and of the States and of the citizens, as they are written in the Constitution, which every judge is bound to

support. . . . The Court is of opinion that the regulations in question are illegal and void, and that the seizure of the goods of the said Carpenter, because he refused to comply with them, cannot be sustained."

The proclamation of the President required by the act issued on August 16, 1861, declared certain States and parts of States to be in insurrection, etc. Under it some licenses were issued to places in Kentucky and Missouri, without any fruitful results. Some strong military and naval expeditions were fitted out to invade us and occupy the ports where cotton and other valuable products were usually shipped. An advance was made up the Cumberland and Tennessee Rivers, and down the Mississippi. The ports of Beaufort, Port Royal, and New Orleans were declared to be open for trade under the new system. Licenses were granted to foreign vessels by United States consuls, and to coasting vessels by the Treasury Department, and the blockade was relaxed as far as related to those ports, except as "to persons, property, and information contraband of war." Collectors were appointed at these ports, and a circular was addressed to the foreign ministers at Washington announcing the reopening of communication with conquered Southern localities.

Again, on March 3, 1863, an act was passed which authorized the Secretary of the Treasury to appoint special agents to receive and collect all abandoned and captured property in any State, or portion of a State, designated as in insurrection. Under this act a paper division of the whole of our territory was made into five special districts, and to each a special agent was appointed with numerous assistants. Abandoned property was declared to be that which had been deserted by its owners, or that which had been voluntarily abandoned by them to the civil or military authorities of the United States. Property which had been seized or taken from hostile possessors by the military or naval forces was also to be turned over to the special agents to be sold. All property not transported in accordance with the Treasury regulations was forfeitable. All expenses incurred in relation to the property were charged upon it.

On September 11, 1863, revised regulations were issued by the Secretary, which divided the country into thirteen districts, from Wheeling, W. Va., to Natchez, on the Mississippi, and a complete system of transportation and trade was organized. In December, 1864, new regulations were issued, which authorized the purchase of our products at certain points, from any person, with bonds furnished by the Treasury. The products were sold, transportation was allowed, and the proceeds were made to constitute a fund for further purchases. A vigorous traffic sprang up under these regulations, which were suspended by an order from General Grant, issued on March 10, 1865, and revoked on April 11th by himself.

On April 29, 1865, all restrictions upon internal, domestic, and coastwise commercial intercourse with all the country east of the Mississippi River were discontinued.

But before these unconstitutional measures were abandoned great distress had arisen among the working-classes of Europe, in consequence of the failure of the supply of cotton to their manufacturing districts. The foreign necessity for our cotton was represented in these words of Her Britannic Majesty's Secretary of State for Foreign Affairs, on May 6, 1862:

> "Thousands are now obliged to resort to the poor-rates for subsistence, owing to this blockade, yet Her Majesty's Government have not sought to take advantage of the obvious imperfection of this blockade in order to declare it ineffective. They have, to the loss and detriment of the British nation, scrupulously observed the duties of Great Britain to a friendly state."

The severity of the distress thus alluded to was such, both in Great Britain and France, as to produce an intervention of the governments of those countries to alleviate it. Instead, however, of adopting those measures required in the exercise of justice to the Confederacy, and which would have been sustained by the laws of nations, by declaring the blockade "ineffective," as it really was, they sought, through informal application to Mr. Seward, the Secretary of State of the United States, to obtain opportunities for an increased exportation of cotton from the Confederacy.

Chapter 65

Military Operations in Virginia

ABOUT he middle of October, 1862, General McClellan crossed the Potomac, east of the Blue Ridge, and advanced southward, seizing the passes of the mountains as he progressed. In the latter part of the month he began to incline eastwardly from the mountains, moving in the direction of Warrenton, about which he finally concentrated.

On November 15th the enemy was in motion, and on the 21st it became apparent that the whole army—now under Burnside, who had superseded McClellan—was concentrating on the north side of the Rappahannock. About November 26th Jackson was directed to advance toward Fredericksburg, and as some of the enemy's gunboats had appeared in the river at Port Royal, and it was possible that an attempt might be made to cross in that vicinity, D. H. Hill's division was stationed near that place, and the rest of Jackson's corps so disposed as to support Hill or Longstreet, as occasion might require. The fords of the Rappahannock above Fredericksburg were closely guarded by our cavalry, and the river above and below Port Royal was watched by W. H. F. Lee's brigade. The interval before the advance of the enemy was employed in strengthening our lines, which extended from the river about a mile and a half above Fredericksburg, along the range of hills in the rear of the city to the Richmond railroad.

As these hills were commanded by the opposite heights, in possession of Burnside's force, earthworks were constructed on their crest at the most eligible positions for artillery. To prevent gunboats from ascending the river, a battery was placed four miles below the city. The plain of Fredericksburg is so completely commanded by the Stafford Heights that no effectual opposition could be made to the passage of the river without exposing our troops to the destructive fire of the numerous batteries on the opposite heights. At the same time the narrowness of the Rappahannock and its winding course presented opportunities for laying down pontoon bridges at points secure from the fire of our artillery. Our position was therefore selected with a view to resist an advance after crossing, and the river was guarded by detachments of sharpshooters to impede the laying of pontoons until our army could be prepared for action.

Before dawn, December 11th, Burnside was in motion. About 2 P.M. he began preparations to throw two bridges over the Rappahannock, opposite Fredericksburg, and one about a mile and a quarter below, near the mouth of the Deep Run. From daybreak until 4 P.M. the troops, sheltered behind the houses on the river-bank, repelled his repeated efforts to lay bridges opposite the town, driving back his working parties and their supports with great slaughter. At the lower point, where there was no such protection, he was successfully resisted until nearly noon, when, being exposed to the severe fire of the batteries on the opposite heights, our troops were withdrawn and the bridge was completed. Soon afterward 150 pieces of artillery opened a furious fire on the city, causing our troops to retire from the river-bank about 4 P.M. The enemy then crossed in boats, and proceeded rapidly to lay down the bridges. His advance into the town was bravely contested until dark, when our troops were recalled, the necessary time for concentration having been gained.

The enemy was prevented from constructing bridges, and his attempts to cross by boats, under the cover of artillery and musketry fire, were repelled until late in the afternoon, when General Barksdale, who commanded our force in Fredericksburg, was ordered to retire. During the night of the succeeding day the enemy crossed in large numbers at and below the town, secured from material interruption by a dense fog.

Shortly after 9 A.M. the partial rising of the mist disclosed a large force moving in line of battle against Jackson. Dense masses appeared in front of A. P. Hill, stretching far up the river in the direction of Fredericksburg. As they advanced, Major Pellham, of Stuart's horse-artillery, opened a rapid and well-directed enfilade fire, which arrested their progress.

Four batteries were immediately turned upon him, and upon his withdrawal the enemy extended his left down the Port Royal road, and his numerous batteries opened with vigor upon Jackson's line. Eliciting no response, his infantry moved forward to seize the position occupied by Lieutenant-Colonel Walker, who, reserving the fire of his fourteen pieces until their line had approached within less than eight hundred yards, opened fire upon it with such destructive effect as to cause it to waver and soon retreat in confusion.

About 1 P.M. the main attack on the right began by a furious cannonade, under cover of which three compact lines of infantry advanced against Hill's front. The contest soon became fierce and bloody. Archer and Lane, who occupied the edge of a wood, repulsed those portions of the line immediately in front of them; but, before the interval between these commands could be closed, the assailants pressed through in overwhelming numbers and turned the left of Archer and the right of Lane. Attacked in front and flank, two regiments of Archer and a brigade of Lane, after a brave resistance, gave way. Archer held his line until the arrival of reinforcements. Thomas came to the relief of Lane, repulsed the column that had broken his line, and drove it back to the railroad. In the meantime a large force had penetrated the wood as far as Hill's reserve, where it was met by a fire for which it was not prepared. The Federals were allowed to approach quite near, when Gregg's South Carolina brigade poured a withering fire into the faces of Meade's men, and Early's division from the second line swept forward. The contest in the woods was short and decisive. The enemy was quickly routed and driven out with very heavy loss, and, though largely reinforced, was pressed back and pursued to the shelter of the railroad embankment. Here he was gallantly charged by the brigades of Hoke and Atkinson, and driven across the plain to his batteries. The attack on Hill's left was repulsed by the artillery on that part of the line, against which a hot fire from twenty-four guns was directed. The repulse of the foe on our right was decisive, and the attack was not renewed, but his batteries kept up an active fire at intervals, and sharpshooters skirmished along the front during the afternoon.

While these events were occurring on our right, the enemy, in formidable numbers, made repeated and desperate assaults upon the left of our line. About 11 A.M., having massed his troops under cover of the houses of Fredericksburg, he moved forward in strong columns to seize Marye's and Willis's Hills. All his batteries on the Stafford Heights directed their fire upon the positions occupied by our artillery, with a view to silence it, and cover the movement of the infantry. Without replying to this furious cannonade, our batteries poured a rapid and destructive fire into the dense lines of the infantry as they advanced to the attack, frequently breaking their ranks, and forcing them to retreat to the shelter of the houses. Notwithstanding the havoc inflicted by our batteries, six times did he press on with great determination to within one hundred yards of the foot of the hill; but here, encountering the deadly fire of our infantry, his columns were broken, and fled in confusion to the town. The last assault was made shortly before dark. This effort met the fate of those that preceded it, and, when night closed in, his shattered masses had disappeared into the town, leaving the field covered with his dead and wounded.

During the night our lines were strengthened by the construction of earthworks at exposed points, and preparations made to receive the enemy on the next day. The 14th passed without a renewal of the attack. The hostile batteries on both sides of the river played upon our lines at intervals, our own firing but little. On the 15th Burnside still retained his position, apparently ready for battle, but the day passed as the preceding. But, on the morning of the 16th, it was discovered that he had availed himself of the darkness of the night and the prevalence of a violent storm of wind and rain to recross the river. The town was immediately reoccupied, and our positions on the river bank were resumed.

In the engagement we captured more than 900 prisoners and 9,000 stand of arms. A large quantity of ammunition was found in Fredericksburg. On our side 458 were killed and 3,743 wounded; total, 4,201. The loss of the enemy was 1,152 killed, 9,101 wounded, and 3,234 missing; total, 13,487.

General Burnside subsequently testified that he "had about 100,000 men on the south side of the river, and every single man of them was under artillery fire, and about half of them were at different times formed in columns of attack."

Less than 20,000 Confederate troops were actively engaged. This number composed about one-fourth of the army under General Lee. The returns of the Army of Northern Virginia show that on December 10,

1862, General Lee had present for duty 78,228, and, on December 20th, 75,524 of all arms.

After the battle of Fredericksburg the Army of Northern Virginia remained encamped on the south side of the Rappahannock until the latter part of April, 1863. The Federal army occupied the north side of the river opposite Fredericksburg, extending to the Potomac. Two brigades of Anderson's division were stationed near United States Mine or Bank Mill Ford. The cavalry was distributed on both flanks. Longstreet, with two divisions, had been detached for service south of James River in February, and did not rejoin the army until after the battle of Chancellorsville.

Excepting a cavalry engagement near Kelly's Ford, on March 17th, nothing of interest occurred during this period of inactivity. But the cavalry movements indicated that the army, now commanded by Hooker, was about to resume active operations.

On the 28th, early in the morning, the enemy crossed the river in boats near Fredericksburg, laid a pontoon-bridge, and built another about a mile below. A considerable force crossed on these bridges during the day, and was massed under the high banks of the river, which afforded protection from our artillery, while the batteries on the opposite heights completely commanded the wide plain between our lines and the narrow river. On the 29th it was reported that he had crossed in force near Kelly's Ford, and that a heavy column was moving from Kelly's toward Germania Ford on the Rapidan, and another toward Ely's Ford. The routes they were pursuing, after crossing the Rapidan, converged near Chancellorsville, whence several roads led to the rear of our position at Fredericksburg. General Anderson proceeded to cover these roads on the 29th, but, learning that the enemy had crossed the Rapidan and was approaching in strong force, he retired early on the next morning to the intersection of the Mine and plank roads near Tabernacle Church, and began to intrench himself. His rear-guard, as he left Chancellorsville, was attacked by cavalry, but, being vigorously repulsed, they offered no further opposition to his march.

The enemy on our front near Fredericksburg continued inactive, and it was now apparent that the main attack would be made upon our flank and rear. It was therefore determined to leave sufficient troops to hold our lines, and with the main body of the army to give battle to the approaching column. Early's division and Barksdale's brigade, with part of the reserve artillery under Pendleton, were intrusted with the defence of our position at Fredericksburg, and at midnight on the 30th McLaws marched with the rest of his command toward Chancellorsville. Jackson followed at dawn next morning with the remaining divisions of his corps, reached the position occupied by General Anderson at 8 A.M., and immediately began to make preparations to advance. At 11 A.M. the troops moved forward on the plank and old turnpike roads. The enemy was soon encountered on both roads, and heavy skirmishing with infantry and artillery ensued, our troops pressing steadily forward. A strong attack upon McLaws was repulsed with spirit by Semmes's brigade; and General Wright, diverging to the left of the plank road, marched by way of the unfinished railroad from Fredericksburg to Gordonsville and turned the Federal right. His whole line thereupon retreated rapidly, vigorously pursued by our troops until they arrived within about one mile of Chancellorsville. Here the enemy had assumed a position of great natural strength, surrounded on all sides by a dense forest filled with a tangled undergrowth, in the midst of which breastworks of logs had been constructed, with trees felled in front so as to form an almost impenetrable abatis. His artillery swept the few narrow roads by which his position could be approached from the front, and commanded the adjacent woods. The left of his line extended from Chancellorsville toward the Rappahannock, covering the Bank Mill Ford, where he communicated with the north bank of the river by a pontoon-bridge. His right stretched westward along the Germania Ford road more than two miles. Darkness was approaching before the strength and extent of his line could be ascertained; and, as the nature of the country rendered it hazardous to attack by night, our troops were halted and formed in line of battle in front of Chancellorsville, at right angles to the plank road, extending on the right to the Mine road, and to the left in the direction of the "Furnace."

 It was evident that a direct attack would be attended with great difficulty and loss, in view of the strength of the enemy's position and his superiority of numbers. It was therefore resolved to endeavor to turn his right flank and gain his rear, leaving a force in front to hold him in check and conceal the movement. The execution of this plan was intrusted to Jackson with his three divisions. The commands of McLaws and

Anderson remained in front of the enemy. Early on the morning of the 2nd, Jackson marched by the Furnace and Brock roads, his movement being effectually covered by Fitzhugh Lee's cavalry under General Stuart. As the rear of his train was passing the Furnace a large force of the enemy advanced from Chancellorsville and attempted its capture, but this advance was arrested. After a long and fatiguing march General Jackson's leading division, under General Rodes, reached the old turnpike about three miles in rear of Chancellorsville at 4 P.M. As the different divisions arrived they were formed at right angles to the road. At 6 P.M. the advance was ordered. The enemy was taken by surprise, and fled after a brief resistance. Position after position was carried, the guns were captured, and every effort of the foe to rally was defeated by the impetuous rush of our troops. In the ardor of pursuit through the thick and tangled woods, the first and second lines at last became mingled and moved on together as one. The fugitives made a stand at a line of breastworks across the road, but the troops of Rodes and Colston dashed over the intrenchments together, and the flight and pursuit were resumed and continued until our advance was arrested by the abatis in front of the line of works near the central position at Chancellorsville. It was now dark. Jackson ordered the third line, under Hill, to relieve the troops of Rodes and Colston, who were completely blended and in such disorder from their advance through intricate woods and over broken ground that it was necessary to reform them. As Hill's men moved forward, Jackson, with his staff and escort, returning from the extreme front, met the skirmishers advancing, and in the obscurity of the night were mistaken for the enemy and fired upon. Captain Boswell and several others were killed, and a number wounded, among whom was General Jackson, who was borne from the field. The command now devolved upon General Hill, whose division, under General Heth, was advanced to the line of intrenchments which had been reached by Rodes and Colston. A furious fire of artillery was opened upon them, under cover of which infantry advanced to the attack, but were handsomely repulsed. Hill was soon afterward disabled, and the command was turned over to Stuart. He immediately proceeded to reconnoitre the ground and make himself acquainted with the disposition of the troops. The darkness of the night and the difficulty of moving through the woods and undergrowth rendered it advisable to defer further operations until morning, and the troops rested on their arms in line of battle.

As soon as the sound of cannon gave notice of Jackson's attack on the enemy's right, the troops in front began to press strongly on the left to prevent reinforcements being sent to the point assailed. They advanced up to the intrenchments, while several batteries played with good effect until prevented by the increasing darkness.

Early on the morning of May 3rd Stuart renewed the attack upon Hooker, who had strengthened his right wing during the night with additional breastworks, while a large number of guns, protected by intrenchments, were posted so as to sweep the woods through which our troops had to advance. Hill's division was in front, with Colston in the second line, and Rodes in the third. The second and third lines soon advanced to the support of the first, and the whole became hotly engaged. The breastworks, at which the attack was suspended on the preceding evening, were carried by assault, under a terrible fire of musketry and artillery. In rear of these breastworks was a barricade, from which the enemy was quickly driven. The troops on the left of the plank road, pressing through the woods, attacked and broke the next line, while those on the right bravely assailed the extensive earthworks behind which General Hooker's artillery was posted. Three times were these works carried, and as often were the brave assailants compelled to abandon them—twice by the retirement of the troops on their left, who fell back after a gallant struggle with superior numbers, and once by a movement of the enemy on their right caused by the advance of General Anderson. The left, being reinforced, finally succeeded in driving back the enemy, and the artillery began to play with great precision and effect. In the meantime, Anderson pressed forward upon Chancellorsville, his right resting upon the plank road and his left extending around the Furnace, while McLaws made a strong demonstration to the right of the road. As the troops advancing upon the enemy's front and right converged upon his central position, Anderson effected a junction with Jackson's corps, and the whole line pressed irresistibly. Hooker's army was driven from all its fortified positions with heavy loss in killed, wounded, and prisoners, and retreated toward the Rappahannock. By 10 A.M. we were in full possession of the field.

The troops, having become somewhat scattered by the difficulties of the ground and the ardor of the contest, were immediately reformed, preparatory to renewing the attack. The enemy had withdrawn to a strong position nearer to the Rappahannock, which he had fortified. His superiority of numbers, the unfavorable nature of the ground, which was densely wooded, and the condition of our troops, after the arduous and sanguinary conflict in which they had been engaged, rendered great caution necessary. Our operations were just completed when further movements were arrested by intelligence received from Fredericksburg.

Before dawn, on the morning of the 3rd, it was known that the enemy had occupied Fredericksburg in large force, and laid down a bridge at the town. He made a demonstration against the extreme right of the force left to hold our lines, which was easily repulsed by General Early. Soon afterward a column moved from Fredericksburg along the river banks, as if to gain the heights on the extreme left which commanded those immediately in rear of the town. This attempt was foiled. Very soon the enemy advanced in large force against Marye's, and the hills to the right and left of it. Two assaults were gallantly repulsed. After the second, a flag of truce was sent from the town to obtain permission to provide for the wounded. Three heavy lines advanced immediately upon the return of the flag and renewed the attack. They were bravely repulsed on the right and left, but the small force at the foot of Marye's Hill, overpowered by more than ten times their number, was captured after an heroic resistance, and the hill carried. The success of the enemy enabled him to threaten our communications by moving down the Telegraph road, or to come upon our rear at Chancellorsville by the plank road. He began to advance on the plank road, his progress being gallantly disputed by the brigade of General Wilcox, who fell back slowly until he reached Salem Church, on the plank road, about five miles from Fredericksburg.

In this state of affairs in our rear, General Lee led General McLaws with his three brigades to reinforce General Wilcox. He arrived at Salem Church early in the afternoon, where he found General Wilcox in line of battle, with a large force of the enemy—consisting, as was reported, of one army corps and part of another—in his front. The enemy's artillery played vigorously upon our position for some time, when his infantry advanced in three strong lines, the attack being directed mainly against General Wilcox, but partially involving the brigades on his left. After a fierce struggle the first line was repulsed with great slaughter.

The second then came forward, but immediately broke under the close and deadly fire which it encountered, and the whole mass filed in confusion to the rear. They were pursued by the brigades of Wilcox and Semmes, which advanced nearly a mile, when they were halted to reform in the presence of the hostile reserve, which now appeared in large force. It being quite dark, General Wilcox deemed it imprudent to push the attack with his small numbers, and retired to his original position, the enemy making no attempt to follow. The next morning General Early advanced along the Telegraph road, and recaptured Marye's and the adjacent hills without difficulty, thus gaining the rear of the enemy's left. In the meantime General Hooker had so strengthened his position near Chancellorsville, that it was deemed inexpedient to assail it with less than our whole force, which had been reduced by the detachment led to Fredericksburg to relieve us from the danger that menaced our rear.

Longstreet had previously been sent with two divisions of Lee's army to co-operate with French in the capture of Suffolk, the occupation of which by the enemy interrupted our collection of supplies in the eastern counties of North Carolina and Virginia. When the advance of Hooker threatened Lee's front, instructions were sent to Longstreet to hasten his return to the army. These instructions were repeated with urgent insistence, yet his movements were so delayed that, though the battle of Chancellorsville did not occur until many days after he was expected to join, his force was absent when it occurred. Had he rejoined his command in due time, Lee need not have diminished his force in front of Hooker, so as to delay the renewal of the attack and force him to a precipitate retreat, involving the loss of his artillery and trains. It was accordingly resolved still further to reinforce the troops in front, in order, if possible, to drive Hooker across the Rappahannock.

Some delay occurred in getting the troops into position, owing to the broken and irregular nature of the ground, and the difficulty of ascertaining the disposition of the opposing forces. The attack did not begin until 6 P.M., when the enemy's troops were rapidly driven across the plank road in the direction of the Rappahannock. The speedy approach of darkness prevented McLaws from perceiving the success of the attack, until the foe began to recross the river a short distance below Banks's Ford, where he had laid one of his pontoon-bridges. His right brigades advanced through the woods in the direction of the firing, but the retreat was so rapid that they could only join in the pursuit. A dense fog settled over the field, increasing the obscurity and rendering great caution necessary to avoid collision between our own troops. Their movements were consequently slow.

The next morning it was found that the enemy had made good his escape and removed his bridges. Fredericksburg was evacuated, and our rear no longer threatened. But, as Hooker had it in his power to recross, it was deemed best to leave a force to hold our lines as before. McLaws and Anderson, directed to return to Chancellorsville, reached their destination during the afternoon, in the midst of a violent storm, which continued throughout the night and most of the following day. Preparations were made to assail the enemy's works at daylight on the 6th, but, on advancing our skirmishers, it was found that, under cover of the storm and darkness of the night, he had retreated over the river. A detachment was left to guard the battle-field, while the wounded were removed and the captured property was collected. The rest of the army returned to its former position.

The loss of the enemy was 1,512 killed and 9,518 wounded; total, 11,030. His dead and a large number of wounded were left on the field. About 5,000 prisoners, exclusive of the wounded, were taken; and 13 pieces of artillery, 19,500 stand of arms, 17 colors, and a large quantity of ammunition fell into our hands.

Our loss was much less in killed and wounded than that of the enemy, but of the number was one—a host in himself—Lieutenant-General Jackson—who was wounded, and died on May 10th.

Of this great captain General Lee, in his anguish, justly said, "I have lost my right arm." As an executive officer he had no superior, and war has seldom shown an equal. Too devoted to the cause he served to have any selfishness, he shared the toils, privations, and dangers of his troops when in chief command; and in subordinate positions his aim was to understand the purpose of his commander and faithfully to promote its success. He was the complement of Lee, united, they had achieved such results that the public felt secure under their shield. To us his place was never filled.

The official return of the Army of Northern Virginia, on March 31,

1863, shows as present for duty 57,112, of which 6,509 were cavalry and 1,621 reserve artillery. On May 20th, two weeks after the battle, and when Pickett's and Hood's divisions had rejoined the army, the total infantry force numbered but 55,261 effective men, from which, if the strength of Hood's and Pickett's divisions is deducted, there would remain 41,358 as the strength of the commands that participated in the battles of Chancellorsville.

The Army of the Potomac numbered 120,000 men, infantry and artillery, with a body of 12,000 well-equipped cavalry and an artillery force of 400 guns.

Chapter 66

Our Foreign Relations

AT the close of the first year of the war the leading Governments of Europe had recognized the Confederate States as a belligerent power, and continued such recognition to the close. Our representative in London was Mr. Mason; in Paris, Mr. Slidell; in Spain, Mr. Rost; in Belgium, Mr. Mann. Competent and zealous, they yet were unsuccessful in obtaining our recognition as an independent power.

Misled by the falsifications of the representatives of the United States the powers of Europe announced their determination to refuse to assume to judge between the conflicting accounts of the two parties as to the true nature of their previous relations. The Governments of Great Britain and France accordingly signified their intention to confine themselves to recognizing the self-evident fact of the existence of a war, and to maintain a strict neutrality during its progress. It soon became evident that by some understanding, express or tacit, Europe had decided to leave the initiative in all action relative to our conflict to England and France, as they had the largest interests involved in it.

This action, although ostensibly neutral, was in fact a decision against us, and injurious in its effects. One immediate and necessary result was the prolongation of hostilities to which our enemies were thereby encouraged; for had those powers promptly admitted our right to be treated as all other independent nations, the moral effect of such action would have been to dispel the pretension under which the Government persisted in their efforts to accomplish our subjugation.

There were other matters in which less than justice was rendered to the Confederacy by "neutral" Europe, and undue advantage conferred on the aggressors in a wicked war; and it was especially in relation to the so-called blockade that the policy of the European powers was so shaped as to cause the greatest injury to the Confederacy, and to confer signal advantages on the United States. A few words in explanation may here be necessary.

Previous to 1856 the principles regulating blockades were often conflicting and uncertain. To remedy the evils resulting from the doubts as to the true rules of maritime law, the five great powers in 1856 adopted a declaration of principles, by which they pledged themselves to be governed in future wars. To these rules every European power yielded its assent; and the United States, while declining to assent to the proposition which prohibited privateering, declared that the three remaining principles were in entire accordance with our own views of international law.

The four principles thus promulgated and adopted by all Europe were that "privateering is and remains abolished;" that "the neutral flag covers enemy's goods, excepting contraband of war;" that "neutral goods, excepting contraband of war, are not liable to capture under enemy's flag;" that "blockades, to be binding, must be effective; that is to say, maintained by a force sufficient really to prevent access to the coast of the enemy."

There is no other instance in history of the adoption of rules of public law under circumstances of like solemnity, with like unanimity, and pledging the faith of nations with a sanctity so peculiar.

When, therefore, this Confederacy was formed, and when neutral powers while deferring action on its demand for admission into the family of nations, recognized it as a belligerent power, Great Britain and France made informal proposals, about the same time, that their own rights as neutrals should be guaranteed by our acceding, as belligerents, to the declaration of principles made by the Congress of Paris. The request was addressed to our sense of justice, and therefore met immediate and favorable response in the resolutions of the Provisional Congress of August, 13, 1861, by which all the principles announced by the Congress of Paris were adopted as the guide of our conduct during the war, with the sole exception of that relative to privateering. As the right to make use of privateers was one in which neutral nations had, as to the then existing war, no interest; as it was a right which the United States had refused to abandon, and which they remained at liberty to use against us; as it was a right of which we were in actual enjoyment, and which we could not be expected to renounce *flagrante bello* against an adversary possessing an overwhelming superiority of naval forces, it was reserved, with entire confidence that neutral nations could not fail to perceive that just reason existed for the reservation. Nor was this confidence misplaced; for the official documents published by the British Government contained the expression of the satisfaction of that Government with the conduct of the officials who transacted successfully the delicate business intrusted to their care.

These solemn declarations of principle, this implied agreement between the Confederacy and the two powers just named, were suffered to remain inoperative against the menaces and outrages on neutral rights committed by the United States with unceasing and progressive arrogance during the whole period of the war. Neutral Europe remained passive while the United States, with a naval force insufficient to blockade effectively the coast of a single State, proclaimed a paper blockade of thousands of miles of coast, extending from the Capes of the Chesapeake to those of Florida, and encircling the Gulf of Mexico from Key West to the mouth of the Rio Grande. Compared with this monstrous pretension of the United States, the blockades known in history under the names of the Berlin and Milan Decrees, and the British Orders in Council, in the years 1806 and 1807, sink into insignificance. Those blockades were justified by the powers that declared them, on the sole ground that they were retaliatory; yet they have since been condemned by the publicists of those very powers as violations of international law. Those blockades evoked angry remonstrances from neutral powers, among which the United States were the most conspicuous, and in their consequences were the chief cause of the war between Great Britain and the United States in 1812. They formed one of the principal motives that led to the declaration of the Congress of Paris in 1856, in the fond hope of imposing an enduring check on the very abuse of maritime power which was renewed by the United States in 1861 and 1862, under circumstances and with features of aggravated wrong without precedent in history.

Repeated and formal remonstrances were made by the Confederate Government to neutral powers against the recognition of that blockade. It was demonstrated by evidence undisputed and indisputable that the blockaded ports were so insufficiently invested that hundreds of entries were effected into them after the declaration of blockade; that the enemy admitted the fact, and made it an excuse for the odious barbarity of destroying a harbor by sinking vessels laden with stone in the entrance of it; that they had not only seized vessels attempting to enter Confederate ports, but captured neutral vessels whenever supposed to be bound to any point on our extensive coast, without inquiring whether a single blockading vessel was to be found at such point; in a word, that every prescription of maritime law and every right of neutral nations to trade with a belligerent under the sanction of principles heretofore universally respected were systematically and persistently violated by the United States.

Neutral Europe received our remonstrances, and submitted in almost unbroken silence to all the wrongs that the United States chose to inflict on its commerce. While every energy of our country was evoked in the struggle for maintaining its existence, the neutral nations of Europe pursued a policy which, nominally impartial, was practically most favorable to our enemies and most detrimental to us.

The exercise of the neutral right of refusing entry into their ports to prizes taken by both belligerents was especially hurtful to us. It was sternly enforced.

The assertion of the neutral right of commerce with a belligerent whose ports were not blockaded by fleets sufficient really to prevent access to them, would have been eminently beneficial to the Confederate States, and only thus hurtful to the United States. It was complaisantly abandoned.

The duty of neutral states to receive with cordiality and recognize with respect any new confederation that independent states might see fit to form was too clear to admit of denial, but its postponement was equally beneficial to the United States and detrimental to the Confederacy. It was postponed.

We did not complain that European nations declared their neutrality; but we did complain that the declared neutrality was delusive, not real; that recognized neutral rights were alternately asserted and waived in such a manner as to bear with great severity on us, while conferring signal advantages on our enemy. Many proofs were given of the friendly spirit of the British Government to the enemy.

The partiality of that Government in favor of our enemies was further evinced in the marked difference in its conduct on the subject of the purchase of supplies by the two belligerents. The difference was conspicuous from the very commencement of the war. As early as May 1, 1861, the British Minister in Washington was informed by the Federal Secretary of State that he had sent agents to England, and that others would go to France to purchase arms; and this fact was communicated to the British Foreign Office, which interposed no objection. Yet, in October of the same year, Earl Russell entertained the complaint of the United States Minister in London that the Confederate States were importing contraband of war from the Island of Nassau, directed inquiry to be made, and obtained a report from the authorities of Nassau denying the allegations, which report was enclosed to Mr. Adams and received by him as satisfactory evidence to dissipate "the suspicion thrown upon the authorities by that unwarrantable act."

So, too, when the Confederate Government purchased in Great Britain, as a neutral country (with strict observance both of the laws of nations and of the municipal law of Great Britain), vessels which were armed and commissioned as vessels of war after they had been removed from English waters, the British Government, in violation of its own laws, and in deference to the importunate demands of the United States, made an ineffectual attempt to seize one vessel, and actually did seize and detain another which touched at the island of Nassau on her way to a Confederate port, and subjected her to an unfounded prosecution, at the very time when cargoes of munitions of war were openly shipped from British ports to New York, to be used in warfare against us. Further instances need not be adduced to show how detrimental to us and advantageous to our enemy was the manner in which England observed its hollow pretension of neutrality toward the belligerents.

Confederate Generals.

CHAPTER 67

MILITARY OPERATIONS IN THE WEST

OPERATIONS in the West now claim attention. General Bragg occupied Chattanooga; General E. K. Smith held Knoxville, in East Tennessee. In August, 1862, he entered Kentucky, and after several small and successful affairs reached Richmond on August 30th, routing a force of the enemy that had collected there to check his progress. The enemy lost several hundred killed and several thousand prisoners, with a large number of small arms, artillery, and wagons. He then advanced on Lexington and Frankfort, and occupied both, creating great alarm for the safety of Cincinnati, which he could have captured had his command been an independent one. As he was but the advance of General Bragg's command, his duty was to co-operate with it, and therefore he could not cross the Ohio.

General Bragg marched from Chattanooga on September 5th without serious opposition, entered Kentucky by the eastern route, compelling General Buell to collect all his forces and retreat rapidly to Louisville, and thus restoring to the Confederacy a large and important territory. By this brilliant piece of strategy, North Alabama and Middle Tennessee were relieved from the presence of the enemy without necessitating a single engagement.

On September 18th General Bragg issued an address to the people of Kentucky. Some recruits joined him, and an immense amount of supplies was obtained. As soon as our army began to retire, the enemy, having received reinforcements, moved out, and pressed so heavily on our rear, under Hardee, that he halted and checked them near Perryville. Bragg then determined to give battle there. Three of the divisions of his old command were concentrated under General Volk, who was ordered to attack on the morning of October 8th. The two armies were formed on opposite sides of the town. The enemy was assailed vigorously, the engagement soon became general, and was continued furiously until dark. Although greatly outnumbered, and although the battle waged with varying success, our men eventually carried every position, and drove the Federals about two miles. Night ended the action. We captured 15 pieces of artillery, killed one and wounded two brigadier-generals, and a very large number of inferior officers and men, estimated at no less than 4,000, and captured 400 prisoners. Our loss was 2,500 killed, wounded, and missing.

The enemy was heavily reinforced during the night. Next morning, therefore, General Bragg withdrew his troops to Harrodsburg. General Smith, with most of his forces, arrived next day, and the whole were then withdrawn to Bryantsville, the enemy following slowly and not closely. General Bragg finally took position at Murfreesboro, and the enemy concentrated at Nashville, General Buell having been superseded by General Rosecrans.

Meanwhile, on November 30th, General Morgan, with 1,300 men, made an attack on a brigade of the enemy at Hartsville. It was found strongly posted on a hill, in line of battle. Our line was formed under fire, and the advance was made with great steadiness. The enemy was driven from his position, losing a battery of Parrott guns. Finally, hemmed in on the river bank, he surrendered. The contest was severe, and lasted an hour and a hall. The prisoners numbered 2,100.

Late in the month of December General Rosecrans commenced his advance from Nashville upon the position of General Bragg at Murfreesboro. His movement began on December 26th, by various routes, but such was the activity of our cavalry as to delay him four days in reaching the battle-field, a distance of twenty-six miles. On the 29th General Wheeler, with his cavalry brigade, gained the rear of Rosecrans's army, and destroyed several hundreds of wagons loaded with supplies and baggage. After clearing the road, he made the circuit of the enemy and joined our left. Their strength was 65,000 men. The number of fighting men we had on the field on December 31st was 35,000, of which 30,000 were infantry and artillery.

Our line was formed about two miles from Murfreesboro, and stretched transversely across Stone River, which was fordable from the Lebanon pike, on the right, to the Franklin road, on the left. As

Rosecrans made no demonstration on the 30th, General Bragg determined to begin the conflict early on the next morning by the advance of his left. The enemy was taken completely by surprise, and his right was steadily driven until his line was thrown entirely back at a right angle to his first position and near the railroad, along which he had massed reserves. After the first surprise the resistance of the enemy was most gallant and obstinate. At night he had been forced from every position except the one on his extreme left, which rested on Stone River, and was strengthened by a concentration of artillery too formidable for assault.

Early next morning (January 1st, 1863,) the cannonading opened on the right centre, and was kept up for a short time. The enemy had withdrawn from the advanced position occupied by his left flank. One or two short contests occurred on the 3rd, but his line was unchanged. Our forces had now been in line of battle five days and nights, with little rest, as there were no reserves. Their tents, packed in wagons, were four miles in the rear. The rain was continuous, and the cold severe. News came that heavy reinforcements were marching rapidly to the enemy. General Bragg therefore decided to fall back to Tullahoma, which he did in good order.

In the series of engagements near Murfreesboro we captured over 6,000 prisoners, 30 pieces of artillery, 6,000 small-arms, a large number of ambulances, horses, and mules, and a large amount of other property. Our losses exceeded 10,000. Those of the enemy were estimated at over 25,000.

After the battle of Shiloh, West Tennessee and North Mississippi were occupied by a force under General Grant. Subsequently this force was increased, and Rosecrans assigned to its command. Many positions were held in West Tennessee and North Mississippi, with garrisons aggregating 42,000 men. The most important of these positions was the fortified town of Corinth.

As part of the plan to subjugate the Southwestern States extensive preparations were made for an advance through Mississippi, and a combined land and naval attack on Vicksburg. A large number of troops occupied Middle Tennessee and North Alabama. To defeat the general plan General Bragg moved his army into Kentucky, which by this time the Federal Government thought it needless to overawe by the presence of garrisons. Van Dorn and Price commanded the Confederate troops then in North Mississippi. General Bragg, when he advanced into Kentucky, had left them with instructions to operate against the Federals in that region, and especially to guard against their junction with Buell in Middle Tennessee.

In September, 1862, General Price learned that Rosecrans was moving to join Buell. He therefore marched to Iuka, which he reached on the 19th. His advance cavalry found the place occupied by a force, which retreated toward Corinth, abandoning a considerable amount of stores. On the 24th General Price received a letter from General Ord stating that "Lee's army had been destroyed at Antietam; that therefore the rebellion must soon terminate; and that, in order to spare the further effusion of blood, he gave him this opportunity to lay down his arms." Price replied, thanking Ord for his kind feeling, but correcting the rumor about Lee, and promising "to lay down his arms whenever Mr. Lincoln should acknowledge the independence of the Southern Confederacy, and not sooner." On that night Price held a council of war, at which it was agreed to fall back next morning and make a junction with Van Dorn, it being now satisfactorily shown that the enemy was holding the line on our left instead of moving to reinforce Buell. The cavalry pickets had reported that a heavy force of the enemy was moving from the south toward Iuka. It proved to be a force commanded by Rosecrans in person. General Little advanced to meet him. A bloody contest ensued. Rosecrans was driven back with a loss of nine guns. Our own loss was very serious. It included General Little, an officer of extraordinary merit, greatly beloved by his troops. The Third Louisiana lost half its men, and every regiment suffered severely. It was afterward ascertained that this movement of Rosecrans was intended to be made in concert with one by Grant moving from the west; but Rosecrans had been beaten before. Grant arrived.

The Confederate force at this time was 22,000. Rosecrans had at Corinth 15,000 men, with 8,000 at various outposts from twelve to fifteen miles distant. In addition to this force the enemy had at Memphis, about 6,000; at Bolivar, about 8,000; at Jackson, Tenn., about 3,000; at other points, from 2,000 to 3,000, making an aggregate of 42,000 in West Tennessee and North Mississippi.

Corinth, although the strongest, was, from its salient position, the most feasible point to attack, and in the circumstances the most important to gain. Van Dorn, therefore, determined to try to take it by surprise.

Our army moved rapidly from Ripley, its point of juncture, cut the railroad between Corinth and Jackson, Tenn., and at daybreak on the 3rd of October was deployed for attack. By ten o'clock our force confronted the enemy inside his intrenchments. In half an hour the whole line of outer works was carried, the obstructions were passed, and the battle opened in earnest. The enemy, obstinately disputing every point, was finally driven from his second line of detached works, and at sunset had retreated to the innermost lines.

The battle had been mainly fought by Price's division, on our left. The troops had made a quick march of ten miles over dusty roads, without water; the line of battle had been formed in forests with undergrowth; the combats of the day had been so severe that General Price thought his troops unequal to further exertion on that day, and it was decided to wait until morning. "One hour more of daylight," said General Van Dorn, "and victory would have soothed our grief for the loss of the gallant dead who sleep on that lost but not dishonored field."

During the night batteries were put in position to open on the town at daybreak. The action was to begin on the left, to be immediately followed by an advance on the extreme right. The order was not executed. The commander of the wing which was to make the attack failed to do so, and another officer was sent to take his place. In the meantime the centre became engaged, and the action extended to the left. The plan had been disarranged; nevertheless the centre and left pushed forward and planted their colors on the last stronghold of the enemy. "His heavy guns were silenced and all seemed about to be ended, when a heavy fire from fresh troops that had succeeded in reaching Corinth was poured into our thin ranks." With this combined assault on Price's exhausted corps, which had sustained the whole conflict, those gallant troops were driven back. The day was lost. Our army retired to Chewalla during the day, without pursuit, and rested during the night without molestation. Our loss both of officers and men was very heavy.

General Van Dorn then moved to near Holly Springs, Miss. In the meantime General Grant massed a heavy force, estimated at 80,000 men, with which he moved through the interior of Mississippi until he encamped near Water Valley. The country was teeming with large quantities of breadstuffs and forage, and he accumulated an immense depot of supplies at Holly Springs, and hastened every preparation necessary to continue his advance southward.

Unless his progress were arrested, the interior of the State, its capital, Jackson, Vicksburg, and its railroads would fall into his hands. As we had no force sufficient to offer battle, our only alternative was to attack his communications. For this purpose Van Dorn (December 15th) quietly withdrew our cavalry—numbering less than 2,500 men—from the enemy's front, and marched for Holly Springs, which was occupied by a brigade of infantry and the Seventh Illinois cavalry. Van Dorn surprised and captured the garrison, and before eight o'clock was in quiet possession of the town. The captured property, amounting to millions of dollars, was burned before sunset. Grant was thus forced to abandon his campaign, and to retreat hastily from the State.

Chapter 68

Naval and Military Operations on the Mississippi

AFTER the battle of Murfreesboro, which closed in the first days of 1863, there was a cessation of active operations in that part of Tennessee, and attention was concentrated on the extensive preparations in progress for a campaign into Mississippi, with Vicksburg as the objective point. The plan was for a combined movement by land and water, the former passing through the interior of the State, to approach Vicksburg in rear, the latter to descend the Mississippi River and attack the city in front.

In the latter part of December, 1862, General Sherman, having descended the Mississippi, entered the Yazoo with four divisions of land troops and five gunboats, for the purpose of reducing our works at Haines's Bluff and turning Vicksburg, so as to attack it in the rear. The first point at which the range of hills extending from Vicksburg up the Yazoo approaches near to the river is at Haines's Bluff, some twenty miles by the course of the Yazoo from the Mississippi River.

On the 27th little progress was made. On the 28th an attempt, by one division, to approach the causeway north of the Chickasaw Bayou was repulsed with heavy loss. The troops were withdrawn and moved down the river to a point below the bayou, there to unite with the rest of the command. At daybreak on the 29th the attack was resumed, and continued throughout most of the day. The enemy was again repulsed with heavy loss. On the next day there was firing on both sides, without conclusive results. On the 31st Sherman sent in a flag of truce to bury the dead. Thereafter nothing important occurred until the latter part of January, 1863, when the troops under General Grant embarked at

Memphis and moved down the Mississippi to Young's Point, on the Louisiana shore, a few miles below Vicksburg.

The expected co-operation of his forces with those of Sherman had been prevented by the brilliant cavalry expedition under Van Dorn, which captured and destroyed the vast supplies collected at Holly Springs for the use of Grant's forces. This compelled Grant to retreat to Memphis, and frustrated the projected combined movement. A new plan of operations was adopted, in which again prominently appears the purpose of turning Vicksburg on the north.

Various attempts to get through to Yazoo above Haines's Bluff were made, but signally failed.

The enemy, after his repeated and disastrous attempts to turn the right flank of Vicksburg, applied his attention to the opposite direction. General Grant first tried to divert the Mississippi from its channel by cutting a canal across the peninsula opposite Vicksburg, so as to make a practicable passage for transport vessels from a point above to one below the city. His attempt was quite unsuccessful. Another attempt to get into the Mississippi without passing the batteries at Vicksburg was by digging a canal to connect the river with the bayou in rear of Milliken's Bend, so as to have water communication by way of Richmond to New Carthage.

On March 19th the flag-ship of Admiral Farragut, with one gunboat from the fleet at New Orleans, passed up the river in defiance of our batteries; but on the 25th four gunboats from the upper fleet attempted to pass down, but were repulsed, two of them completely disabled. On April 16th a fleet of ironclads, with barges in tow, Admiral Porter commanding, under cover of the night ran the Vicksburg batteries. One of the vessels was destroyed, and another crippled, but towed out of range. On the 26th a fleet of transports with loaded barges was floated past Vicksburg. One or more of them was sunk, but enough escaped to give the enemy abundant supplies below Vicksburg, and boats enough for ferriage uses. On April 20th the movement of the enemy commenced through the country on the west side of the river to their selected point of crossing below Grand Gulf. On the 29th the enemy's gunboats came down and took their stations in front of our batteries and rifle-pits at Grand Gulf. A furious cannonade was continued for many hours, and the fleet withdrew, having one gunboat disabled, but otherwise receiving and inflicting little damage. In a short time the fleet reappeared from behind a point which had concealed them from view. The gunboats now had their transports lashed to their farther side, and, protected by their iron shields, ran by our batteries at full speed, losing but one transport on the way.

On the evening of April 29th the enemy commenced ferrying over troops from the Louisiana to the Mississippi shore, to a landing just below the mouth of Bayou Pierre. General Green attacked them with his brigade with so much vigor as to render their march both cautious and slow. Reinforcements coming to the enemy, General Green retired, skirmishing, until joined by Generals Tracy and Baldwin, who had made forced marches to reach him. A serious conflict followed, after which, step by step disputing the ground, Green retired to the range of hills southwest of Port Gibson, where General Bowen joined him, and formed a new line of battle. Although the enemy's force was steadily augmented, and outflanked both our right and left, our troops continued most valiantly to resist until their condition became almost hopeless, when, by a movement to which desperation gave a power quite disproportionate to the numbers, the right wing of the enemy was driven back, and our forces made good their retreat over Bayou Pierre. The relative forces engaged in the battle of May 1st were, as nearly as I have been able to learn, 5,500 Confederates and 20,000 Federals. Fresh troops were reported to be joining Grant's army, and one of his corps had been seen to cross by a ford above, so as to get in rear of our position.

To divert notice from this movement to get in the rear of Bowen, on the morning of the 2nd Grant ordered artillery fire to be opened on our intrenchments across Bayou Pierre. During the forenoon Bowen sent a flag of truce to ask a suspension of hostilities for the purpose of burying the dead. The request was refused, and a demand made for surrender. This was promptly rejected; but, as the day wore away without the arrival of reinforcements, Bowen, under cover of night, commenced a retreat toward Grand Gulf. General Loring, with his division, soon joined him. On the morning of the 3rd Grant commenced a pursuit of the retreating forces, but only unimportant skirmishes resulted.

While these events were happening, Colonel Grierson, with three regiments of cavalry, made a raid through the northern border of Mississippi, through the interior of the State, and joined General Banks at Baton Rouge, La. Among the expeditions for pillage and arson this stands prominent for savage cruelties against defenceless women and children, constituting a record unworthy of a soldier and a man.

Grant, with his large army, was now marching into the interior of Mississippi. The country through which he had to pass was for some distance composed of abrupt hills, and all of it had poor roads. With such difficult communication with his base of supplies, and with the physical obstacles to his progress, there was reasonable ground to hope that he might be advantageously encountered at many points and finally defeated. In such warfare as this, that portion of the population who were exempt from or incapable of full service in the army could be very effective as an auxiliary force. I therefore wrote to Governor Pettus, requesting him to use all practicable means to get every man and boy, capable of aiding their country in its need, to turn out, mounted or on foot, with whatever weapons they had, to aid the soldiers in driving the invader from our soil. The facilities which the enemy possessed in river transportation, and the aid which their ironclad gunboats gave to all operations where land and naval forces could be combined, were lost to Grant in this interior march which he was making.

After the retreat of Bowen, General Pemberton, anticipating an attack on Vicksburg from the rear, concentrated all the troops of his command for its defence.

All previous demonstrations had indicated that the special purpose of the enemy was its capture. Its strategic importance justified the belief that he would concentrate his efforts upon that object, and this opinion was enforced by the difficulty of supplying his army in the region into which he was marching, and the special advantages of Vicksburg as his base. The superior force of the enemy enabled him, while moving the main body of his troops through Louisiana to a point below Vicksburg, to send a corps to renew the demonstration against Haines's Bluff. Finding due preparation made to resist an attack there, this demonstration was merely a feint, but, had Pemberton withdrawn his troops, that feint could have been converted into a real attack, and the effort, so often foiled, to gain the heights above Vicksburg would have become a success. When that corps retired, and proceeded to join the rest of Grant's army, which had gone toward Grand Gulf, Pemberton commenced energetically to prepare for what was now the manifest object of the enemy. On the 23rd of April, from his headquarters at Jackson, Miss., he directed Major-General Stevenson, commanding at Vicksburg, "that communications, at least for infantry, should be made by the shortest practicable route to Grand Gulf." "All troops not absolutely necessary to hold the works at Vicksburg should be held as a movable force for either Warrenton or Grand Gull." On the 28th Brigadier-General Bowen, commanding at Grand Gulf, reported that "transports and barges loaded down with troops are landing at Hard-Times on the west bank." At this time the small cavalry force remaining in Pemberton's command compelled him to keep infantry detachments at many points liable to be attacked by raiding parties of the enemy's mounted troops, a circumstance seriously interfering with the concentration of the forces of his command. Instructions were sent to all the commanders of his cavalry detachments to move toward Grand Gulf, to harass the enemy in flank and rear, obstructing, as far as might be, communications with his base. A despatch was sent to General Buckner, commanding at Mobile, asking him to protect the Mobile and Ohio Railroad, as Pemberton required all the troops he could spare to strengthen General Bowen. A despatch was also sent to General J. E. Johnston, saying that the Army of Tennessee must be relied on to guard the approaches through North Mississippi. To Major-General Stevenson, at Vicksburg, he sent a despatch: "Hold five thousand men in readiness to move to Grand Gulf, and, on the requisition of Brigadier-General Bowen, move them; with your batteries and rifle-pits manned, the city front is impregnable." At the same time he telegraphed General Bowen: "I have directed General Stevenson to have five thousand men ready to move on your requisition, but do not make requisition unless absolutely necessary for your position. I am also making arrangements for sending you two or three thousand men from this direction in case of necessity."

The policy was here manifested of meeting the enemy in the hills east of his point of debarkation; yet all unfriendly criticism has treated General Pemberton's course on that occasion as having been voluntarily to withdraw his troops to within the intrenchments of Vicksburg. His published reports show that he made early and consistent efforts to avoid that result.

After General J. E. Johnston had recovered from the wound received at Seven Pines, he had been assigned, on the 24th of November,

1862, to the command of a geographical department including the States of Tennessee, Mississippi, Alabama, Georgia, and North Carolina. When the events that have been narrated were occurring in Pemberton's command, he felt severely the want of cavalry, and much embarrassed by the necessity for substituting portions of his infantry to supply the deficiency of cavalry.

Finding it impossible to procure cavalry from General Johnston, Pemberton commenced to concentrate all his forces for the great effort of checking the invading army.

Large bodies of troops continued to descend the river, land above Vicksburg, and, to avoid our batteries at that place, to move on the west side of the river to reinforce General Grant. This seemed to justify the conclusion that the main effort in the West was to be made by that army; and, supposing that General Johnston would be convinced of the fact if he repaired to that field in person, as well as to avail ourselves of the public confidence in his military capacity, he was ordered, on May 9, 1863, to "proceed at once to Mississippi and take chief command of the forces."

When he reached Jackson, hearing that the enemy, was between that place and the position occupied by General Pemberton's forces, about thirty miles distant, he halted there and opened correspondence with Pemberton, from which a confusion, with a consequent disaster, resulted, which might have been avoided had he, with or without his reinforcements, proceeded to Pemberton's headquarters in the field.

On the same day General Pemberton called a council of war of all the general officers present. He then reversed his column so as to return to Edward's Depot and take the Brownsville road, and notified General Johnston of the retrograde movement and the route to be followed. Just as this movement began the enemy drove in the cavalry pickets and opened an artillery fire. As soon as the demonstration of the enemy became serious, orders were issued to form a line of battle, with Loring on the right, Bowen in the centre, and Stevenson on the left. The line of battle was quickly formed in a position naturally strong, and the approaches to the front were well covered. After a lively artillery duel for an hour or more a large force was thrown against the left, and skirmishing became heavy. About ten o'clock the battle began in earnest along Stevenson's entire front. Stevenson soon found that unless reinforced he would be unable to resist the heavy and repeated attacks along his line. Aid was sent to him from Bowen, and for a time the tide of battle turned in our favor. The enemy still continued to move troops from his left to his right, thus increasing on that flank his vastly superior force. At 4 P.M. a part of Stevenson's division broke badly and fell back. Some assistance finally came from Loring; but it was too late to save the day, and the retreat was ordered.

Though defeated they were not routed. Stevenson's single division for a long time resisted a force described by him as more than four times his own. Cockerell, commanding the First Missouri division, fought with like fortitude under like disadvantage.

Though some gave way in confusion, and others failed to respond when called on, the heroism of the rest shed lustre on the field, and "the main body of the troops retired in good order." The gallant brigades of Green and Cockerell covered the rear.

Chapter 69

The Campaign Against Vicksburg

ONE of the immediate results of the retreat from the Big Black was the necessity of abandoning our defences on the Yazoo at Snyder's Mills, as that position and the line of the Chickasaw Bayou were no longer tenable. All stores that could be transported were ordered to be sent into Vicksburg rapidly, the rest, including heavy guns, to be destroyed. On the morning of the 18th the troops were disposed from right to left on the defences. On the entire line 102 pieces of artillery of different calibre, principally field-guns, were placed in position. Previously instructions had been given that all live stock belonging to private parties and likely to fall into the hands of the enemy should be driven within our lines. Grant's army appeared on the 18th.

The development of the intrenched line from our extreme right was about eight miles, the shortest possible line of which the topography of the country admitted. It consisted of a system of detached works—redans, lunettes, and redoubts—on the prominent and commanding points, with the usual profile of raised field-works, connected in most cases with rifle-pits. To hold the entire line there were about 18,500 infantry; but these could not all be put in the trenches, as it was necessary to keep a reserve always ready to reinforce any point heavily threatened.

The campaign against Vicksburg had begun as early as November, 1862. General Grant had now, by a circuitous march, reached the rear of the city, established a base on the Mississippi River a few miles below, had a fleet of gunboats on the river, and controlled the navigation of the Yazoo up to Haines's Bluff, and was relieved from all danger in regard to supplying his army. Pemberton, by wise provision, had endeavored to secure supplies for the duration of an ordinary siege, and relied for the co-operation of a relieving army to break any investment that might be made. The ability of the Federals to send reinforcements was so much greater than ours that the necessity for prompt action was fully realized to increase as far as possible the relieving army; therefore, when General Johnston, on May 9, 1863, was ordered to proceed to Mississippi, he was directed to take from the Army of the Tennessee 3,000 good troops, and informed that he would find reinforcements from Beauregard. On May 12th he was telegraphed that in addition to 5,000 from Beauregard, already sent, 4,000 more would follow, and that it was feared no more could be spared. On June 1st General Johnston telegraphed to me that the troops at his disposal available against Grant amounted to 24,100, not including Jackson's cavalry command and a few hundred irregular cavalry. On May 18th General Pemberton received by courier a communication from General Johnston containing these words:

> "If Haines's Bluff is untenable, Vicksburg is of no value and cannot be held. If you are invested in Vicksburg, you must ultimately surrender. Under these circumstances, instead of losing both place and troops, we must, if possible, save the troops. If it is not too late, evacuate Vicksburg and its dependencies, and march to the northeast."

Pemberton, in his report, remarked: "This meant the fall of Port Hudson, the surrender of the Mississippi River, and the severance of the Confederacy."

Confident in his ability, with the preparations that had been made, to stand a siege, and firmly relying on the desire of the President and of General Johnston to raise it, General Pemberton called a council of war, laid Johnston's communication before them, and desired their opinion "on the question of practicability." The opinion was unanimous that "it was impossible to withdraw the army from this position with such *morale* and material as to be of further service to the Confederacy." He then announced his decision to hold Vicksburg as long as possible.

While the council of war was assembled the guns of the enemy opened on the works, and the siege proper commenced.

Making meagre allowance for a reserve, it required the whole force to be constantly in the trenches, and even when they were all on duty they did not furnish one man to the yard of the developed line.

On May 19th two assaults were made on the left and centre. Both were repulsed, and heavy loss was inflicted; our loss was small. At the same time the mortar fleet of Admiral Porter, from the west side of the peninsula, kept up a bombardment of the city.

Chapter 70

The Defence of Vicksburg

VICKSBURG is built upon hills rising successively from the river. The intrenchments were upon ridges beyond the town, only approaching the river on the right and left flanks, so that the fire of Porter's mortar fleet was mainly effective upon private dwellings, and the women, the children, and other noncombatants.

The hills on which the city is built are of a tenacious calcareous clay, and caves were dug in these in which to shelter the women and children, many of whom lived in them during the entire siege. From these places of shelter, heroically facing the danger of shells incessantly bursting over the streets, gentlewomen hourly went forth on the mission of humanity to nurse the sick and wounded, and to soothe the death-beds of their defenders who were collected in numerous hospitals. Without departing from the softer character of their sex, it was often remarked that, in discharge of the pious duties assumed, they seemed as indifferent to danger as any of the soldiers who lined the trenches.

During May 20th, 21st, and the forenoon of the 22nd a heavy fire of artillery and musketry was kept up by the besiegers, as well as by the mortar- and gun-boats in the river. On the afternoon of the 22nd preparations were made for a general assault.

The attacking columns were allowed to approach within good musket-range, when every available gun was opened with grape and canister, and our infantry, "rising in the trenches, poured into their ranks volley after volley with so deadly an effect that, leaving the ground literally covered with their dead and wounded, they (the enemy) precipitately retreated." One of our redoubts had been breached by their artillery previous to the assault, and a lodgement made in the ditch at the foot of the redoubt, on which two colors were planted. General Stevenson thus writes of this period of the conflict:

"The work was constructed in such a manner that the ditch was commanded by no part of the line, and the only means by which they could be dislodged was to retake the angle by a desperate charge, and either kill or compel the surrender of the whole party by the use of hand-grenades. A call for volunteers for this purpose was made, and promptly responded to by Lieutenant-Colonel E. W. Pettus, Twelfth Alabama regiment, and about forty men of Waul's Texas Legion. A more gallant feat than this charge has not illustrated our arms during the war. The preparations were quietly and quickly made, but the enemy seemed at once to divine our intentions, and opened upon the angle a terrible fire of shot, shell, and musketry. Undaunted, this little band rushed upon the work, and, in less time than is required to describe it, the flags were in our possession. Preparations were then quickly made for the use of hand-grenades, when the enemy in the ditch, being informed of our purpose, immediately surrendered. From that time forward the enemy relinquished all idea of assaulting us, and confined himself to the more cautious policy of gradual approaches and mining."

His force was not less than 60,000 men.

Thus affairs continued until July 1st, when General Pemberton thus describes the causes which made capitulation necessary:

"It must be remembered that for forty-seven days and nights these heroic men had been exposed to burning suns and drenching rains, damp fogs and heavy dews, and that during all this period they never had by day or night the slightest relief. The extent of our works required every available man in the trenches, and even then in many places they were insufficiently manned. It was not in my power to relieve any portion of the line for a single hour. Confined to the narrow limits of trench, with their limbs cramped and swollen, constantly exposed to a murderous storm of shot and shell . . . is it strange that the men grew weak and attenuated? They had held the place against an enemy five times their number, admirably clothed and fed, and abundantly supplied with all the appliances of war. Whenever the foe attempted an assault they drove him back discomfited, covered the ground with his dead and wounded, and already had they torn from his grasp five stands of colors as trophies of their prowess, none of which were allowed to fall again into his hands."

The General became satisfied that the time had come when it was necessary either to evacuate the city by cutting his way out or to capitulate. It was found that the troops were unequal to the fatigues necessary to accomplish a successful sortie.

It was therefore resolved to seek terms of capitulation. These were obtained, and the city was surrendered to General Grant on July 4th.

Our loss in killed, wounded, and missing, from the landing of the enemy on the east to the capitulation, was 5,632; that of the enemy was 8,875. The number of prisoners surrendered, as near as we can tell, did not exceed 28,000.

Chapter 71

Surrender of Port Hudson

PORT HUDSON is situated on a bend of the Mississippi about twenty-two miles above Baton Rouge, La., and one hundred and forty-seven miles above New Orleans. The defences in front, or on the water side, consisted of three series of batteries situated on a bluff and extending northward along the river. General Banks with a large force landed on May 21, 1863, and on the 27th an assault was made on the works, and repulsed. A bombardment from the river was then kept up for several days, and on June 14th another unsuccessful assault was made. This was the last assault; but the enemy, resorting to mines and regular approaches, was slowly progressing with these when the news of the surrender of Vicksburg was received. General Gardner then made a proposal to General Banks to capitulate, which was accepted, and the position was yielded to the Federal commander on the next day (July 9).

The surrender included about 6,000 persons all told, 51 pieces of artillery, and a quantity of ordnance stores. Our loss in killed and wounded in the assaults was small compared with that of the enemy, and by the fall of Vicksburg the position of Port Hudson had ceased to have much importance. For more than six weeks the garrison, which had resisted a vastly superior force, attacking by both land and water, had cheerfully encountered danger and fatigue without a murmur, had borne famine and repulsed every assault, and they yielded Port Hudson only when the fall of Vicksburg had deprived the position of its importance. A chivalric foe would have recognized the gallantry of the defence in the terms usually given under like circumstances; such, for instance, as were granted to Major Anderson in Fort Sumter, or, at the least, have paroled the garrison. But no such consideration was shown to the gallant band by the Federal commander.

CHAPTER 72

BATTLE OF CHICKAMAUGA

AFTER the battle of Murfreesboro there ensued a period of inactivity, interrupted only by occasional expeditions of small bodies on each side. Two such expeditions of the enemy—that of Colonel Colburn and that of Colonel Streight—were captured, Colburn losing 1,300 men, and Streight 1,700. We soon withdrew our forces from Middle Tennessee and returned to the occupation of Chattanooga. Buckner held Knoxville, and General Samuel Jones had his headquarters at Abingdon, Va. Between the two was Cumberland Gap, supposed to be the only pass by which an army could march from the north to East Tennessee or Southwest Virginia. It was therefore partially fortified, and the command assigned to General I. W. Frazier, with 1,700 effective infantry and artillery, and about 600 cavalry,

About August 20th it was ascertained that Rosecrans, with an army of 70,000 men, had crossed the mountains to Stevenson and Bridgeport; Burnside about the same time advanced from Kentucky and approached Knoxville, with a force estimated at 25,000 men. General Buckner therefore evacuated Knoxville, and took position at Loudon with about 5,000 men. This rendered the occupation of Cumberland Gap hazardous and of comparatively little value, and it was surrendered to Burnside's vastly superior force on September 9, 1863.

The movements of Rosecrans made it impossible for us to hold Chattanooga, where the main body of our army had been encamped. It took position from Lee and Gordon's Mill to Lafayette, on the road leading to Chattanooga, and fronting the east slope of Lookout Mountain. After various changes in the position of our men and the enemy's forces, made necessary by the condition of the roads and other causes, our trains and supplies were put in a safe position, and all our forces were concentrated along the Chickamauga, threatening the opposing force in front. General Wheeler with two divisions of cavalry occupied the extreme left, vacated by Hill's corps. To divert his attention from the real movement General Forrest covered the movement on our front and right. General B. R. Johnson was moved from Ringgold to the extreme right of the line; Walker's corps formed on his left, opposite Alexander's Bridge; Buckner's next, near Tedford Ford; Polk opposite Lee and Gordon's Mill; and Hill on the extreme left. Orders were issued to cross the Chickamauga at 6. A.M. on September 18th, commencing by the extreme right.

The movement was unexpectedly delayed by the difficulty of the road and the resistance of the enemy's cavalry. The right column did not effect its crossing until late in the afternoon of the 18th. At this time General Hood, from the Army of Northern Virginia, arrived and assumed command of the column. General W. H. T. Walker had a severe skirmish at Alexander's Bridge, from which he finally drove the enemy, but not before he had destroyed it. General Walker then found a ford, and crossed. Hood united with him after night. The advance was resumed at daybreak on the 19th, when Buckner's corps, with Cheatham's division, crossed the Chickamauga, and our line of battle was formed. Forrest, with his cavalry, being in advance to the right, soon became engaged with such a large force that two brigades were sent to his support. Fighting with unusual tenacity Forrest desperately held in check the immense force opposing him. General Walker, being ordered to open the attack on the right, boldly advanced, and soon encountered opposing forces greatly superior to his own. He drove them back handsomely, capturing several batteries of artillery by dashing charges. Being repulsed, however, in his turn by the superior numbers of the enemy, Cheatham's division was ordered to his support. It came too late. Before it could reach him, assailed on both flanks, he was forced back to his first position; but the two commands united, though yet greatly outnumbered, and by a spirited attack recovered our advantage. These movements on our right were in such direction as to create an opening between the left of Cheatham's division and the right of Hood's. To fill this, Stewart's division, the reserve of Buckner's corps, was ordered up, and soon became engaged, as did Hood's whole front. The enemy had transferred forces from his extreme right so as to concentrate his main body on his left, acutely perceiving the probability of an effort on our part to gain his rear and cut off his communications with his base at Chattanooga. The main part of the battle, therefore, was fought on the opposite flank from that on which both armies had probably expected it. General Polk was now directed to move the remainder of his corps across the stream, and to assume command in person. Hill's corps was directed to move to our right. Stewart, by a gallant assault, broke the enemy's centre, and pushed forward until he became exposed to an enfilading fire. Cleburne, immediately on reaching the right, closed so impetuously with the enemy as to create surprise, and drove him in great disorder.

Our troops slept upon the field they had so bravely contested. A part of the forces on our extreme left had not reached the field of actual conflict in time to participate in the engagement of the day. They, with the remainder of Longstreet's corps, were brought up and put in position to renew the battle in the morning. From prisoners and otherwise the commanding general became satisfied that the whole Federal force had been fought on the field of Chickamauga. The Confederate troops engaged on the right numbered 33,583 men.

On the night of the 19th our whole force (including 5,000 effective infantry sent for temporary service from Virginia) was organized as two corps, the right being assigned to General Polk, and the left to General Longstreet. The aggregate of both wings was 47,321. The forces under Rosecrans numbered 64,392. On the night before the battle General Bragg gave orders that the attack should be commenced at daybreak on the right, and be taken up successively to the left. From various mishaps the attack did not open until nine or ten o'clock in the day, and, what was still more unfortunate, the troops from right to left did not engage in the rapid succession necessary to have that effectiveness which would have resulted from concert of action. Partial successes were made in the beginning of the battle; but in the first operations the troops so frequently moved to the assault without the necessary cohesion in a charging line that nearly all the early assaults by our right wing were successively repulsed with loss. Though at first invariably successful, our troops were subsequently compelled to retire before the heavy reinforcements constantly brought up.

About 4 P.M. a general assault was made by the right, and the attack was pressed from right to left until the enemy gave way at different points, and finally, about dark, yielded along the whole line. Our army bivouacked on the ground it had so gallantly won. The foe, though driven from his lines, continued to confront us when the action closed. But he withdrew in the night, and his main body was soon within his lines at Chattanooga.

We captured over 8,000 prisoners, 51 pieces of artillery, 15,000 stand of small-arms, and quantities of ammunition, with wagons, ambulances, teams, medicines, and hospital stores in large quantities. The victory was complete. But pride in the gallantry of our heroes, rejoicing in the repulse of the invader, was subdued by the memory of our fallen brave. The loss of the enemy in the conflicts at Chattanooga was 757 killed, 4,529 wounded, and 337 missing—total, 5,616. Our loss in killed and wounded was much less than theirs. General Bragg explained the reason why the enemy was not promptly pursued. "Our supplies of all kinds were greatly reduced, the railroad having been constantly occupied in transporting troops, prisoners, and our wounded, and the bridges having been destroyed to a point two miles south of Ringgold. These supplies were ordered to be replenished, and as soon as it was seen that we could be subsisted, the army was moved forward to seize and hold the only communication the enemy had with his supplies in the rear. . . . These dispositions, faithfully sustained, insured the enemy's evacuation of Chattanooga for want of food and forage.

CHAPTER 73

MISSIONARY RIDGE

THESE reverses caused the enemy to send reinforcements from the army at Vicksburg, and also to assign General Grant to the command in Tennessee. It was on October 23rd that General Grant arrived at Chattanooga, and then only in time to save their army from starvation or evacuation. The investment by General Bragg had been so close, and the enemy's communications had been so destroyed, that Bragg was on the point of realizing the evacuation of Chattanooga which he had anticipated. General Grant thus described the situation:

> "Up to this period our forces in Chattanooga were practically invested, the enemy's lines extending from the Tennessee River, above Chattanooga, to the river at and below the point of Lookout Mountain, below Chattanooga, with the south bank of the river picketed nearly to Bridgeport, his main force being fortified in Chattanooga Valley, at the foot of and on Missionary Ridge and Lookout Mountain, and a brigade in Lookout Valley. True, we held possession of the country north of the river, but it was from sixty to seventy miles over the most impracticable roads to army supplies. The artillery horses and mules had become so reduced by starvation that they could not be relied upon for moving anything. An attempt at retreat must have been with men alone, and with only such supplies as they could carry. A retreat would have been almost certain annihilation; for the enemy, occupying positions within gunshot of and overlooking our very fortifications, would unquestionably have pursued retreating forces. Already more than 10,000 animals had perished in supplying half rations to the troops by the long and tedious route from Stevenson and Bridgeport to Chattanooga over Waldron's Ridge. They could not have been supplied another week."

Grant's first movement was to establish a shorter line of supplies. Preliminary operations to this end ensued, during one of which we lost the remaining heights held by us west of Lookout Creek. Further operations of the enemy were delayed until the arrival of Sherman's forces from Memphis. After his arrival, on November 23rd, an attempt was made to feel our lines, and it was done with so much force as to obtain possession of Indian Hill and the low range of hills south of it. That night Sherman began to move to obtain a position just below the mouth of the South Chickamauga; and by daylight on the 24th he had 8,000 men on the south side of the Tennessee and fortified in rifle-trenches. By noon pontoon-bridges were laid across the Tennessee and Chickamauga, and the remainder of his forces crossed. During the afternoon he took possession of the whole northern extremity of Missionary Ridge. On the same day Hooker scaled the western slope of Lookout Mountain. On the 25th he took possession of the mountain-top with a part of his force, and with the remainder crossed Chattanooga Valley to Rossville. Our most northern point was assailed by Sherman, and the attack kept up all day. He was reinforced by a portion of Howard's corps. In the afternoon the whole of the enemy's centre, four divisions, was moved to the attack. They got possession of the rifle-pits at the foot of Missionary Ridge, and began the ascent of the mountain from right to left, and continued it until the summit was reached, notwithstanding the volleys of grape and canister discharged at them. Our forces retreated from the Ridge as the multitudinous assailants neared the thin line on the crest, and during the night withdrew from the positions on the plain below. General Grant, after advancing a short distance from Chattanooga, despatched a portion of his forces to the relief of Burnside in East Tennessee, where he was closely besieged by Longstreet in Knoxville. Longstreet moved east into Virginia, and ultimately joined General Lee. He had left the army of Lee, and moved to the west with his force, on the condition that he should return when summoned. This summons had been sent.

Chapter 74

The Battle of Gettysburg

IN May, 1863, the enemy, under General Hooker, occupied his former position before Fredericksburg in great strength, the force present being 136,704. His objective point was Richmond.

General Lee's forces had been reorganized into the First, Second, and Third Army Corps, commanded respectively by Longstreet, Ewell, and A. P. Hill.

In view of the enemy's great superiority in numbers, it was considered inadvisable to allow him to choose his own time for attacking us, and it was therefore decided, by a bold movement, to attempt to transfer hostilities to the north side of the Potomac, by crossing the river into Maryland and Pennsylvania; simultaneously driving the foe out of the Shenandoah Valley, which he occupied in considerable force.

With this view our forces, on June 3, 1863, advanced to Culpeper Court-House, leaving Hill to occupy the lines in front of Fredericksburg.

On the 5th Hooker, having discovered our movement, crossed an army corps to the south side of the Rappahannock; but, as this manœuvre was apparently for observation, it was not thought necessary to oppose it. On the 9th a large force of the enemy's cavalry crossed at Beverly's and Kelly's Fords and attacked General Stuart. A severe engagement ensued. Stuart forced his assailant to recross the river, with heavy loss, leaving 400 prisoners, 3 pieces of artillery, and several stands of colors in our hands.

On June 13th General Ewell advanced directly upon Winchester, driving the enemy into his works around the town. Next day he stormed the works, and the whole army of General Milroy was captured or put to flight. Most of those who attempted to escape were made prisoners.

General Rhodes captured Martinsburg on the 14th, with 700 prisoners, 5 pieces of artillery, and a considerable quantity of stores.

Thus the valley was cleared of the enemy. Our loss was small.

On the night that Ewell appeared at Winchester, the enemy at Fredericksburg recrossed the Rappahannock, and disappeared behind the hills of Stafford.

Hooker, in retreating, pursued the roads near the Potomac, and offered no favorable opportunity for attack. On the 17th, near Aldie, Stuart encountered and drove back the enemy's cavalry. The engagement was renewed on the 18th. Finding that the Federal cavalry was now strongly supported by infantry, Stuart retired, having taken in these engagements about 400 prisoners and a considerable number of horses and arms.

Meanwhile General Ewell had entered Maryland, and Jenkins, with his cavalry, had penetrated as far as Chambersburg, Pa. Longstreet and Hill crossed the Potomac, to be within supporting distance of Ewell, and, advancing into Pennsylvania, encamped near Chambersburg on June 27th. On the same day it was ascertained that Hooker had crossed the Potomac and was marching northward, thus menacing our communications. It was determined therefore to arrest his further progress by concentrating our army at Gettysburg.

Heth's, the leading division of Hill's corps, met the enemy in front of Gettysburg on the morning of July 1st, driving him back within a short distance of the town. There the advance encountered a larger force, with which two of Hill's divisions became engaged. Ewell came up, with two of his divisions, and took part in the engagements. The Federals were driven through Gettysburg with heavy loss, including about 5,000 prisoners and several pieces of artillery.

Our troops bivouacked on the ground they had won.

The position at Gettysburg was not the choice of either side. South of the town an irregular, interrupted line of hills runs, which is sometimes called the "Gettysburg Ridge." This ridge, at the town, runs eastward and then southward. At the turn eastward is Cemetery Hill, and at the turn southward, Culp's Hill. From Cemetery Hill the line runs southward about three miles in a well-defined ridge, called Cemetery Ridge since the battle, and terminates in a high, rocky, and wooded peak named Round-Top, which was the key of the enemy's position, as it flanked their line. The less elevated position, near where the crest rises into Round-Top, is termed Little Round-Top, a rough and bold spur of the former. Thus, while Cemetery and Culp's Hills require the formation of a line of battle to face northward, the direction of Cemetery Ridge requires the line to face westward. The crest has a good slope to the rear, while to the west it falls off in a cultivated and undulating valley, which it commands. About a mile distant is a parallel crest, known as Seminary Ridge, which our forces occupied during the battle. Longstreet, with the divisions of Hood and McLaws, faced Round-Top and a good part of Cemetery Ridge; Hill's three divisions continued the line from the left of Longstreet, fronting the remainder of Cemetery Ridge; while Ewell with his three divisions held a line through the town, and sweeping round the base of Cemetery Hill terminated the left in front of Culp's Hill.

These were the positions of the three corps after the arrival of General Longstreet's troops.

The main purpose of the movement across the Potomac was to free Virginia from the presence of the enemy. It had not been intended to fight a general battle at such a distance from our base as Gettysburg; but, being unexpectedly confronted by the opposing army, it became a matter of difficulty to withdraw through the mountains with our large trains. At the same time, in the presence of the main army of the enemy, the country was unfavorable for collecting supplies.

Encouraged by the successful issue of the engagement of the first day, and in view of the valuable results that would ensue from the defeat of the Federal army, General Lee decided to renew the attack on the next day, July 2nd.

General Meade held the high ridge above described, along which he had moved a large amount of artillery. Ewell held our left, Hill the centre, Longstreet the right. In front of Longstreet the enemy held a position from which, if he could be driven, it was thought that our army could gain Round-Top beyond, and thus enable our guns to rake the crest of the ridge. Longstreet was ordered to try to carry this position, while Ewell should attack the high grounds on the enemy's right, which had already been partially fortified. Hill was instructed to threaten the centre, to prevent reinforcements to either wing, and to avail himself of any opportunity that might present itself to attack.

After a severe struggle, Longstreet succeeded in getting possession of the ground in his immediate front and holding it. Ewell also carried some of the strong positions he assailed; and the result was such as to lead to the belief that he would ultimately be able to dislodge the force in his front. The battle ceased at dark.

These partial successes determined Lee to continue the assault on the next day, July 3rd. Pickett with three brigades joined Longstreet next morning, and our batteries were moved forward to the positions gained by him on the day before.

In the meantime General Meade had strengthened his line with earthworks. The morning was occupied in necessary preparations, and the battle reopened in the afternoon and raged with great violence until sunset. Our troops succeeded in entering the advanced works of the enemy; but, our artillery having nearly expended its ammunition, the attacking columns became exposed to the heavy force of the numerous batteries near the summit of the ridge, and, after a most determined and gallant struggle, were compelled to relinquish the advantage and fall back to their original positions with severe loss.

Owing to the strength of the enemy's position and the exhaustion of our ammunition, a renewal of the engagement could not be hazarded, and the difficulty of procuring supplies rendered it impossible to continue longer where we were. Such of the wounded as could be removed were ordered to Williamsport.

The army remained at Gettysburg during the 4th, and at night began to retire by the road to Fairfield, carrying with it about 4,000 prisoners. Nearly 2,000 had been previously paroled; but the numerous wounded who had fallen into our hands after the first and second day's engagements were left behind.

Little progress was made that night, owing to a severe storm, which greatly embarrassed our movements. The rear of the column did not leave its position near Gettysburg until after daylight on the 5th. The march was continued during the day without interruption by the enemy, except one unimportant demonstration upon our rear, which was easily checked.

After a tedious march, rendered more difficult by the rains, our army reached Hagerstown on the 6th and the morning of the 7th of July.

The Potomac was unfordable. It had been swollen by the rains that had fallen almost incessantly since our army entered Maryland. The pontoon-train sent from Richmond was inadequate. By the 13th a good bridge was thrown over at Falling Waters. On the 12th Meade's army approached. An attack was awaited during that and the following day, yet, although the two armies were in close proximity, no collision occurred, the enemy being occupied in fortifying his own lines.

On the night of the 13th, our preparations being completed, the army commenced to cross the Potomac. The crossing was not completed until 1 P.M. on the 14th, when the bridge was removed. The enemy offered no serious interruption, and the movement was attended with the loss of only a few disabled wagons and two pieces of artillery, which the horses were unable to move through the deep mud.

The strength of our army at Gettysburg is stated at 62,000 of all arms. The report of the Army of the Potomac under Meade, on June 30th, states the force present at 112,988 men. General Meade stated to a Congressional Committee that, "including all arms of the service, my strength [at Gettysburg] was a little under 100,000 men—about 95,000."

If the strength of Lee's forces, according to the last accessible report before his movement northward, be compared with that made after his return to Virginia, there is a decrease of 19,000 of the brave men who had set the seal of invincibility on the Army of Northern Virginia.

Thus closed the campaign in Pennsylvania. The wisdom of the strategy was justified by the result. The battle of Gettysburg was unfortunate; though the loss sustained by the enemy was greater than our own, theirs could be repaired, ours could not.

The battle of Gettysburg has been the subject of an unusual amount of discussion, and the enemy has made it a matter of extraordinary exultation. As an affair of arms it was marked by mighty feats of valor to which both combatants may point with military pride. It was a graceful thing in President Lincoln, as reported, when, on being shown the steeps which the Northern men persistently held, he answered, "I am proud to be the countryman of the men who assailed those heights."

The consequences of the battle have justified the amount of attention it has received. It may be regarded as the most eventful struggle of the war. By it the drooping spirit of the North was revived. Had their army been there defeated, those having better opportunities to judge than I or anyone who was not among them, have believed it would have ended the war. On the other hand, a drawn battle, where the Army of Northern

Virginia made an attack, impaired the confidence of the Southern people so far as to give the malcontents a power to represent the government as neglecting for Virginia the safety of the more southern States.

In all free governments the ability of its executive branch to prosecute a war must depend largely upon public opinion; in an infant republic this is peculiarly the case. The volume given to the voice of disaffection was therefore most seriously felt by us.

Chapter 75

After Gettysburg

SHATTERED, it is true, but not disheartened, the Army of Northern Virginia, after recrossing the Potomac, rose, like the son of Terra, with renewed vigor, and valor undiminished by reverses.

Early in October General Lee, with two corps, crossed the Rapidan to attack the flank of the enemy or compel him to retreat. He forced Meade's army back to Alexandria and Centreville, and captured 1,500 prisoners. With the exception of a rash and ill-conducted affair at Bristoe Station, where our advance engaged a corps, and was repulsed, the campaign was an unbroken success. Without a general battle a large portion of the State was for the time liberated from the power of the invader.

On November 7th the enemy advanced upon our force at Kelly's Ford, of the Rappahannock River, effected a crossing, and rushing upon two brigades who were at Rappahannock Station, defending the bridges, overwhelmed and captured most of them, taking between 1,200 and 1,500 men and 4 pieces of artillery. The movements of the enemy were concealed by darkness, and his attack was a surprise.

On November 26th the army under General Meade crossed the Rapidan, with the intention of interposing between the widely separated wings of his adversary. The movement resulted in an entire failure. General Meade found Lee's army posted behind Mine Run, and ready to receive an attack whenever he was disposed to make it. Lee had inaugurated that system of breastworks which did him good service in his long campaign with Grant. When the troops were halted in a wood the men felled the large trees; heavy logs were dragged without loss of time to the prescribed line, where they were piled upon one another in double walls, which were filled in rapidly with earth; so that in a short space of time defences that would turn a cannon-ball were often constructed. In front, for some distance, the felled timber made a kind of abatis.

As General Meade did not attack, General Lee, on the night of December 1st, determined to assail his adversary on the following morning; but when the dawn broke, his camps were seen to be abandoned.

General Meade had abandoned the campaign and was in full retreat. Pursuit was immediately made, but he had too much the start, and reached the north side of the Rapidan before he could be overtaken. Both armies then returned to their original positions.

We captured about 700 prisoners, 400 mules and horses, and destroyed or secured 120 wagons.

Chapter 76

The Subjugation of Tennessee and Louisiana

THE saddest pages of a history of the war between the States are those that must tell of the subjugation of the State Governments by the Federal Government. That the work of the fathers of the Republic, that the most magnificent system of constitutional government which the wisdom of man has devised, should be turned from its object, changed from its order, rendered powerless to protect the individual rights and sovereignty of the people, and made the instrument by which to establish and maintain imperialism is a revolution unlike any other that may be found in the history of mankind.

The governments of the States were instituted to secure certain unalienable rights of the citizens with which they were endowed by their Creator. Where must the American citizen look for the security of these rights? To his State Government.

The powers which a State Government possesses for the security of his life, his liberty, his property, his safety, and his happiness are "just powers." They have been derived from the unconstrained consent of the governed, and they have been organized in such form as seems most likely to effect these objects.

The entire order of the State Government is founded on the free consent of the governed. From this it springs; from this it receives its force and life. It is this consent alone from which "just powers" are derived. They can come from no other source, and their exercise secures a true republican government. All else are usurpations, their exercise is a tyranny, and their end is the safety and security of the usurper, to obtain which the safety and security of the people are sacrificed. The "just powers" thus derived are organized in such form as seems most likely to effect safety and happiness. It is the governed who determine the form of the government, and not the ruler or his military force, unless he comes as a conqueror to make the subjugated do his will.

What, then, is the Government of the United States? It is an organization of a few years' duration. It might cease to exist and yet the States and the people continue prosperous, peaceful, and happy. Unlike the governments of the States, which find their origin deep in the nature of man, it sprang from certain circumstances which existed in the course of human affairs. Unlike the governments of the States and of separate nations, which have a divine sanction, it has no warrant for its authority but the ratification of the sovereign States. Unlike the governments of the States, which were instituted to secure generally the unalienable rights of man, it has only the enumerated objects, and is restrained from passing beyond them by the express reservation of all undelegated functions. It keeps no record of property, and guarantees to no one the possession of his estate. Marriage it can neither confirm nor annul. It is an anomaly among governments, and arose out of the articles of agreement made by certain friendly States which proposed to form a society of States, and invest a common agent with specified functions of sovereignty. Its duration was intended to be permanent, as it was hoped thus to promote the peaceful ends for which it was established; but to have declared it perpetual would have been to deny the right of the people to alter or abolish their government when it should cease to answer the ends for which it was instituted.

The objects which its creation was designed to secure to the States and their people were of a truly peaceful nature, and commended themselves to the approbation of men:

> "To form a more perfect union, establish justice, insure domestic tranquillity, provide for the common defence, promote the general welfare, and secure the blessings of liberty to ourselves and our posterity."[111]

Mankind must contemplate with horror the fact that an organization established for such peaceful and benign ends did, within the first century of its existence, lead the assault in a civil war that brought nearly four

---

111. Preamble to the Constitution of the United States.

millions of soldiers into the field, and destroyed thousands and thousands of millions of treasure, trampled the unalienable rights of the people under foot, subverted the governments of the States, and ended by establishing itself as supreme and sovereign over all.

Now let us proceed to notice the acts of the Federal Government which subjugated the State Governments. In the case of Tennessee, already noted, the Government of the State—which derived its powers from the consent of the governed, so that they were "just powers"—found, in the discharge of its duty to protect the institutions of its people, that there were no means by which it could fulfil that duty but by a withdrawal from the Union, so as to be rid of the Government of the United States, and thus escape the threatened dangers of usurpation and sectional hostility. It therefore resolved to withdraw from the Union, and the people gave their assent to that resolution; so that the State no longer considered itself a member of the Union, nor recognized the laws and authority of its Government.

The Government of the United States then, with a powerful military force, planted itself at Nashville, the State capital. It refused to recognize the laws and authority of its Government, or any organization under it, as having any existence, or to recognize the people otherwise than as a hostile community. It said to them, in effect, "I am the sovereign, and you are the subjects. If you are stronger than I am, then drive me out of the State; if I am stronger than you are, then I command an unconditioned surrender to my sovereignty." It is evident that the Government of the United States was not there by the consent of those who were to be governed. It had not, therefore, any "just powers" of government within the State of Tennessee. "For," says the Declaration of Independence of our fathers, "governments derive their just powers from the consent of the governed." By this action; therefore, the Federal Government not only subverted the State Government, but annihilated it. It proceeded to establish a new order of affairs, founded on the assumption of Federal sovereignty. It appointed its military governor to be the head of the new order, and recognized no civil or political existence in any man except some of its notorious adherents, until, by betraying the State, he had taken an oath of allegiance to the sovereignty of the United States. Then unalienable rights were systematically denied, freedom of speech was suppressed, freedom of the press was suspended, personal liberty was destroyed. Citizens were arrested, imprisoned, and exiled without the process of law.

Finally an effort was made to erect a form of State Government that should be subject and subservient to the Federal Government. No one was allowed to vote until he had taken an oath to support and defend the Government of the United States. Under the State Government manhood and residence were deemed sufficient qualifications. The right to cast a ballot, therefore, no longer was granted as an unalienable right, but rested upon the permission of the Federal Government. A little later a similar oath, with additional conditions, was required before a man was permitted to vote for a State Constitutional Convention or for delegates to it. These, conditions were that he should faithfully support all acts of Congress and all proclamations of the President of the United States, passed or made during the rebellion, with reference to slaves. These conditions, sustained by military force, were exacted by the Federal Government as the lord paramount—as the sovereign within the State.

Thus the Government of the State of Tennessee was subverted and overthrown, and the people were subjugated. The approval by Tennessee, under such circumstances, of Article XIII, as an amendment of the Constitution of the United States, prohibiting the institution of slavery, was of no force; for consent given by a party under constraint has neither legal nor moral validity. The State Constitution, which was amended to meet the demands of the Federal Government, was so altered by a so-called Convention of delegates elected by a handful only of the people of Tennessee. Admitting even that those who voted for the amended Constitution were the only legal voters in the State, the Government of the United States was no less an unlawful intruder and usurper when it prescribed the amendments of the Constitution and designated the voters. Nevertheless, the work was recognized by it as constituting a republican State Government under the Constitution.

One of the earliest steps in the subversion of the State Government of Louisiana, after the occupation of New Orleans, was to make a registration of voters. The Federal Government was in possession by military force, and the object was to secure its permanent supremacy. Therefore every applicant for registration was required to take an oath that he was "loyal to the Government of the United States." It was announced that any person swearing falsely to any material part of the oath would be deemed guilty of perjury and liable to its penalties. The effect of this measure was to secure the registration of such persons only who would maintain the supremacy of the Federal Government. A proclamation was next issued by the commander of the United States forces for an election of State officers under the Federal laws and Constitution. It was declared that these officers, when thus elected, would constitute the civil government of the State under the Constitution and laws of Louisiana, "except so much of the said Constitution and laws as recognize, regulate, or relate to slavery."

The effect of these acts was to establish as the only qualified voters in the State a number of persons pledged to support the Federal Government, and to elect by their ballots so-called State officers, and delegates to a so-called Constitutional Convention. But this was a work that could be rightfully done only by the sovereign people acting through their lawful State Government. It was not so done because the Government of the United States, with a powerful military force, had taken possession of New Orleans, refused to recognize the officers of the State Government, and sought to capture and imprison them, although it professed to recognize the validity of the State Constitution and commanded these things to be done as if it was the ultimate sovereign over all.

Then the Government of the State was subverted, the Constitution of the State in part set aside, and the sovereignty of the people trampled down by a power that had no rightful authority for such acts.

Subsequently a so-called Convention was held, a so-called new Constitution adopted, complying with the views of the Federal Government; the amendment to the Constitution of the United States was adopted, the State representatives were admitted to seats in Congress, and the people submitted to the fraud which they had not the power to correct.

Chapter 77

The Subjugation of Maryland

IT has already been shown how the State Government of Maryland was subjugated and her sovereignty ignored by the action of the Federal Executive. A Federal military force occupied Baltimore at a time when no invasion of the State was threatened, and when there had been no application of the Legislature or of the Executive for protection against domestic violence—circumstances which alone could have given constitutional authority for the occupation by this organized military force. Soon the commanding General, Schenck, issued an order declaring the establishment of martial law in the city and county of Baltimore, and in all the counties of the Western Shore of Maryland. All the State civil courts were to continue in the discharge of their duties as in times of peace, "only in no way interfering with the exercise of the predominant power assumed and asserted by the military authority." There was no constitutional warrant whatever for this usurpation of power.

A further subversion of the State Government was now commenced by an invasion and denial of some of the unalienable rights of the citizens for the security of which that Government was instituted. Immediately upon the issue of the order of the commanding general, the arrest of citizens by provost-marshals commenced. The family residence of a lady was broken open; she was seized, put on board a steamer, and sent to the Confederate States. A man was arrested for being "disloyal" to the United States Government, and held for examination. Another was charged with interfering with the enrolment; he was held for further examination. Another, charged with being "disloyal" to the United States Government, took the oath of allegiance and was released. Another, charged with having given improper information to enrolling officers, was released on furnishing the information. Another, charged with having powder in his possession, was released on taking the oath of allegiance. Another, charged with rendering assistance to wounded Confederate soldiers and expressing treasonable sentiments, took the oath of allegiance and was released. Another, charged with being a soldier in the Confederate army and paroled, was ordered to be sent across the line. Another citizen, charged with "treasonable language," was ordered to be sent across the line. Two men, charged with cheering for Jefferson Davis, took the oath and were released. These are a few instances of illegal arrests and punishments, out of hundreds that occurred. During the month of July 361 persons were arrested by the military authorities, on charges similar to those just noted. Of this number 317 took the oath of allegiance to the Government; 5 were sent to Fort McHenry, 3 to Washington for the action of the authorities, 11 to the North, 6 across the lines; and 19 were held for further examination.

On September 11, 1863, one of the Baltimore City papers published a poem called "The Southern Cross." The editor and publisher were arrested and sent across the lines, with the understanding that they should not return during the war. On July 2nd an order was issued forbidding the citizens of Baltimore to keep arms unless they were enrolled as volunteer companies. A Massachusetts regiment, placed at the disposal of the provost-marshal and chief of police, was formed into squads of three and four, which were soon diligently engaged in searching houses. Large wagons were provided, and muskets, carbines, rifles, revolvers, sabres, bayonets, swords, and bird or ducking guns in considerable quantities were gathered. The Constitution of the United States says:

> "The right of the people to keep and bear arms shall not be infringed."

A still further subversion of the State Government of Maryland was made by a direct interference with the elections. On November 3, 1863, an election was to be held in the State for members of the Legislature and members of Congress. On October 27th the commanding General issued an order to all marshals and military officers to cause their direct interference with the voters. Governor Bradford appealed to President Lincoln to revoke the order, and protested against any person who offered to vote being put to any test not found in the laws of Maryland. President Lincoln refused the request.

"On Monday evening preceding the election," said Governor Bradford, "I issued a proclamation giving the judges of election the assurance of the protection of the State to the extent of its ability. Before the following morning orders were sent to the Eastern Shore directing its circulation to be stopped; the public papers were forbidden to publish it. An embargo was laid on all steamers in port trading with that part of the State, lest they might carry it. On the day preceding the election the officer in command of the regiment which had been distributed among the counties of the Eastern Shore commenced his operations by sending across the Bay some ten or more of the most estimable and distinguished of its citizens, including several of the most steadfast and most uncompromising loyalists of the Shore. The jail of the county was entered, the jailer seized, imprisoned, and afterward sent to Baltimore, and prisoners confined therein under indictment set at liberty. The commanding officer issued a proclamation in which he invited all the truly loyal to avail themselves of that opportunity, and establish their loyalty 'by giving a full and ardent support to the Union League Convention;' declaring that 'none other is recognized by the Federal authorities as loyal or worthy of the support of anyone who desires the peace and restoration of the Union.'

"The Government ticket was in several, if not all, of those counties designated by its color. It was a yellow ticket; and armed with that a voter could safely run the gauntlet of the sabres and carbines that guarded the entrance to the polls, and known sympathizers with the rebellion were allowed to vote unquestioned if they would vote that ticket; while loyal and respected citizens ready to take the oath were turned back by the officer in charge, without even allowing them to approach the polls. In one district the military officer took his stand at the polls before they were opened, declaring that none but the 'yellow ticket should be voted,' and excluded all others throughout the day. In another district a similar officer caused every ballot offered to be examined, and unless it was the favored one the voter was required to take the oath, and not otherwise. In another district, after one vote only had been given, the polls were closed, the judges were all arrested and sent out of the county, and military occupation taken of the town."

The result was the election of a majority of members of the Legislature in favor of a State Constitutional Convention. The acts necessary for the purpose were passed. At the election of delegates the military authority again interfered in order to secure a majority in favor of immediate and unconditional emancipation. The so-called Convention assembled and drafted a so-called Constitution, which prohibited the existence of slavery in the State.

Notwithstanding the aid of the President, which was asked and obtained to help on the ratification of the new Constitution; notwithstanding the soldiers' vote, a most stringent oath, and the exclusion of every person who had in any manner, by word or act, aided the cause of the Confederacy, the majority for the so-called Constitution was only 375. The total vote was 59,973. In 1860 the vote of the State was 92,502.

Thus was the State Government of Maryland subjugated and made an instrument of destruction to the people; thus were their rights ruthlessly violated, and property, millions of dollars in value, annihilated.

Chapter 78

The Subjugation of Kentucky

IN Kentucky the first open and direct measures taken by the Federal Government for the subjugation of the State Government and people, thereby to effect the emancipation of the slaves, consisted in an interference with the voters at the State election in August, 1863. A military force was stationed at the polls to sustain and enforce the action of some of the servants of the Government of the United States, in order to overawe the judges of election, secure the administration of a rigid oath of allegiance, and thereby the rejection of as many opposition votes as possible. It was intended that none but the so-called "Union men" should vote—that is, men who were willing to approve of every measure which the Government of the United States might adopt to carry on the war and revolutionize the State. No man was allowed to be a candidate or to receive any votes unless he was a well-known advocate of the Government of the United States. These measures excluded the largest portion of the former Democratic party, although they might be practically "Union men," and placed everything in the hands of the Administration party, where, by the use of similar machinery, it remained a great many years after the war closed.

Meanwhile, on July 31, 1863, the commanding General of the Department of the Ohio issued an order declaring the State under martial law, and said, "It is for the purpose only of protecting, if necessary, the rights of loyal citizens and the freedom of elections." The General in command in the western part of the State issued an order to regulate the election in that quarter, and the colonels at every post did likewise. In Louisville, on the day of election, there were ten soldiers at each voting-place, who, with crossed bayonets, stood at the doors, preventing all access of voters to the polls but by their permission, and who arrested and carried to the military prison all whom they were told to arrest. Out of some 8,000 votes in the city, less than 5,000 were taken. The interpretation generally put on the order of the commanding officer by the opposition party was that no man was to have the privilege of having his right to vote tested by the judges of election if he was pointed out to the guard by any one of the detectives as a proper person to be arrested. As the commanding officer had not the semblance of legal or rightful power to interfere with the election, the most sinister suspicions were naturally aroused, and very many were said to have been detained from going to the polls through fear that they might be made the victims of personal or party malice. Similar intimidation was practised in other parts of the State. The result was that there was not only direct military interference with the election, but it was conducted in most of the State under the intimidation of the bayonets of the Government of the United States. The total vote was 85,695. In 1860 the vote of the State was 146,216.

The Federal Government was now ready to move forward in its design to destroy one of the most valuable institutions of the State. Steps were taken by its officers to enroll all the able-bodied male negroes in the State between the ages of twenty and forty-five years, that they might form a part of its forces. The effect of this measure was to break up the labor system of the State; and meanwhile the pseudo-philanthropists furnished food for powder, and indulged their ideas of freedom at their neighbors' expense. The excitement produced caused the Governor to visit Washington and effect agreements by which all recruiting should cease when a county's quota was full, all recruits should be removed from the State, and other similar provisions. A year later he said to the Legislature: "Had these agreements been carried out, a very different state of feeling would have existed in Kentucky. But, instead of carrying them out, the most offensive and ingenious modes were adopted to violate them."

The next step taken by the Federal Government in this work of subversion was the destruction of the unalienable right of personal liberty of the citizen, which the State was in duty bound to protect. The Union Governor of Kentucky, whose election was aided by the military force, bears witness to the Federal usurpations in his message to the Legislature of January, 1865. He complains of the outrage committed by the military in "the arrest, imprisonment, and banishment of loyal citizens without a hearing, and even without a knowledge of the charges against them. There have been a number of this class of arrests, merely for partisan political vengeance, and to force them to pay heavy sums to purchase their liberation." He proves his accusation by citing the cases of General Huston, Colonel Wolford, and Lieutenant-Governor Jacobs, whose "acts are part of the glorious history of loyal heroism."

Next came the proclamation of martial law throughout the State, and the suspension of the writ of *habeas corpus*. A large number of eminent Kentuckians, of all professions and pursuits, were arrested and imprisoned. A group of persons, consisting of judges, magistrates, wealthy merchants, and young women, were banished from the State without having been allowed a hearing or trial, or any opportunity to vindicate themselves. The State Government was passive; indeed, it was powerless to resist. A State election was held on the first Monday of August for local officers and a Judge of the High Court of Appeals from one district. Chief Justice Duvall was one of the two candidates. On July 29th an order was issued by the Major-General, commanding, to the sheriffs of the counties concerned, as follows:

> "You will not allow the name of Alvin Duvall to appear upon the poll-books as a candidate for office at the coming election."

Another name was substituted.

The Presidential election occurred in November, but as the vote of Kentucky was not regarded as necessary to insure Republican success, the Federal Government refrained from interference.

By enlistment over 22,000 of the most valuable slaves in the State had gone into the service of the United States. On March 3, 1865, Congress passed an act declaring that the wives and children of all such soldiers should be free.

Mrs. Henry's House, near the center of the battlefield of Manassas, in which the wounded were nursed by Bishop Wilmer of Ala.—as it appeared after the Battle.

Chapter 79

The Subjugation of Missouri

THE subjugation of the State Government of Missouri by the Federal Government was more rapid and more desperate than in the case of Kentucky. But the bravery of the Governor and the determination of the Legislature caused the Government of the United States to depart from its usually stealthy progress in the invasion of the State Government and the sovereignty of the people, and to adopt bolder measures. For his attempt faithfully to discharge his duties the Governor was charged with purposes of treason and secession. Troops were poured into the State so rapidly as to render the successful operation of the lawful authorities impossible, and the control of a large portion of the State was soon held by the military forces. Unable to resist these usurpations the Governor retired to the southern part of the State.

Meanwhile the State Convention reassembled at the call of its committee. Entirely forgetful of the object for which the people had called it together, it proceeded to declare the State offices vacant and to elect a provisional Governor and other officers entirely subservient to the will and interests of the administration at Washington. The commanding General now declared martial law in the State, and the emancipation of all slaves belonging to persons who had taken active part with us. This proclamation was modified by the President as in advance of the times.

The attention of the reader is called to the numerous usurpations and violations of constitutional principles and laws thus rapidly voted, many invasions with military force, the expulsion of the lawful State Government, the assumption by the State Convention of unlawful powers, the election and introduction of persons into offices not vacant, the declaration of martial law without any authority for it, and the attempt to emancipate the slaves in violation of every law and constitutional principle.

The severity of the Federal Executive now began to be felt by the citizens of the State. All disaffected persons were silenced or arrested, prisoners of war were treated as criminals, and every obstacle to complete subjugation to the will of the conqueror was sought to be removed. The State Government was represented by a prominent Governor; and a State Convention, which adjourned its sessions from year to year, after dallying periodically with the subject of the emancipation of the slaves, finally passed an ordinance for that purpose, to take effect in 1870. This was not immediate emancipation; so the disturbances were kept up in the State until, at a session of the Legislature, in February, 1864, a bill was passed for a so-called State Convention to revise the State Constitution, and the election of delegates in November. The delegates were elected, the so-called Convention assembled January 6, 1865, an immediate emancipation ordinance was passed, and the State organization was subjugated to do the will of the usurper and to disregard the will of the sovereign people.

Chapter 80

The Subjugation of the State of New York

NOW follows the humiliating spectacle of the subjugation of the State Government of New York, where, with all her men and treasures, it might have been supposed that some, stanch defenders of constitutional liberty would have sprung up. On the contrary, under the pretext of "preserving the Union" her deluded children aided to destroy the Constitution on which the Union was founded, and to put forth all their strength to exalt the Government of the United States to supremacy. Thus the States were brought to a condition of subjugation, and their governments subverted from the protection of the rights for which they were instituted. These unalienable rights of the people were left without a protector or shield against the cunning hand of the usurper; the sovereignty of the people was set aside, and in its place arose the sovereignty of the Government of the United States.

To show how the laws were disregarded, and how despotically the personal liberty of the citizen was invaded, let this example bear witness: The Secretary of State at Washington, William H. Seward, a favorite son of New York, would "ring a little bell," which brought to him a messenger, to whom was given a secret order to arrest and confine in Fort Lafayette a person designated. The order was sent by telegraph to the United States Marshal of the district in which would be found the person to be arrested. The arrest being forcibly made by the marshal, with armed attendants, without even the form of a warrant, the prisoner, without the knowledge of any charge against him, was conveyed to Fort Hamilton and turned over to the commandant.

An aid, with a guard of soldiers, then conveyed him in a boat to Fort Lafayette, and delivered him to the keeper in charge, who gave a receipt for the prisoner. He was then divested of the weapons, money, valuables, or papers in his possession. His baggage was opened and searched. A soldier then took him in charge to the designated quarter, which was a portion of one of the casemates for guns, lighted only from the port-hole, and occupied by seven or eight other prisoners. All were subjected to prison fare. Some were citizens of New York, and others of different States. This manner of imprisonment was subsequently put under the direction of the Secretary of War, and continued at intervals until the close of hostilities.

Between July 1 and October 19, 1861, Mr. Seward made such diligent use of his "little bell" that one hundred and seventy-five of the most respectable citizens of the country were consigned to imprisonment in this Fort Lafayette, a strong fortress in the lower harbor of New York.

Ample safeguards had been provided in the Constitution for the protection of the personal liberty of the citizen, in addition to the guarantees afforded by the constitutions of the several States.[112]

Yet all these safeguards, State and Federal, proved to be of no avail to secure and enforce the right of the citizens in the hour of trial.

The writ of *habeas corpus* was issued by some of the State courts directing the officer in command at the fort to bring some one or other of the prisoners into court for an investigation of the cause and authority for his detention. No attention was given to any of these writs by the officer. Neither did the Governor of the State make any effort to enforce the processes of the courts.

Thus the Constitution, the laws, the courts, the Executive of the State of New York were subverted, turned aside from the end for which they were instituted, and all the specific arrangements were of no avail to secure this guaranteed right of its citizens. Probably every one of the prisoners was entirely innocent of any act whatever that was criminal under the laws of either the State or the United States.

Finally, the prison in New York harbor became so full that many prisoners were sent to Fort Warren, in Boston harbor. At this time the Government of the United States used the old Capitol at Washington, Fort McHenry at Baltimore, Fort Lafayette at New York, and Fort Warren at Boston for the confinement of those whom the usurper

---

112. See Art. 1, Sec. 9; Art. 5, amendment; Art. 6, amendment.

designated as "state prisoners." Despite the distinct provision in the Constitution, these prisoners were refused the assistance of counsel, and officially notified that the Government "will not recognize anyone as an attorney for political prisoners, and will look with distrust upon all applications for release through such channels."

In every Northern State victims of this violence were to be found. It was demonstrated in the most decisive manner that there was no just cause for these invasions of the rights of the States. At this time (November 4, 1862) the administration party was decisively defeated at the elections. On the 22nd of November ensuing, the War Department issued an order releasing all prisoners except prisoners of war. Thus these arrests were for a short period suspended; then they were vigorously renewed.

Many of the persons thus illegally imprisoned commenced suits for damages. Congress then, on March 3, 1863, passed an act, giving the defence the power of simply filing a petition, verified by affidavit, to remove the case from any State court to the Circuit Court, thus terminating the jurisdiction of all the courts of the State of New York upon the simple word of the defendant accompanied by an affidavit.

The subjugation of the Government of the State of New York was made in another section of the same act, which declared that the President was authorized, whenever in his judgment the public safety might require it, to suspend the privilege of the writ of *habeas corpus* in any case throughout the United States, or any part thereof.

By the Constitution the power to suspend the writ of *habeas corpus* is vested in Congress alone, which cannot delegate the power either of suspension or of determining that the public safety requires it.

On the 15th of September the President issued a proclamation declaring that, in his judgment, the public safety required that the privilege of the writ of *habeas corpus* should be suspended throughout the United States in cases where, by the authority of the President or of the military, naval, or civil officers of the United States, or either of them, persons were held in custody, either as prisoners of war, spies, or aiders and abettors of the enemy, or officers, soldiers, or seamen enrolled, drafted, or numbered, or enlisted in the land or naval forces of the United States, etc.: "Therefore, I do hereby proclaim that the privilege of the writ of *habeas corpus* is suspended throughout the United States in the several cases before mentioned throughout the duration of said rebellion."

No autocrat ever issued an edict more destructive of the natural right to personal liberty. Not only was the State Government of New York deprived of the power to fulfil its obligations to protect and preserve this right of its citizens, but every State Government of the Northern States was in like manner subverted.

Another step in the subjugation of the Government of the State of New York was made by the domination over it of the military power of the Government of the United States. This took place in a time of peace in the State, when the courts were all open and the civil administration of affairs was unobstructed. On July 30, 1863, General Dix, commanding General of the Department, addressed a letter to Governor Seymour, asking whether the military power of the State could be relied on to enforce the execution of the "draft" law, in case of forcible resistance, and stating that, if the Act would be enforced under the authority of the Governor, he need not ask the War Department to put at his disposal, for the purpose, troops in the service of the United States.

Governor Seymour replied, on August 3rd, that he had addressed a letter to the President, the answer to which he believed would release him and the General from the painful questions growing out of an armed enforcement of the conscription law in New York.

On August 8th General Dix again addressed Governor Seymour, stating that it was his duty as commanding officer, if called on, to aid enrolling officers in resisting forcible opposition to the execution of the law; that he wished to see the draft enforced by the military power of the State, in case of organized resistance; and that he designed to ask the General Government for a force that would be adequate to enforce the law and meet any emergency growing out of it.

Meanwhile Governor Seymour had received no answer to his letter to the President, in which he had asked for a suspension of the draft on account of errors in estimates, and failures to give credit for the past enrolments. He therefore replied to General Dix that he would take care that all executive officers of the State should perform their duties vigorously and thoroughly, and that, if need be, the military power would be called into requisition.

On August 18th General Dix notified the Governor that he had applied for a force, and that his call had been promptly responded to, and that he would be ready to meet all opposition to the draft. The force thus sent to subjugate the people amounted to forty-two regiments and two batteries. No occasion arose for the exercise of their powers, but the wrong to the State of New York was none the less gross.

Another act soon made manifest the subjugation of the Government of the State of New York by the domination of the military power of the Government of the United States. A spurious proclamation, purporting to have been issued by the President, appeared in two New York morning papers—the *Journal of Commerce* and the *World*—on May 18, 1864. It was immediately contradicted by the authorities at Washington, and orders were issued under which the offices of these papers were entered by armed men, the property of the owners was seized, the premises were held by force for several days, and the publication was suspended. The operators were taken into custody, and the proprietors of the newspapers were ordered to be arrested and imprisoned. At the same time the office of the independent telegraph line was occupied by a military force in the name of the Government of the United States.

Governor Seymour immediately instructed the District Attorney to proceed against the offenders. An investigation was made by one of the city judges, and warrants were issued for the arrest of General Dix and several of his officers. They voluntarily appeared by counsel. The result of the arguments was that the officers were held to await the action of the Grand Jury, who, however, took no action on the charges. Two or three days after the appearance of the proclamation, the guilty person was arrested and imprisoned in Fort Lafayette, the newspapers and telegraph offices were restored to their owners, and publication was resumed. But the Government of New York never obtained any indemnification for these losses by its citizens.

Another subversion of the State Government was brought about by military interference, on the part of the Government of the United States, with the State election. This was in 1864, when President Lincoln and General McClellan were the candidates for the Presidency of the United States. As usual in all these cases, in order to work up a pretended necessity for interference on the part of the United States Government, proceedings were commenced by the appearance of a grandiloquent proclamation from the commanding General, telling what horrible designs, there was reason to believe, the agents of the Confederate States in Canada had prepared to be executed on election day, by an invasion of voters from Canada to colonize different points. At the same time the State Department issued a despatch saying that information had been received from the British Provinces that there was a conspiracy to set fire to the principal cities in the Northern States on the day of the Presidential election. Thus was created an apparent necessity for this military force to be very active on the day of election.

General B. F. Butler was sent to take command in the city of New York, 7,000 additional men were placed in the forts of the harbor, and proclamations were issued by the United States Government threatening the severest punishment upon everyone who might attempt improperly to vote at the election in the State of New York.

The proposed limits will not permit me to present further details of the subjugation of the State Government by the Government of the United States. Neither can space be spared to relate the details of the subjugation of the government of each Northern State. In many the events were similar to those in New York; in others the circumstances were dissimilar; but in all the sovereignty of the people was entirely disregarded, and the operation of the institutions which had been established for the protection of their rights was suspended or nullified by a military force of the Government of the United States.

Only such events can be stated as serve to show how universal and how complete was the work done by the United States Government to secure a recognition of its supremacy over not only the acts but even the words of every citizen. All were its subjects: the "loyal," as some were called, were its friends; the "disloyal" were its disaffected subjects, to be watched by spies and informers, and, if necessary, to be put in prison to secure their passive submission.

Under the pretext of securing the arrest of deserters from the army, a military domination was established in all the Northern States. This was accomplished on September 24, 1862, by the appointment of a Provost-Marshal General of the War Department at Washington, and in each State one or more special provost-marshals, who were required to report to the Provost-Marshal and to receive instructions from him.

In utter disregard of the principles of civil liberty a military control was established in every Northern State, the declarations of right in their

Constitutions were violated, and the authority of their governments was subverted by an absolute and direct usurpation on the part of the Government of the United States.

CHAPTER 81

THE MILITARY COMMISSION AT WASHINGTON

DURING 1865 the country was filled with horror by two trials held before a Military Commission in the city of Washington.

The specification charged eight men and one woman with conspiracy to murder President Lincoln, Vice-President Johnson, General Grant, and William H. Seward, Secretary of State. The President had been assassinated, and Secretary Seward badly wounded with a knife. The sentence of the commission was that Harold, Atzerott, Payne, and Mrs. Surratt should be hanged by the military authority under the direction of the Secretary of War on the 7th of July. The others were sentenced to imprisonment at hard labor for a term of years or for life. With only one day's delay the sentences were carried into execution. John H. Surratt, the son of Mrs. Surratt, escaped before trial. He was sought for by the spies of the War Department half round the world, and, after a long time, was found serving as a soldier in the corps of Papal Zouaves at Rome. He was brought back to Washington, tried, and acquitted.

The insertion of my name with those of others, honorable gentlemen, as "inciting and encouraging" these acts, served as an exhibition of the malignant spirit with which justice was administered by the authorities in Washington at that time. The case of Mrs. Surratt awakened much sympathy. Some of the accused had boarded at her house. She was spoken of by her counsel, Reverdy Johnson, of Maryland, as "a devout Christian, ever kind, affectionate, and charitable," a testimony which was confirmed by evidence and uncontradicted. On the day of her execution her affectionate and devoted daughter sought to obtain an audience with President Johnson, to implore, at least, a brief suspension of the sentence on her mother. She was obstructed and prevented from seeing the President by Ex-Senator Preston King, of New York, and Senator James H. Lane, of Kansas, who were reported to have been stationed at the Executive Mansion to keep guard over President Johnson. Each of these senators afterward committed suicide.

The trial of Major Henry Wirz was the next in importance which came before the Military Commission. In April, 1865, President Johnson issued a proclamation stating that from evidence in possession of the "Bureau of Military Justice," it appeared that I, Jefferson Davis, was implicated in the assassination of President Lincoln, and for that reason he offered a reward of one hundred thousand dollars for my capture. That testimony was subsequently found to be entirely false, having been a mere fabrication. Meanwhile certain persons of influence and public position at that time, either aware of the fabricated character of this testimony, or convinced of its insufficiency to secure my conviction at a trial, sought to find ample material to supply this deficiency, in the great mortality of the soldiers we had captured and imprisoned at Andersonville. The military authorities therefore arrested Captain Henry Wirz, a foreigner by birth, poor, friendless, and wounded, and held as prisoner of war, as he had been included in the surrender of General Johnson. Doomed before he was tried, the poor man was denied permission to be heard according to law.

Captain Wirz had been in command of the Confederate prison at Andersonville. The first charge against him was that of conspiring with Jefferson Davis, Secretary Seddon, General Howell Cobb, General Winder, and others to cause the death of thousands of prisoners through cruelty, etc. The second charge was against himself for murder, in violation of the laws and customs of war.

The Military Commission before which he was tried was convened by order of President Johnson, and met August 20th. Wirz pleaded not guilty. The trial lasted three months. No evidence whatever was produced to show the existence of such a conspiracy as had been charged. Wirz, however, was pronounced guilty, and executed November 10, 1865.

After his death, Mr. Schade, his attorney at the trial, in compliance with his client's request, shortly before his execution, made a public statement in vindication of his character. In this statement Mr. Schade said:

"On the night previous to the execution of the prisoner some parties came to the confessor of Wirz (Rev. Father Boyle) and also to me. One of them informed me that a high Cabinet officer wishes to assure Wirz that if he would implicate Jefferson Davis with the atrocities committed at Andersonville his sentence should be commuted. He requested me to inform Wirz of this. In presence of Father Boyle I told him next morning what had happened. The Captain simply and quietly replied: 'You know that I have always told you that I do not know anything about Jefferson Davis. He had no connection with me as to what was done at Andersonville. If I knew anything of him, I would not become a traitor against him or anybody else to save my life.'"

Thus ended the attempt to suborn Captain Wirz against Jefferson Davis.

Captain C. B. Winder, who saw Wirz a few days before his execution, confirmed the statement of Mr. Schade. He stated that Wirz, at the time of the offer made to him, informed him that his life should be spared and his liberty restored if he would implicate me, directly or indirectly, with the condition and treatment of prisoners of war as charged by the Federal authorities, and that he had indignantly spurned the propositions.

As to the other evidence alleged to have been held against me, it will surely suffice to say that at the session of Congress of 1865-66 a committee was appointed by the House of Representatives "to inquire into and report upon the alleged complicity of Jefferson Davis with the assassination of the late President Lincoln," or words to that effect. George S. Boutwell was the chairman, and the majority of the members were extreme advocates of the war. The charge emanated from the "Bureau of Military Justice," an institution similar to the "Secret Committee" of the French Revolution. After an investigation, continued through several months, a majority of that committee made their report to Congress.

"The report not only failed to establish the charge, but the committee were forced to confess in it that the witnesses on whose testimony Holt (chief of the bureau) had affected to rely, were wholly untrustworthy. Shortly after this report was submitted, Mr. Rogers, of New Jersey, a member of the committee, made a minority report in which he stated that much of the evidence had been wholly suppressed; that the witnesses, who had received large sums of money from Holt for testifying to the criminality of Mr. Davis, recanted their evidence before the committee, and acknowledged that they had perjured themselves by testifying to a mass of falsehoods, and had been tutored to do so by one, S. Conover; and that, from him down through all the miserable list, the very names under which these hired informers were known to the public were as false as the narratives to which they had sworn."[113]

---

113. Baltimore *Gazette*, September 25, 1866.

Chapter 82

Free Speech Suppressed in the North

ON April 13, 1863, General Burnside, commanding the Department of Ohio, issued an order declaring that,

> "Hereafter all persons found within our lines who commit acts for the benefit of the enemies of our country will be tried as spies or traitors, and, if convicted, will suffer death. . . . The habit of declaring sympathies for the enemy will no longer be tolerated in this department. Persons committing such offences will be at once arrested with a view to being tried as above stated, or sent beyond our lines into the lines of their friends."

Mr. Vallandigham commented upon this order at a public meeting of citizens on May 1st. Three days afterward a body of soldiers broke into his house with violence before daylight, hurried him to the cars, and conveyed him to Cincinnati, where he was committed to a military prison. Tried before a Military Commission, he was pronounced guilty, and sentenced to confinement in Fort Warren during the war, a sentence changed by President Lincoln to banishment to the Confederate States.

A number of such arrests were made in Ohio. Newspapers were suspended and editors imprisoned.

In Pennsylvania arrests were made, newspapers suspended, editors put in jail, and offices destroyed.

In New Hampshire, Vermont, and Wisconsin many similar scenes occurred.

The Provost-Marshal system was used as a weapon of vindictiveness against influential citizens of opposite political views throughout all the Northern States. No one of such persons knew when he was safe. A complaint of his neighbors, supported by affidavit of "disloyal" words spoken or "disloyal" acts approved, received prompt attention from all marshals. Everything was brought into subjection to the will of the Government of the United States and its military officers.

In view of all the facts here presented relative to the Northern States, let the reader answer where the sovereignty *de facto* resided. Most clearly in the Government of the United States. That presided over the ballot-box, held the keys of the prisons, arrested all citizens at its pleasure, suspended or suppressed newspapers, and did whatever it pleased under the declaration that the public welfare required it. But, under the principles of American liberty, the sovereignty is inherent in the people as an unalienable right; and for the preservation and protection of this and other rights, the State Governments were instituted. If, therefore, the people have lost this inherent sovereignty, it is evident that the State Governments have failed to afford that protection for which they were instituted. If they have thus failed, it has been in consequence of their subversion and loss of power to fulfil the object for which they were established. This subversion was achieved when the General Government, under the pretext of preserving the Union, made war on its creators, the States, thus changing the nature of the Federal Union, which could rightfully be done only by the sovereign, the people of the States, in like manner as it was originally formed. If they should permit their sovereignty to be usurped and themselves to be subjugated, individuals might remain, States could not. Of their wrecks a nation might be built, but there could not be a Union, for that implies entities united, and of the State which has lost its sovereignty there may be only written, "*It was.*"

Chapter 83

Military Operations in Virginia

BOTH the Federal and Confederate armies remained in a state of comparative quiet during the months of January and February, 1864.

On February 26th, two corps of the enemy left their camp for Madison Court-House, part of a concerted plan to capture Richmond; a movement in which General Butler was to make a demonstration upon the city on the east, while Custer, Kilpatrick, and Dahlgren were to attack and enter it on the west and north. Further forces were soon sent to Madison Court-House. At the same time General Custer marched for Charlottesville, for the purpose of destroying the Orange and Alexandria Railroad, running by Charlottesville to Gordonsville. The capture of the army stores there, and the destruction of the railroads and telegraphs would have severed the communication between Lee's army and Richmond by this route. The different movements, if successful, would have isolated Lee's army from its base of supplies.

A few hours after General Custer started, General Kilpatrick, with 5,000 picked cavalry and a battery of 6 guns, left Stevensburg for the lower fords of the Rapidan. His object was to make a dash upon Richmond, release the United States prisoners, and do whatever injury might be possible. He moved rapidly, destroying railroads and depots, and plundering the country, until he reached the line of the defences of Richmond. There he was attacked in the rear by a company of 60 Marylanders, under Colonel Bradley T. Johnson, who had followed and harassed him during the raid, and opposed in front by Colonel Stevens, who, with a detachment of engineer troops, manned a few sections of light artillery. After an engagement of thirty minutes Kilpatrick's entire force began to retreat. At night his camp-fires were discovered by

General Wade Hampton, who dismounted 100 men to act as infantry, and, supported by the cavalry, opened his two-gun battery on the enemy at short range. He then attacked the camp of Davies and of a part of two other brigades. The camp was taken, and the whole force of Kilpatrick fled at a gallop, leaving 105 prisoners and more than 100 horses.

Colonel Dahlgren started with General Kilpatrick, but at Spottsylvania Court-House was despatched with 500 men to Frederick's Hall, a depot of the Central Railroad, where some 80 pieces of our reserve artillery had been parked. Finding the artillery too well guarded he moved onward until he reached within 22 miles west of Richmond. Then he moved toward the city, pillaging and destroying dwelling-houses, outbuildings, mills, canal-boats, grain, and cattle, and cutting one lock on the canal.

After overcoming a small battalion of General G. W. C. Lee's force, which fell back until it joined a battalion of Treasury clerks, led by Captain McIlhenney, Dahlgren moved on Richmond. Captain McIlhenney charged him with such impetuosity that Dahlgren and his men were routed, and rapidly retreated, leaving 18 killed, 20 to 30 wounded, and as many more prisoners on our hands. About 100 horses and equipments, a number of small-arms, and one 3-inch napoleon gun were captured. Our loss, was 3 officers killed, and 3 lieutenants and 7 privates wounded. Dahlgren, to increase his chances of escape, divided his force into two parties, he leading one party in the direction of King and Queen County. The Home Guard of the county turned out against the raiders, and, being reinforced by some furloughed cavalrymen of Lee's army, surprised and attacked Dahlgren's retreating column, killing the leader, and capturing nearly 100 prisoners, with negroes, horses, etc.

On the body of Dahlgren was found an address to his officers and men, another paper giving special orders and instructions, and one giving his itinerary, the whole disclosing the unsoldierly means and purposes of the raid, such as disguising the men in our uniform, carrying supplies of oakum and turpentine to burn Richmond, and, after releasing their prisoners on Belle Isle, to exhort them to destroy the hateful city; while on all was impressed the special injunction that the city must be burned, and "Jeff Davis and cabinet killed."

The prisoners, having been captured in disguise, were, under the usages of war, liable to be hanged as spies; but their protestations that their service was not voluntary, and the fact that as enlisted men they were subject to orders, and could not be held responsible for the infamous instructions under which they were acting, saved them from the death penalty they had fully incurred.

Photographic copies of the papers found on Dahlgren's body were taken and sent to General Lee, with instructions to communicate them to General Meade, with an inquiry whether such practices were authorized by his Government, and also to say that, if any question was raised as to the copies, the original papers would be submitted. No such question was then made, and the denial that Dahlgren's conduct had been authorized was accepted.

Many sensational stories, having not even a basis of truth, were put in circulation to exhibit the Confederate authorities as having acted with unwarrantable malignity toward the deceased Colonel Dahlgren. The fact was that his body was sent to Richmond and decently buried in Oakwood Cemetery, where other Federal soldiers were buried. The enormity of his offence was not forgotten, but resentment against him ended with his life. It was also admitted that, however bad his previous conduct had been, he met his fate gallantly, charging at the head of his men when he found himself inextricably encompassed by his foes.

Custer and Kilpatrick, who were to have co-operated with Dahlgren, rapidly retreated, but not before Kilpatrick was met and routed by our gallant cavalier, General Wade Hampton, near the Chickahominy. This ended the combined movement with which Northern papers had regaled their readers by announcing as made "with instructions to sack the rebel capital."

Chapter 84

Butler Bottled Up

DURING the first week in May, 1864, General B. F. Butler landed at Bermuda Hundred with a considerable force, and moved up so as to reach, by a raiding party, the railroad between Richmond and Petersburg. General Ransom, with a small force, attacked this advance of General Butler, and after a sharp skirmish compelled him to withdraw.

Meantime General Ransom was summoned to Richmond to resist an impending assault by General Sheridan on the outer works north of the city. Taking two brigades he hastened forward, arriving at the fortifications on the Mechanicsville turnpike just in time to see a battery of artillery, then entirely unsupported, repulse the advance of Sheridan. During the night the clerks and citizens, under General G. W. C. Lee, had formed a thin line along part of the fortifications on the west side of the city. As the day advanced Sheridan withdrew from before our defences, and the two brigades returned to the vicinity of Drury's Bluff, the approach on the south side of James River, by forces under Butler, being then considered the most imminent danger to Richmond.

After the battle of the Wilderness, on May 4th and 5th, Grant moved his army toward Spottsylvania Court-House, and Lee made a corresponding movement. At this time Sheridan, with a large force of cavalry, passed around and to the rear of our army, so as to place himself on the road to Richmond, which, in the absence of a garrison to defend it, he may have not unreasonably thought might be surprised and captured.

Stuart, our most distinguished cavalry commander, soon knew of Sheridan's movement, perceived its purpose, and, hastily collecting such of his troops as were near, pursued Sheridan. He fell upon Sheridan's rear and flank at Beaver Dam Station, and drove it before him. The route of the enemy being unmistakably toward Richmond, Stuart, to protect the capital, or at least to delay attack, made a detour around Sheridan, and by a forced march got in front of him, taking position at a place called Yellow Tavern, about seven or eight miles from Richmond. Here, notwithstanding the great inequality between his force and that of his foe, he decided to make a stand (May 11th). The respective strength of the two commands (as given by Colonel Heros von Borke, chief of Stuart's staff) was, Stuart, 1,100; Sheridan, 8,000. While engaged in this desperate service, Stuart sent couriers to Richmond to give notice of the approach of the enemy, so that the defences might be manned.

Notwithstanding the great disparity of force, the contest was obstinate and protracted, and fickle fortune cheered our men with several brilliant successes, Stuart was always a leader when his cavalry charged. On this occasion he is represented to have been quite in advance when he was wounded, to have fired the last load in his pistol, and to have been shot by a fugitive whom he found cowering under a fence, and ordered to surrender. The "heavy battalions" at last prevailed, our line was broken, and our leader, though mortally wounded, still kept in his saddle, invoking his men to continue the fight. Our gallant chieftain was brought wounded into Richmond, where he died a few hours later (May 12th).

Grant's plan of campaign was to continue his movement against Lee's army, and, if he should be unable to defeat it and move directly to his objective point, Richmond, he was to continue his efforts so as to reach the James River below Richmond, and thus to connect with the army under Butler moving up on the south side of the James. The topography of the country favored that design. The streams in the country in which he was operating all tended toward the southeast, and his changes of position were frequently made under cover of them. Butler, in the meantime, was ordered, with the force of his department—about 20,000—reinforced by Gilmer's division of 10,000, to move up to City Point, there intrench, and concentrate all his troops as rapidly as possible. From this base he was expected to operate so as to destroy the railroad connections between Richmond and the south. On the 7th of May he telegraphed that he had "destroyed many miles of railroad, and got a position which, with proper supplies, we can hold against the whole of Lee's army."

At this time General Robert Ransom was in command at Richmond, including Drury's Bluff. His force for the defence of both places consisted of the men serving the stationary or heavy artillery, and three brigades of infantry. To these, in cases of emergency, the clerks and artisans in the departments and manufactories were organized, to be called out as an auxiliary force when needed for the defence of the capital. It was with this field force that Ransom moved on Butler, and drove him from the railroad, the destruction of which he had so vauntingly announced.

A few days thereafter he emerged from his cover, but changed his objective point, and, diverging from the south bank of the James River, moved toward Petersburg, and reached the railroad at Port Walthal Junction. Here he encountered some of General Beauregard's command, which had been ordered from Charleston, and was driven from the railroad and turnpike. The troops ordered from Charleston with Beauregard had, by May 14th, reached the vicinity of Drury's Bluff. In connection with the works and rifle-pits on the bluff, which were to command the river and prevent the ascent of gunboats, an intrenched line had been constructed on a ridge about a mile south of the bluff, running across the road from Richmond to Petersburg. This ridge was higher than the ground on which the fort was built, and was designed to check an approach of the enemy from the south, as well as to cover the rear of the fort. On the afternoon of the 14th I rode down to visit General Beauregard.

My first question on meeting him was to learn why the intrenchments were abandoned. He answered that he thought it better to concentrate his troops. Upon my stating to him that there was nothing then to prevent Butler from turning his position, he said he would desire nothing better, as he would then fall upon him, cut him off from his base, etc.

According to my uniform practice never to do more than make a suggestion to a general commanding in the field, the subject was pressed no further. We then passed to the consideration of the operations to be undertaken against Butler, who had already advanced from his base at Bermuda Hundred. I offered, for the purpose of attacking Butler, to send General Ransom with the field force he had for the protection of Richmond. He reported to General Beauregard on the 15th, received his orders for the battle which was to occur the next day, and about 10 P.M. was, with a division of four brigades and a battery of light artillery, in position in front of the breastworks. Colonel Dunovant, with a regiment of cavalry not under Ransom's orders, was to guard the space between his left and the river, so as to give him information of any movement in that quarter. General Whiting, with some force, was holding a defensive position at Petersburg. General Beauregard proposed that the main part of it should advance and unite with him in an attack upon Butler, wherever he should be found between Drury's and Petersburg. To this I offered distinct objection, because of the hazard, during a battle, of attempting to make a junction of troops moving from opposite sides of the enemy, and proposed that Whiting's command should move at night by the Chesterfield road, where they would not probably be observed by Butler's advance. This march I supposed they could make so as to arrive at Drury's by or soon after daylight. The next day being Sunday, they could rest, and, all the troops being assigned to their positions, they could move to make a concerted attack at daylight on Monday.

On Monday morning I rode down to Drury's, where I found that the enemy had seized our line of intrenchments, it being unoccupied, and that a severe action had occurred, with serious loss to us, before he could be dislodged. He had crossed the main road to the west, entering a dense wood, and our troops on the right had moved out and were closely engaged with him. We drove him back, frustrating the attempt to turn the extreme right of our line. The day was wearing away, a part of the force had been withdrawn to the intrenchments, and there was no sign of purpose to make any immediate movement. General Beauregard said he was waiting to hear Whiting's guns, and had been expecting him for some time to approach on the Petersburg road. Soon after this, the foe, in a straggling, disorganized manner, commenced crossing the road, moving to the east, which indicated a retreat, or perhaps a purpose to turn our left and attack Fort Drury in rear. He placed a battery in the main road and threw some shells at our intrenchments, probably to cover his retiring troops. General Ransom, in an unpublished report, says that, at the time he received the order of battle, General Beauregard told him, "As you know the region, I have given you the moving part of the army, and you will take the initiative." He further states that at dawn of day he moved to the south of Kingsland Creek, formed two lines with a short interval, and at once advanced to the attack. A dense fog suddenly enveloped him, so as to obscure all distant objects. Moving forward, the skirmishers were quickly engaged, and the fighting was pressed so vigorously that by sunrise he had captured a brigade of infantry, a battery of artillery, and occupied about three-quarters of a mile of the enemy's temporary breastworks, which were strengthened by wire interwoven among the trees in their front. This result was not effected, however, without considerable loss in killed and wounded, and much confusion, owing to the denseness of the fog. On the next morning our troops moved down the river road as far as Howlett's, about three or four miles, but saw no enemy. The "back-door" of Richmond was closed, and Butler was "bottled up."

Soon after the affair at Drury's Bluff, General Beauregard addressed to me a communication, proposing that he should be heavily reinforced from General Lee's army, so as to enable him to crush Butler in his intrenchments, and then, with the main body of his own force, together with the detachment from General Lee's army, that he should join General Lee, overwhelm Grant, and march to Washington. I knew that General Lee was then confronting an army vastly superior to his in numbers, fully equipped, with inexhaustible supplies, and a persistence in attacking of which sufficient evidence had been given. I could not, therefore, expect that General Lee would consent to the proposition of General Beauregard; but, as a matter of courteous consideration, his letter was forwarded with the usual formal endorsement. General Lee's opinion on the case was shown by the instructions he gave directing General Beauregard to straighten his line so as to reduce the number of men requisite to hold it, and send the balance to join the army north of the James.

Chapter 85

Battles of the Wilderness

IN March, 1864, Lieutenant-General Grant assumed command of the armies of the United States. He subsequently proceeded to Culpeper and assumed personal command of the Army of the Potomac, although the nominal command remained with General Meade. From every military department of the United States reinforcements were rapidly gathered to strengthen the Federal army in Virginia.

On May 3rd Lee held the south bank of the Rapidan, with his right resting near the mouth of Mine Run, and his left extending to Liberty Mills. Ewell's corps was on the right, Hill's on the left, and two divisions of Longstreet's corps were encamped in the rear. The Federal army had occupied the north bank of the Rapidan, with the main body encamped in Culpeper County and on the Rappahannock River.

While Grant, with his immense and increasing army, was thus posted, Lee with a comparatively small force—to which few reinforcements could be furnished—confronted him on a line stretching from near Somerville Ford to Gordonsville. To Grant was left the choice to move directly on Lee and attempt to defeat his army—the only obstacle to the capture of Richmond, which his vast means rendered supposable—or to cross the Rapidan above or below Lee's position. The second would fulfil the condition, so imperatively imposed on McClellan, of covering Washington; the third would be in the more direct line to Richmond. Of the three, he chose the last, and so felicitated himself on his unopposed passage of the river as to suppose that he had, unobserved, turned the flank of Lee's army, got between it and Richmond, and necessitated the retreat of the Confederates to some point where they might resist his further advance. So little did he comprehend the genius of Lee that he expected him to be surprised, as appears from his arrangements contemplating only combats with the rear-guard covering the retreat.

Lee, dauntless as he was sagacious, seized the opportunity which Grant's movement offered, to meet him where his artillery would be least available, where his massive columns would be embarrassed in their movements, and where Southern individuality and self-reliance would be specially effective.

Grant's object was to pass through "the Wilderness" to the roads between Lee and Richmond. Lee resolved to fight him in those pathless woods, where mind might best compete with matter.

In order to cross the Rapidan, Grant's army moved, on May 3rd, to Germania Ford, ten to twelve miles from our right. He succeeded in seizing the ford and crossing. When Grant had crossed the river he was nearer than Lee to Richmond. From Orange Court-House there are two nearly parallel roads running eastward to Fredericksburg. The road nearest the river is called the "Stone Turnpike," and the other "the Plank Road." This road from the ford to Spottsylvania Court-House crosses the old "Stone Turnpike" at the Old Wilderness Tavern, and, two or three miles farther on, it crosses the Plank Road.

As soon as Grant's movements were known, Lee's troops were put in motion. Ewell's corps moved on the Stone Turnpike, and Hill's corps on the Plank Road, into which Longstreet's force also came from his camp near Gordonsville. Ewell's corps crossed Mine Run and encamped at Locust Grove, four miles beyond, on the afternoon of the 4th. On the morning of the 5th it was again in motion, and encountered Grant's troops, in heavy force, at a short distance from the Old Wilderness Tavern, and Jones's and Battle's brigades were driven back in some confusion. Early's division was ordered up, advanced through a dense pine thicket, and, with other brigades of Rodes's division, drove the enemy back with heavy loss, capturing several hundred prisoners and gaining a commanding position on the right. Meanwhile Johnson's division, on the left of the pike, and extending across the road to Germania Ford, was heavily engaged in front, and Hays's brigade was sent to the left to participate in a forward movement. It advanced, encountered a large force, and, not meeting with the expected co-operation, was driven back. Subsequently Pegram's brigade took position on Hays's left. Just before night an attack was made on their front, which was repulsed with severe loss to the enemy. There was hot skirmishing all along the line during the afternoon, and several attempts were made by the enemy to regain the position from which he had been driven. At the close of the day Ewell's corps had captured over 1,000 prisoners, besides inflicting on the enemy very severe loss in killed and wounded. Two pieces of artillery had been abandoned and were secured by our troops.

On the 4th A. P. Hill, with two divisions, moved eastwardly along the Plank Road. They bivouacked near Verdiersville, and resumed their march on the 5th. At 1 P.M. musketry was heard in front. Kirkland's brigade deployed on both sides of the Plank Road, and the column proceeded to form in line of battle on its flanks. Hill's advance had followed the Plank Road, while Ewell pursued the Stone Turnpike. These parallel movements were from three to four miles apart.

The country intervening and round about for several miles is known as "the Wilderness." It consists almost wholly of a forest of dense undergrowth of shrubs and small trees. To open communication with Ewell, Wilcox's division moved to the left and effected a junction with Gordon's brigade on Ewell's extreme right. The line of battle thus completed extended from the right of the Plank Road through a succession of open fields and dense forest to the left of the Stone Turnpike. It presented a line of six miles, and the thicket that lay along the whole front of our army was so impenetrable as to exclude the use of artillery save only at the roads. Heth's skirmishers were driven in about 3 P.M. by a massive column that advanced, firing rapidly. The struggle, thus commenced in Heth's front, continued unabated for two or three hours. The contest continued till night closed over our force still in the position it had originally taken, although greatly reduced.

This stubborn and heroic resistance was made by the divisions of Heth and Wilcox, 15,000 strong, against the repeated and desperate assaults of five divisions numbering about 45,000 men. During the day the Ninth Corps of the enemy, under General Burnside, had come on the field. The third division of Hill's corps, under General Anderson, and the two divisions of Longstreet's corps did not reach the scene of conflict until dawn on the morning of the 6th.

Simultaneously the attack on Hill was renewed with great vigor. In addition to the force he had so successfully resisted, a fresh division of the enemy had secured position on Hill's flank, and co-operated with the column assaulting in front.

After a severe contest the left of Heth's division and the right of Wilcox's were overpowered before the advance of Longstreet's column reached the ground, and were compelled to retire. The repulsed portions of the divisions were in considerable disorder. General Lee now came up, and, appreciating the impending crisis, dashed amid the fugitives, calling on the men to rally and follow him.

> "The soldiers, seeing General Lee's manifest purpose to advance with them, and realizing the great danger in which he then was, begged him to go to the rear, promising that they would soon have matters rectified. The General waved them on with some words of cheer."[114]

The assault was checked.

Longstreet had now come up with his divisions. He deployed them in line of battle, and gallantly advanced to recover the lost ground. The enemy was driven back over the ground he had gained by his assault on Hill's line, but reformed in the position previously held by him. About midday Longstreet ordered an attack on his left flank and rear. For this purpose three brigades were detached, and, on moving forward, were joined by General J. R. Davis's brigade, which had been the extreme right of Hill's line. Making a detour to avoid observation, and rushing precipitately to attack the enemy in flank and reverse, while he was preparing to resist the movement in front, he was taken completely by surprise. The assault resulted in his utter rout with heavy loss.

Preparations were now made to follow up the advantages gained, by the forward movement of the whole line under General Longstreet's personal directions. When advancing at the head of Jenkins's brigade, with that officer and others, a body of Confederates in the wood on the roadside, supposing the column to be a hostile force, fired into it, killing, General Jenkins and severely wounding General Longstreet. The valuable services of Longstreet were thus lost to the army at a critical moment, and caused the suspension of a movement promising the most important results; and time was thus afforded to the enemy to rally and find shelter behind his intrenchments. In these circumstances the

---

114. Col. Walter Taylor's *Four Years with General Lee*.

commanding General deemed it inadvisable to attack.

On the morning of the 6th the contest was renewed on the left, and a heavy attack was made on the front, occupied by Pegram's brigade, but it was handsomely repulsed, as were several subsequent attacks at the same point. In the afternoon an attack was made on the enemy's right flank, resting in the woods, when Gordon's brigade, with Johnson's in the rear, and followed by Pegram's, succeeded in throwing it into great confusion, doubling it up and forcing it back some distance, capturing two brigadier-generals and several hundred prisoners. Darkness closed the contest.

On the 7th an advance was made. It disclosed the fact that Grant had given up his line of works on his right. During the day there was some skirmishing, but no serious fighting.

The result of these battles was the infliction of severe loss on the enemy, the gain of ground, and the capture of prisoners, artillery, and other trophies. But the cost to us was so serious as to enforce, by additional considerations, the policy of Lee to spare his men as much as possible.

A rapid flank movement was next made by Grant to secure possession of Spottsylvania Court-House. Lee comprehended Grant's purpose, and on the night of the 7th a division of Longstreet's corps was sent as an advance to that point. Stuart, then in observation on the flank, dismounted his troops, and, felling trees, obstructed the roads so as materially to delay the march of the enemy.

The head of the opposing forces arrived almost at the same moment on the 8th; theirs, being a little in advance, drove back our cavalry, but in turn were quickly driven from the strategic point by the arrival of our infantry.

On the 9th the two armies, each forming on its advance as a nucleus, swung round and confronted each other in line of battle.

The 10th and 11th passed in comparative quiet.

On the morning of the 12th the enemy made a very heavy attack on Ewell's front, and broke the line where it was occupied by Johnson's division.

A portion of the attacking force swept around Johnson's line to Wilcox's left, and was checked by a prompt movement on that flank. Several brigades sent to Ewell's assistance were carried into action under his orders. They all suffered severely. Subsequently, on the same day, some brigades were thrown to the front for the purpose of moving to the left and attacking the flank of the column which broke Ewell's line, to relieve the pressure upon him, and recover the part of the line which had been lost. These soon encountered Burnside's Ninth Corps, advancing to the attack. They captured over 300 prisoners and three battle flags. Their attack on the enemy's flank, taking him by surprise, contributed materially to his repulse.

On the 12th an attacking column advanced, under cover of a pine thicket, to within a very short distance of a salient defended by Walker's brigade. A heavy fire of musketry and artillery, from a considerable number of guns on Heth's line, opened with tremendous effect upon the column. It was driven back with severe loss, leaving its dead in front of our works.

Several days of comparative quiet ensued. During this time the army of Grant was heavily reinforced. "In numerical strength his army so much exceeded that under General Lee that, after covering the entire Confederate front with double lines of battle, he had in reserve a large force with which to extend his flank and compel a corresponding movement on the part of his adversary, in order to keep between him and his coveted prize, the capital of the Confederacy."[115]

On the 18th another assault was made on our lines. It made no impression.

On the 20th of May, after twelve days of skirmish and battle at Spottsylvania against a superior force, General Lee's information led him to believe that the enemy was about to attempt another flanking movement, and to interpose his army between the Confederate capital and its defenders. To defeat this purpose Longstreet was ordered to move at midnight in the direction of Hanover Junction, and on the following day and night Ewell's and Hill's corps marched for the same point.

The Confederate commander, deeming that Grant's objective point was the intersection of the two railroads leading to Richmond at a point two miles south of the North Anna River, crossed his army over that stream and took up a line of battle which frustrated the movement.

---

115. From *Four Years with General Lee*.

Grant began his flanking movement on the night of the 20th, marching in two columns, the right crossing the North Anna at Jericho Ford without opposition. On the 23rd the left, crossing four miles further down, was obstinately resisted by a small force, and the passage was not made till the 24th.

After crossing the North Anna, Grant discovered that his movement was a blunder, and that his army was in a position of much peril.

The Confederate commander established his line of battle on the south side of the river, both wings reformed, so as to form an obtuse angle, with the apex resting on the river between the two points of the enemy's crossing. Longstreet's and Hill's corps formed the two sides; the Little River and the Hanover Marshes the base; Ewell's corps held the apex or centre.

The hazard of Grant's position appears not to have been known to him until he attempted to unite his two columns—four miles apart—by establishing a connecting line along the river. Foiled in the attempt; he discovered that the Confederate army was interposed between his two wings, which were also separated by the North Anna, and that the one could give no support to the other except by a double crossing of the river. Profiting by the lessons of Spottsylvania and the Wilderness, Grant, with cautious, noiseless movement, withdrew, under cover of the night of the 26th, to the north side of the North Anna, and moved eastward down to the Pamunkey River.

At Hanover Junction Lee was joined by Pickett's division and by a small force under Breckinridge. Hoke's brigade, 1,200 strong, here also rejoined Early's division. On the 29th the whole of Grant's army was across the Pamunkey, while Lee's army the next day was in line of battle, with his left at Atlee's Station. By another movement, eastward, the two armies were brought face to face at Cold Harbor, on June 3rd.

Here Grant made fruitless efforts to pierce or drive back the forces of Lee. Our troops were protected by temporary earthworks, and while under this cover were assailed by the enemy.

"The carnage on the Federal side," writes General Taylor,[116] "was fearful. I well recall having received a report from General Hoke, after the assault. His division reached the army just previous to the battle. The

---

116. *Four Years with General Lee.*

ground in his entire front, over which the enemy had charged, was literally covered with their dead and wounded; and, up to that time, Hoke had not had a single man killed. No wonder that, when the command was given to renew the assault, the Federal soldiers sullenly and silently declined. 'The order[117] was issued through the officers to their subordinate commanders, and from them descended through the wonted channels; but no man stirred, and the immobile lines pronounced a verdict, silent yet emphatic, against further slaughter. The loss on the Union side in this sanguinary action was over 13,000, while on the part of the Confederates it is doubtful whether it reached that many hundreds.' After some disingenuous proposals, General Grant finally asked a truce to enable him to bury his dead. Soon after this he abandoned his chosen line of operations, and moved his army so as to secure a crossing to the south side of James River. The struggle from the Wilderness to this point covered a period exceeding a month, during which time there had been an almost daily encounter of arms; and the Army of Northern Virginia had placed *hors de combat* of the army under Grant a number exceeding the entire numerical strength of Lee's army at the commencement of the campaign, and, notwithstanding its own heavy losses and the reinforcements received by the enemy, it still presented an impregnable front to its opponent."

On the 1st of May, 1864, two days before he crossed the Rapidan, Grant had 120,380 men, and in the Ninth Army Corps, 20,780; or an aggregate, with which he marched against Lee, of 141,160 men. To meet this vast force Lee had, on the Rapidan, less than 50,000 men. Grant had a reserve, upon which he could draw, of 137,672. Lee had practically no reserve; for he was compelled to make detachments from his army for the protection of West Virginia and other points about equal to all the reinforcements he received. In the *Southern Historical Papers*,[118] upon the very trustworthy authority of the editor, there appears this statement:

> "Grant says he lost, in the campaign from The Wilderness to Cold Harbor, 39,000 men; but Swinton puts his loss at over 60,000, and a careful examination of the figures will show that his real loss was nearer 100,000. In other words, he lost about twice as many men

---

117. Swinton's *Army of the Potomac*, p. 487.
118. Vol. 6, p. 144.

as Lee had, in order to take a position which he could have taken at first without firing a gun or losing a man."

On June 12th the movement for crossing the James River was commenced by Grant. On the 14th and 15th of June the crossing of Grant's army was completed. It had therefore taken him more than a month to reach the south side of the James. In this campaign he had sacrificed a hecatomb of men, a vast amount of artillery, small-arms, munitions of war, and supplies, to reach a position to which McClellan had already demonstrated there was an easy and inexpensive route.

After an unsuccessful attempt to capture Petersburg by a surprise, General Grant concentrated his army south of the Appomattox River.

CHAPTER 86

EARLY'S ADVANCE ON WASHINGTON AND CHAMBERSBURG

BEFORE the opening of the campaign of 1864, Sigel held the Lower Shenandoah by a force with which Grant determined to renew the attempt to destroy the railroad west of Lynchburg in order to isolate Richmond. With about 15,000 men, Sigel began the movement up the Valley (May 3rd). Breckinridge, commanding in southwestern Virginia, marched to meet Sigel, his two infantry brigades reinforced by the reserves of Augusta County, the cadets of the Military Institute at Lexington, numbering 200, and a few hundred cavalry under General Imboden—Breckinridge's force of infantry not much exceeding 3,000. At this time Lee was engaged with the greatly superior force of Grant, who had crossed the Rapidan, and Sigel's was a movement to get on our flank and thus co-operate in the capture of Richmond. The hazard incurred by an attack on Sigel's force was great, but the necessity of the case justified it. Breckinridge's force was only enough to form one line of battle in two' ranks, the cadets holding the centre between the two brigades. There were no reserves. Skirmish lines were promptly engaged, and soon thereafter the enemy fell back beyond New Market, where Sigel, assuming the defensive, took a strong position, in which to wait for an attack. Our artillery was moved forward and opened with effect upon the enemy's position; then our infantry advanced, "with the steadiness of troops on dress parade, the precision of the cadets serving well as a color-guide for the brigades on either side to dress by.... The Federal line had the advantage of a stone wall which served as a breastwork." Sigel's cavalry attempted to turn our right, but was repulsed disastrously, and in a few moments the enemy was in full retreat, crossing the Shenandoah and burning the bridge behind him.

Breckinridge captured 5 pieces of artillery and over 500 prisoners, exclusive of the wounded left on the field. Our loss was several hundred killed and wounded. General Lee, on receiving notice of this engagement, ordered Breckinridge to transfer his command as rapidly as possible to Hanover Junction.

The battle was fought on May 15th, and the command reached Hanover Junction on the 20th.

After Breckinridge's departure, General W. E. Jones had come from Southwestern Virginia with a small cavalry force, and this, with the command of Imboden, only sufficient for observation, was all that remained in the Valley when the Federal General, David Hunter, with a larger force than his predecessor, succeeded Sigel. Jones, with his cavalry and a few infantry, encountered this force at Piedmont, and was defeated and killed. On the receipt of this news Breckinridge, with his command, was sent back to the Valley.

On June 13th General Early, with the Second Corps of Lee's army, numbering a little over 8,000 muskets and two battalions of artillery, commenced a march to strike Hunter's force in the rear, and, if possible, destroy it; then to move down the Valley, cross the Potomac, and threaten Washington.

On the 17th he reached Lynchburg. Hunter arrived there at the same time. Preparations were made for the attack on Hunter on the 19th, when he began to retreat. He was pursued, with much loss, until he escaped by taking the route to the Kanawha River. On the 27th Early's force reached Staunton on its march down the Valley. It now amounted to 10,000 infantry and about 2,000 cavalry, having been joined by Breckinridge, and by Colonel Bradley T. Johnson with a battalion of Maryland cavalry. The advance was rapid. Railroad bridges were burned, the track was destroyed, and stores were captured. The Potomac was crossed on the 5th and 6th of June, and a move was made through the gaps of South Mountain to the north of Maryland Heights, which were occupied by a hostile force. A brigade of cavalry was sent north of Frederick to strike the railroads from Baltimore to Harrisburg and Philadelphia, burn the bridges over the Gunpowder, cut the railroad between Washington and Baltimore, and threaten the latter place. The other troops moved forward toward Monocacy Junction, where a considerable body of Federal troops under General Wallace was found posted on the eastern bank of the Monocacy, with an earthwork and two block-houses commanding both bridges. The position was attacked in front and on the flank; it was carried, and the garrison put to flight. Between 600 and 700 unwounded prisoners fell into our hands, and the enemy's loss in killed and wounded was far greater than ours, which was about 700.

An advance was made on the 10th nearly to Rockville, which was continued next day to Washington, with the hope of getting into the fortifications before they could be manned. But the heat and the dust impeded the progress greatly. Fort Stevens was approached soon after mid-day, and appeared to be lightly manned; but before our force could get into the works a column of the enemy from Washington filed into them on the right and left, skirmishers were thrown out in front, and an artillery fire was opened on us from a number of batteries. An examination made to determine if it were practicable to carry the defences by assault, reported that they were "exceedingly strong, and consisted of what appeared to be inclosed forts for heavy artillery, with a tier of lower works in front of each, pierced for an immense number of guns, the whole being connected with curtains, with ditches in front, and strengthened by palisades and abatis. The timber had been felled within cannon-range all around, and left on the ground, making a formidable obstacle, and every possible approach was raked by artillery." As far as the eye could reach the works appeared to be of the same impregnable character. The exhaustion of our force, the lightness of its artillery, and the information that two corps of the enemy's forces had just arrived in Washington, in addition to the veteran reserves and hundred-day men, and the parapets filled with troops, led us to refrain from making an attack and to retire during the night of the 12th. On the morning of the 14th Early recrossed the Potomac, with all his prisoners and other captures, in safety. There was some skirmishing in our rear between our cavalry and the Federal cavalry that was following us, and on the afternoon of the 14th there was artillery-firing across the river at our cavalry watching the fords.

In the meantime General Hunter had united with Sigel at Harper's Ferry, and some skirmishing took place. Early determined to concentrate near Strasburg; and, crossing Cedar Creek, so posted his force as to cover all the roads from the direction of Winchester. Learning next day that the Army of West Virginia was at Kernstown, he resolved to attack it.

After the enemy's skirmishers had been driven in, it was discovered that his left flank was exposed, and Breckinridge was ordered to move a division under cover of some ravines and attack that flank. This movement was made and resulted in the complete rout of the enemy. He was pursued by the artillery and infantry beyond Winchester. Our loss was very light; his loss in killed and wounded was severe. The whole defeated force crossed the Potomac and took refuge at Maryland Heights and Harper's Ferry. The road was strewed with débris of the rapid flight, 12 caissons and 72 wagons having been abandoned, and most of them burned.

On the 26th the Confederate force moved to Martinsburg.

"While at Martinsburg," says General Early in his memoir, "it was ascertained beyond all doubt that Hunter had been again indulging in his favorite mode of warfare, and that, after his return to the Valley, while we were near Washington, among other outrages the private residences of Andrew Hunter, a member of the Virginia Senate, Alexander R. Boteler, an ex-member of the Confederate Congress, as well as of the United States Congress, and Edmund I. Lee, a distant relative of General Lee, all in Jefferson County, with their contents, had been burned by his orders, only time enough being given for the ladies to get out of the houses. A number of towns in the South, as well as private country-houses, had been burned by Federal troops, and the accounts had been heralded forth in some of the Northern papers in terms of exultation, and gloated over by their readers, while they were received with apathy by others. I now came to the conclusion that, we had stood this mode of warfare long enough, and that it was time to open the eyes of the people of the North to its enormity by an example in the way of retaliation. I did not select the cases mentioned as having more merit or greater claims for retaliation than others, but because they had occurred within the limits of the country covered by my command, and were brought more immediately to my attention.[119]

"The town of Chambersburg was selected as the one on which retaliation should be made, and McCausland was ordered to proceed with his brigade and that of Johnson, and a battery of artillery, to that place, and demand of the municipal authorities the sum of $100,000 in gold, or $500,000 in United States currency, as a compensation for the destruction of the houses named and their contents; and in default of payment to lay the town in ashes, in retaliation for the burning of those houses and others in Virginia, as well as for the towns which had been burned in other Southern States. A written demand to that effect was also sent to the municipal authorities, and they were informed what would be the result of a failure or a refusal to comply with it. I desired to give the people of Chambersburg an opportunity of saving their town, by making compensation for part of the injury done, and hoped that the payment of such a sum would have the desired effect, and open the eyes of people of other towns at the North to the necessity of urging upon their Government the adoption of a different policy.

"On July 30th McCausland reached Chambersburg, and made the demand as directed, reading to such of the authorities as presented themselves the paper sent by me. The demand was not complied with, the people stating that they were not afraid of having their town burned, and that a Federal force was approaching. The policy pursued by our army on former occasions had been so lenient that they did not suppose the threat was in earnest at this time, and they hoped for speedy relief. McCausland, however, proceeded to carry out his orders, and the greater part of the town was laid in ashes. He then moved in the direction of Cumberland, but found it defended by a strong force. He then withdrew and crossed the Potomac, near the mouth of the South

---

119. "I had often seen delicate ladies who had been plundered, insulted, and rendered desolate by the acts of our most atrocious enemies, and, while they did not call for it, yet in the anguished expressions of their features while narrating their misfortunes, there was a mute appeal to every manly sentiment of my bosom for retribution, which I could no longer withstand. On my passage through the Lower Valley into Maryland, a lady had said to me, with tears in her eyes: 'Our lot is a hard one, and we see no peace; but there are a few green spots in our lives, and they are when the Confederate soldiers come along, and we can do something for them.' May God defend and bless these noble women of the Valley, who so often ministered to the wounded, sick, and dying Confederate soldiers, and gave their last morsel of bread to the hungry! They bore with heroic courage the privations, sufferings, persecutions, and dangers to which the war, which was constantly waged in their midst, exposed them, and upon no portion of the Southern people did the disasters which finally befell our army and country fall with more crushing effect an on them."

Branch, capturing the garrison and partly destroying the railroad bridge. Averill pursued from Chambersburg, and surprised and routed Johnson's brigade, and caused a loss of 4 pieces of artillery and about 300 prisoners from the whole command."

Chapter 87

Battle of Winchester

MEANTIME a large force of the Federal army, consisting of the Sixth, Nineteenth, and Crook's Corps, had concentrated at Harper's Ferry under General Sheridan. Early had 8,500 infantry fit for duty, nearly 3,000 mounted men, 3 battalions of artillery, and a few pieces of horse-artillery. Sheridan's force, according to the best information, consisted of 10,000 cavalry, 35,000 infantry, and artillery that greatly outnumbered ours both in men and guns.

On the morning of September 19th, 1864, the enemy began to advance on Ramseur's position, about a mile and a half from Winchester, on the Berryville road. Nelson's artillery was posted on Ramseur's line, covering the approaches as far as practicable; and Lomax, with Jackson's cavalry and a part of Johnson's, was on the right, while Fitzhugh Lee was on the left with cavalry. These troops held the enemy's main force in check until Gordon's and Rodes's divisions arrived, a little after 10 A.M. Gordon was placed under cover in rear of a piece of woods. Rodes formed on Gordon's right, in rear of another piece of woods. We soon discovered very heavy columns, which had been massed under cover, moving to attack Ramseur on the left flank, while another force pressed him in front. Rodes and Gordon were immediately hurled upon the flank of the advancing columns. But Evans's brigade, of Gordon's division, on the extreme left of our infantry, was forced back through the woods from behind which it had advanced, by a column which followed to the rear of the woods and within musket range of seven pieces of Braxton's artillery. Braxton's guns stood their ground and opened with canister. The fire was so well directed that the column staggered, halted, and commenced falling back. Just then Battle's brigade moved forward and swept through the woods, driving the enemy before it, while Evans's brigade was rallied and co-operated. Our advance was resumed, and the enemy's attacking columns, the Sixth and the Nineteenth Corps, were thrown into great confusion and fled from the field. General Early exclaims:

> "It was a grand sight to see this immense body hurled back in utter disorder between my two divisions, numbering very little over 5,000 muskets!"

This affair occurred about 11 A.M., and a splendid victory had been gained. But the enemy had a small corps which had not been engaged, and there remained his heavy force of cavalry. Our lines were now formed across from Abraham's Creek to Red Bud, and were very attenuated. There were still seen in front a formidable force, and away to the right a division of cavalry massed, with some artillery, overlapping us at least a mile. Late in the afternoon two divisions of the enemy's cavalry drove in the small force that had been watching on the Martinsburg road; and Crook's corps, which had not been engaged, advanced at the same time on the north side of the Red Bud and forced back our brigade of infantry and cavalry. A considerable force of cavalry then swept along the Martinsburg road to the skirts of Winchester, thus getting in the rear of our left flank. They were soon driven back by two of Wharton's brigades, and subsequently another charge of cavalry was also repulsed. But many of the men in the front line, hearing the fire in the rear, and thinking they were flanked and about to be cut off, commenced to fall back. At the same time Crook's corps advanced against our left, and Evans's brigade was thrown into line to meet it; but after an obstinate resistance that brigade also retired. The whole front line had now given way, but was rallied and formed behind some old breastworks, and with the aid of artillery the progress of the enemy's infantry was arrested. Their cavalry afterward succeeded in getting round on our left, producing great confusion, for which there was no remedy.

We now retired through Winchester, a new line was formed, and the hostile advance checked until nightfall. We then retired to Newtown without serious molestation.

This battle had lasted from daylight until dark, and at the close of it we had been forced back two miles, after having repulsed the first attack with great slaughter, and subsequently contested every inch of ground with unsurpassed obstinacy. Our loss was severe for the size of our force, but only a fraction of that ascribed to us by the foe; while his was very heavy.

Chapter 88

Military Operations After Winchester

SEVERAL minor engagements without important results followed the battle of Winchester. On October 5th Rosser, with 600 mounted men, joined Early, who moved forward to New Market on the 7th. Rosser pushed forward on the back and middle roads in pursuit of Federal cavalry, which, in executing Sheridan's orders, were burning houses, mills, barns, and stacks of wheat and hay, and he had several skirmishes with it.

The enormous damage done by Sheridan's campaign of arson may be seen from the fact that a committee of citizens and magistrates, appointed by the County Court of Rockingham to estimate the damage, reported, after a careful investigation, as follows:

> "Dwelling-houses burned, 30; barns burned, 450; mills burned, 31; fences destroyed (miles), 100; bushels of wheat destroyed, 100,000; bushels of corn destroyed, 50,000; tons of hay destroyed, 6,233; cattle carried off, 1,750; horses carried off, 1,750; sheep carried off, 4,200; hogs carried off, 3,350; factories burned, 3; furnaces burned, 1. In addition there was an immense amount of farming utensils of every description destroyed, many of them of great value, such as reapers and thrashing-machines; also household and kitchen furniture, and money, bonds, plate, etc., pillaged."

Early, having learned that Sheridan was preparing to send a part of his troops to Grant, moved down the Valley and found the enemy in strong force on the north bank of Cedar Creek. As it was necessary to attack him or move back for provisions and forage, Early determined to engage him, and drove him from his position to a new one about two miles north of Middletown, where he formed a line of battle behind breastworks.

"It was now apparent," says General Early, "that it would not do to press my troops further. They had been up all night, and were much jaded. In passing over rough ground to attack the enemy at dawn their own ranks had been much disordered and the men scattered, and it required time to reform them. Their ranks were much thinned by the absence of the men engaged in plundering the enemy's camps."

It was therefore determined to hold what had been gained, and orders were given to carry off the captured and abandoned artillery, small-arms, and wagons. A number of bold attempts were made by the enemy's cavalry to break our line, but they were invariably repulsed (Oct. 19th).

Late in the afternoon the Federal infantry advanced against the lines of Ramseur, Kershaw, and Gordon. The attacks on Ramseur's and Kershaw's fronts were handsomely repulsed. But a portion of the assailants had penetrated an interval between Evans's brigade, on the extreme left, and the rest of the line, when that brigade gave way, and Gordon's other brigades soon followed. General Gordon vainly tried to rally his men.

The affair was soon known with exaggerations along Kershaw's and Ramseur's lines, and their men, fearing to be flanked, began to fall back in disorder. Observing the disorder in our ranks the enemy's cavalry made another charge on our right, but were again repulsed. Every effort was made to rally the men, but the mass of them refused to stand, Three hundred men of Ramseur's division, and about the same number from Conner's brigade, aided by several pieces of artillery, held the whole force on our left in check for an hour and a half, until Ramseur was shot down, and the artillery ammunition was exhausted. Then the force that had continued steady gave way also. Every effort to rally the men in the rear having failed, the troops were ordered to retire. Wharton's divisions and Wofford's brigade had remained steadfast. The disorder soon extended to them.

The troops were halted at New Market, seven miles from Mount Jackson. Our loss in the battle of Cedar Creek was 23 pieces of artillery, some ordnance and medical wagons, and ambulances, about 1,860 killed and wounded, and something over 1,000 prisoners. Fifteen hundred prisoners were captured from the enemy and brought off, and his loss in killed and wounded was very heavy. We had in this battle about 8,500 muskets and a little over 40 pieces of artillery. Sheridan's cavalry numbered 8,700, and his infantry force was fully as large as at Winchester.

Subsequently General Early confronted Sheridan's whole force, north of Cedar Creek, for two days without any attack being made on him. On November 27th the fortified post at New Creek, on the Baltimore & Ohio Railroad, was surprised and captured by General Rosser. Two regiments of Federal cavalry, with their arms and colors, were taken, and 8 pieces of artillery and a very large amount of ordnance, quartermaster's, and commissary stores fell into our hands. Eight hundred prisoners, 4 pieces of artillery, and some wagons and horses were brought off.

When the campaign closed the invader held precisely the same position in the Valley which he held before the opening of the campaign in the spring.

Confederate Generals.

Chapter 89

The Red River Campaign

IN the Red River country of Louisiana it became certain, in February, 1864, that the enemy was about to make an expedition against our forces there under General Richard Taylor. The Federal forces were to be commanded by General N. P. Banks, augmented by a portion of Sherman's Vicksburg army, and to be accompanied by a fleet of gunboats under Admiral Porter. With these the force of General Steele, in Arkansas, was to co-operate.

On March 12th Admiral Porter, with 19 gunboats and 10,000 men of Sherman's army, entered the Red River. On the 15th the advance of Porter reached Alexandria, and on the 19th General Franklin left the Lower Teche with 18,000 men to meet him. General Steele reported his force at 7,000 men. General Taylor's army had been increased to 5,300 infantry, 500 cavalry, 300 artillerymen; and Liddell had about the same number of cavalry, and a four-gun battery.

General Taylor selected, three miles from Mansfield, a position in which to wait for an expected attack from the enemy, who were reported to be advancing in force to assail him. Taylor's force now amounted to 5,300 infantry, 3,000 mounted men, and 500 artillery—total, 8,800. Banks's force was estimated at 25,000.

As the enemy showed no disposition to advance, a forward movement of our whole line was made (April 8th). On the left our forces crossed the field under a heavy fire and entered the wood, where a bloody contest ensued, which resulted in gradually turning their right, which was forced back with loss of prisoners and guns. On the right little resistance was encountered until the wood was entered. Finding that our force outflanked the opponent's left, the right brigade was kept advanced, and we swept everything before us.

His first line, consisting of all the mounted force and one division of the Thirteenth Corps, was in full flight, leaving in our hands prisoners, guns, and wagons. Two miles to the rear of the first position the Second Division of the Thirteenth Corps was brought up. It was speedily routed, losing guns and prisoners. The advance was continued. Four miles from the original position the Nineteenth Army Corps was found drawn up on a ridge overlooking a stream. Sharp work followed; but as our force persisted, his fell back at nightfall. Twenty-five hundred prisoners, 20 pieces of artillery, several stands of colors, many thousands of small arms, and 250 wagons were taken.

On the next morning the enemy was found about a mile in front of Pleasant Hill, which occupies a plateau a mile wide from west to east along the Mansfield road. His lines extended across the plateau from the highest ground on the west; his left, to a wooded height on the right of the Mansfield road. Winding in front of this position was a dry gully cut by winter rains, bordered by a thick grove of young pines. This was held by his advanced cavalry, his main lines and guns being on the plateau. The forces of General Taylor—Churchill's brigade having joined him—amounted to 12,500 men, against 18,000 of General Banks, among them the fresh corps of General A. J. Smith. The action opened about 4.30 A.M. An obstinate battle ensued, with much confusion. Night ended the conflict on our right, and both sides occupied their original positions. Banks made no attempt to recover the ground from which his left and centre had been driven. During the night he retreated, leaving 400 wounded, and his dead unburied. Next morning he was pursued twenty miles before his rear was overtaken. On the road were found stragglers and burning wagons and stores. Our loss in the two actions of Mansfield and Pleasant Hill was 2,200. At Pleasant Hill the loss was 3 guns and 426 prisoners. The loss of the enemy in killed and wounded was larger than ours. We captured, not including stragglers, 2,800 prisoners and 20 guns. Their campaign was defeated.

Chapter 90

Fort Pillow

ON April 12, 1864, an attack was made by two brigades of General N. B. Forrest's force, under General J. R. Chalmers, upon Fort Pillow. Fort Pillow was an earthwork on a bluff on the east side of the Mississippi, at the mouth of Coal Creek. It was garrisoned by 400 men and 6 pieces of artillery. General Chalmers promptly gained possession of the outer works and drove the garrison to their main fortifications. The fort was crescent-shaped, the parapet 8 feet in height and 4 feet across the top, surrounded by a ditch 6 feet deep and 12 feet in width. About this time General Forrest arrived, and he soon ordered his forces to move up. The brigade of Bell, on the northeast, advanced until it gained a position in which the men were sheltered by the conformation of the ground, which was intersected by a ravine. The other brigade, under McCulloch, carried the intrenchments on the highest part of the ridge, immediately in front of the southeastern face of the fort, and occupied a cluster of cabins on its southern face and about sixty yards from it. The line of investment was now short and complete, within an average distance of one hundred yards. It extended from Coal Creek on the north, which was impassable, to the river-bank south of the fort. In the rear were numerous sharpshooters, well posted on commanding ridges, to pick off the garrison whenever they exposed themselves. At the same time our forces were so placed that the artillery could not be brought to bear upon them with much effect except by a fatal exposure of the gunners. During all this time a gunboat in the river kept up a continuous fire in all directions, but without effect. General Forrest, confident of his ability to take the fort by assault, which it seemed must be perfectly apparent to the garrison, and desiring to prevent further loss of life, sent a demand for an unconditional surrender, with the assurance that they would be treated as prisoners of war. The answer written with a pencil on a slip of paper: "Negotiations will not attain the desired object." Meantime three boats were seen to approach, the foremost of which was apparently laden with troops; and, as an hour's time had been asked for to communicate with the officers of the gunboat, it seemed to be a pretext to gain time for reinforcements. General Forrest, understanding that the enemy doubted his presence and pronounced the demand to be a trick, also declared himself and demanded an answer within twenty minutes, whether the commander would fight or surrender. Meanwhile the foremost boat indicated an intention to land, but a few shots caused her to withdraw to the other side of the river, along which they all passed up. The answer from the fort was a positive refusal to surrender. Three companies on the left were now placed in an old rifle-pit and almost in the rear of the fort, and on the right a portion of Barton's regiment of Bell's brigade was also under the bluff and in the rear of the fort.

The works were carried without a halt. As the troops poured into the fortification the enemy retreated toward the river, arms in hand and firing back, and their colors flying, expecting the gunboat to shell us away from the bluff and protect them until they could be taken off or reinforced. As they descended the bluff an enfilading and deadly fire was poured in upon them from right to left by the forces in rear of the fort, of whose presence they were ignorant. To this was now added the destructive fire of the regiments that had stormed the fort. Fortunately some of our men cut down the flag, and the firing ceased. Our loss was 20 killed and 60 wounded. Of the enemy 228 were buried that evening, and quite a number next day. We captured 6 pieces of artillery and about 350 stand of small-arms. The gunboat escaped up the river.

CHAPTER 91

JOHNSTON'S RETROGRESSIVE CAMPAIGN

ON December 16, 1863, I directed General Joseph E. Johnston to transfer the command of the Department of Mississippi and East Louisiana to General Polk, and to proceed to Dalton, Ga., and there assume command of the Army of the Tennessee, representing at that date an effective force of 43,094 men. My information led me to believe that the condition of that army was satisfactory in all that constitutes efficiency—that the men were eager for an opportunity to retrieve the loss of prestige sustained in the disastrous battle of Missionary Ridge. I was also informed that the enemy's forces were weaker than at any time since that battle, and especially deficient in cavalry, artillery, and train horses. The Federal army occupied Chattanooga, Bridgeport, and Stevenson, with a detached force at Knoxville. I desired that prompt and vigorous measures should be taken to enable our troops to begin active operations against the enemy as early as practicable, not only because it was important to guard against the injurious results to the morale of the troops which always attend a prolonged season of inactivity, but because, also, the recovery of the territory in Tennessee and Kentucky which we had been forced to abandon, and on the supplies of which the proper subsistence of our armies mainly depended, imperatively demanded an onward movement. I believed that by a rapid concentration of our troops between the scattered forces of the enemy, without attempting to capture his intrenched positions, we could compel him to accept battle in the open field, and that, should we fail to draw him out of his intrenchments, we could move upon his line of communication. I repeatedly urged on General Johnston, both by letter and by officers of my staff, the importance of a prompt aggressive movement.

General Johnston cordially approved of an aggressive movement, and notified me of his purpose to make it as soon as reinforcements and supplies then on the way should reach him. He did not approve of the proposed advance into Tennessee, but preferred to stand on the defensive until strengthened; "to watch, prepare, and strike" as soon as possible. He declared his purpose, as soon as reinforced, to advance to Ringgold, attack there, and, if successful, to strike at Cleveland, cut the railroad, control the river, isolate East Tennessee, and consequently force his antagonist to give battle on this side of the Tennessee River. Simultaneously with this movement, and to aid it, General Johnston proposed that a large cavalry force should be sent to Middle Tennessee, in the rear of the enemy. By these operations he believed that the Federal army would be forced to evacuate the Tennessee Valley, when an advance into the heart of the State would be safely practicable.

The irreparable loss of time in making any forward movement having allowed the combinations which rendered an advance across the Tennessee River no longer practicable, I took prompt measures to enable General Johnston to carry out immediately his own proposition, to strike first at Ringgold and then at Cleveland, proposing that General Buckner should threaten Knoxville, General Forrest advance into and threaten Middle Tennessee, and General Roddy hold the enemy in Northern Alabama. This movement might have been successful if it had been promptly executed, although it held out no such promise as did the plan of advance before the enemy had had time to make his combinations, General Johnston's belief that General Grant would be ready to assume the offensive before he could be prepared to do so, proved too well founded; while his purpose that we should take the initiative if the Federal army did not attack, was never carried out.

On May 2, 1864, Johnston discovered that the enemy was advancing against him under the command of General Sherman; and two days later it was reported that he had reached Ringgold, about fifteen miles, north of Dalton, in considerable force.

According to official returns the effective strength of General Johnston's army, including Polk's command, then *en route*, was not less than 68,620 men of all arms, excluding from this estimate the thousands of men employed on extra duty, amounting, as General Hood states, to 10,000 when he assumed command.

No effort was spared by the Government to enable Johnston to repulse the hostile advance and assume the offensive. Almost all the available military strength of the South and West, in men and supplies, was pressed forward to him. The supplies of the commissary, quartermaster, and ordnance departments of his army were represented as ample and suitably located. The troops were eager to advance, and confident in their power to achieve victory and recover the territory they had lost. Their position warranted the confidence of successful resistance at least. Long mountain ranges, penetrated by few and difficult roads and paths, and deep and wide rivers, seemed to render our position one which could not be turned, and from which we could not be dislodged; while that of the enemy was manifestly perilous, as he was dependent for his supplies upon a single line of railroad from Nashville. Both the country and the Government shared the hope that a decisive victory would soon be won in the mountains of Georgia, which would free the South and West from invasion, open to our occupation and the support of our armies the productive territory of Tennessee and Kentucky, and so recruit our army in the West as to render it impracticable for the enemy to accumulate additional forces in Virginia.

On May 6th the Confederate army was in position in and around Dalton, in daily expectation of an attack from Sherman's whole force. No attack was made. On the evening of the 12th of May Johnston withdrew his troops and fell back on Resaca, eighteen miles south of Dalton, a strong position on a peninsula formed by the junction of two rivers, and further fortified by continuous rifle-pits and earthworks; but he soon abandoned it and withdrew toward Adairsville, thirteen miles south on the railroad. General Johnston, not finding the narrow valley north of Adairsville to be as advantageous as he had hoped, again ordered a further retreat to Cassville, seventeen miles further south, where he announced his intention to do battle with the enemy at Kingston. He supposed that the enemy would divide his forces into two columns before reaching Kingston; and as that point would be the place of their greatest distance from each other, he proposed to assail them there. The battle was announced in orders to each regiment.

But the Federal army, instead of dividing, united for the purpose of attacking our forces. Johnston thereupon ordered another retreat (May 19th) beyond Etowah.

The next stand of our army was at Allatoona, in the Etowali Mountains, south of the river of that name; but the rapid extension of the Federal army, threatening Marietta, was deemed to necessitate the evacuation of that strong position.

Engagements with the enemy at New Hope Church (May 27th and 28th), although distinguished by many acts of gallantry, did not result in any advantage to our army.

Falling back slowly, General Johnston made his next stand in that mountainous country that lies between Acworth and Marietta. Here the greatest blow to the country that had been felt since Albert Sidney Johnston fell at Shiloh, and Stonewall Jackson at Chancellorsville, was experienced, in the death of that noble Christian and soldier, General Polk. On June 14th he was killed by a shot from a Federal battery on Pine Mountain, as he was reconnoitring near the Confederate outposts.

On June 18th, heavy rain having so swollen Nose's Creek as to render it impassable, the Federal army, under cover of this stream, extended its lines several miles beyond Johnston's left flank, causing a further retrograde movement by a portion of his force. For several days brisk fighting occurred at various points of our line. A cavalry attack on Wheeler's cavalry on the 20th, and a general assault on the Confederate position on the 27th, were handsomely repulsed. On July 5th General Johnston deemed it necessary to abandon his position at Kenesaw; and on the 9th, General Sherman having thrown two corps across the Chattahoochee on the previous day, the Confederate army crossed that river and established itself two miles in the rear.

Thus from Dalton to Resaca, from Resaca to Adairsville, from Adairsville to Allatoona (involving by the evacuation of Kingston the loss of Rome, with its valuable mills, foundries, and large quantities of military stores), from Allatoona to Kenesaw, from Kenesaw to the Chattahoochee, and then to Atlanta—retreat followed retreat during seventy-four days of anxious hope and bitter disappointment, until at last the Army of Tennessee fell back within the fortifications of Atlanta. The Federal army soon occupied the arc of a circle extending from the railroad between Atlanta and the Chattahoochee River to some miles south of the Georgia Railroad (from Atlanta to Augusta) in a direction north and northeast of Atlanta. We had suffered a disastrous loss of territory.

Chapter 92

Fall of Atlanta

WHEN it became known that our army had been driven from one strong position to another, until finally it had reached the earthworks of the exterior defence of Atlanta, the popular disappointment was extreme, and from many quarters came petitions, letters, and delegations, urging me to remove General Johnston, and put someone in command who would resolutely hold Atlanta, and the railroads, threatened with destruction, on which we mainly depended for indispensable supplies for the armies then fighting the main battles of the war in Virginia. These demands came from many who had urged his appointment. While sharing the disappointment that pervaded the whole country at General Johnston's failures, and more keenly conscious of the disasters likely to result from them—because I was in a position to estimate more accurately their probable extent—I resisted the clamors that had steadily increased with each successive retreat from Dalton to Atlanta, because conscious of the danger of a change of commanders in the presence of the enemy. I only issued the order to revoke his assignment after I became satisfied that his declared purpose to occupy the works of Atlanta with militia levies, and withdraw his army into the open country for freer operations, would eventually result in the loss of Atlanta, in which event it was impossible to foretell where the retreat would cease. I gave my permission to issue the order relieving General Johnston, and directing him to turn over his force to General Hood, in the hope that the impending danger of the loss of Atlanta might be averted.

General Hood assumed command on July 18th. He reported that the effective strength of his force on that day was 48,750 men of all arms.

Feeling that the only chance of holding Atlanta consisted in assuming the offensive by forcing the enemy to accept battle, General Hood determined, on July 20th, to attack the corps of Generals Thomas and Schofield, who were in the act of crossing Peachtree Creek, hoping to defeat Thomas before he could fortify himself, then to fall on Schofield, and finally to attack McPherson's corps, which had reached Decatur, on the Georgia Railroad, driving the enemy back to the creek and into the narrow space included between that stream and the Chattahoochee River. Owing to a misapprehension of the order of battle, and consequent delay in making the attack, the movement failed. On the 21st, finding that McPherson's corps was threatening his communications, General Hood resolved to attack him at or near Decatur, in front and on flank, turn his left, and then, following up the movement from the right to the left with his whole army, force the enemy down Peachtree Creek. This engagement was the hottest of the campaign, but it failed to accomplish any other favorable result than to check McPherson's movement on the communications of our army, while it cost heavily in the loss of many officers and men.

Beyond expeditions by the enemy, for the most part by cavalry, to destroy the lines of railroad by which supplies and reinforcements could reach Atlanta, and successful efforts on our part to frustrate their movements, resulting in the defeat and capture of General Stoneman and his command near Macon, the utter destruction of the enemy's cavalry force engaged by General Wheeler at Newnan, and the defeat of Sherman's design to unite his cavalry at the Macon & Western Railroad, and effectually destroy that essential avenue for the conveyance of stores and ammunition for our army, no movement of special importance took place between July 22nd and August 26th, at which latter date it was discovered that Sherman had abandoned his works upon our right, and, leaving a considerable force to hold his intrenched position at the railroad bridge over the Chattahoochee, was marching his main body to the south and southwest of Atlanta, to use it, as he himself has expressed it, "against the communications of Atlanta, instead of against its intrenchments."

On the 30th, it being known that he was moving on Jonesboro, the county town of Clayton County, about twenty miles south of Atlanta, General Hood sent two corps under Hardee, in the hope that he could drive him across Flint River, oblige him to abandon his works on the left, and then be able to attack him successfully in flank. The attack at

Jonesboro was unsuccessful. Hardee was obliged, on September 1st, to fall back to Lovejoy's, seven miles south of Jonesboro, on the Macon & Western Railroad.

Thus, the main body of the Federal army was between Hardee and Atlanta, and the immediate evacuation of that city became a necessity. There was an additional and cogent reason for that movement. Owing to the obstinately cruel policy which the United States Government had pursued for some time, of refusing on any terms to exchange prisoners of war, upward of thirty thousand prisoners were at Andersonville in Southwestern Georgia at this time. To guard against the release and arming of these prisoners, General Hood thought it necessary to place our army between them and the enemy, and abandon the project, which he thought feasible, of moving on Sherman's communications and destroying his depots of supplies at Marietta.

Chapter 93

Hood's Campaign from Atlanta to Nashville

UPON abandoning Atlanta, Hood marched his army in a westerly direction, and formed a junction with the two corps which had been operating at Jonesboro and Lovejoy's under Hardee.

Sherman, desisting from any further aggressive movement in the field, returned to Atlanta, which had been formally surrendered by the Mayor on September 2nd, with the promise, as reported, on the part of the Federal commander, that non-combatants and private property should be respected. Shortly after his arrival, the commanding general of the Federal forces, regardless of this promise, and on the pretence that the exigencies of the service required that the place should be used exclusively for military purposes, issued an order directing all civilians living in Atlanta, male and female, to leave the city within five days from the date of the order (September 5th).

Since Alva's atrocious cruelties to the non-combatant population of the Low Countries, in the sixteenth century, the history of war records no instance of such barbarous cruelty as that which this order designed to perpetrate. It involved the immediate expulsion from their homes and only means of subsistence of thousands of unoffending women and children, whose husbands and fathers were either in the army, in Northern prisons, or had died in battle. In vain were appeals made to Sherman by the civil authorities to revoke or modify this inhuman order. His reply was, "I give full credit to your statements of the distress that will be occasioned by it, and yet I shall not revoke my order, because my orders are not designed to meet the humanities of the case."

At the time appointed the women and children were expelled from their homes; and before they were passed within our lines complaint was generally made that the Federal officers and men who were sent to guard them had robbed them of the few articles of value they had been permitted to take from their homes. Thus the order was executed with a cowardly dishonesty in perfect harmony with its temper and spirit.

During September the Federal army made no movements beyond strengthening the defences of Atlanta and collecting within it large quantities of military supplies. Hood held his troops near Jonesboro. With a view to judge better of the situation, and then determine the best course to pursue, I visited General Hood's headquarters at Palmetto. The crisis was grave. It was not to be expected that Sherman would remain long inactive. His movements indicated that he contemplated a movement farther south, making Atlanta a secondary base. To rescue Georgia, save the Gulf States, and keep possession of the lines of our supplies, it became necessary that the lines of railroad in Sherman's rear should be effectually torn up, the Bridgeport railroad bridge destroyed, and the communications between Atlanta, Chattanooga, and Nashville completely cut off. If this could be done, all the fruits of Sherman's successful campaign in Georgia would be blighted, his capture of Atlanta would become a barren victory, and he would probably be compelled to retreat toward Tennessee, at every mile of which he might be harassed by our army. Or if, on the other hand, relying on Atlanta as a base, he should push forward through Georgia to the Atlantic coast, our army, having cut his communications north of Atlanta, could fall upon his rear, and with our better knowledge of the country and the devotion of the surrounding population, and our superiority in cavalry, it was not unreasonable to hope that retributive justice might overtake the ruthless invader.

After I had conferred with prominent citizens of Georgia, with Generals Hardee, Cobb, and Beauregard, and a plan of campaign had been adopted, General Hood moved upon the enemy's line of communication. His successes at Big Shanty and Acworth, in capturing those stations and thoroughly destroying the railroad between them, and his partial success at Allatoona, caused Sherman, leaving one corps to garrison Atlanta, to move out with his main body to restore his communications. Hood further succeeded in destroying the railroad from Resaca to Tunnel Hill, capturing the enemy's posts at Tilton, Dalton, and Mill-Creek Gap. Not deeming his army in a condition to risk a general engagement, Hood withdrew his forces toward Gadsden, which he reached October 20th, and where he found supplies adequate for the wants of his troops. Sherman had returned to Atlanta, and Hood, instead of hanging on his rear, and not allowing him to repair the damage to the railroad, and otherwise harassing him in his march, after conference with General Beauregard decided to continue his march into Tennessee, supposing that thus he could force Sherman to follow him beyond the limits of Georgia.

After overcoming many vexatious detentions, General Hood, on November 20th, crossed the Tennessee River at Gunter's Landing, and moved forward on the route to Nashville, where General Sherman had sent General Thomas for the protection of his depots and communications against an apprehended attack by cavalry under Forrest.

Chapter 94

Sherman's March to the Sea

THOMAS having been sufficiently reinforced in Tennessee to enable him to hold Hood in check, Sherman, thus relieved from the necessity of defending himself against an active army and protecting a long line of railroad communication with a fortified line in his rear, resolved upon his march to the sea; abandoning Atlanta, after having first utterly destroyed that city by fire. Not a house was spared, not even a church. Similar acts of vandalism marked the progress of the Federal army at Rome, Kingston, Acworth, Marietta, and every town or village along the route, thus carrying out General Sherman's order "to enforce a devastation more or less relentless" along the line of his march, where he only encountered helpless women and children. The arson of the dwelling-houses of non-combatants, and the robbery of their property, extending even to the trinkets worn by women, made the devastation as relentless as savage instincts could suggest.

On November 16th Sherman left his intrenchments around Atlanta, and dividing his army into two bodies, each from 25,000 to 30,000 strong, the one followed the Georgia Railroad in the direction of Augusta, and the other took the line of the Macon & Western Railroad to Jonesboro. Avoiding Macon and Augusta, they passed through central Georgia, taking Milledgeville on the way, marching in compact column, and advancing with extreme caution, although only opposed by detachments of Wheeler's cavalry and a few hastily formed regiments of raw militia. Partial efforts were made to obstruct and destroy the roads in the front and on the flanks of the invading army, and patriotic appeals by prominent citizens were made to the people to remove all provisions from its path; but no formidable opposition was made except at the railroad bridge over the Oconee, where Wheeler, with a portion of his command and a few militia, held the enemy in check for two or three days. With his small force Wheeler daringly and persistently harassed and, when practicable, delayed the enemy's advance, attacking and defeating exposed detachments, deterring his foragers from venturing far from the main body, defending all cities and towns along the railroad lines, and affording protection to depots of supplies, arsenals, and other important government works. The report of his operations from November 14th to December 20th displays a dash, activity, vigilance, and consummate skill which justly entitles him to a prominent place on the roll of great cavalry leaders. By his indomitable energy, operating on all sides of Sherman's columns, he was enabled to keep the Government advised of the enemy's movements; and by preventing foraging parties from leaving the main body, he saved from spoliation all but a narrow tract of country, and from the torch millions' worth of property which would otherwise have been certainly consumed.

It soon became manifest that Savannah was Sherman's objective point. That city was occupied by General W. J. Hardee, with about 18,000 men, a considerable portion of whom were militia, local troops, reserves, and hastily organized regiments and battalions made up of convalescents from the hospitals and artisans from the Government shops.

On December 10th the enemy's columns reached the immediate vicinity of Savannah, and on the 12th they occupied a semicircular line extending from the Savannah River to the Savannah & Gulf Railroad. The defences of the city were strong; the earthworks and other fortifications were flanked by inundated rice swamps extending across the peninsula formed by the Savannah and Ogeechee rivers; and the causeways leading through them were well fortified by works mounting heavy guns. With a sufficient force to occupy his long lines of defence, General Hardee could have sustained a protracted siege. The city was amply supplied, and its lines of communication were still open. Although Sherman had reached Savannah he had not yet opened communication with the Federal fleet. Fort McAllister, situated on the right side of the Ogeechee, about six miles from Ossabaw Sound, was a serious obstacle in his way, as it was a work of considerable strength, mounting twenty-one heavy guns, with a deep and wide ditch extending along its front, and every avenue of approach swept by the guns mounted upon its bastions. The fort was held by a garrison of 250 men, under the command of experienced officers. The work was attacked on the evening of the 13th, and carried by assault after a short and feeble resistance. Having obtained possession of the fort, Sherman speedily opened communication with the fleet, and became perfectly secure against any future want of supplies. The fleet also enabled him to obtain heavy ordnance for use against the city. He proceeded immediately to take measures to invest Savannah, and in a few days had succeeded in doing so on every side of the city except that fronting the river. While Hardee's troops had not yielded a single position or lost a foot of ground, with the exception of Fort McAllister, he discovered, on December 20th, that Sherman had put heavy siege guns in position near enough to bombard the city, and that the enemy was threatening Union Causeway, which runs across the large swamps that lie between Savannah and Charleston, and offered the only practicable line of retreat. He determined therefore, to evacuate the city rather than expose it and its inhabitants to bombardment. He also thought that holding it had ceased to be of any special importance, and that his troops could do more valuable service in the field. Accordingly, on the night of December 20th, having destroyed the navy-yard and other Government property, and razed the fortifications below the city, he withdrew his army and reached Hardeeville on the evening of the 22nd, without hindrance or molestation on the part of the enemy.

Let us now return to follow the fortunes of General Hood. Owing to an accidental delay in the transmission of orders, General Hood, who had not cavalry enough to protect his trains, was obliged to wait three weeks at Florence for the coming of Forrest. This unfortunate delay gave the enemy time to repair the railroad to Chattanooga, and to accumulate supplies at Atlanta for the march to the Atlantic coast. Forrest's cavalry joined on the 21st of November, and the movement began. The enemy's forces were concentrated at Pulaski and Lawrenceburg. Hood tried to place his army between these forces and Nashville, but our cavalry, having driven off the enemy at Lawrenceburg, gave notice of our advance, and on the 23rd he evacuated Pulaski and moved rapidly by the turnpike and railroad to Columbia. On the evening of November 27th our army took position in front of the works at that place. During the night the town was evacuated, and a strong position was taken on the opposite side of the river, about a mile and a half distant.

On the evening of the 28th General Forrest crossed Duck River a few miles above Columbia, and in the morning of the 29th Stewart's and Cheatham's corps followed, leaving General Stephen D. Lee's corps confronting the enemy at Columbia. The cavalry and the two infantry corps moved in light marching order, the object being, by advancing rapidly on roads parallel to the Columbia and Franklin turnpike, at or near Spring Hill, to cut off that portion of the foe at Columbia. The movement having been discovered after Hood's forces had got well on the flank of the enemy, he began to retreat along the turnpike toward Spring Hill. About noon of that day the cavalry attacked his trains, but found them too strongly guarded to be captured. The retreat was rapidly conducted along the turnpike, with flankers thrown out to protect the main column. About two miles from Spring Hill General Cheatham commenced to come in contact with the retreating column. He was ordered to attack vigorously, and get possession of the turnpike. This order was so feebly executed that it failed, and the enemy passed on toward Spring Hill. Though the golden opportunity had passed with daylight, Hood did not abandon the hope of effecting by a night movement the end he sought. Accordingly, General Stewart was ordered to move his corps beyond Cheatham's, and place it across the road beyond Spring Hill. In the dark and confusion he did not succeed in getting the position desired. About midnight, ascertaining that the enemy was moving in disorder, with artillery, wagons, and troops intermixed, Hood sent instructions to General Cheatham to advance a heavy line of skirmishers, still further to impede the retreat. "This was not accomplished. The enemy continued to move along the road in hurry and confusion nearly all the night. Thus was lost a great opportunity for striking him for which we had labored so long—the greatest this campaign had offered, and one of the greatest during the war. General S. D. Lee, left in front of the enemy at Columbia, was instructed to press him the moment he abandoned his position at that point. He did not abandon his works until dark, showing that his trains obstructed the road for fifteen miles during the day and a great part of the night." At daylight Hood pursued the enemy so rapidly as to compel him to burn a number of his wagons. On the hills about four miles south of Franklin he made demonstrations as if to give battle, but when our forces deployed for the attack he retired to Franklin.

From despatches captured at Spring Hill, Hood learned that Schofield was instructed by Thomas to hold that position until Franklin could be made secure, and thus knew that it was important to attack Schofield promptly, and concluded that, if he should escape at Franklin, he would gain the fortifications about Nashville. Hood reports that "the nature of the position was such as to render it inexpedient to attempt any other flank movement, and I therefore determined to attack him in front and without delay."

On November 30th he formed his line of battle. At 4 P.M. he gave the order to advance; his troops moved gallantly forward, carried the first line, and advanced against the interior works; here the engagement was close and fierce; the combatants occupied the opposite sides of the intrenchments, our men carrying them in some places, many being killed entirely inside the enemy's works. Some of the Tennesseeans, after years of absence, saw again their homes, and strove with desperation to expel the invader from them. The contest continued till near midnight, when the enemy abandoned his works and crossed the river, leaving his dead and wounded behind him. We had won a victory, but it was purchased at fearful cost. It was one of the bloodiest battles of the war. General Hood reported his loss at about 4,500, and among them were Generals Cleburne, Gist, John Adams, Strahl, and Granberry, whose loss we could ill afford. Around Cleburne thickly lay the gallant men who, in his desperate assault, followed him with the implicit confidence that, in another army, was given to Stonewall Jackson; and, in the one case as in the other, a vacancy was created which could never be filled. The dead left by the enemy indicated that his loss was equal to our own. Those of our men who were captured were inside the enemy's works.

The next morning at daylight, the wounded being cared for and the dead buried, Hood moved forward toward Nashville, about eighteen miles distant. Forrest with his cavalry closely pursued the enemy.

Chapter 95

The Battle of Nashville

On the 2nd of December our army took position in front of Nashville, about two miles from the city, Lee's corps in the centre resting on the Franklin turnpike, Cheatham's on the right, Stewart's on the left, and the cavalry on each flank. Hood then commenced to construct detached works to cover the flanks.

Nothing of importance occurred until the morning of the 15th, when the enemy, having been reinforced by about 15,000 men from the trans-Mississippi country, attacked simultaneously both flanks of our line. On our right he was repulsed with heavy loss, but on our left, toward evening, he carried some of our partially completed redoubts. During the night of the 15th our line was shortened and strengthened. Cheatham's corps was transferred from our right to our left. Early on the 16th the enemy made a general attack on our lines, accompanied by a heavy fire of artillery. All his assaults were repulsed with heavy loss until 3.30 P.M., when a portion of our line to the left of the centre suddenly gave way.

Up to this time no battle ever progressed more favorably—the troops in excellent spirits, waving their colors, and bidding defiance to the enemy; but the position he then gained being such as to enfilade us, caused our entire line to give way in a few moments, and our troops to retreat in the direction of Franklin, most of them in great confusion. Our loss in killed and wounded, however, was small.

During the 17th the enemy's cavalry pressed boldly on the retreating column, the open character of the country being favorable to cavalry operations. The retreat continued, and on the 25th, 26th, and 27th the army crossed the Tennessee River at Bainbridge. After crossing the river the army moved by easy stages to Tupelo, Miss.

General Hood reported his losses in the Tennessee campaign to have been about 10,000, including prisoners, and when he arrived at Tupelo he had 18,500 infantry and artillery, and 2,306 cavalry.

Chapter 96

Exchange of Prisoners

THAT we of the Confederate States should dare to resort to arms for the preservation of our rights, and to "secure the blessings of liberty to ourselves and our posterity," was regarded as most improbable by the Government of the United States. The true character and intentions of that Government were clearly exposed in the treatment of the question of the exchange of prisoners. Their aspirations for dominion and sovereignty, through the Government of the Union, had become so deep-seated as to cause that Government, at its first step, to assume the haughtiness and imperiousness of an absolute sovereign. The term "loyal," or its opposite, has no signification except as applied to the sovereign of an empire or kingdom. To say, therefore, that the agent of the sovereign people, the representative of the system they have organized to conduct their common affairs, composed the real sovereign, and that loyalty or disloyalty was of signification or relation to that sovereign alone, was an error that led straight to the subversion of all popular Government, and the establishment of the monarchial or consolidated form. The Government of the United States, said President Lincoln (in his proclamation calling for 75,000 men), is now the sovereign here, and loyalty consists in the maintenance of that sovereignty against its foes. The sovereignty of the people and of the several and distinct States, in his mind, was only a weakness and an enthusiasm of the fathers. The States and the people thereof had become consolidated into a National Union. "I appeal," he said, "to all loyal citizens to favor, facilitate, and aid this effort to maintain the honor, the integrity, and the existence of our National Union."

The Confederate States not only refused to aid this effort, but took up arms to defeat the consummation of such a monstrous usurpation. It was evident that, if no efforts for a rescue were made, the time would come when the rights of all the States might be denied, and the hope of mankind in constitutional freedom be forever lost. This was usurpation. This lay at the foundation of the war. Every subsequent act tended palpably to supremacy for the Federal Government, the subjugation of the States, and the submission of the people.

That we dared to draw our swords to vindicate the rights and sovereignty of the people, and to resist and deny all sovereignty as inherently existing in the Government of the United States, was adjudged an infamous crime, and we were denounced as "rebels." It was asserted that those of us "who were captured should be hung as rebels taken in the act." Crushing the corner-stone of the Union, the independence of the States, the Federal Government assumed toward us a position of haughty arrogance, refusing to recognize us otherwise than as insurrectionists and "rebels," who resisted and denied its usurped sovereignty, and who were entitled to no amelioration from the punishment of death except such as might proceed only from the promptings of mercy.

In April, 1861, I issued a proclamation offering to grant letters of marque and reprisal to seamen. Two days afterward President Lincoln issued a counter-proclamation, declaring that, "if any person, under the pretended authority of said States, or under any other pretence, should molest a vessel of the United States, or the persons or cargo on board of her, such person shall be held amenable to the laws of the United States for the prevention and punishment of piracy," which was death.

Some small vessels obtained these letters of marque, and were captured. The crews were the first prisoners that fell into the hands of the enemy. They were imprisoned, and held for trial as pirates.

As soon as the treatment of these prisoners was known in Richmond, as early as July 6, 1861, I sent a special messenger to President Lincoln, with a communication in which, after quoting the uncontradicted statements that had been published respecting these prisoners, I announced the policy of the Confederate Government in case the threats made against them were carried out. I said:

> "It is the desire of this Government so to conduct the war now existing as to mitigate its horrors as far as may be possible, and, with this intent, its treatment of the prisoners captured by its forces has been marked by the greatest humanity and leniency consistent

with public obligation. Some have been permitted to return home on parole, others to remain at large, under similar conditions, within this Confederacy, and all have been furnished with rations for their subsistence, such as are allowed to our own troops. It is only since the news has been received of the treatment of the prisoners taken on the *Savannah* that I have been compelled to withdraw these indulgences, and to hold the prisoners taken by us in strict confinement.

"A just regard to humanity and to the honor of this Government now requires me to state explicitly that, painful as will be the necessity, this Government will deal out to the prisoners held by it the same treatment and the same fate as shall be experienced by those captured on the *Savannah*; and, if driven to the terrible necessity of retaliation by your execution of any of the officers or crew of the *Savannah*, that retaliation will be extended so far as shall be requisite to secure the abandonment of a practice unknown to the warfare of civilized man, and so barbarous as to disgrace the nation which shall be guilty of inaugurating it. With this view, and because it may not have reached you, I now renew the proposition made to the commander of the blockading squadron, to exchange for the prisoners taken on the *Savannah* an equal number of those now held by us, according to rank."

The bearer of this communication, Colonel Thomas Taylor, was denied an audience, and was obliged to content himself with a verbal reply from General Scott that President Lincoln had received the communication and would reply in writing. No letter ever came. We were therefore compelled to select by lot from among the prisoners in our hands a number to whom we proposed to mete out the same fate which might await the crew of the *Savannah*.

These measures of retaliation arrested the cruel and illegal purposes of the enemy.

Meanwhile (in May, 1861) the Confederate Congress had passed an act directing the transfer of all prisoners of war to the War Department by their captors, and enacting that the rations to be furnished to prisoners "shall be the same in quantity and quality as those furnished to enlisted men in the army of the Confederacy."

This law was embodied in orders issued from the Department and from the headquarters in the field, and no order was ever issued in conflict with its humane provisions.

Nevertheless, the Government of the United States stubbornly refused all consideration of the question of exchange of prisoners, or to accept any interchange of courtesy. An exchange was occasionally made by the various commanders in the field, under the paltry pretence that the Federal Government knew nothing of it. We released numbers at different points on parole, and the matter was compromised in various ways. On September 3rd an exchange was made by General Pillow and Colonel Wallace of the United States Army. On October 23rd a similar exchange was made between General McClernand and General Polk. Subsequently, in November, General Grant offered to surrender to General Polk certain wounded men and invalids unconditionally. On November 1st General Frémont made an agreement with General Price, in Missouri, by which certain persons named were authorized to negotiate for the exchange of any persons who might be taken prisoners of war, upon a plan previously arranged. General Hunter succeeded him, and he repudiated Frémont's agreement.

A proposition was made in the Confederate Congress to return without any formality whatever the Federal prisoners captured at Manassas. But for the difficulty in reference to the crew of the *Savannah* it would doubtless have prevailed.

But the determination of the Federal Government not to meet us on an equal footing was shaken by the clamor of the Northern people for a restoration of their friends, and both Houses of Congress united in a request that the President should take immediate steps for a general exchange. The President, however, instead of complying with the request, appointed two respectable commissioners to visit the prisoners we held, and provide for their comfort at the expense of the United States. The commissioners arrived at Norfolk, Va., but were not allowed to proceed any farther. A readiness to negotiate for a general exchange was manifested on our part, and our proposals were agreed to by them, and subsequently approved at Washington. Soon afterward an arrangement was made between General Howell Cobb, on our part, and General Wool, the commander at Fortress Monroe, by which the prisoners on both sides were to be exchanged, man for man, the officers to be assimilated as to rank. The privateersmen were to be exchanged on the footing of prisoners of war. Any surplus remaining on either side were to be released; and during the continuance of hostilities prisoners on either side were to be paroled.

The exchange proceeded, and about 300 in excess had been delivered by us when it was discovered that not one of our privateersmen had been released, and that our men taken prisoners at Fort Donelson, instead of being paroled, had been sent into the interior. Some of the hostages we held for our privateers had gone forward, but the remainder were retained. Being informed of this state of affairs I recommended to Congress that all of our men who had been paroled by the United States Government should be released from the obligations of their parole, so as to bear arms in our defence, in consequence of this breach of good faith on the part of that Government.

The only unadjusted point between Generals Cobb and Wool was that the latter was unwilling that each party should agree to pay the expenses of transporting their prisoners to the frontier, and this he promised to refer to his Government. At a second interview General Wool said that his Government would not consent to pay these expenses, and thereupon General Cobb agreed to the terms proposed by the other side. General Wool now stated that his Government had changed his instructions. Thus the negotiations were abruptly broken off, and the matter was left where it was before.

After these negotiations had begun, the capture of Forts Henry and Donelson had given to the United States a considerable preponderance in the number of prisoners held by them, and they immediately returned to their original purpose of unequal treatment.

A suspension of exchanges for some months followed. Finally, a storm of indignation beginning to arise among the Northern people at the conduct of their Government, it was forced to yield its absurd pretensions, and on July 22, 1862, a cartel for the exchange of prisoners was executed. The exchanges were immediately renewed, and by the middle of August most of the officers of rank on either side who had been for any long period in captivity were released.

Chapter 97

Federal Barbarities, and Threatened Retaliation

ON the same day on which the cartel was signed an order was issued by the Federal Secretary of War, empowering the military commanders "to seize and use any property, real or personal, which may be necessary or convenient for their several commands for supplies or for other military purposes," and "to keep accounts sufficiently accurate and in detail to show quantities and amounts, and from whom it shall come, as a basis upon which compensation can be made in proper cases." This was simply a system of plunder, for no compensation would be made to any person unless he could prove his fidelity to the Government of the United States.

On the next day General Pope, in command of the Federal forces near Washington, issued a general order directing the murder of our peaceful citizens as spies, if found quietly tilling the land in his rear, even outside of his lines; and one of his brigadier-generals seized innocent and peaceful inhabitants to be held as hostages, to the end that they might be murdered in cold blood if any of his soldiers were killed by some unknown persons whom he designated as "bushwhackers." Upon this state of facts I issued a general order recognizing General Pope and his commissioned officers to be in the position they had chosen for themselves—that of robbers, and murderers, not that of public enemies, entitled, if captured, to be treated as prisoners of war. Some of the military authorities of the United States seemed to suppose that better success would attend a savage war, in which no quarter was to be given, and no age or sex spared, than had hitherto been secured by such hostilities as were alone recognized to be lawful by civilized men. We renounced our right of retaliation on the innocent, and continued to treat the soldiers of Pope's army as prisoners of war, confining our repressive measures to the punishment only of such commissioned officers as were willing participants in such crimes. Pope was soon afterward removed from command.

In August a letter involving similar principles was addressed by General Lee to the commanding General at Washington, General Halleck, making inquiries as to the truth of the case of William B. Mumford, reported to have been murdered at New Orleans by order of General Butler; and of Colonel Owen, reported to have been murdered in Missouri by order of General Pope. I had also been credibly informed that many other Federal officers within the Confederacy had been guilty of felonies and capital offences. It was announced that General Hunter had armed slaves for the murder of their masters, and had thus done all in his power to inaugurate a servile war. He had boasted in June that he hoped to organize before winter "from 48,000 to 50,000 of these hardy and devoted soldiers." General Phelps had imitated at New Orleans the example of Hunter in South Carolina. General G. N. Fitch was stated, in the public journals, to have murdered in cold blood two peaceful citizens, because one of his men, while invading our country, was killed by some unknown person while defending his home.

General Lee was directed by me to say that if a reply was not received in fifteen days, it would be assumed that the alleged facts were true, and that on the United States Government would rest the responsibility of retaliatory measures. General Halleck declined to receive the papers because "couched in language insulting to the Government of the United States."

On August, 20, 1862, I issued an order threatening retaliation for the lives of peaceful citizens reported to have been executed by General Fitch. The report was subsequently found to be untrue, and on the next day I issued another order, which, after reciting the principal facts, directed that Generals Hunter and Phelps should be treated no longer as public enemies, but as outlaws, and that in the event of the capture of either of them, or of any other commissioned officer employed in drilling, organizing, or instructing slaves, with a view to their armed service in the war, he should not be regarded as a prisoner of war, but should be held in close confinement for execution as a felon, at such time and place as might be ordered.

In the case of Mumford a letter dated August 7, 1862, was received from General Halleck stating that "no authentic information had been received in relation to" his execution, "but measures will be immediately taken to ascertain the facts." Subsequently, on November 25, 1862, our Commissioner of Exchange notified the Federal agent that if no answer was received within fifteen days it would be considered that an answer was declined. No answer was received at the expiration of the limit thus indicated. Besides, I had received evidence that said Mumford was publicly executed in cold blood, by hanging, after the occupation of New Orleans by the forces under General Butler, and for no offence ever alleged to have been committed subsequent to the occupation of the city.

It appeared that the silence of the Federal Government, and its maintenance of Butler in high office under its authority, afforded evidence too conclusive that it sanctioned his conduct, and was determined that he should remain unpunished for these crimes.

I therefore pronounced and declared the said Butler a felon, deserving capital punishment, and ordered that he be no longer considered as a public enemy of the Confederate States, but as an outlaw and common enemy of mankind, and that, in the event of his capture, the officer in command should cause him to be immediately executed by hanging.

These measures of retaliation were in conformity with the usages of war, and were adopted to punish and check the cruelties of our adversary.

At length so many difficulties were raised, and so many complaints made, in the execution of the cartel, that, for the sake of the unfortunate prisoners, I resolved to seek an adjustment through the authorities of Washington.

Chapter 98

Mission of Vice-President Stephens

VICE-PRESIDENT ALEXANDER H. STEPHENS, of Georgia, offered his services as Commissioner.

He was furnished with two letters of authority, identical in terms, but the first signed by me as Commander-in-Chief of the land and naval forces of the Confederate States, and addressed to Abraham Lincoln as Commander-in-Chief of the land and naval forces of the United States, and the duplicate addressed to him as President and signed by me as President. In Mr. Stephens's letter of instructions I stated:

> "You will perceive from the terms of the letter (of authority) that it is so worded as to avoid any political difficulties in its reception. Intended exclusively as one of those communications between belligerents which public law recognizes as necessary and proper between hostile forces, care has been taken to afford no pretext for refusing to receive it on the ground that it would involve a tacit recognition of the independence of the Confederacy. Your mission is simply one of humanity, and has no political aspect.
>
> "If objection is made to receiving your letter on the ground that it is not addressed to Abraham Lincoln as President, instead of Commander-in-Chief, etc., then you will present the duplicate addressed to him as President and signed by me as President. To this latter, objection may be made on the ground that I am not recognized as President of the Confederacy. In this event you will decline any further attempt to confer on the subject of your mission, as such conference is admissible only on the footing of perfect equality."

Mr. Stephens was authorized to arrange and settle all differences and disputes that had arisen, or might arise, in the execution of the cartel for the exchange of prisoners of war; to agree to all just modifications that might be found necessary to prevent future misunderstandings; and finally, to enter into such arrangement about the mode of carrying on hostilities as should confine the severities of the war within such limits as are rightfully imposed not only by modern civilization, but by our common Christianity.

On July 3, 1863, Mr. Stephens proceeded to Newport News, where his progress was arrested by the orders of the Admiral of the enemy's fleet. The object of Mr. Stephens's mission, with a request for permission to go to Washington, was communicated to the Government there, and the reply transmitted by telegraph was:

> "The request is inadmissible. The customary agents and channels are adequate for all needful military communication and conference between the United States forces and the insurgents."

This was all the notice ever taken of our humane proposition. The door was shut in our faces.

From the date of the cartel, July 22, 1862, until the summer of 1863 we had an excess of prisoners. During the interval the deliveries were made as fast as the enemy furnished transportation. On more than one occasion he was urged to send increased means of transportation. When he had the excess we never failed or neglected to make prompt deliveries of prisoners who were not held under charges.

On the other hand, the cartel was openly and notoriously violated by the Washington authorities. Officers and men were kept in confinement, sometimes in irons or doomed to cells, without charge or trial. Many officers were kept in confinement even after the notices published by the enemy had declared them to be exchanged.

In the summer of 1863 the Federal authorities insisted upon limiting the exchanges to such as were held in confinement on either side. This was resisted as in violation of the cartel. Such a construction kept in confinement the excess on either side, but ignored all paroles held by the Confederate Government. These were very many, being the paroles of officers and men who had been released on capture. The Federal Government at that time held no or few paroles. All, or nearly all, had been surrendered. We gave prisoners as equivalents for them. As long as we had the excess of prisoners matters went on smoothly enough; but as soon as the position of affairs in that respect was reversed, the cartel would no longer be observed by the Federal Government. So long as that Government held the paroles of Confederate officers and men, they were respected and made the basis of exchange; but when equivalents were obtained for them, and no more were in hand, they would not recognize the paroles which were held by us.

In consequence of the position thus assumed by the Government of the United States, the requirement of the cartel, that all prisoners should be delivered within ten days, was practically nullified. The deliveries which were afterward made were the results of special agreements.

Chapter 99

War Prisons, Northern and Southern

THE wish of the Confederate Government was the prompt release of all prisoners on both sides, either by exchange, or parole. When, in 1864, the cartel was so disregarded by the enemy as to indicate that prisoners would be held in long confinement, Andersonville, Ga., was selected for the location of a principal prison. General Howell Cobb employed a large number of negro laborers in the construction of a temporary shelter for the number of prisoners it was expected would be assembled there. The number, however, rapidly increased, and by the middle of May gangrene and scurvy made their appearance. General John H. Winder went to Andersonville in June, and found disease prevailing to such an extent that he immediately advised the removal of prisoners to other points. In September, with the main body of the prisoners, he removed first to Millen, Ga., and then to Florence, S. C.

Major Wirz thereafter remained in command at Andersonville. This unfortunate man—who, under the severe temptation to which he was exposed before his execution, exhibited honor and fidelity strongly in contrast with his tempters and persecutors—it now appears, was the victim of men whom, in his kindness, he paroled to take care of their sick comrades, and who, after having violated their parole, appeared to testify against him.

In like manner has calumny pursued the memory of General Winder, a man too brave to be cruel to anything in his power. Adjutant-General Samuel Cooper, a man as pure in heart as sound in judgment, in a letter of July 9, 1871, wrote that "General Winder was an honest, upright, and humane gentleman. He had the reputation, in the Confederacy, of treating the prisoners confided to his supervision with great kindness and consideration."

In order to alleviate the hardships of confinement on both sides, our Commissioner, on January 24, 1863, addressed a communication to General E. A. Hitchcock, United States Commissioner of Exchange, in which he proposed that all prisoners on each side should be attended by a proper number of their own surgeons, who should be permitted to take charge of their health and comfort. These surgeons were also to act as commissaries, receiving and distributing such food, clothing, money, and medicines as might be forwarded to them. They were to be selected by their own Government, with full liberty to make reports of their own acts and any matters relating to the welfare of the prisoners. No reply was received. In a communication published August, 1868, Commissioner Ould says:

> "About the last of March, 1864, I had several conferences with General B. F. Butler, and we reached what we both thought a tolerably satisfactory basis. The day I left there General Grant arrived. General Butler says he communicated to him the state of the negotiations, and 'most emphatic verbal directions were received from the Lieutenant-General not to take any step by which another able-bodied man should be exchanged until further orders from him;' and that on April 30, 1864, he received a telegram from General Grant 'to receive all the sick and wounded the Confederate authorities may send you, but send no more in exchange.'"

On October 1st, when the number of prisoners was large on both sides, General Lee addressed a note to General Grant, saying:

> "With a view of alleviating the sufferings of our soldiers, I have the honor to propose an exchange of the prisoners of war belonging to the armies operating in Virginia, man for man, or upon the basis established by the cartel."

On the next day General Grant replied:

> "I could not of right accept your proposition further than to exchange prisoners captured within the last three days, and who have not yet been delivered to the commanding General of prisoners. Among those lost by the armies operating against Richmond were a number of colored troops. Before further

negotiations are had upon the subject, I would ask if you propose delivering these men the same as white soldiers."

General Lee said in rejoinder:

"Deserters from our service and negroes belonging to our citizens are not considered subjects of exchange."

On October 20th General Grant finally answered:

"I regard it my duty to protect all persons received into the army of the United States, regardless of color or nationality; when acknowledged soldiers of the Government are captured, they must be treated as prisoners of war, or such treatment as they receive inflicted upon an equal number of prisoners held by us."

In a despatch from General Grant to General Butler, August 18, 1864, the former had said:

"It is hard on our men held in Southern prisons not to exchange them, but it is humanity to those left in the ranks to fight our battles. At this particular time to release all rebel prisoners North would insure Sherman's defeat, and would compromise our safety here."

We then proposed to the Government of the United States to exchange prisoners, officer for officer, and man for man. We had previously declined this proposal, and insisted on the terms of the cartel, which required the delivery of the excess on either side on parole. No answer being received to this proposal a communication was sent, August 22, 1864, to Major-General Hitchcock, United States Commissioner of Exchange, containing the same proposal. No answer was received to either of these letters.

Thus having ascertained that exchanges could not be made, we offered the United States their sick and wounded without any equivalents. Although the offer was made in the summer, the transportation did not arrive till November. Why was there this delay in sending vessels for the transportation of sick and wounded, for whom no equivalents were asked? Were Federal prisoners left to suffer, and afterward photographed as specimen prisoners, "to aid in firing the popular heart of the North"?

One final effort was now made to obtain an exchange. This consisted in my sending a delegation from the prisoners at Andersonville to plead their cause at Washington. It was of no avail. President Lincoln refused to see them. They carried back the sad tidings that their Government held out no hope of their release.

The following extracts are from the official report of Major-General Butler to "the Committee on the Conduct of the War:"

> "General Grant visited Fortress Monroe on April 1st (1864). To him the state of the negotiations as to exchange[120] was verbally communicated, and most emphatic directions were received from the Lieutenant-General not to take any step by which another able-bodied man should be exchanged, until further orders from him.
>
> "After conversation with General Grant, in reply to the proposition of Mr. Ould to exchange all prisoners of war on either side held, man for man, officer for officer, I wrote an argument showing our right to our colored soldiers. This argument set forth our claims in the most offensive form possible, consistently with ordinary courtesy of language, for the purpose of carrying out the wishes of the Lieutenant-General that no prisoners of war should be exchanged."

The report continues:

> "In case the Confederate authorities should yield to the argument, and formally notify me that their former slaves captured in our uniform would be exchanged as other soldiers were, and that they were ready to return us all our prisoners at Andersonville and elsewhere in exchange for theirs, then I had determined, with the consent of the Lieutenant-General, as a last resort to prevent exchange, to demand that the outlawry against me should be formally reversed and apologized for, before I would further negotiate the exchange of prisoners. But the argument was enough, and the Confederates never offered to me afterward to exchange the colored soldiers who had been slaves, held in prison by them."

---

120. "The negotiations to which General Butler refers were the points of agreement between General Butler and myself, under which exchanges of all white and free black soldiers, man for man and officer for officer, were to go on, leaving the question as to slaves to be disposed of by subsequent arrangement" (Letter of Mr. Ould, June, 1879).

The conclusion of the report is as follows:

> "The great importance of the questions; the fearful responsibility for the many thousands of lives which, by the refusal to exchange, were sacrificed by the most cruel forms of death, from cold, starvation, and pestilence of the prison-pens of Raleigh and Andersonville . . . have compelled me to this exposition, so that it may be seen that those lives were spent as a part of the system of attack upon the rebellion, devised by the wisdom of the General-in-Chief of the armies, to destroy it by depletion, depending upon our superior numbers to win the victory at last."

Sufficient facts have been presented to satisfy every intelligent and candid mind of our entire readiness to surrender, for exchange, all the prisoners in our possession, whenever the Government of the United States would honestly meet us for that purpose.

During all this time Northern prisons were full of our brave soldiers, of whom there were about 60,000. The privations they suffered, the cruelties, inspired by the malignant spirit of the Government, which were inflicted upon them, surpass any records of modern history; yet we have had no occasion to seek out a Wirz for public trial before an illegal court, that we might conceal behind him our own neglect and cruel sacrifice of them. Finally, to the allegations of ill-treatment of prisoners on our side, and humanity on that of our opponents, it is only necessary to offer two facts. First, the report of the Secretary of War, E. M. Stanton, made July 19, 1866, shows that of all the prisoners in our hands during the war only 22,576 died; while, of the prisoners in our opponents' hands, 26,246 died. Second, in round numbers, the number of Confederate prisoners on their hands amounted to 220,000; the number of United States prisoners in our hands amounted to 270,000. Thus, more than twelve per cent of the prisoners in our opponents' hands died, and less than nine per cent of the prisoners in our hands died.

CHAPTER 100

ABORTIVE NEGOTIATIONS

THAT the purpose of the Government of the United States was to subjugate the Southern States and the Southern people, under the pretext of a restoration of the Union, is established by the terms and conditions offered us in all the conferences relating to a settlement of differences. Several efforts were made by us to communicate with the authorities at Washington without success. Commissioners were sent before hostilities were begun, but the Government of the United States refused to receive them. A second time I sent a military officer with a communication addressed by myself to President Lincoln. The letter was received by General Scott, who did not permit the officer to see Mr. Lincoln. No answer was ever received. Vice-President Stephens made a tender of his services, and although little belief was entertained of his success, I cheerfully yielded to his suggestion that the experiment be tried. He was stopped before he reached Fortress Monroe.

If we would break up our Government, dissolve the Confederacy, disband our armies, emancipate the slaves, and take an oath of allegiance to it, the Government of the United States would pardon us, and not deprive us of anything more than the property already stolen from us, and such slaves as still remained.

The next movement relating to the accommodation of differences occurred in July, 1864, and consisted in the appearance at Richmond of Colonel James F. Jacques, of the Seventy-eighth Illinois Infantry, and James R. Gilmore, of Massachusetts, soliciting an interview with me. They had crossed our lines through a letter of General Grant to Colonel Ould. Colonel Jacques expressed the ardent desire he felt, in common with the men of their army, for a restoration of peace. Mr. Gilmore conveyed the information that the two gentlemen had come to Richmond impressed with the idea that the Confederate Government would accept peace on the basis of the reconstruction of the Union, the abolition of slavery, and the grant of an amnesty to the people of the Confederate States as repentant criminals. The abolition of slavery was to be accomplished, and all other disputed questions were to be settled, by a general vote of all the people of both federations. These were stated to be Mr. Lincoln's views. I answered that, as the people of the North were a majority, this offer was, in effect, a proposal that the Confederate States should surrender at discretion, and that Mr. Lincoln ought to have known that it was out of the power of the Confederate Government to act upon the subject of the domestic institutions of the several States. Having no disposition to discuss questions of state with such persons, especially as they bore no credentials, I terminated the interview.

The opening of the spring campaign of 1864 was deemed a favorable conjuncture for the employment of diplomacy. Political developments at the North favored the adoption of some action by us that might influence popular sentiment in the hostile section. A commission of three persons was accordingly appointed to visit Canada, with a view to negotiation with such persons in the North as might be relied upon to aid in the attainment of peace. The commissioners—Messrs. Clay, of Alabama; Holcombe, of Virginia; and Thompson, of Mississippi—established themselves at Niagara Falls, and on the 12th of July commenced a correspondence with Horace Greeley. Mr. Lincoln at first appeared to favor an interview, but finally refused, on the ground that the commissioners were not authorized to treat for peace. Hence this movement, like all others which had preceded it, was a failure.

On December 30, 1864, I received a request from Mr. Francis P. Blair, of Maryland, for permission to visit Richmond for certain personal objects, which was granted. On January 12, 1865, he visited me. In explanation of his position he stated that he, being a man of Southern blood, felt very desirous to see the war terminated, and hoped by an interview with me to effect something to that end. He was without credentials or any instructions from Mr. Lincoln which would enable him to speak for him. He read portions of a rough draft of a letter he had prepared to send me, in the event of his not being able to obtain a personal interview. When he had finished, I inquired as to his main proposition, the cessation of hostilities and the union of the military forces for the common purpose of maintaining the "Monroe doctrine"—how that object was to be reached. He said that both political parties asserted the "Monroe doctrine" as a cardinal point in their creed, and that there was a general desire to apply it in the case of Mexico. For that purpose a secret treaty might be made, etc. I called his attention to my past efforts for negotiation, and my inability to see how we were to take the first step. He expressed the belief that Mr. Lincoln would now receive commissioners, though he could not give any assurance on that point. For himself he avowed an earnest desire to stop the further effusion of blood. He expressed the hope that the pride, the power, and the honor of the Southern States should suffer no shock; and reiterated the idea of State sovereignty. He admitted the necessity of a new channel for the bitter waters, and another bond than that of former memories and interests. This was supposed to be contained in the proposed common effort to maintain the "Monroe doctrine" on the American continent. The only difficulty which he spoke of as insurmountable was that of existing engagements between European powers and the Confederate States.

This was met by me with a statement that we had now no such complication, and were free to act as to us should seem best. Our conference ended with no other result than an agreement that he would learn whether Mr. Lincoln would adopt his (Mr. Blair's) project, and send or receive commissioners to negotiate for a peaceful solution of the questions at issue, and that he would report to him my readiness to enter upon negotiations.

The following letter was given by me to Mr. Blair:

> "F. P. Blair, Esq., Sir: I have no disposition to find obstacles in forms, and am willing now, as heretofore, to enter into negotiations for the restoration of peace, and ready to send a commission whenever I have reason to suppose it will be received, or to receive a commission if the United States Government shall choose to send one. That, notwithstanding the rejection of our former offers, I would, if you could promise that a commissioner, minister, or other agent would be received, appoint one immediately, and renew the effort to enter into conference with a view to secure peace to the two countries. Yours, etc., Jefferson Davis."

> "F. P. Blair, Esq., Sir: You having shown me Mr. Davis's letter to

you of the 12th instant, you may say to him that I have constantly been, am now, and shall continue ready to receive any agent whom he or any other influential person now resisting the national authority may informally send to me with the view of securing peace to the people of our one common country. Yours, etc., A. Lincoln."

When Mr. Blair returned and gave me this letter of Mr. Lincoln, of January 18th, he said it had been a fortunate thing that I gave him that note, as it had created greater confidence in Mr. Lincoln regarding his efforts at Richmond. Further reflection, he said, had modified the views he formerly presented to me. He then unfolded to me the embarrassment of Mr. Lincoln on account of the extreme men in Congress and elsewhere, who wished to drive him into harsher measures than he was inclined to adopt; whence it would not be feasible for him to enter into any arrangement with us by the use of political agencies. He therefore, suggested that Generals Lee and Grant might enter into an arrangement by which hostilities would be suspended, and a way paved for the restoration of peace. I responded that I would willingly intrust to General Lee such negotiation. Mr. Blair subsequently informed me that the idea of a military convention was not favorably received at Washington, so it only remained for me to act upon the letter of Mr. Lincoln.

I determined to send, as commissioners for the informal conference, Messrs. Alexander H. Stephens, R. M. T. Hunter, and John A. Campbell. A letter of commission for each was prepared by the Secretary of State. Despite Mr. Lincoln's letter expressing a willingness to receive any agent I might send to Washington, the commissioners were not allowed to proceed farther than Hampton Roads, where Mr. Lincoln, accompanied by Mr. Seward, met them. Why Mr. Lincoln changed his purpose, and, instead of receiving the commissioners at Washington, met them at Hampton Roads, I cannot, of course, explain. I think the views of Mr. Lincoln had changed after he wrote the letter to Mr. Blair of Jan. 18th, and that the change was mainly produced by the report which Mr. Blair made of what he saw and heard at Richmond on the night he stayed there. Mr. Blair had many acquaintances among the members of the Confederate Congress; and all those of the class who of old fled to the cave of Adullam "gathered themselves unto him." That

Mr. Blair saw and noted a serious inclining of many of his old friends and associates to thoughts of peace, scarcely admits of a doubt; and if he believed the Congress to be infected by a cabal undermining the Executive in his efforts successfully to prosecute the war, Mr. Lincoln may be naturally supposed thence to have reached the conclusion that he should accept nothing but an unconditional surrender.

The report of the commissioners, dated February 5, 1865 (condensed), was as follows:

> "The conference took place on the 30th ult., on board a steamer anchored in Hampton Roads, where we met President Lincoln and the Hon. Mr. Seward, Secretary of State of the United States. We understood from President Lincoln that no terms or proposals of any treaty or agreement, looking to an ultimate settlement, would be entertained or made by him with the authorities of the Confederate States, because that would be a recognition of their existence as a separate power, which under no circumstances would be done; and, for a like reason, that no such terms would be entertained by him for the States separately; that no extended truce or armistice would be granted without a satisfactory assurance in advance of the complete restoration of the authority of the Constitution and laws of the United States over all places within the States of the Confederacy; that whatever consequences may follow from the re-establishment of that authority must be accepted; but that individuals subject to pains and penalties under the laws of the United States might rely upon a very liberal use of the power confided to him to remit those pains and penalties if peace be restored. The proposed amendment to the Constitution of the United States, adopted by Congress on the 31st ultimo, was brought to our notice. This amendment provides that neither slavery nor involuntary servitude, except for crime, should exist within the United States or any place within their jurisdiction. Very respectfully, etc., Alexander H. Stephens, R. M. T. Hunter, John A. Campbell."

This closed the conference and all negotiations with the Government of the United States for the establishment of peace.

On March 4, 1861, President Lincoln appeared on the western portico of the Capitol at Washington, and in the presence of a great multitude of witnesses took the following oath:

> "I do solemnly swear that I will faithfully execute the office of President of the United States, and will, to the best of my ability, preserve, protect, and defend the Constitution of the United States."

The first section of the fourth article of the Constitution of the United States is in these words:

> "No person held to service or labor in one State, under the laws thereof, escaping into another, shall, in consequence of any law or regulation therein, be discharged from such service or labor, but shall be delivered up on claim of the party to whom such service or labor may be due."

Thus the Constitution itself nullified Mr. Lincoln's emancipation proclamation, and made it of no force whatever. Yet he assumed and maintained, with all the military force he could command, that it set every slave free. The Constitution says:

> "This Constitution, and the laws of the United States which shall be made in pursuance thereof, shall be the supreme law of the land."

Was it thus obeyed by Mr. Lincoln as the supreme law of the land? It was not obeyed, but set aside, subverted, and overturned by him. Of what value, then, are paper constitutions, and oaths binding officers to their preservation, if there is not intelligence enough in the people to discern the violations, and virtue enough to resist the violators?

The Constitution of the United States says, in Article X:

> "The powers not delegated to the United States by the Constitution, nor prohibited by it to the States, are reserved to the States respectively, or to the people."

Within the purview of this article the States are independent, distinct, and separate bodies—that is, in their reserved powers they are as sovereign, separate, and supreme as the Government of the United States is in its delegated powers. One of these reserved powers is the right of the people to alter or abolish any form of government, and to institute a new one such as to them shall seem most likely to effect their safety and happiness; that power is neither "delegated to the United

States by the Constitution nor prohibited by it to the States." No one will venture to say that a sovereign State, by the mere act of accession to the Constitution, delegated the power of secession. The assertion would be of no validity if it were made; for the question is one of fact as to the powers delegated or not delegated to the United States by the Constitution.

The Convention of the State of New York, which ratified the Constitution of the United States on July 26, 1788, in its resolution of ratification, said:

> "We do declare and make, known that the powers of the Government may be reassumed by the people, whensoever it shall become necessary to their happiness; that every power, jurisdiction, and right, which is not by the said Constitution clearly delegated to the Congress of the United States, or to the departments of the Government thereof, remains to the people of the several States, or to their respective State governments."

The resolution of Rhode Island asserts the same reservation in regard to the reassumption of powers.

When Mr. Lincoln issued his proclamation calling for seventy-five thousand men to subjugate certain "combinations too powerful to be suppressed by the ordinary course of judicial proceedings," he not only thereby denied the validity of the Constitution, but sought to resist, by military force, the exercise of a power clearly reserved in the Constitution, and reaffirmed in its Tenth Amendment, to the States respectively, or to the people for their exercise. Thus any recognition of the Confederate States, or either of them, in his negotiations, would have exposed the groundlessness of his fiction. But the Constitution required him to recognize each of them, for they had simply exercised a power which it expressly reserved for their exercise.

It has been stated that the conditions offered to our soldiers, whenever they proposed to capitulate, were only those of subjugation. When General Buckner, on February 16, 1862, asked of General Grant to appoint commissioners to agree upon terms of capitulation, he replied:

> "No terms, except unconditional and immediate surrender, can be accepted."

When General Lee asked the same question, April 9, 1865, General Grant replied:

> "The terms upon which peace can be had are well understood. By the South laying down their arms, they will hasten that most desirable event, save thousands of human lives and hundreds of millions of property, not yet destroyed."

General Sherman wrote to General Johnston:

> "I demand the surrender of your army on the same terms as were given to General Lee at Appomattox, on April 9th, purely and simply."

The Government which spurned all these proposals for peace, and gave no terms but unconditional surrender, was instituted and organized for the objects expressed in the following extract:

> "We, the people of the United States, in order to form a more perfect union, establish justice, insure domestic tranquillity, provide for the common defence, promote the general welfare, and secure the blessings of liberty to ourselves and our posterity, do ordain and establish this Constitution for the United States of America."

Chapter 101

Sherman's March Northward

AFTER the evacuation of Savannah, it soon became known that Sherman was making preparations to march northward through the Carolinas, with the supposed purpose of uniting his forces with those of Grant before Richmond.

Sherman lest Savannah January 22, 1865, and reached Pocotaligo on the 24th. On February 3rd he crossed the Salkekatchie with slight resistance, and thence pushed forward to the South Carolina Railroad at Midway, Bamberg, and Graham's. After thoroughly destroying the railroad between these places, which occupied three or four days, he advanced slowly along the line of the railroad, threatening Branchville, the junction of the railroads from Augusta to Columbia and Charleston. For a short time it was doubtful whether he proposed to attack Augusta, Ga., where we had our principal powder-mill, many important factories and shops, and large stores of army supplies; but on the 11th it was found that he was moving north to Orangeburg, on the road from Branchville to Columbia, the latter city being the objective point of his march. Early on the morning of the 16th the head of his columns reached the Congaree, opposite Columbia. The bridge over that stream had been burned by our retreating troops, but a pontoon-bridge, built by the enemy under cover of strong detachments who had crossed higher up at Saluda Factory, enabled the main body to pass the river and enter the city on the morning of the 17th, the Confederate troops having previously evacuated it. On the same day the Mayor formally surrendered the city to Colonel Stone, commanding a brigade of the Fifteenth Corps, and claimed for its citizens the protection which the laws of civilized war always accord to non-combatants. In infamous disregard not only of the established rules of war, but of the common dictates of humanity, the defenceless city was burned to the ground, after the dwelling-houses had been robbed of everything of value, and their helpless inmates subjected to insult and outrage of a character too base to be described.

General Sherman has endeavored to escape the reproaches for the burning of Columbia by attributing it to General Hampton's order to burn the cotton in the city, that it might not fall into the hands of the enemy. General Hampton has proved circumstantially that General Sherman's statement is untrue, and hundreds of unimpeachable witnesses have testified that the burning of Columbia was the deliberate act of the Federal soldiery, and that it was certainly permitted, if not ordered, by the commanding General.

In order that General Hardee's command might become available in the field, it was now deemed advisable to evacuate Charleston, and thus that noble city and its fortresses, which the combined military and naval forces of the United States during an eighteen months' siege had failed to reduce, were, on February 21, 1865, without resistance, occupied by the Federal forces under General Gillmore.

Fort Sumter, though it now presented the appearance of a ruin, was really better proof against bombardment than when first subjected to fire. The upper tier of masonry, from severe battering, had fallen on the outer wall, and shell only served to solidify and add harder material to the mass. Over its rampart the Confederate flag defiantly floated until the city of Charleston was evacuated.

Every effort that our circumstances permitted was immediately made to collect troops for the defence of North Carolina. Hood's army, the troops of General D. H. Hill at Augusta, Hardee's force, a few thousand men under Bragg, and the cavalry commands of Hampton and Wheeler constituted our entire available strength to oppose Sherman's advance. They were collected as rapidly as our broken communications and the difficulty of gathering and transporting supplies would permit.

General J. E Johnston was assigned to the command of the troops in North Carolina, under the supervision and control of General R. E. Lee. He relieved Beauregard and assumed command at Charlotte, February 23rd. The force of which he now had the command amounted to about 30,500 men of all arms.

General Lee's first instructions to him were to "concentrate all available forces and drive back Sherman." The first part of the instructions was well executed, the last part of it was more desirable than practicable.

After leaving Columbia, the course of Sherman's army through Winnsboro, across the Catawba at Rocky Mount, Hanging Rock, and Peay's Ferry, indicated that he would attempt to cross the Cape Fear River at Fayetteville, N. C. a town sixty miles south of Raleigh, and of special importance as containing an arsenal, several Government shops, and a large portion of the machinery which had been removed from Harper's Ferry—and effect a junction at that point with Schofield's command, then at Wilmington.

The advance of the enemy's columns across the Catawba, Lynch's Creek, and the Pedee, though retarded as much as possible by our cavalry, under Hampton, Butler, and Wheeler, was steady and continuous. Johnston's hope that he might find an opportunity to strike one of Sherman's columns when the other was not in supporting distance, was unhappily disappointed.

On March 6th, near Kinston, General Bragg, with a reinforcement of less than 2,000 men, attacked and routed three divisions of the enemy under Cox, capturing 1,500 prisoners and 3 field-pieces, and inflicting heavy loss in killed and wounded. During the march from the Catawba to the Cape Fear River, several brilliant cavalry affairs took place, in which our troops displayed their wonted energy and dash.

As it was not known whether Sherman would march to Goldsboro or Raleigh, Johnston, with a portion of his command, took position at Smithfield, nearly equidistant from each of these places, leaving Hardee to follow the road from Fayetteville to Raleigh, and posting one division of his cavalry on the Raleigh road, and another on the road to Goldsboro.

On the 16th of March Hardee was attacked by two corps of the enemy at Averysboro, a place nearly half-way between Fayetteville and Raleigh. Falling back a few hundred yards to a stronger position, Hardee easily repelled the repeated attacks of those two corps during the day, and in the night, to check a threatening movement of the enemy, he withdrew toward Smithfield.

On the 18th Johnston obtained definite information that Sherman was marching on Goldsboro, the right wing of his army being about a day's march distant from the left. Johnston took immediate steps to attack the head of the left wing on the morning of the 19th, and ordered the troops at Smithfield and Hardee's command to march at once to Bentonville and take position between that village and the road on which the enemy was advancing. An error in the estimate as to the relative distances caused the failure to concentrate our troops in time to attack the enemy's left wing while in column; but when General Hardee's troops reached Bentonville in the morning, the attack was commenced. The battle lasted through the greater part of the day, resulting in the enemy's being driven from two lines of intrenchments, and his taking shelter in a dense wood, where it was impracticable for our troops to preserve their line of battle or to employ the combined strength of the three arms.

On the 20th the two wings of the Federal army, numbering upward of 70,000, came together and repeatedly attacked a division of our force (Hoke's) which occupied an intrenched position parallel to the road to Averysboro; but every attack was handsomely repulsed.

On the next day (21st) an attempt by the enemy to reach Bentonville, in the rear of our centre, and thus cut off our only route of retreat, was gallantly defeated by an impetuous and skilful attack, led by Generals Hardee and Hampton, on the front and both flanks of the enemy's column, by which he was compelled to retreat as rapidly as he had advanced. On the night of the 21st our troops were withdrawn across Mill Creek, and in the evening of the 22nd bivouacked near Smithfield. On the 23rd the forces of General Sherman and those of General Schofield were united at Goldsboro, where they remained inactive for upward of two weeks.

Chapter 102

Siege of Petersburg

AFTER the battle of Cold Harbor the geography of the country no longer enabled Grant, by a flank movement to his left, to keep himself covered by a stream, and yet draw nearer to his objective point. He had now reached the Chickahominy; to move down the east bank of that stream would be to depart farther from the prize he sought—Richmond. His overland march had cost him the loss of more men than Lee's army contained at the beginning of the campaign. He now decided to seek a new base on the James River, and to attempt the capture of our capital by a movement from the south. With this view, on the night of June 12, 1864, he commenced a movement by the lower crossings of the Chickahominy toward the James River. Lee learned of the withdrawal on the next morning, and moved to our pontoon-bridge above Drury's Bluff.

While Grant's army was making this march to James River, General Smith, with his division, which had arrived at Bermuda Hundred, was, on the night of the 14th, directed to move against Petersburg, with an additional force of two divisions, it being supposed that this column would be sufficient to effect what Butler's previous attempts had utterly failed to accomplish—the capture of Petersburg and the destruction of the Southern Railroad. On the morning of the 15th the attack was made, the exterior redoubts and rifle-pits were carried, and the column advanced toward the inner works, but the artillery was used so effectively as to impress the commander of the assailants with the idea that there must be a large supporting force of infantry, and the attack was suspended so as to allow the columns in rear to come up.

Hancock's corps was on the south side of the James River before the attack on Petersburg commenced, and was ordered to move forward, but not informed that an attack was to be made, nor directed to march to Petersburg until late in the afternoon, when he received orders to move to the aid of General Smith. It being night when the junction was made, it was deemed prudent to wait until morning. Had they known how feeble was the garrison, it is probable that Petersburg would have been captured that night; but with the morning came another change, as marked as that from darkness to light. Lee crossed the James River on the 15th, and by a night march his advance was in the intrenchments of Petersburg before the morning for which the enemy was waiting. The artillery now had other support than the old men and boys of the town.

The Confederates promptly seized the commanding points and rapidly strengthened their lines, so that the morning's reconnaissance indicated to the enemy the propriety of postponing an attack until all his force should arrive.

On the 17th an assault was made with such spirit and force as to gain a part of our line. The assailants suffered severely. Lee had constructed a line in rear of the one first occupied, having such advantages as gave to our army much greater power to resist. On the morning of the 18th Grant ordered a general assault, but finding that the former line had been evacuated, and that a new one on more commanding ground had been constructed, the assault was postponed until the afternoon; then attacks were made by heavy columns on various parts of our line, with some partial success; but the final result was failure everywhere, and with extraordinary sacrifice of life.

With his usual persistence, he had made attack after attack, and for the resulting carnage had no gain to compensate. The eagerness manifested leads to the supposition that it was expected to capture the place while Lee with part of his force was guarding against an advance on Richmond by the river road. The four days' experience seems to have convinced Grant of the impolicy of assault, for thereafter he commenced to lay siege to the place. On the 21st a heavy force of the enemy was advanced more to our right, in the vicinity of the Weldon Railroad, which runs southward from Petersburg. But General Lee, observing an interval between the left of the Second and right of the Sixth of the enemy's corps, sent forward a column under Gen. A. P. Hill, which, entering the interval, poured a fire into the flank of one corps on the right and the other on the left, doubling their flank divisions up on their centre, and driving them with disorder and with heavy loss. Several entire regiments, a battery, and many standards were captured, when Hill, having checked the advance which was directed against the Weldon Railroad, withdrew with his captures to his former position, bringing with him the guns and nearly 3,000 prisoners.

On the same night, a cavalry expedition, consisting of the divisions of Generals Wilson and Kautz, numbering about 6,000 men, was sent west to cut the Weldon, Southside, and Danville Railroads, which connected our army with the south and west. This raid resulted in important injury to our communications. The enemy's cavalry tore up large distances of the tracks of all three of the railroads, burning the woodwork and laying waste the country around. But they were pursued and harassed by a small body of cavalry under General W. H. F. Lee, and, on their return near Ream's Station, were met, near Sapponey Church, by a force of 1,500 cavalry under General Hampton. That officer at once attacked. The fighting continued fiercely throughout the night, and at dawn the enemy's cavalry retreated in confusion. Near Ream's Station, at which point they attempted to cross the Weldon Railroad, they were met by General Fitzhugh Lee's horsemen and a body of infantry under General Mahone, and this force completed their discomfiture. After a brief attempt to force their way, they broke in disorder, leaving behind them twelve pieces of artillery, more than 1,000 prisoners, and many wagons and ambulances. The railroads were soon repaired, and the enemy's cavalry was for the time rendered unfit for service.

.Every attempt made to force Lee's lines having proved unsuccessful, Grant determined upon the method of slow approaches, and proceeded to confront the city with a line of earthworks; and, by gradually extending the line to his left, he hoped to reach out toward the Weldon and Southside Railroads. To obtain possession of these roads now became the special object with him, and all his movements had regard to that end. Petersburg is twenty-two miles south of Richmond, and is connected with the south and west by the Weldon and Southside Railroads, the latter of which crosses the Danville Railroad, the main line of communication between Richmond and the Gulf States. With the enemy once holding these roads and those north of the city, Richmond would be isolated, and it would have been necessary for the Confederate army to evacuate eastern Virginia.

General Grant had crossed a force into Charles City, on the north bank of the James, and thus menaced Richmond with an assault from that quarter. His line extended thence across the neck of the peninsula of Bermuda Hundred, and east and south of Petersburg, where it gradually stretched westward, approaching nearer and nearer to the railroads bringing the supplies for our army and for Richmond. The line of Lee conformed to that of Grant. In addition to the works east and southeast of Richmond, an exterior line of defence had been constructed against the hostile forces at Deep Bottom, and, in addition to a fortification of some strength at Drury's Bluff, obstructions were placed in the river to prevent the ascent of the Federal gunboats. The lines thence continued facing those of the enemy north of the Appomattox, and, crossing that stream, extended around the city of Petersburg, gradually moving westward with the works of the enemy. The struggle that ensued consisted chiefly of attempts to break through our lines. These it is not my purpose to notice seriatim; some of them, however, it is thought necessary to mention.

While, at Petersburg, the assaults of the enemy were met by a resistance sufficient to repel his most vigorous attacks, our force confronting Deep Bottom was known to be so small as to suggest an attempt to capture Richmond by a movement on the north side of the James. On the 26th of July a corps of infantry was sent over to Deep Bottom to move against our pontoon-bridges near Drury's Bluff, so as to prevent Lee from sending reinforcements to the north side of the James, while Sheridan with his cavalry moved to the north side of Richmond to attack the works which, being poorly garrisoned, it was thought might be taken by assault. Lee, discovering the movement after the enemy had gained some partial success, sent over reinforcements, which drove him back and defeated the expedition. On the night of the 28th the infantry corps (Hancock's) was secretly withdrawn from the north side of the river, to co-operate in the grand assault which Grant was preparing to make upon Lee's intrenchments. The uniform failure of the assaults upon our lines had caused the conclusion that they could only succeed after a breach had been made in the works. For that purpose a subterranean gallery for a mine was run under one of our forts. General Burnside, who conducted the operation, thus describes the work:

"The main gallery of the mine is five hundred and twenty-two feet in length, the side-galleries about forty feet each. My suggestion is that eight magazines be placed in the lateral galleries, two at each end, say a few feet apart, at right angles to the side gallery, and two more in each of the side-galleries, similarly placed by pairs, situated equidistant from each other and the end of the galleries, thus:

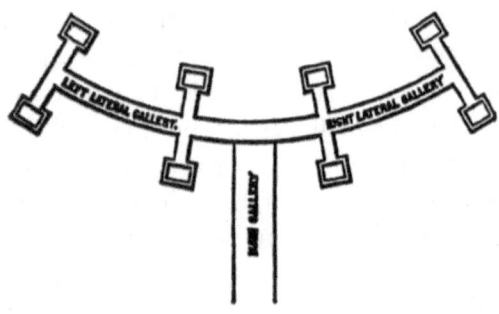

"I proposed to put in each of the eight magazines from twelve to fourteen hundred pounds of powder, the magazines to be connected by a trough of powder instead of a fuse."

It appears that it was decided that the charge should be eight thousand pounds instead of the larger amount proposed.

Between four and five o'clock on the morning of the 30th of July the mine was exploded, and simultaneously the enemy's batteries commenced firing, when, as previously arranged, the column of attack moved forward to the breach, with instructions to rush through it and seize the crest of a ridge in rear of our fort, so as to interpose a force between our troops and in rear of our batteries. A question had arisen as to whether the assaulting column should consist of white or negro troops; there were brigades of each in General Burnside's division, which occupied that part of the line nearest to the mine, and therefore seems to have been considered as the command from which the troops to constitute the storming column must be selected The explosion was destructive to our artillery and its small supporting force immediately above the mine.

An opening, one hundred and fifty feet long, sixty feet wide, and thirty feet deep, suddenly appeared in the place of the earthworks, and the division of the enemy selected for the charge rushed forward to pierce the opening. John Esten Cooke thus describes what ensued:

> "The white division charged, reached the crater, stumbled over the débris, were suddenly met by a merciless fire of artillery enfilading them right and left, and of infantry fusillading them in front; faltered, hesitated, were badly led, lost heart, gave up the plan of seizing the crest in rear, huddled into the crater man on top of man, company mingled with company; and upon this disordered, unstrung, quivering mass of human beings, white and black—for the black troops had followed—was poured a hurricane of shot, shell, canister, musketry, which made the hideous crater a slaughter-pen, horrible and frightful beyond the power of words. All order was lost; all idea of charging the crest abandoned. Lee's infantry was seen concentrating for the carnival of death; his artillery was massing to destroy the remnants of the charging divisions; those who deserted the crater, to scramble over the débris and run back, were shot down; then all that was left to the shuddering mass of blacks and whites in the pit was to shrink lower, evade the horrible *mitraille*, and wait for a charge of their friends to rescue them or surrender."

The forces of the enemy finally succeeded in making their way back, with a loss of about four thousand prisoners, and General Lee, whose casualties were small, re-established his line without interruption.

Attacks continued to be made on our lines during the months of August and September, but they were promptly repulsed. On August 18th the enemy seized on a portion of the Weldon Railroad near Petersburg, and on the 25th this success was followed up by an attempt, under Hancock, to take possession of Ream's Station on the same road, farther south. He was defeated by Heth's division and a portion of Wilcox's, under the direction of A. P. Hill, and, having lost heavily, was compelled to retreat. These events did not materially affect the general result. The enemy's left gradually reached farther and farther westward, until it had passed the Vaughan, Squirrel Level, and other roads running southwestward from Petersburg, and in October was established on the left bank of Hatcher's Run. The movement was designed to reach the Southside Railroad. A heavy column crossed Hatcher's Run, and made an obstinate attack on our lines, in order to break through to the railroad. This column was met in front and flank by Hampton and W. H. F. Lee, with dismounted sharpshooters. Infantry was hastened forward by Lee, and the enemy was driven back. This closed for the winter active operations against our lines at Petersburg.

Chapter 103

Fort Fisher

WHEN the campaign opened on the Rapidan, Lee's effective strength was in round numbers 60,000 of all arms; that of Grant at the same time, 140,000. Although in the many battles fought in this campaign Grant's loss had been a multiple of that sustained by Lee, yet Grant's losses were so rapidly repaired by reinforcements, both before and after he crossed the James River, that the numerical disparity must have been increased. Yet the long-projected movement for the reduction of Fort Fisher and the capture of Wilmington was delayed because of Grant's unwillingness, notwithstanding the great superiority in the number of his force, to detach any troops for that purpose until after active operations before Petersburg had been suspended.

The enemy seems about this time to have conceived a new means of destroying forts. It was to place a large amount of powder in a boat, and, having anchored off the fort, to explode the powder and so destroy the works and incapacitate the garrison as to enable a storming party to capture them. How near to Fort Fisher it was expected to anchor the ship I do not know, nor how far it was supposed the open atmosphere could be made to act as a projectile. General Whiting, who commanded the defences of Wilmington, stated that the powder ship did not come nearer to Fort Fisher than twelve or fifteen hundred yards. No effect was produced by the explosion on the fort.

The combined force of this expedition was 6,500 land troops and 50 vessels of war of various sizes and classes, several ironclads, and the ship charged with 235 tons of powder. Some of the troops landed, but after a reconnaissance of the fort, which then had a garrison of 6,500 men, the troops were re-embarked. Thus the expedition ended.

On January 15, 1863, the attempt was renewed with a larger force, amounting, after the arrival of General Schofield, to twenty-odd thousand, Porter's fleet also received additional vessels, making the whole number 58 engaged in the attack. The garrison of Fort Fisher had been increased to probably more than the number of men there on December 24th. The iron-clad vessels of the enemy approached nearer the fort than on the former occasion, and the fire of the fleet was more concentrated and vastly more effective. Many of the guns in the fort were dismounted, and the parapets seriously injured, by the fire. The garrison stood bravely to their guns, and, when the assault was made, fought with such determined courage as to repulse the first column, and obstinately contended with another approaching from the land side, continuing the fight long after they had got into the fort. Finally, overwhelmed by numbers, and after the fort and its armament had been mainly destroyed by a bombardment—I believe greater than ever before concentrated on a fort—the remnant of the garrison surrendered. The other forts, of necessity, fell with the main work, Fisher, and were abandoned. Hoke, after destroying the public vessels and property, slowly fell back through Wilmington, and finally made a junction with General Johnston.

Chapter 104

Evacuation of Petersburg

THE fixed purpose of Grant's campaign of 1864 was the capture of Richmond. For this he had assembled the large army with which he crossed the Rapidan, and fought the numerous battles between that river and the James. For this he had moved against Petersburg, which was not valuable in itself, but only because it was on the line of communication with the more southern States, and afforded another approach to Richmond.

In the opening of the campaign of 1865 be continued to extend his line to the left, seeking to reach the railroad connecting Petersburg with the Richmond and Danville Railroad. With a well-deserved confidence in his troops, and his usual intrepidity, Lee drew from his lines of defence men enough to enable him for a long time to defeat the enemy in these efforts.

During the months of February and March, Lee's army was materially reduced by the casualties of battle and the frequency of absences without leave. These absentees were not deserters—they did not join the enemy; for the most part they had gone to their necessitous families, with the intention of returning to resume their places in the line of battle. Lee's cavalry force was also diminished by the absence of General Hampton's division, which had received permission to return to South Carolina to get fresh horses and to recruit.

Early in March General Lee, in a full and free conference with me, stated his belief that the evacuation of Petersburg was but a question of time. As one of the expedients for avoiding retreat—a movement to which he was instinctively averse—a short time subsequent to this conversation he submitted the plan of a sortie against the enemy's right. This sortie, if entirely successful, would threaten Grant's line of communication with his base; if only partially successful, it would relieve our right, and delay the impending disaster for a more convenient season for retreat.

Fort Steadman was the point against which the sortie was directed. The distance from our lines was less than two hundred yards, but an abatis covered its front. For this service, requiring equal daring and steadiness, General John B. Gordon was selected. His command was the remnant of Ewell's corps, troops often tried in the fiery ordeal of battle, and always found true.

Before daylight on the morning of the 25th of March, Gordon moved his troops silently forward. His pioneers were sent in advance to make openings through the obstructions, and the troops rushed forward, surprised and captured the garrison, then turned their guns on the adjacent works, and soon drove the enemy out of them. A detachment was now sent to seize the commanding ground and works in the rear, the batteries of which, firing into the gorges of the forts on the right and left, would soon make a wide opening in Grant's line. The guides to this detachment misled it in the darkness of a foggy dawn far from the point to which it was directed. In the meantime the enemy, recovering from his surprise and the confusion into which he had been thrown, rallied and with overwhelming power concentrated both artillery and infantry upon Gordon's command. The supporting force which was to have followed him failed to come forward, and Gordon's brilliant success, like the Dead Sea fruit, was turned to ashes at the moment of possession. Unsupported, it was hopeless to retain the position he had gained. He was compelled to withdraw. In doing so, some of his men were killed and many taken prisoners—all, or nearly all, who had been detached to seize other works.

Immediately after the sortie an extensive attack was made upon our lines on the left of Fort Steadman, but without any decisive results. On the 27th of March the main part of Grant's forces confronting Richmond were moved over to the lines before Petersburg, and on the same day his left was joined by Sheridan's division of cavalry.

On the 31st of March Grant, strengthened by two corps, made a determined movement to gain the right of Lee's position. Before he was ready to make the assault, however, Lee, with a comparatively small force, took the initiative, struck the enemy's advance, and repulsed him in great confusion.

A strategic position of recognized importance was that known as Five Forks. Lee had there stationed General Pickett with his division, and some additional force. On April 1st this position was assaulted, and our troops were driven from it in confusion. The unsettled question of time was now solved.

Grant's massive columns, advancing on the right, left, and centre, compelled our forces to retire to the inner line of defence; so that, on the morning of the 2nd, the enemy was in a condition to besiege Petersburg in the true sense of that term. Battery Gregg made an obstinate defence, and with a garrison of about 250 men held a corps in check for a large part of a day. The arrival of Longstreet's troops, and the strength of the shorter line now held by Lee, enabled him to make several attempts to dislodge his opponent from positions he had gained, in one of which, however, General A. P. Hill was killed.

Retreat was now a present necessity. All that could be done was to hold the inner lines during the day, and make needful preparations to withdraw at night.

Chapter 105

Evacuation of Richmond

ON the forenoon of Sunday, April 2nd, I received when in church a telegram announcing that the army would retire from Petersburg at night. I went to my office to give the needful directions for the evacuation of Richmond, the greatest difficulty of which was the withdrawal of the troops east of the city and along the James River.

The event had come before Lee had expected it. For, while it had been foreseen as a coming event that might possibly, though not probably, be averted, it was not believed to be so near at hand.

At nightfall our army commenced crossing the Appomattox, and before dawn was far on its way to Amelia Court-House, Lee's original purpose being, as agreed on in our conference, to march to Danville, Va. Prevented from carrying out this purpose, he directed his march to Lynchburg.

Lee had never contemplated surrender. He had long before expressed to me the belief that in the mountains of Virginia he could carry on the war for twenty years, and in directing his march toward Lynchburg it may well be that, as an alternative, he hoped to reach those mountains, and, with the advantage which the topography would give him, yet baffle the hosts that were pressing him.

On the evening of the 8th General Lee decided, after conference with his corps commanders, that he would advance the next day beyond Appomattox Court-House, and if the force reported there should prove to be only Sheridan's cavalry, to disperse it and continue the march toward Lynchburg; but if infantry should be found in large force, the attempt to break through it was not to be made, but propositions for an interview with General Grant were to be made to arrange the terms of capitulation.

Gordon, whose corps formed the rear-guard from Petersburg, and who had fought daily for the protection of the trains, had now been transferred to the front. Next morning, before daybreak, General Lee sent a staff officer to learn his opinion as to the chance of a successful attack. Gordon replied that his corps was "reduced to a frazzle," and that, unless he was supported by Longstreet heavily, he did not think we could do anything more. When this answer was reported to Lee he said: "Then there is nothing left me but to go and see General Grant."

As at that time Longstreet, covering the rear, was threatened by Meade with a numerically superior force, it was impossible for him to reinforce Gordon; hence General Lee realized that the emergency had arisen which on the day previous he did not believe existed.

When Colonel Venable, who carried Lee's inquiry to Gordon, left his headquarters to return, the general was forming his line of battle to attack the enemy. Gordon had 5,000 infantry, 1,500 cavalry under Fitzhugh Lee, and a battalion of artillery, with whom he was then preparing to assail the enemy in his front, who were supposed to be Sheridan's cavalry. The assault was made with such vigor and determination as to drive Sheridan a considerable distance; and if he had been the only obstacle the road would have been opened for Lee to resume the march to Lynchburg. But, after Gordon had advanced nearly a mile, he found himself confronted by a body of eighty thousand infantry.

To attack such a force was hopeless. Gordon therefore began to fall back. The enemy advanced as he retreated. Suddenly the pursuing enemy came to a halt.

Lee had sent a flag to Grant, who had thereupon ordered a suspension of hostilities.

Chapter 106

The Surrender at Appomattox

A LEADER less resolute than General Lee, an army less heroically resisting fatigue, constant watching, and starvation, would long since have reached the conclusion that surrender was a necessity. Men and horses all reduced below the standard of efficiency by exposure and insufficient supplies of clothing, food, and forage, only the mutual confidence between the men and their commander could have sustained either under the trials to which they were subjected. It is not a matter of surprise that the army should have wasted away to a mere remnant, but rather that it had continued to exist as an organized body still willing to do battle. All the evidence we have proves that the proud, cheerful spirit both of the army and its leader had resisted the extremes of privation and danger, and never sank until confronted by surrender.

General Grant, in response to a communication under a white flag made by General Lee, came to Appomattox, where a suitable room was provided for their conference; and, the two generals being seated at a small table, General Lee opened the interview thus: "General, I deem it due to proper candor and frankness to say at the very beginning of this interview that I am not willing even to discuss any terms of surrender inconsistent with the honor of my army, which I am determined to maintain to the last."

General Grant replied that he had no idea of proposing dishonorable terms, but he would be glad if General Lee would state what be considered honorable terms.

General Lee then briefly stated the terms upon which he would be willing to surrender. General Grant expressed himself as satisfied with them, and Lee requested that he would formally reduce the propositions to writing.

These propositions were substantially the same as had been stated in General Grant's letter of the 8th. They required

> "The officers to give their individual parole not to take arms against the Government of the United States until properly exchanged, and each company or regimental commander to sign a like parole for the men of their commands.
>
> "The arms, artillery, and public property to be parked and stacked and turned over to the officers appointed by me to receive them.
>
> "This will not embrace the side-arms of the officers, nor their private horses or baggage.
>
> "This done, each officer and man will be allowed to return to their homes, not to be disturbed by the United States authority so long as they observe their parole and the laws in force where they may reside."

General Lee accepted these terms, and the surrender and dispersion of the gallant Army of Northern Virginia was accomplished.

Chapter 107

Evacuation of Richmond

WHEN, on the morning of April 2nd, the main line of the defences of Petersburg was broken, General Lee telegraphed the advice that Richmond should be evacuated that night simultaneously with the withdrawal of his troops. This left little time for preparation, especially in the matter of providing transportation for the troops holding the eastern defences of Richmond. To supply the cavalry, artillery, and army-wagons with horses had so exhausted the stock of Virginia as to leave the quartermaster's department little ability to supplement the small transportation possessed or required by troops regarded as a stationary defence. Hence their withdrawal had to be made under circumstances involving unusual embarrassments on the march; but soldiers, sailors, and citizens, constituting the "reserves," all vied with each other in the performance of the hard duty to which they were called—a night march over unknown roads, pursued by a powerful enemy having large bodies of cavalry.

Overcoming the great obstacles, and not without several conflicts with the enemy, Ewell's corps, G. W. C. Lee's division, and the remainder of the defenders of Richmond withdrew to the different points assigned to them.

On the withdrawal of our troops there was a serious conflagration in Richmond, but neither army was responsible for that calamity.

On Sunday, April 2nd, while I was in St. Paul's church, General Lee's telegram, announcing his speedy withdrawal from Petersburg, and the consequent necessity for evacuating Richmond, was handed to me. I quietly rose and left the church. The occurrence probably attracted attention, but the people of Richmond had been too long beleaguered, had known me too often to receive notice of threatened attacks, and the congregation of St. Paul's was too refined, to make a scene at anticipated danger. I went to my office and assembled the heads of departments and bureaus, as far as they could be found on a day when all the offices were closed, and gave the needful instructions for our removal that night, simultaneously with General Lee's withdrawal from Petersburg. The event was not unforeseen, and some preparation had been made for it, though, as it came sooner than was expected, there was yet much to be done. The executive papers were arranged for removal. This occupied myself and staff until late in the afternoon. By this time the report that Richmond was to be evacuated had spread through the town, and many who saw me walking toward my residence left their houses to inquire whether the report was true.

Upon my admission of the painful fact, qualified, however, by the expression of my hope that we should under better auspices again return, they all, the ladies especially, with generous sympathy and patriotic impulse, responded, "If the success of the cause requires you to give up Richmond, we are content."

The affection and confidence of this noble people in the hour of disaster were more distressing to me than complaint and unjust censure would have been.

In view of the diminishing resources of the country on which the Army of Northern Virginia relied for supplies, I had urged the policy of sending families as far as practicable to the south and west, and had set the example by requiring my own to go. If it was practicable and desirable to hold the south side of the James, then, even for merely material considerations, it was important to hold Richmond, and this could best have been done if there had been none there save those who could aid in its defence. If it was not practicable and desirable to hold the south side of the James, then Richmond would be isolated; and if it could have been defended, its depots, foundries, workshops, and mills could have contributed nothing to the armies outside, and its possession would no longer have been to us of military importance. Ours being a struggle for existence, the indulgence of sentiment would have been misplaced.

Being alone in Richmond, the few arrangements needful for my personal wants were soon made after reaching home. Then, leaving all else in care of the housekeeper, I waited until notified of the time when the train would depart; then, going to the station, started for Danville, whither I supposed General Lee would proceed with his army.

Though the occupation of Danville was not expected to be permanent, immediately after arriving there rooms were obtained, and the different departments resumed their routine labors. Nothing could have exceeded the kindness and hospitality of the patriotic citizens. They cordially gave us an "Old Virginia welcome," and with one heart contributed in every practicable manner to cheer and aid us in the work in which we were engaged.

The town was surrounded by an intrenchment as faulty in location as construction. I promptly proceeded to correct the one and improve the other, while energetic efforts were being made to collect supplies of various kinds for General Lee's army.

The design, as previously arranged with General Lee, was that, if he should be compelled to evacuate Petersburg, he would proceed to Danville, make a new defensive line of the Dan and Roanoke Rivers, unite his army with the troops in North Carolina, and make a combined attack upon Sherman; if successful, it was expected that reviving hope would bring reinforcements to the army, and Grant, being then far removed from his base of supplies, and in the midst of a hostile population, it was thought we might return, drive him from the soil of Virginia, and restore to the people a government deriving its authority from their consent.

While thus employed, little if any reliable information in regard to the Army of Northern Virginia was received, until a son of General Henry A. Wise came to Danville, and told me that, learning Lee's army was to be surrendered, he had during the night mounted his fleet horse, and, escaping through and from the enemy's cavalry, had come quite alone to warn me of the approaching event. Other unofficial information soon followed, and of such circumstantial character as to prove that Lieutenant Wise's anticipation had been realized.

Our scouts now reported a cavalry force to be moving toward the south around the west side of Danville, and we removed thence to Greensboro, passing a railroad-bridge a very short time before the enemy's cavalry reached and burned it. I had telegraphed to General Johnston from Danville the report that Lee had surrendered, and, on arriving at Greensboro, conditionally requested him to meet me there, where General Beauregard at the time had his headquarters, my object being to confer with both of them in regard to our present condition and future operations.

Chapter 108

Surrender of General Johnston

In compliance with my request General Johnston came to Greensboro, N. C., and with General Beauregard met me and most of my Cabinet at my quarters there. Though fully sensible of the gravity of our position, seriously affected as it was by the evacuation of the capital, the surrender of the army of Northern Virginia, and the consequent discouragement which those two events would produce, I did not think that we should despair. We still had effective armies in the field, and a rare extent of rich and productive territory both east and west of the Mississippi, whose citizens had shown no disposition to surrender. Ample supplies had been collected in the railroad depots, and much still remained to be placed at our disposal when needed.

At the first conference of the members of my Cabinet and the generals, in command, General Johnston expressed a desire to open a correspondence with General Sherman with a view to a suspension of hostilities, and thereby permit the civil authorities to enter into the needful arrangements to end the war. I had never contemplated a surrender, except upon such terms as a belligerent might claim, as long as we were able to keep the field, and never expected a Confederate army to surrender while it was able either to fight or to retreat. Lee had surrendered only when it was impossible for him to do either; and in the face of overwhelming numbers had proudly rejected Grant's demand until he found himself surrounded and his line of retreat blocked by a force much larger than his own. I was not at all hopeful of any success in the attempt to provide for negotiations between the civil authorities of the United States and those of the Confederacy, believing that, even if Sherman should agree to such a proposition, his government would not ratify it; but after having distinctly announced my opinion, I yielded to the judgment of my constitutional advisers, and consented to permit Johnston, as he desired, to hold a conference with Sherman,

After this decision, Johnston left for his army headquarters, and I, expecting that he would soon take up his line of retreat, which his superiority in cavalry would protect from harassing pursuit, proceeded with my cabinet and staff to Charlotte, N. C. While on my way a dispatch was received from Johnston stating that Sherman had agreed to a conference, and asking that the Secretary of War, General Breckinridge, should return to co-operate in it.

When we arrived at Charlotte, on April 18, 1865, we received a telegram announcing the assassination of President Lincoln. A vindictive policy was speedily substituted for his, which avowedly was to procure a speedy surrender of our forces in the field upon any terms, and to stop the further effusion of blood.

On the same day Sherman and Johnston united on a memorandum, or basis of agreement, which contained the following provisions:

> "That both of the contending armies should maintain their *status quo* until either of the commanding Generals should give notice of its termination, and allow reasonable time to his opponent.
>
> "That the Confederate armies should be disbanded and conducted to the several State capitals and deposit their arms and public property in the State arsenal; each officer and man to file an agreement to cease from acts of war, and abide the action of both Federal and State authorities.
>
> "That there should be recognition by the Executive of the United States of the several State Governments on their officers and legislatures taking the oaths prescribed by the Constitution of the United States, and, where conflicting State Governments have resulted from the war, the legitimacy of all shall be submitted to the Supreme Court of the United States,
>
> "That all Federal Courts should be re-established in the several States, with powers as defined by the Constitution of the United States and of the States respectively.
>
> "That the people and inhabitants of all States should be guaranteed, so far as the Executive can, their political rights and franchises, as well as their rights of person and property, as defined by the Constitution of the United States and of the States respectively.
>
> "That the Executive authority of the Government of the United States should not disturb any of the people by reason of the

late war, so long as they live in peace and quiet, abstain from acts of armed hostility, and obey the laws.

"That, in general terms, war should cease; a general amnesty, so far as the Executive of the United States could command, on condition of the disbandment of the Confederate armies, the distribution of arms, and resumption of peaceful pursuits by the officers and men hitherto composing said armies. Not being fully empowered by our respective principals to fulfil these terms, we individually and officially pledge ourselves to promptly obtain necessary authority, and to carry out the above programme. W. T. Sherman, Major-General, etc. J. E. Johnston, General, etc."

I notified General Johnston that I approved his action. In doing so I doubted whether the agreement would be ratified by the United States Government. The opinion I entertained in regard to President Johnson and Stanton, his venomous Secretary of War, did not permit me to expect that they would be less vindictive after a surrender of our army had been proposed than when it was regarded as a formidable body defiantly holding its position in the field. Whatever hope others entertained that the war was about to be peacefully ended was soon dispelled by the rejection of the basis of agreement by the Government of the United States, and a notice from Sherman of the termination of the armistice in forty-eight hours after noon of the 24th of April. On the 26th General Johnston again met General Sherman, who offered the same terms which had been made with General Lee. Johnston accepted the terms, and the surrender was made, with the condition of his troops being paroled, and the officers being permitted to retain their side-arms, baggage, and private horses.

The total number of prisoners thus paroled at Greensboro, N. C., as reported by General Schofield, was 36,817; in Georgia and Florida, as reported by General Wilson, 52,543; in all, under General Johnston, 89,360.

On May 8th General Richard Taylor agreed with General Canby for the surrender of the land and naval forces in Mississippi and Alabama, on terms similar to those made between Johnston and Sherman.

On the 26th of May the Chiefs of Staff of General Kirby Smith and General Canby arranged similar terms for the surrender of the troops in the trans-Mississippi Department.

The total number thus paroled by General Canby in the Department of Alabama and Mississippi was 42,293, to which may be added less than 150 of the navy; while the number surrendered by General Kirby Smith of the trans-Mississippi Department was 17,686.

Chapter 109

Capture of President Davis

AFTER the expiration of the armistice I rode out of Charlotte, attended by all but two members of my Cabinet, my personal staff, and the cavalry that had been concentrated from different fields of detached service. The number was about 2,000. They represented five brigade organizations. Though so much reduced in number they were in a good state of efficiency, and among their officers were some of the best in our service.

We proceeded at easy stages. After two halts of half a day each, we reached the Savannah River.

I crossed early in the morning of the 4th of May, with a company which had been detailed as my escort, and rode some miles to a farmhouse, where I halted to get breakfast and have our horses fed. Here I learned that a regiment of the enemy were moving upon Washington, Ga., which was one of our depots of supplies, and I sent back a courier with a pencil-note addressed to General Vaughan, or the officer commanding the advance, requesting him to come on and join me immediately. After waiting a considerable time I determined to move on with my escort, trusting that the others would overtake us, and that, if not, we should arrive in Washington in time to rally the citizens to its defence. When I reached there scouts were sent out on the different roads, and my conclusion was that we had had a false alarm. The Secretary of State, Mr. Benjamin, being unaccustomed to travelling on horseback, parted from me at the house where we stopped to breakfast, to take another mode of conveyance and a different route from that which I was pursuing, with intent to rejoin me in the trans-Mississippi Department. At Washington the Secretary of the Navy, Mr. Mallory, left me temporarily, to attend to the needs of his family. The Secretary of

War, Mr. Breckinridge, had remained with the cavalry at the crossing of the Savannah River. During the night after my arrival in Washington he sent in an application for authority to draw from the treasure, under the protection of the troops, enough to make to them a partial payment. I authorized the acting Secretary of the Treasury to meet the requisition by the use of the silver coin in the train. When the next day passed without the troops coming forward, I sent a note to the Secretary of War, showing the impolicy of my longer delay, having then heard that General Upton had passed within a few miles of the town on his way to Augusta to receive the surrender of the garrison and military material at that place, in conformity with orders issued by General Johnston. This was my first positive information of his surrender. Not receiving an immediate reply to the note addressed to the Secretary of War, General Breckinridge, I explained to Captain Campbell, of Kentucky, commanding my escort, the condition of affairs, and, telling him that his company was not strong enough to fight, and too large to pass without observation, asked him to inquire if there were ten men who would volunteer to go with me without question wherever I should choose. He brought back for answer that the whole company volunteered on the terms proposed. Gratifying as this manifestation was, I felt it would expose them to unnecessary hazard to accept the offer, and told him, in any manner he might think best, to form a party of ten men. With these ten men and five of my personal staff, I left Washington. Secretary Reagan remained for a short time to transfer to Mr. Semple and Mr. Tidball the treasure in his hands, except a few thousand dollars, and then rejoined me on the road.

Mr. Reagan overtook me in a few hours, but I saw no more of General Breckinridge, and learned subsequently that he was following our route, with a view to overtake me, when he heard of my capture, and, turning to the east, reached the Florida coast unmolested. On the way he met J. Taylor Wood, and, in an open boat, they crossed the straits to the West Indies. No report reached me at that time, or until long afterward, in regard to the cavalry command left at the Savannah River; then it was to the effect that paroled men from Johnston's army brought news of its surrender, and that the condition of returning home and remaining unmolested embraced all the men of the department who would give their parole, and that this had exercised a great influence over the troops, inclining them to accept those terms. Had General Johnston obeyed the order sent to him from Charlotte, and moved on the route selected by himself, with all his cavalry, so much of the infantry as could be mounted, and the light artillery, he could not have been successfully pursued by General Sherman. His force, united to that I had assembled at Charlotte, would, it was believed, have been sufficient to vanquish any troops which the enemy had between us and the Mississippi River.

Had the cavalry with which I left Charlotte been associated with a force large enough to inspire hope for the future, instead of being discouraged by the surrender in their rear, it would probably have gone on, and, when united with the forces of Maury, Forrest, and Taylor, in Alabama and Mississippi, have constituted an army large enough to attract stragglers, and revive the drooping spirits of the country. In the worst view of the case it should have been able to cross to the trans-Mississippi Department, and, there uniting with the armies of E. K. Smith and Magruder, to form an army which, in the portion of that country abounding in supplies and deficient in rivers and railroads, could have continued the war until our enemy, foiled in the purpose of subjugation, should, in accordance with his repeated declaration, have agreed, on the basis of a return to the Union, to acknowledge the Constitutional rights of the States, and by a convention, or *quasi* treaty, to guarantee security of person and property. To this hope I persistently clung, and, if our independence could not be achieved, so much, at least, I trusted might be gained.

Those who have endured the horrors of "reconstruction," who have, under "carpet-bag rule," borne insult, robbery, and imprisonment without legal warrant, can appreciate the value which would have attached to such limited measure of success.

When I left Washington, Ga., with the small party which has been enumerated, my object was to go to the south far enough to pass below the points reported to be occupied by Federal troops, and then turn to the west, cross the Chattahoochie, and go on to meet the forces still supposed to be in the field in Alabama. If, as now seemed probable, there should be no prospect of a successful resistance east of the Mississippi, I intended then to cross to the trans-Mississippi Department, where I believed Generals E. K. Smith and Magruder would continue to uphold our cause.

After leaving Washington in the manner and for the purpose heretofore described, I overtook a commissary and quartermaster's train, having public papers of value in charge, and, finding that they had no experienced woodsman with it, I gave them four of the men of my small party, and went on with the rest. On the second or third day after leaving Washington I heard that a band of marauders, supposed to be stragglers and deserters from both armies, were in pursuit of my family, whom I had not seen since they left Richmond, but who, I heard at Washington, had gone with my private secretary and seven paroled men, who generously offered their services as an escort, to the Florida coast. Their route was to the east of that I was pursuing, but I immediately changed direction and rode rapidly across the country to overtake them. About nightfall the horses of my escort gave out, but I pressed on with Secretary Reagan and my personal staff. It was a bright moonlight night; and just before day, as the moon was sinking below the treetops, I met a party of men in the road, who answered my questions by saying they belonged to an Alabama regiment; that they were coming from a village not far off, on their way homeward. Upon inquiry being made, they told me they had passed an encampment of wagons, with women and children, and asked me if we belonged to that party. Upon being answered in the affirmative, they took their leave. After a short time I was hailed by a voice which I recognized as that of my private secretary, who informed me that the marauders had been hanging around the camp, and that he and others were on post around it, and were expecting an assault as soon as the moon went down. A silly story had got abroad that it was a treasure-train, and the *auri sacra fames* had probably instigated these marauders, as it subsequently stimulated General J. H. Wilson to send out a large cavalry force to capture the same train. For the protection of my family I travelled with them two or three days, when, believing that they had passed out of the region of marauders, I determined to leave their encampment at nightfall, to execute my original purpose. My horse and those of my party proper were saddled preparatory to a start, when one of my staff, who had ridden into the neighboring village, returned and told me that he had heard that a marauding party intended to attack the camp that night. This decided me to wait long enough to see whether there was any truth in the rumor, which I supposed would be ascertained in a few hours. My horse remained saddled and my pistols in the holsters, and I lay down, fully dressed, to rest. Nothing occurred to rouse me until just before dawn, when my coachman, a free colored man, who faithfully clung to our fortunes, came and told me there was firing over the branch, just behind our encampment. I stepped out of my wife's tent and saw some horsemen, whom I immediately recognized as cavalry, deploying around the encampment. I turned back and told my wife these were not the expected marauders, but regular troopers. She implored me to leave her at once. I hesitated, from unwillingness to do so, and lost a few precious moments before yielding to her importunity. My horse and arms were near the road on which I expected to leave, and down which the cavalry approached; it was therefore impracticable to reach them. I was compelled to start in the opposite direction. As it was quite dark in the tent, I picked up what was supposed to be my "raglan"—a water-proof light overcoat without sleeves; it was subsequently found to be my wife's, so very like my own as to be mistaken for it; as I started, my wife thoughtfully threw over my head and shoulders a shawl. I had gone perhaps fifteen or twenty yards when a trooper galloped up and ordered me to halt and surrender, to which I gave a defiant answer, and, dropping the shawl and raglan from my shoulders, advanced toward him; he levelled his carbine at me, but I expected, if he fired, he would miss me, and my intention was in that event to put my hand under his foot, tumble him off on the other side, spring into his saddle, and attempt to escape. My wife, who had been watching, when she saw the soldier aim his carbine at me, ran forward and threw her arms around me. Success depended on instantaneous action, and, recognizing that the opportunity had been lost, I turned back, and, the morning being damp and chilly, passed on to a fire beyond the tent. Our pursuers had taken different roads, and approached our camp from opposite directions; they encountered each other and commenced firing, both supposing they had met our armed escort, and some casualties resulted from their conflict with an imaginary body of Confederate troops. During the confusion, while attention was concentrated upon myself, except by those who were engaged in pillage, one of my aides, Colonel J. Taylor Wood, with Lieutenant Barnwell, walked off unobserved. His daring exploits on the sea had made him an object of special hostility on the part of the Federal Government, and rendered it quite proper that he should avail himself of every possible means of escape. Colonel Pritchard went over to their battle-field, and I did not see him for a long time, surely more than an hour after my capture. He subsequently claimed credit, in a conversation with me, for the forbearance shown by his men in not shooting me when I refused to surrender.

Wilson and others have uttered many falsehoods in regard to my capture, which have been exposed in publications by persons there present—by Secretary Reagan, by the members of my personal staff, and by the colored coachman, Jim Jones, which must have been convincing to all who were not given over to believe a lie. For this reason I will postpone to some other time, and more appropriate place, any further notice of the story and its variations, all the spawn of a malignity that shamed the civilization of the age. We were, when prisoners, subjected to petty pillage, as described in the publications referred to, and in others; and to annoyances such as military *gentlemen* never commit or permit.

On our way to Macon we received the proclamation of President Andrew Johnson offering a reward for my apprehension as an accomplice in the assassination of the late President A. Lincoln. Some troops by the wayside had the proclamation, which was displayed with vociferous demonstrations of exultation over my capture. When we arrived at Macon I was conducted to the hotel where General Wilson had his quarters. A strong guard was in front of the entrance, and, when I got down to pass in, it opened ranks, facing inward, and presented arms.

A commodious room was assigned to myself and family. After dinner I had an interview with General Wilson. After some conversation in regard to our common acquaintance, he referred to the proclamation offering a reward for my capture. Taking it for granted that any significant remark of mine would be reported to his Government, and fearing that I might never have another opportunity to give my opinion of A. Johnson, I told him there was one man in the United States who knew that proclamation to be false. He remarked that my expression indicated a particular person. I answered that it did, and the person was the one who signed it, for he at least knew that I preferred Lincoln to himself.

Having several small children, one of them an infant, I expressed a preference for the easier route by water, supposing then, as he seemed to do, that I was to go to Washington City. He manifested a courteous, obliging temper, and, either by the authority with which he was invested or by obtaining it from a higher power, my preference as to the route was accorded. I told him that some of the men with me were on parole, that they all were riding their own horses—private property—and that I would be glad they should be permitted to retain them; and I have a distinct recollection that he promised me it should be done. But I have since learned that they were all deprived of their horses; and some who were on parole, viz., Major Moran, Captain Moody, Lieutenant Hathaway, Midshipman Howell, and Private Messec, who had not violated their obligations of parole, but had been captured because they were found voluntarily travelling with my family to protect them from marauders, were sent with me as prisoners of war, and all incarcerated, in disregard of the protection promised when they surrendered.

At Augusta we were put on a steamer, and there met Vice President Stephens; Honorable C. C. Clay, who had voluntarily surrendered himself upon learning that he was included in the proclamation for the arrest of certain persons charged with complicity in the assassination of Mr. Lincoln; General Wheeler, the distinguished cavalry officer, and his adjutant, General Ralls. My private secretary, Burton N. Harrison, had refused to be left behind, and, though they would not allow him to go in the carriage with me, he was resolved to follow my fortunes, as well from sentiment as the hope of being useful. His fidelity was rewarded by a long and rigorous imprisonment. At Port Royal we were transferred to a sea-going vessel, which, instead of being sent to Washington City, was brought to anchor at Hampton Roads. One by one all my companions in misfortune were sent away, we knew not whither, leaving on the vessel only Mr. Clay and his wife and myself and family. After some days' detention Clay and myself were removed to Fortress Monroe, and there incarcerated in separate cells. Not knowing that the Government was at war with women and children, I asked that my family might be permitted to leave the ship and go to Richmond or Washington City, or to some place where they had acquaintances; but this was refused. I then requested that they might be permitted to go abroad on one of the vessels lying at the Roads. This also was denied. Finally, I was informed that they must return to Savannah on the vessel by which we came. This was an old transport ship, hardly seaworthy. My last attempt was to get for them the privilege of stopping at Charleston, where they had many personal friends. This also was refused—why, I did not then know, have not learned since, and am unwilling to make a supposition, as none could satisfactorily account for such an act of inhumanity. My daily experience as a prisoner shed no softer light on the transaction, but only served to intensify my extreme solicitude. Bitter tears have been shed by the gentle, and stern reproaches have been made by the magnanimous, on account of the needless torture to which I was subjected, and the heavy fetters riveted upon me, while in a stone casemate and surrounded by a strong guard; but all these were less excruciating than the mental agony my captors were able to inflict. It was long before I was permitted to hear from my wife and children, and this, and things like this, was the power which education added to savage cruelty. But I do not propose now and here to enter upon the story of my imprisonment, or more than merely to refer to other matters which concern me personally, as distinct from my connection with the Confederacy.

Chapter 110

The Cost of the War; and the Northern Methods of Warfare

ON April 25th, at Raleigh, N. C., General Johnston surrendered and disbanded his army. On May 4th General Richard Taylor capitulated, with the last of our forces east. On May 26th General E. Kirby Smith surrendered the last of our forces across the Mississippi. The military contest had ended. The war between the States was ended.

The number of men brought into the field by the Government of the United States during the war was 2,678,967. In addition to these 86,724 paid a commutation. During the last eighteen months of the war the Federal Government made calls for 1,257,134, and they were furnished; 1,427,833 men had been furnished from April 15, 1861, to October 17, 1863. Kentucky, Maryland, Missouri, and Tennessee furnished to the armies of the United States 262,601 men—equal to 225,031 three-years' men.

The public debt of the United States rose from $90,867,828.68, in July, 1861, to $2,682,593,026.53, in July, 1865—an increase, in four years, of $2,591,725,197.85.

The manner in which our adversaries conducted the war I thus characterized in my message to Congress, on August 15, 1862:

> "Rapine and wanton destruction of private property, war upon non-combatants, murder of captives, bloody threats to avenge the death of an invading soldiery by the slaughter of unarmed citizens, orders of banishment against peaceful farmers engaged in the cultivation of the soil, are some of the means used by our ruthless invaders to enforce the submission of a free people to a foreign

sway."

Again, in January, 1863, I said:

> "It is my painful duty to inform you of the renewed examples of every conceivable atrocity committed by the armed forces of the United States at different points within the Confederacy, and which must stamp indelible infamy, not only on the perpetrators, but on their superiors, who, having the power to check these outrages on humanity, have not yet in a single instance, of which I am aware, inflicted punishment on the wrong-doers."

The war, which in its inception was waged for forcing us back into the Union, having failed in accomplishing that purpose, passed into a second stage, in which it was attempted to conquer and rule our States as dependent provinces. Defeated in this design, our adversaries entered upon another, which could have no other purpose than revenge and plunder of private property. In May, 1864, it was still characterized by the barbarism with which it had been previously conducted. Aged men, helpless women and children, appealed in vain to the humanity which should be inspired by their condition, for immunity from arrest, incarceration, or banishment from their homes. Plunder and devastation of the property of non-combatants, destruction of private dwellings, and even of edifices devoted to the worship of God; expeditions organized for the sole purpose of sacking cities, consigning them to the flames, killing the unarmed inhabitants, and inflicting horrible outrages on women and children, were some of the constantly recurring atrocities of the invader.

One single illustration, and by no means the worst out of thousands of similar testimonies, must suffice, owing to our restricted limits, to enforce this grave impeachment.

On June 19, 1864, Major-General Hunter began his retreat from before Lynchburg down the Shenandoah Valley. Lieutenant-General Early, who followed in pursuit, thus describes the destruction he witnessed along the route:

> "Houses had been burned, and helpless women and children left without shelter. The country had been stripped of provisions, and many families left without a morsel to eat. Furniture and bedding

had been cut to pieces, and old men and women and children robbed of all the clothing they had, except that on their backs. Ladies' trunks had been rifled, and their dresses torn to pieces in mere wantonness. Even the negro girls had lost their little finery. At Lexington he had burned the Military Institute, with all its contents, including its library and scientific apparatus. Washington College had been plundered, and the statue of Washington stolen. The residence of ex-Governor Letcher at that place had been burned by orders, and but a few minutes given Mrs. Letcher and her family to leave the house. In the county a most excellent Christian gentleman, a Mr. Creigh, had been hung, because, on a former occasion, he had killed a straggling and marauding Federal soldier while in the act of insulting and outraging the ladies of his family."

Jefferson Davis when captured.

CHAPTER 111

RE-ESTABLISHMENT OF THE UNION BY FORCE

WITH the capture of the capital, the dispersion of the civil authorities, the surrender of the armies in the field, and the arrest of the President, the Confederate States of America disappeared as an independent power, and the States of which it was composed, yielding to the force of overwhelming numbers, were forced to rejoin the Union from which, four years before, they had one by one withdrawn. Their history henceforth became a part of the history of the United States.

With the cessation of all hostilities against the power of the Government of the United States nothing remained to be done but for the sovereigns, the people of each State, to assert their authority and to restore order. If the principle of the sovereignty of the people—the corner-stone of our political institutions—had survived and was still in force, it was necessary only that the people of each State should reconsider and revoke their ordinances of secession, and again recognize the Constitution of the United States as the supreme law of the land. This simple process would have placed the Union on its original basis, and have restored what had ceased to exist—the Union by consent. Unfortunately, such was not the intention of the conqueror. The union of free wills and brotherly hearts, under a compact ordained by the people, was not his object. Henceforth there was to be established a Union by force. Sovereignty was to pass from the people to the Government of the United States, and to be upheld by those who had furnished the money and the soldiers for the war.

Standing defenceless, stripped of their property, and exposed, as it was asserted, to the penalties of insurrection on the one hand, and that of treason on the other, the people of the late Confederate States were disfranchised; not their official representatives only, but large and influential classes; unconstitutional oaths were required of them before they could regain their civil rights; the negro population was invested with the right to vote, whereby governments were established in many of the States which were officered exclusively by blacks and by aliens elected to power by negro votes—governments whose sole purpose seemed to be to plunder and oppress the people under the forms of law, and the record of whose misrule will forever form one of the most discreditable chapters in the history of the country. But it would require a separate volume to narrate the oppressions inflicted on the people of the South after the cessation of hostilities; and my task is done.

My object in this work has been to prove by historical authority that each of the States, as sovereign parties to the compact of Union, had the reserved power to secede from it whenever it was found not to answer the ends for which it was established. If this has been done, it follows that the war, on the part of the Government of the United States, was a war of aggression and usurpation; and on the part of the South was for the defence of an inherent and unalienable right.

My next purpose was to show, by the gallantry and devotion of the Southern people in their unequal struggle, how thorough was their conviction of the justice of their cause; that by their humanity to the wounded and captives they proved themselves the worthy descendants of chivalric sires, and fit to be free; and that, in every case, as when our army invaded Pennsylvania, by their respect for private rights, their morality and observance of the laws of civilized war, they were entitled to the confidence and regard of mankind.

In asserting the right of secession, it has not been my wish to incite to its exercise. I recognize the fact that the war showed it to be impracticable; but this did not prove it to be wrong; and now that it may not be again attempted, and that the Union may promote the general welfare, it is needful that the truth, the whole truth, should be known, so that crimination and recrimination may forever cease; and then, on the basis of fraternity and faithful regard for the rights of the States, there may be written on the arch of the Union, *Esto perpetua*.

The End

Want to learn more about Lincoln's War on the Constitution and the American people? Then you will be interested in Lochlainn Seabrook's popular titles:

- ABRAHAM LINCOLN WAS A LIBERAL, JEFFERSON DAVIS WAS A CONSERVATIVE
- EVERYTHING YOU WERE TAUGHT ABOUT THE CIVIL WAR IS WRONG, ASK A SOUTHERNER!
- ALL WE ASK IS TO BE LET ALONE: THE SOUTHERN SECESSION FACT BOOK
- EVERYTHING YOU WERE TAUGHT ABOUT AMERICAN SLAVERY IS WRONG, ASK A SOUTHERNER!
- CONFEDERATE FLAG FACTS: WHAT EVERY AMERICAN SHOULD KNOW ABOUT DIXIE'S SOUTHERN CROSS
- LINCOLN'S WAR: THE REAL CAUSE, THE REAL WINNER, THE REAL LOSER

Available from Sea Raven Press and wherever fine books are sold

ALL OF OUR BOOK COVERS ARE AVAILABLE AS 11" X 17" COLOR POSTERS, SUITABLE FOR FRAMING

SeaRavenPress.com

www.ingramcontent.com/pod-product-compliance
Lightning Source LLC
Chambersburg PA
CBHW021147230426
43667CB00006B/288